FROM WALTON TO THE WORLD

THE STORY OF A FARM BOY FROM WALTON

SIR DRYDEN SPRING

BALLYRAEMEEN PUBLISHING

Copyright © 2024 Dryden Spring

Dryden Spring asserts his moral right to be identified as the author of this work.

All rights reserved. No part of this publication may be reproduced or transmitted in any form or by any means without permission in writing from the copyright holder.

Published by Ballyraemeen Publishing

A catalogue record for this book is available from the National Library of New Zealand.

ISBN 978-0-473-71613-4 (Paperback)
ISBN 978-0-473-71614-1 (EPUB)

Credits: Cover design, Kalee Jackson. Cover image of Fonterra's Darfield plant used with permission. All images are from the author's collection except as otherwise noted. Thanks to Martin Taylor and Brian O'Flaherty for their help in producing and editing this book.

To my family

My parents: Maurice and Violet, who made me what I am.

My children: Mark, Julie-Ann, Gregory, Kevin, Lisa-Jane and Annemarie for their love and support.

My grandchildren: Adam, Melanie, Sean, Jessica, James, Hannah, Ruby, Joel, Olivia, Sophie, Nicholas and Harry, so that they may know something of our family history.

The future belongs to those who see opportunity
and have the ability to turn it into reality.

CONTENTS

Introduction   xi

PART ONE
WHERE WE CAME FROM

1. TO NEW ZEALAND THEY CAME   3
    The Springs   3
    The McBrides   7
    The Edges   8
    The Davises   9

PART TWO
EARLY YEARS

2. GROWING UP   13
3. DAD COMES HOME   25
4. FARMING BEGINS   31
5. PARATU BECKONS   37
6. WALTON SCHOOL   48
7. COLLEGE   55
8. FARMING CALLS   61
9. SPORT   68
10. WORK EXPERIENCE   78

PART THREE
A FARMER POLITICIAN

11. FEDERATED FARMERS   87
12. HIGHER OFFICE BECKONS   95
13. THE PRESIDENT   100
14. WAIKATO FARMERS TRADERS   105
15. A BIG YEAR   111

PART FOUR
THE BUSINESSMAN

16. A COMPANY DIRECTOR	119
17. OVERSEAS EXPERIENCE	126
18. ELSTOW	136
19. THE RURAL BANK	142
20. FERTILISER	149

PART FIVE
DAIRY BUSINESS

21. EARLY DAYS AT NEW ZEALAND COOPERATIVE DAIRY CO	161
22. A COAL MINER	170
23. THE CHAIRMAN	176
24. TOWN MILK: A BIG OPPORTUNITY	195
25. UNION ISSUES	213
26. PERSONNEL	219
27. A STRONG FINISH	228
28. PORT REFORM	233
29. USA FOREIGN LEADER GRANT	239

PART SIX
NEW ZEALAND DAIRY BOARD

30. INTERNATIONAL BUSINESS	249
31. CHAIRMAN OF THE NEW ZEALAND DAIRY BOARD	261
32. ANNUAL CHAIRMAN'S EUROPEAN TRIP	270
33. EARLY TIMES	280
34. TRADE REFORM	289
35. THE TRAVELLER	303
36. A NEW CHIEF EXECUTIVE	312
37. CUSTOMS ISSUES	320
38. RUCTIONS AT NEW ZEALAND DAIRY COMPANY	329
39. AN EMINENT PERSON	336
40. INDIA	344

41. THE GOING GETS TOUGH	350
42. THE END GAME	361
43. A FINAL SALVO	385
44. THE AFTERMATH	395

PART SEVEN
A NEW BUSINESS CAREER

45. MAJOR CHANGES IN LIFE AND CAREER	407
46. ASIAN ENGAGEMENT	414
47. GOODMAN FIELDER	429
48. ANZ	448
49. BACK TO THE WAIKATO	465
50. WEL NETWORKS	473
51. FLETCHER CHALLENGE	481
52. FLETCHER FORESTS	488
53. FLETCHER BUILDING: THE PHOENIX	499
54. SKY CITY	509
55. PORT OF TAURANGA	519
56. CODA: THE LAST STANZA	528
57. BLESSINGS	534
About the Author	545

INTRODUCTION

If, as a boy growing up on a farm at Paratu, Walton, I had ever dreamed that I would have an international business career, rising to the top of the three largest businesses in New Zealand, that I would meet some of the most influential people, not only in New Zealand but in the world, that having left school at age fifteen with no educational qualifications, not even School Certificate, I would receive two honorary doctorates, from Massey and Waikato Universities, that I would be honoured by Her Majesty the Queen with a knighthood, I would have brought myself back to reality with the admonition, "But I am going to be a farmer." That is all I ever wanted to be.

I did become a farmer and enjoyed it immensely. I am a creature of open air and the countryside. Even today when travelling, wherever I am, I prefer the countryside to cities. But I have also had an amazing business career which I have equally enjoyed. Being at the heart of decision making is exhilarating. Like all careers, mine has been a mix of excitement, unique experiences and just plain hard work. There were highs, many of them, some disappointments but few regrets. Much of what I came to regard as ordinary, others would regard as extraordinary. I believe that you make your own luck, but I have been extraordinarily lucky to have been in the right place at the right time as opportunities presented themselves.

For some time, I have thought about recording my experiences in a book. Such thoughts were usually more whimsical than a belief that I would ever do so. During my long career I did not keep a diary. Had I done so, it would have made the writing of my story much easier, and this book would likely have been written much earlier. But I did not keep a diary, principally because I have always focussed on the future not the past. Given the huge workload I carried for most of my career, the last thing I needed was to each night use up valuable time to write down what I had done during the day. I preferred to focus on and prepare for what I had to do the next day. My story would probably have never actually seen the light of day but for my daughter Julie-Ann who reminded me that my career had been so rich and varied, so full of unique experiences which few would know about, much of which even my own family probably did not know about. She cajoled me to write my story. She has usually been able to persuade me. She has done so again.

This is my story; it is not a story of my personal life but one which is largely about my professional career. It is written mainly for my wonderful children, Mark, Julie-Ann, Gregory, Kevin, Lisa-Jane and Annemarie, and their families. It is they who paid the price of my career with a father frequently absent, thus giving them less time than they deserved and much less than I now wish I had. But they have all grown into fine people of whom I am immensely proud.

While I do record my family's arrival in New Zealand and my early life, which will provide for my family a record of the early New Zealand Spring, McBride, Edge and Davis families, I largely cover the organisations and roles I have occupied through my professional career, and some of the issues and experiences in those roles and during those times. It is written largely from memory and is not intended to be a detailed reference source of events, but rather my perspective on the roles I have occupied and events I experienced. As I became electronically literate and the internet made access to information easier, I have been more able to check information to bolster my recall for the latter part of my career. But it is my memory of events on which I have mainly relied. I have largely followed the chronology of my life, but there was considerable time overlap with many of my roles. As I traverse my commercial career, I cover the most significant roles and organisations.

It was not all plain sailing. In my first leadership role farming faced a perfect storm of several successive years of drought, inflation taking off to reach 18 per cent in 1980 and declining product prices. Then there was a necessary economic restructuring of the Lange Government, which was devasting for famers and working people. But thank God they did it. It released farming and business from the shackles of regulation and dramatically increased our national efficiency and economic performance. There was the Asian economic crisis of 1987 and then the grandaddy of them all, the Global Financial Crisis of 2008–2012 at a time when I was chairman of a bank. They were all crisis times which had to be weathered and which tested one's mettle and judgement.

There will be others who will have a different perspective than mine on some of the issues I have commented on, particularly where I have made judgements. I make no apology for that for this is my story, written from my perspective. It contains my honest views as best as I can recall events. One of my great strengths was that I was frank with people. I always told it like I saw it. Few did not understand what I meant or what my position was. That was why farmers trusted me and unreservedly supported me. I have applied the same standard of frankness to my comments in this manuscript. But I have also tried to avoid exaggeration.

Most of my career, almost forty years, was in agriculture, both on and off farm. Most of it was in service to farmers. If I had a vocation, it was to serve my farmers, and I gave them everything I had. Farmers run risky and complex businesses. They work hard, are efficient, are smart business people and they keep doing the job. For most of New Zealand's history it has been farming which has paid our nation's import bills. It still is. Dairying is an industry which is systemically important to New Zealand. It has been a privilege to serve New Zealand farming families, to represent them and fight for their interests, which I did to the best of my ability. I was privileged to be entrusted by dairy farmers with the leadership of their industry and of their cooperative commercial enterprises. I was honoured to receive their support and thank them for it.

I regard my roles as chairman of New Zealand Dairy Company and the New Zealand Dairy Board as the peak of my career. Farmers make good directors as they need to think long term, plan, have a sound understanding of a wide range of disciplines, be able to balance conflicting demands and priorities, be able to deal with the unexpected, get the job done regardless of the difficulties, be able to understand and manage finance, and above all display good judgement. Those qualities are also all essential requirements for effective directors. Over many generations, the record of achievement of those responsible for governing the dairy industry has been formidable. The achievement by farmers in building the farmer-owned cooperative dairy companies into the New Zealand Dairy Board and now Fonterra, a substantial international business, is an amazing achievement, one unmatched in any other country in the world. In Fonterra, New Zealand's dairy farmers have a priceless asset protecting their interests. It is one that is able to foot it with the large commercial enterprises which dominate world food markets and international commerce. Today's dairy farmers benefit from the foresight and wisdom of their forebears. I am proud to have been part of that achievement.

After my retirement, I had the good fortune to have a new career as a director or chairman of some of the largest companies in Australia and New Zealand. After the parochial conflict of the latter years with the Dairy Board, it was a welcome change to be a director of companies where that attitude was absent. To work with director colleagues who were single-mindedly focussed on creating value for shareholders was much more enjoyable. Despite that, it is worth recording my experience that the overall achievements of the dairy industry at least matched the performance of the best companies I have been involved with and exceeded that of most.

While my career has been amazing it could not have occurred without the support of Christine and our children, Mark, Julie-Ann, Gregory, Kevin, Lisa-Jane and Annemarie, and in more recent years, Marg. I express my heartfelt gratitude to them for their selfless love and support.

Sir Dryden Spring

PART ONE
WHERE WE CAME FROM

ONE
TO NEW ZEALAND THEY CAME

THE SPRINGS

My father always proudly proclaimed that the "Springs were 100 per cent pure Irish", but he usually added: "Until your mother diluted the strain with Welsh and English." However, I discovered in the 1980s, much to my father's chagrin, that this was not completely true as the Springs were originally a Lavenham, Suffolk, England family of comfortable means, engaged in the clothing and wool trade.

We can trace our lineage back to Thomas Spring, clothier of Lavenham, who died in 1440. The grandson of Thomas Spring, Sir Thomas Spring "The Rich Wool Merchant", was a major benefactor of St Peter & St Paul's Church in Lavenham. It has a chapel which is named after him. The Spring coat of arms is prominently displayed in several places in the church.

Successive generations of the family seemed to prosper, there being a significant number of knights, with at least three holding the office of High Sherriff of Suffolk, from 1578 until 1654. Sir William Spring, a

Member of Parliament and Privy Councillor, became Baron Askeaton in 1641. The Spring baronetcy ended in 1769 on the death of Sir John Spring who had no heirs.

Spring crest. Non mihi sed Patriae (not for me but for my fatherland)

A Thomas Spring went to Kerry with Sir Walter Raleigh in 1578, and so the Irish Springs began. Thomas was Captain and Constable of Castlemaine, as was his son, Thomas. In those early days the Springs were agents for 16,000 acres but eventually lost the agency. I do not know why or when, but it is likely that the staunchly Catholic family were on the wrong side when Oliver Cromwell conquered Ireland and confiscated most Catholic landholdings in the seventeenth century.

My great-grandfather, Arthur Francis Spring, was born in Ballyraemeen, County Kerry in 1837, one of a family of nine children – six boys and three girls. Arthur emigrated to New Zealand around 1873, with his brother Alexander and cousin John. There is quite a story about why they left Ireland. The Springs were widely renowned for horse breeding. The family owned a very good stallion which earned a good income for the family, servicing mares. It would be taken to the regular horse fairs around Kerry, where for a fee it would service as many mares as possible. In those days horses were the main means of transport, travel and war. Ireland was a huge supplier of horses to the armies of England and Europe. One day in 1873 the boys decided to ride the stallion down to the river, but on the way it put its leg into a hole, broke it, and had to be put down. This had serious economic consequences for the family who depended on the income earned by the stallion. The father was so infuriated that he made the boys bury the horse, and what is more, bury it standing up. He then banished them from the farm and home. They got on a vessel and came to New Zealand. In those days Irish people were emigrating in great numbers all over the world so they could have gone anywhere, Australia, USA, Canada, Chile, Argentina, but for whatever reason the young men ended up here. Probably it was as simple as the fact a boat was leaving for New Zealand on the day.

When I became chairman of the Dairy Board it was news throughout the world's dairy industries. Willie Spring, whom I did not know, phoned our London Office and asked that I visit him when I was next in Ireland. I was unable to do so but invited him to a reception we were holding in Dublin. As soon as he walked in the door, the resemblance was striking and both I and my colleagues instantly recognised him as a Spring.

Ballyraemeen House, Ireland. Birthplace of Arthur Francis Spring

I have been to the Spring farm at Ballyraemeen, which until his death in 2022 was farmed by Willie Spring and now by his son Lachtain. Naturally, we went down the farm to view the site where the "hoss" was buried.

The Spring boys arrived in Timaru, New Zealand in 1873. Arthur Francis married Mary McCarthy who died four years later in 1880. They had three children, William who drowned at Opotiki in 1919, my grandfather John James, and Frank who died in infancy. In 1886 Arthur Francis remarried, to Mary Crennan from County Kilkenny. They appear to have had no children.

At that time there was no means for migrants to keep in touch with home, so the boys completely lost contact with their family in Kerry. Alexander and cousin John remained in the South Canterbury region and Springs farmed at Seadown, Timaru. My father recounted that "being Irish my grandfather soon had a row with both Sandy and John and never spoke to them again, so in one fell swoop we lost both our Irish and New Zealand relations".

Cousin John married Margaret Brosnahan. They had sixteen children. One of their sons was Father Leo Spring, a Marist priest whom I met on several occasions. He was a most charming man and was renowned as a very popular and respected chaplain to the New Zealand Expeditionary Force during the Second World War. Recognising his leadership qualities, he attained the rank of lieutenant colonel and was awarded an OBE.

My grandfather, John James Spring, was born in in Christchurch in 1878. He married my grandmother, Katherine Clare McBride, at Pahiatua in 1907. They met when John was a patient in Pahiatua Hospital and my grandmother was a nurse. In 1910 they purchased a small farm at Nireaha in the Seventy Mile Bush district, which they had been allocated in a ballot. My grandfather also established a cartage business. In those days, of course, horses were the means of both travel and transport.

My grandparents had seven children: John (Jack), Arthur who died in 1940 at age thirty-two, my dad Maurice, born in 1911, Ronald or Pat as he was known, Bill, Brian and Izabel. Jack married Mona Ryan and they had a carrying business in Eketahuna. My father, Maurice, married Violet Grace Edge on Boxing Day 1938. Pat married Kate Bradley and they farmed in Opunake, Taranaki. Bill was captured and killed in Crete in 1941. I have visited his grave in the Suda Bay War Cemetery. Brian served in the RNZAF during the war and married Dorothy Muldrew. His family still farm the Spring family farm at Nireaha. Izabel married Keith Perry and they settled in Waipukurau, Hawke's Bay.

THE MCBRIDES

The McBride family hailed from Antrim in Ulster, James from Culfeightrin near Ballycastle and his wife Annie (née McQuaig) from the most northern extreme of Ireland, Rathlin Island. Together with two of James's brothers they arrived in New Zealand on the *Christian McAusland* in 1875 and settled in Queenstown. The McBride brothers established a sawmill at the Greenstone River where it joined Lake Wakatipu. They seemed to be very successful.

James and Annie had six children: two boys and four girls. My grandmother Katherine Clare was born in 1881. But when she was three years old her mother Annie died. Within a year further tragedy was to strike the family when her father James was drowned in Lake Wakatipu, leaving the six children, aged from fifteen months to eight years, orphans. When the youngest, Isabella, was five the children were placed in St Mary's School and Orphanage in Nelson.

The eldest son James was killed in France during the First World War. Michael remained around Nelson and today there are McBride relations there. Annie became a nun and died in 1926 from cholera, in what is now Bangladesh.

Alicia, or Cis as she was known, was a nurse, who was matron and owner of the Eketahuna Maternity Hospital. She married Mynot Berry. Her daughter Anne was also a nurse who married Cliff Robinson and was the mother of Toby, Norah (now Cowley) and Bill Robinson. They farmed at Manawaru in the Waikato.

The youngest, Isabella (Bell), married Don Ratcliffe. They lived in Wellington and had twin boys, Ben and Don Ratcliffe.

Nana Kathryn Clare Spring

THE EDGES

My mother's father, Thomas Field Edge, was born in Stretton-en-le-field, Leicestershire England in 1872, one of eight children of Benjamin and Elizabeth Edge.

He became a skilled butter maker and managed a butter factory. He served in the British Army during the Boer War, was discharged in South Africa in 1903 and came to New Zealand. He purchased a small farm in Newman, Eketahuna where he farmed until retiring to join Mum and Dad in Waitara about 1940. He served as chairman of the Newman Cheese Co-op. He married Margaret Ellen Davis. They had one child: my mother Violet Grace Edge born in 1913. Sadly, Margaret Ellen died in 1923 when my mother was only ten years of age. Tom never remarried, so my mother became "housekeeper" for her father at a very early age. Grandad lived with us from 1940 until he died at Walton in 1954 at the age of eighty-four.

Grandad Thomas Edge

I have managed to trace Grandad's family in the UK. One of his brothers, John George (Jack), was a cattle station manager for Sir Stanley Kidman ("the Cattle King") in South Australia and Queensland.

THE DAVISES

My grandmother, Margaret Ellen Davis, was born in Tawa in 1883. Her mother was an Irish girl, Ellen Madigan, and her father was George Davis. However, George died in 1890 and Ellen remarried to William Henry Morgan in St Mary of the Angels in Wellington the following year. Ellen died in 1893 when my grandmother was ten years of age. So, my father's comment that Mum diluted the "pure Irish of the Springs" was hardly correct as her grandmother was "pure Irish". However, I am not sure that either Mum or Dad were aware of that.

Mum appears to have no New Zealand relations. She always referred to her "Uncle" Phil Davies who farmed at Hamua in the Eketahuna district. Uncle Phil and Auntie Mabel retired to Te Puke. They had eleven children. I only knew Nell (later Hawkes), Dulcie, Jimmy and Phyllis. Jimmy and Dad were best mates, and they played rugby and boxed together. Dulcie was a bridesmaid at Mum and Dad's wedding. Uncle Phil proposed the toast to Mum and Dad at my wedding. However, I can find no links between my maternal grandmother and the Davies family.

PART TWO
EARLY YEARS

TWO
GROWING UP

I was born at Waitara on 6 October 1939, 33 days after war on Germany was declared. I was christened Dryden Thomas. I don't know why I was called Dryden, but I did hear Mum and Dad talk about a Dryden who they knew in Eketahuna, so they probably just liked the name. My second name, Thomas, was after Mum's father, Thomas Edge. Of course, it was also a long-standing name used by generations of Springs.

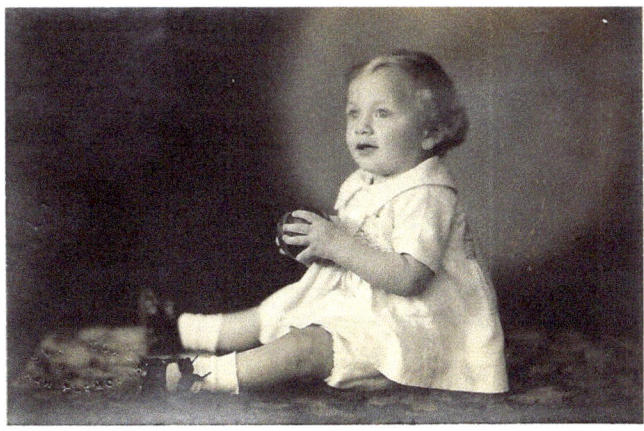

Dryden – A lot of promise

My parents Maurice Spring and Violet Edge were raised on farms in Eketahuna in the northern Wairarapa or "Bush" district. The Spring family farm was at Nireaha next to Nireaha School, while Mum's father had a farm at Newman right next to the Newman Railway Station.

When my parents were growing up, times were tough. Farms were small and had been recently hewn out of the bush, so were not overly productive. Butterfat prices were only a few pence per pound. There was little money to spare. Education was limited by today's standards with Mum and Dad leaving school, as most children did, after two years' secondary school.

Dad actually worked on a farm in the district while he was still at school. He and another person would milk thirty cows by hand, and he would then walk three miles to school, walk home again after school and milk in the evening. After leaving school, he worked on farms milking cows, but studied at tech, mostly by night, to qualify as an electrician.

Dad was a good sportsman. He played his first game of senior rugby at age fourteen. He represented Bush and Wairarapa Bush for seven years, playing in the front row even though he was only ten and a half stone (66 kg). At that time, Wairarapa Bush were a strong team, one year defeating Wellington, Hawke's Bay, Manawatu and Horowhenua, all much larger unions. They also defeated the visiting Australian side in 1936.

Dad was a very good boxer, winning numerous provincial championships. His first was the Wairarapa, Middle to Heavy Weight Title, when he defeated a 15 stone (95 kg) opponent having his last fight as an amateur before turning professional. When an Australian team visited New Zealand in 1934, Dad defeated the Australian Middleweight Champion. He was also runner-up in the New Zealand Middleweight Boxing Championships in 1936.

Maurice the boxer

Mum was a very good pianist and she earned a few shillings by playing at the local picture theatre (movies were silent then), and as a member of a dance band. It was while doing the latter that she first met Winston McCarthy who was later to become my father-in-law. Mum also represented Bush at hockey as did Auntie Izabel who was a New Zealand reserve.

When Dad qualified as an electrician, he and Mum married on Boxing Day 1938 and moved to Waitara where he had secured a job with the Waitara Borough Council. As was usual in those days, the council was responsible for electricity supply in the town of Waitara. They lived in a small cottage down by the beach then moved into a state house on Cracroft Street where their neighbours were Jim and Edna Freebairn (Roslyn's parents). Jim was a Scotsman with a very strong Scottish accent. They were lovely people with whom Mum and Dad became lifelong friends.

Mum and Dad's wedding

They then purchased their own house at 76 Domett Street. It was a 1930s-built house which was relatively comfortable with three bedrooms, a large kitchen, a living room, and as they were called then, a sitting room. It had a flush toilet, although this was outside in a garden shed close to the back door. Michael was born in 1942.

In 1941, Dad's father John was visiting us when he died, just a few months after Dad's brother Arthur had died at the age of thirty-two. Grandad was buried in the Waitara Cemetery. It was a tough year for the Springs as another of Dad's brothers, Bill, was killed on Crete in 1941 at the age of twenty-seven.

With the war not going well for the Allies, Dad joined the army two and a half months after Michael was born in 1942 and went overseas with the Second New Zealand Expeditionary Force in 1943. By that time Mum was expecting Denise. Dad was not actually required to go overseas to war as he had two young children, soon to be three, but he chose to go because he believed it was his duty to do so.

I was only four at the time and do not remember very much. However, I do recall that before he went Dad dug a neat underground hut in our garden. It was, of course, an air-raid shelter and was a wonderful place to play. I also remember vividly the day my dad went to war. He sailed from Wellington on the *New Amsterdam*. Here was this huge ship with soldiers like ants over every inch of it, on the decks, the roof and in the rigging. Every vantage point was taken, with all the soldiers waving furiously at the huge crowd gathered to farewell them. I was told to wave to Daddy and did so, even though I could not actually see him. And then as the ship sailed away, noticing Mum and Auntie Izabel crying. It upset me to see my Mum cry and I did not like seeing her upset, so I cried too. They were still crying when we got back to Uncle Don and Aunt Bell Ratcliffe's place in Hobson Street Flats. I could not understand what they were crying about. In my innocence it was a time of pride for me, as I had complete confidence that my dad was going to kill that bad man Hitler and the war would soon be over.

Michael was only about fifteen months old when Dad went overseas, and Denise was born in August 1943 while Dad was still on the boat en route to Egypt. Times were tough during the war years, and it must have been particularly difficult for Mum, with three young children under the age of four to bring up, with her husband away at the war and having to get by on a soldier's wartime pay. Fortunately, my grandfather Tom Edge (Mum's father) moved to Waitara to live with us. He was of considerable help to Mum during those difficult years. Grandad was a wonderful gardener who kept us in fresh vegetables and eggs the year round, looked after the house and section, and I guess contributed to the household from his small pension. He was a significant influence on my life until he died in 1954.

Dryden – Angelic

The war dominated my early life. Food was rationed, and "stamps" were allocated to every person and were required to purchase food and clothing. There were no luxuries; you took what you could get and were grateful for it. We purchased our meat – with little choice, only what was available on the day – from the freezing works shop down the road. We seemed to have a lot of tripe which I could not eat, and mutton which Mum boiled and served with parsley sauce to make it edible. We did not know what lollies were as sugar was very tightly rationed. There were no fat kids around in those days. We never went hungry, although I would not be surprised if Mum and Grandad went short on occasions to ensure that we kids were properly nourished.

There were few cars and of course we did not have one. It was walk or bike to get around and bus or train for longer journeys. There were few telephones; our neighbours the Becketts had one and, as was common in those days, were generous in allowing those without a phone to use theirs. If either we, or they, wanted to contact the other, someone would lean out the window and lob small pebbles onto the roof next door to attract their attention. The postal service, though, was rather better than now and for urgent communications telegrams were the mode.

Modern nutritionists would have thought that they were in heaven as fat was in short supply, but sufficient fat is an essential part of a good diet. So, we had a spoonful of cod liver oil each every day, foul stuff but we had to have it. Every bit of fat off any meat we were lucky enough to get was saved and spread on bread or toast and was a real luxury. On very rare occasions Mum would come home from the grocer with an extra half pound of homemade butter and we considered ourselves to be very lucky. I can also recall seeing the grocer taking it out from under the counter, so it was probably "black market" and highly illegal, as every ounce of butter and cheese had to be supplied to the government.

Our national anthem was "God Save The King" and everyone stood at attention when it was played, which occurred often during the war years. I can remember being in bed one night when "God Save The King" was played on the radio and standing to attention in my bed. I was probably about five. There was no New Zealand radio news, but BBC bulletins were played once or twice a day. I remember the BBC call sign "This is London Calling" as we listened eagerly to the Bulletin to find out how the war was going.

When I started school, I went to the convent school run by Sisters of The Missions nuns. Mum took me to school on my first day, but after that I was on my own. In those days the school and church were just on the edge of Waitara's main street and were about a twenty-minute walk from home. No mothers driving kids to school then, as we all walked, or rode our bikes if we were old enough (and lucky enough to have one), except for the country kids who came by bus. I was a pretty well-behaved kid and can remember being chosen to be the priest in a tableau the school was putting on. I had to dress in small but proper priest's vestments and learn to put them on in the proper way. However, my priestly career was short lived as unfortunately I got sick and missed the tableau.

Since I first learned to read, I have loved books and reading. I started reading the daily newspaper while we were at Waitara when I was about seven. The first newspaper I was aware of was the *Southern Cross*. It was a paper published by or sympathetic to the Labour Party (not that I was aware of that) and lasted only a few years before ceasing publishing. I soon developed the practice of reading the newspaper from cover to cover every day, something I have continued to do all of my life.

We did not have much organised sport but played rugby with "pick-up" sides and, of course, Bullrush. On one occasion we went up to the dreaded public school for running races. I did not really know what to do but managed to come second, which qualified me for the final. Grandad told me that I was faster than the kid who beat me and before the final told me to run as fast as I could from the word "Go", as straight as I could to the finish line and I would win. He was right; I did, and he told me, "You won going away."

At school holiday time I was usually sent to either Opunake or Eketahuna. Uncle Pat and Auntie Kate were sharemilking at Pihama, Opunake. Pat was a stern disciplinarian and I was sent to the bathroom on occasions for committing some misdemeanour of which I was usually unaware. Uncle Pat was also a keen crayfish fisherman and one evening when I was only four or five, I was shut in the bathroom with a huge live crayfish in the bath for company. It was a terrifying-looking creature which kept trying to climb out of the bath. I was sure that it was coming to get me. It would climb the slippery bath almost to the top and just when I thought it was going to get out and come after me, it would slither back down in the bath. I was petrified.

To get to Eketahuna you had to catch a small local train from Waitara to Lepperton about five miles away, then change trains there to Palmerston North and once there catch another train to Eketahuna. Nana Spring lived in Eketahuna. She had a small cottage with an outside bathroom. Saturday was bath day so this tiny little lady would put on her boots, take the axe and chop enough wood to heat the water for our bath. I used to love staying with her as she used to make such a fuss of me and there were so many new places to explore around her place. Sometimes she would have my cousin Kevin Perry, with whom I got on very well, stay at the same time. Those were great times.

The other place I used to go to was Monaghans, whom we regarded as family. Grandad Edge's farm was right next to the Newman Railway Station, about three miles north of Eketahuna. The Monaghan farm was straight across the road next to the Newman Hall. Mum's mother died when she was ten and Mrs Monaghan

(Auntie Dolly) virtually brought Mum up. She was so kind and loving. The Monaghans had quite a large farm. At that time, it was being run by Uncle Jack and son Peter. The eldest son Jackie (John's father) was away at war, and another son Dave was working down in Wairarapa. There were two girls, Kathleen who had been bridesmaid at Mum and Dad's wedding and Margaret who had been flower girl. (Mum's other bridesmaid was her cousin Dulcie Davies). I loved those two girls; they were such fun and so kind to me. I was very disappointed when they got a little older and went away to work so were not there when I visited.

I used to go to Monaghans most holidays so it was on their farm that I received my early experience of living on a farm. I loved it and wanted to get out on the farm as much as possible. Hay making was great fun, and it was there that I saw my first hay baler, a stationary machine. You had to manually put wooden dividing panels into the chamber to separate each bale which was tied with wire. Very advanced for the times, though. Each morning after milking the milk had to be transported in 30-gallon cans to the Newman cheese factory about three miles away by horse and cart. There the cans were unloaded, the milk poured into a large weighing vat and weighed, the cans put through the can washer and loaded back on the wagon to be taken home. I loved getting onto the wagon for the journey to the factory and sometimes was allowed to hold the reins and guide the horses.

Monaghans also had a car, which was a new experience for me. At home Mum either walked or biked everywhere. I would ride on the pillion seat behind her. When Michael got old enough, he was "doubled" on the bike with Mum while I rode my trike.

When Denise was, I think, about two, she had a serious accident. Mum was doubling her on the bike and Denise put her leg through the wheel. She was in hospital for several weeks. Mum packed

Michael and me off, me to Monaghans and Michael to Auntie Izabel's at Waipukurau. It was the summer holidays and when it was time for school to start it was decided that I should go to school at Newman until Denise was out of hospital and Mum was able to cope with having us all at home. I had only ever been taught by nuns and the thought of going go to a public school terrified me. After all, in Waitara the public-school kids intimidated us. They used to give us cheek and chant "Catholic dogs stink like frogs in their mother's bathing togs". We were terrified of them. As we walked to school, we always walked on the opposite side of the road away from them. However, I was saved as it was agreed that I would go to Auntie Izabel's at Waipukurau, where Michael was staying, and go to the convent school there, which I did for the first term.

From time to time, I used to get lovely cards from Dad sent from Italy. I still have some of them. He used to ask me to look after Mum, Michael and Denise which I tried to do. I can recall vividly hearing his voice when troops overseas were allowed about half a minute to broadcast to their families back home. Dad asked me to "be a good boy for Mum, and help her, and look after Michael and Denise for him". Mum was a wonderful mother but strict. When we had a disagreement, I would sometimes threaten to "tell Dad when he gets home" (the thought that he might not come home never occurred to me). Of course, I never ever got round to doing so.

One day in March 1944 the most dreaded event occurred. A telegraph boy arrived at the door with a telegram. That was how bad news from the war was delivered to the family. Mum was seriously worried, but relieved when she read it to find that while it was bad news it could have been worse. Dad had been seriously wounded at Cassino in Italy, but thank God he was alive and in hospital. Edna Freebairn happened to be at our place when the telegram arrived so was there to support Mum, even though she was pretty cut up also.

As an electrician Dad had been assigned to NZ Divisional Signals or Div. Sigs. Radios were not particularly good or reliable so telephones were the major means of communication. The role of Div. Sigs was to keep the telephones working. At Cassino the Germans occupied the mountain which had to be taken before the Allies could push on towards Rome. The New Zealand forces were at the foot of the mountain being heavily shelled. The shelling kept breaking the telephone lines so Dad and his mates had to continually repair and relay the lines as they were continuously broken, all the time under heavy fire. Dad was caught in a shell blast and seriously wounded. Till the end of his life, pieces of shrapnel would work their way out of his body, mostly from his head. Dad was taken to the field hospital by his officer Bob Milne, who an hour later was lying alongside Dad in hospital with one of his arms blown off. Dad was awarded the Military Medal for his bravery at Cassino. More about that later.

THREE
DAD COMES HOME

I CAN JUST REMEMBER THE DAY THE WAR WAS DECLARED over in 1945 when I was just six. Mum and Grandad were in really high spirits, had a drink of sherry, which was pretty rare, and told me that Dad would be coming home soon. But it would be several months before he did.

There was great excitement on the day of his homecoming. We caught the train from Waitara to Lepperton and waited for his train to arrive. It seemed like forever, but it finally arrived and a large group of soldiers in uniform with their kit bags over their shoulder alighted, although many more stayed on as the train was going on to New Plymouth.

I saw my dad coming towards us and was excited to see the hilt of a sword protruding from the top of his kit bag. We caught the train back to Waitara and then walked home to Domett Street. I was keen to see the sword. Later Denise was to use it when she learned Scottish dancing. It was a bit strange for a while having a father we really did not know in the house. The morning after he arrived home, Michael and Denise rushed into Mum's room as they did first thing every morning, only to find a strange man in bed with Mum. They retreated outside the door and had to be coaxed to come back in. It was good having a father again; life changed and became more interesting as there were many more activities we could engage in.

Dad went back to work at the Waitara Borough Power Board. A lot of what he did was erecting new lines. There were no motorised augers then to bore holes for power poles; they were dug by hand and he had to dig a sloping channel so he could go down to get the hole deep enough, and then use it to slide the pole into the hole, using a rope tied to the truck to stand it up and then ram the pole tight by hand. If he were working close to home, Mum would sometimes take his lunch or afternoon tea to him on the job.

Me and my dad

In whitebait season Dad made a whitebait net for himself and a small one for me. We would go whitebaiting together, either off the river bank, which was very close to our house, or the Waitara wharf. My net was too small for me to catch much, but I used to do rather better when with my friends. When the tide was low, we would go up some of the very small tributaries which ran into the river, put our net in the middle, dam the stream, then go upstream and chase the whitebait downstream into our net. Enterprising even if illegal.

In the autumn months we would gather firewood. Dad and a friend, Jim Oliver, who had a car and trailer, would make arrangements with a farmer for us to cut down a tree, cut it up and split it for firewood. Mum and Mrs Oliver would prepare a picnic lunch, we would go out to the farm, Dad and Jim would cut down a tree and cut it into lengths, by handsaw (there were no chainsaws then). Then the really exciting part would commence. They would hand drill a hole large enough to take a splitting gun in the log. A splitting gun was a very heavy metal pipe, solid at one end and open at the other, with a small hole at the closed end. The gun would be packed with explosives, then driven into the hole in the log with a sledge hammer and a fuse inserted into the small hole. We would then all be shepherded a couple of hundred metres away, the fuse would be lit and there would be a spectacular explosion and the log would be split open. It would then be all hands on deck as we searched for the splitting gun which could be thrown fifty metres or so away. Having found it, the process was repeated on the next log again and again. Mr Oliver and Dad would then saw the split logs into the correct lengths and split them into fireplace-sized pieces. Then Grandad, Mum, Mrs Oliver and we kids would load the trailer with the split wood. We would have a picnic lunch, and morning and afternoon tea breaks, sitting on a tarpaulin. It was great fun.

Food rationing continued until 1950 and there were shortages for many years thereafter. There were no sweets available. The best substitute we had was broken biscuits. At that time goods came into the grocer's shop in bulk, with no pre-packaging. Flour, sugar, tea and other grocery items were weighed by the grocer to order, into brown paper bags. Biscuits came in large square tins of about 20 lbs (9 kg) and were weighed out to order. That left the grocer to deal with the biscuits which were broken. For a penny you could get a bag of broken biscuits, and for threepence a very big bag. Occasionally, if you were very, very lucky you might even get a piece of chocolate biscuit. Broken biscuits were a real treat.

We would watch Clifton play rugby at the Camp Reserve in winter, while during the summer there would be twilight athletic meetings including wood chopping. These were professional events. Occasionally there would be a kids race. I was pretty quick so usually picked up a threepence which to me was a real fortune.

Sometime in 1946 an Avro Lancaster bomber came into Bell Block Air Base and was available to viewing by the public. I got to climb all over the Lancaster, sit in the pilot's seat and in the gunner's cockpit where we pretended to fire the machine guns and shoot down the German fighters.

A similar event was held at Port Taranaki when HMS *Achilles*, of the Battle of the River Plate fame when the German pocket battleship *Graf Spee* was sunk, berthed and held an open day. We were allowed to go on board and all over the ship including the bridge and the gunnery cockpits. How excited we were on those occasions.

One extremely exciting event for me was when I was allowed to attend Dad's Investiture with his Military Medal. I was seven years of age and to go out at night with Mum and Dad was itself a real treat. Governor-General Sir Bernard Freyberg presented the medals. He had been the Commanding General of the New Zealand forces during the war and Dad greatly admired him. The whole event took about two hours and Lady Freyberg stood beside him for the whole time. I was bursting with pride when my dad was called up onto the stage, the citation was read out (even though I did not really understand it), the Governor-General pinned the medal onto Dad's army uniform and then he and Lady Freyberg shook hands with Dad and spoke to him for a short time. When Dad returned to his seat with us, I was allowed to hold his medal which I clutched tightly while bursting with pride.

The citation read:

> *Signalman Spring was a linesman attached to Head Quarters 5, NZ Infantry Brigade. On the night of 19/20 March 1944 he was detailed to assist in laying lines from Brigade HQ forward to the Battalions in Cassino. The only route available was along Highway 6, the main road leading into town. This had been registered accurately by the enemy and was under heavy and continuous artillery and mortar fire. This fire became even more concentrated in the area of the town where the Battalion Headquarters were situated. Under this fire and without any cover or protection, Signalman Spring worked with the party and the line was laid. Meanwhile, however, it had been cut in several places by enemy shelling. Signalman Spring at once returned along the line coolly repairing the breaks en route, persisting in his work rather than take cover. While so engaged he was severely wounded by shell splinters. Under conditions which he knew to be extremely dangerous, Signalman Spring displayed courage and devotion to duty, disregarding his own personal safety in his efforts to establish vital communications. His courage and devotion to duty deserve the highest praise.*

There was to be an unusual sequel to this about sixty years later at Dad's funeral. During my eulogy I referred to Dad's decoration for bravery during the war and quoted part of the citation. As is usual at Returned Service personnel funerals, a representative of the RSA stood up to pay tribute to Dad and read the Ode. He had known Dad for many years but was unaware that Dad had been awarded the Military Medal. He told an amazing story.

"I was at Cassino on the evening of 19th March 1944. My section and I were under heavy artillery fire and were sheltering near the railway station. A soldier came down the road laying out the telephone wire. He said his name was Maurie and he sheltered with us waiting for the shelling to ease, but it did not; it actually became more intense. After a short while Maurie said that he had to get the line to Battalion HQ and went out into the heavy shellfire. I never saw him again and often wondered what happened to him. I thought that he had probably been killed as I could not see how anyone could survive in that intense shellfire. Now I know that he was Maurice Spring," he said.

Mum and Dad loved dancing and went to a lot of dances and balls with Jim and Elsie Freebairn all over northern Taranaki. The Freebairns had a car, a Morris 8. Petrol was rationed and scarce, and if you could get your hands on a bottle of petrol you kept it and squirreled it away. There were many occasions that the car ran out of petrol on the way home so Dad, Mum and Mrs Freebairn would be out in their ball finery pushing the car home.

FOUR
FARMING BEGINS

When war ended hundreds of thousands of soldiers were being demobbed, many with no skills and most with no job. New Zealand had a huge shortage of skills and infrastructure, particularly houses. The Returned Soldiers Rehabilitation Scheme (the "Rehab Scheme") was designed to assist in the rehabilitation of returned soldiers and to increase the skills available in New Zealand. Adult trade training schemes were introduced and a land-settlement programme initiated. Under it, the government acquired large farms, compulsorily if necessary, and subdivided them into small one-man farms.

Mum and Dad had both been brought up on farms and wanted to do the same with their family. They realised that the Rehab Scheme provided an opportunity to go farming again and to have their own farm so Dad applied to be settled on a farm. Returned soldiers had to register, be approved and then apply for individual farms as they became available for settlement. A ballot would then be held for each property and the winning applicant had the opportunity to purchase the farm on either a freehold basis, or a 33-year Crown Lease at a very modest rent. State Advances Corporation lent each farmer the money, at an interest rate of 3%, to purchase the farm. Most chose leasehold as this required much less to get started and few had any money. Of course, there were usually many applicants for each property so one had to be fortunate to win a ballot.

Dad began applying for ballots around Taranaki and we looked at many farms, with high hopes but no luck. He knew that many more farms were becoming available in the Waikato which might provide better chances of winning a ballot, but with no money and a young family it would have been a big gamble to go to the Waikato without a job lined up. He heard about a man called Bill Preece who lived in South Taranaki but also had several farms in Waikato. His Waikato farms were being taken for rehab settlement. Dad contacted him and arranged to see him as he passed through Waitara on the way to Waikato. Bill Preece had four farms at what is now Toa Road (off No 1 Road), Waitoa. He agreed to give Mum and Dad a job managing one of them. Dad hoped that he might be able to get the inside running to buy one of them under rehab.

So, one day in 1947 the great adventure for us all commenced. We were all thrilled that we were going to live on a farm. Our furniture was loaded onto a truck and away we went. I was allowed to travel in the furniture truck with Dad, while Mum, Grandad, Michael and Denise had to take the bus. Roads then were not nearly as good as they are now so it was a long and arduous journey but, eventually, we arrived at the farm in Waitoa.

We lived in a very old and rather small cottage which was pretty basic. There was an outside "short drop" toilet which was cold in winter, hot in summer and always smelly. Dad had to empty it and bury the contents every week. But we were all in heaven, enjoying living on a farm and the space, experiences and adventures that went with it. We often played along the Ohine Stream which is the back boundary of our Elstow farm. We did not have a car but fortunately the beautiful little Springdale Church was about four miles up the road so we would bike to Mass on Sundays. There would be Dad with Michael on his bike, Mum with Denise on her bike, while I was a big boy with my own bike. It was great fun except when it rained.

Horses provided the mobile power; there was no tractor, although not long before we left Mr Preece provided a Case tractor to service the four farms he owned. We had two draught horses, a mare called Kate which we used to ride, and a stroppy but very strong gelding called Duke. I would have to catch Kate in the paddock, which was not always easy, put the reins around her neck and lead her over to the fence. I could then climb onto the fence and put her bridle on and then climb up the fence to get onto her back to ride her.

Each milking we had to take the milk in cans on a wagon towed by the two horses to the "dump" on No.1 Road. Dumps were stages situated three or four miles apart, where the local farmers took their milk to be collected by the dairy company trucks. The trucks dropped off the empty cans from the previous day and the farmers took them back to the farm. This was initially a real adventure. To be on a horse-drawn wagon and sometimes to be allowed to take the reins and guide the horses was an exciting experience, but it must have been a most onerous chore for Dad, especially when the weather was adverse.

I cannot remember how many cows there were but probably around sixty or so. In those days the cows had to be "stripped"; that is, after the cups were removed each cow was hand milked to extract every last drop of milk. There would be several buckets of milk each milking which had a much higher butterfat content so stripping was considered to be worthwhile. But it was an onerous and time-consuming practice. A year or two later, research showed that the practice was uneconomic so it was discontinued.

In addition to a dray, a two-wheeled cart with shafts drawn by one horse, and a wagon, four wheels drawn by two horses, we also had a konaki. This was a small low cart with two wheels and a single skid at the front. It was towed by a single horse using chains. It was the tractor carrying tray of the time. It was used when pulling ragwort which was loaded onto it, or to transport small volumes of fencing or other gear. I was often allowed to drive the horse by myself so it was great fun.

Waitoa was a flat and fertile area which had previously been a swamp so drainage was essential. Virtually every paddock was ringed by drains which had to be cleaned every year. Drain cleaning was a two-man job, as there was no machinery. One man slashed the vegetation off the side, and then forked it on to the bank and the other dug a spit out of the bottom of the drain. It was a big job which went on for many weeks.

Haymaking was a communal effort and several farmers worked together to harvest and stack hay. The grass was mown by a horse-drawn mower, turned and when dry, windrowed by a horse-drawn tedder (which stirred and spread the hay). It was then swept to the stack by a two-horse sweep. Another man handled the ropes controlling the stacker, which was a crane with a metal grab that lifted the hay onto the stack. Another man walked a horse backwards and forwards to pull the grab-load of hay up onto the stack. Two other men were on the stack building it. Stack building was a real art so the stackers were top of the hierarchy. It took seven or eight men to carry out all of those functions. After one farm was finished, the gang moved on to the next farm and so on. Haymaking went on for about two months. Occasionally, I would be allowed to lead the horse back and forth to pull the grab up and down.

When haymaking was being carried out the women brought lunch and morning and afternoon tea for all of the men. As most of the haymaking occurred during the summer school holidays, it was wonderful time for us kids. Many would come with their fathers so we would have plenty of playmates, interesting haymaking activities to watch, and a picnic lunch each day.

When we moved to Waitoa, Mum and Dad were keen for me to go to a convent school. The Morrinsville College bus came past our place so I caught that and walked from the college to Morrinsville's convent school, St Joseph's. However, the bus was full and preference was given to the college students, so after one day we were informed that I could not travel to Morrinsville on that bus.

Another option was to catch the same college bus to Waitoa and then transfer to the Te Aroha convent school bus. That worked well in the mornings but not so well on the way home, as often the college bus had left Waitoa before the convent bus arrived there so I missed the connection. Mrs Prime (Paul Brown's grandmother) was very kind in allowing me to go to their home in Waitoa until Dad finished milking, borrowed a car and came to get me. So that did not work either. I then tried catching the train from Waitoa to Te Aroha, but there was the same problem on the way home so that lasted only one day.

So, at the end of the week Mum and Dad reached the inevitable conclusion: that I would have to go to Waitoa School. I had gone to Morrinsville convent school for one day, Te Aroha convent school for one week but ended up going to a "dreaded" public school. Despite my apprehension, it worked out just fine. I enjoyed my time at Waitoa School and made some good friends.

In late 1947 there was a poliomyelitis epidemic in New Zealand. It is a disease in which a virus attacks the spinal cord and can cause paralysis of limbs or muscles, usually permanently. It occasionally attacked the lung functions so was sometimes fatal. It seemed to be more prevalent in younger children so for many years was called infantile paralysis. It was a particularly nasty disease and we all knew somebody unfortunate to have contracted it. My cousin John Spring caught it when he was about seven and had a partially paralysed leg for the rest of his life. In the 1950s a vaccine was developed which, within a few years, had virtually eliminated it.

In 1948, with the poliomyelitis epidemic raging, the government decided that New Zealand schools would not open at the start of the year, and they remained closed until Easter, by which time the peak of the epidemic had passed. So, we had an extended holiday that year, although correspondence lessons were organised for all children in a very short time. It must have been a difficult time for Mum in particular, having to supervise lessons for Michael who by now had started school, and me, as well as running the house and milking.

Mum and Dad continued to seek an opportunity to purchase a farm and entered many ballots all over the Waikato and Thames Valley. As a family we looked at many farms, some of which were very appealing and some less so, but without luck. At last, we were fortunate to have our name drawn in a ballot for Paratu Estate, Walton. That particular block was not high on Dad's list of priorities, and in fact he included Paratu almost as an afterthought at the last minute before submitting his ballot applications. But we were extraordinarily lucky as we drew a very good farm in what proved to be a great district to farm, live and grow up in. So, in May 1949 the moving truck came, our furniture and possession were loaded on to it and a new adventure commenced.

FIVE
PARATU BECKONS

Paratu Estate was a large corporately owned farm running sheep and cattle. It had a manager's cottage, single men's accommodation, large woolshed and sheep and cattle yards, located on what later became Trevor Jones's property. It was acquired by the government under the Returned Servicemen's Rehabilitation Act and subdivided into sixteen dairy farms and two sheep farms. The first settlers, as they were called, moved on in 1948 and we were in the second lot in 1949. Percy Collins (Judith's father) and his family moved in a few months later.

We were fortunate that our farm was without doubt the most attractive piece of land on the estate, with either flat or gently contoured topography. It had a brand-new three-bedroom house which was heaven for Mum after the basic cottage we had at Waitoa. It was the same as the many state houses being built at that time, of good solid construction and well built. Many materials were in short supply so it had spouting which had been constructed from wood and painted with tar as there was no galvanised spouting available. Inevitably, after a few years this began to leak and Dad replaced it with high-quality copper spouting which was installed free of charge by my cousin Shea who was a plumber. As soon as they could afford to do so, Mum and Dad had a fourth bedroom built, which with Grandad and three growing kids we really needed.

The farm of 103 acres had only two paddocks of around fifty acres each. The house, cowshed and implement shed sat forlornly in the middle of one of the paddocks. Apart from the good seven-wire and batten fences around each of the two paddocks there were no other fences, and no races, trees or hedges. A very limited number of troughs had been installed and a restricted water-reticulation system was in place.

When we moved in, we had no telephone, no car and no electricity, so we lived for a few days by candlelight with Mum cooking over the open fireplace which was also the only source of heating. Of course, there was no hot water for baths and Mum heated water over the fire for washing and washing the dishes. When electricity was connected after about three days, we certainly appreciated it. Oh, the sheer joy of a hot bath.

It took close to year before we got a telephone, and until then we had to go to our neighbours, Manningtons, Feists or Harrises who had phones, if we needed to make a call. Getting a telephone was not easy. Equipment was in short supply and no line network existed; it had to be built. There was a manual telephone exchange in the Walton Post Office staffed between 6 am and 10 pm by local girls. The telephones were large, old-fashioned crank-operated units with connections on a party line, which had several households on it. Each household was allocated a line number (ours became 56) and an individual letter (ours became U). So, our telephone number was 56U. Individual calls were routed by the exchange operator plugging into line 56 and ringing the Morse code sequence for the letter (U was dit dit dah). With a party line it was possible to listen into other people's calls and during the peak-use period of 6 to 8 pm the line was usually continuously engaged so getting a clear line was often not easy. For that reason, there was a limit (I think of about six) on the number of houses which could be on any line. Our problem was that there were already about ten on the line we wanted to join so the Post Office were reluctant to add another two (us and the Collinses). But Paratu settlers were very supportive of one another and all agreed to sign a letter indicating that they backed us being connected.

Dryden and Rory

The herd was sixty heifers which were quite wild as they had been run on the estate as a large mob and thus had not been handled much. Breaking them in and milking them was going to be challenging, to say the least. Given the absence of fences, getting them into the shed was going to be an even bigger hurdle, so Dad built a wing fence out from the cowshed to enable the heifers to be herded into the shed and run through it to get them used to being handled. It was initially about 80% effective which of course meant that about 20% escaped as we yarded them, a process which required Mum, Dad, Grandad, Michael, Denise and me to participate. The first few efforts resembled a wild west rodeo with heifers and people dashing madly about, but the process improved as we conducted the exercise time and time again till, at last, we could get every heifer into the yard each time.

A fencing contractor came onto the farm to subdivide it into nine paddocks. The government supplied mostly silver birch posts, which, while not ideal, did the job. Wire was a different matter. In the immediate post-war years, almost everything was in very short supply and many commodities, such as food, clothing and petrol, were rationed. The only wire which could be obtained was the surplus army barbed wire. It was high tensile so could not be tied or bent, about 10 or 12 gauge, and ungalvanised which meant that it rapidly corroded, weakened and broke easily. Each loop was fixed to the next loop by a permanent metal clip so that when pulled out it opened out in coils like a spring. To use it for fencing each clip had to be cut by holding it onto the edge of an axe blade and hitting it with a hammer. It also had long barbs about twice as close together as the barbed wire in use today. It was horrible stuff to handle and use and did not last well when used for fencing. But the good news was that, despite its faults, it was better than having no wire and there was plenty of it.

We relied on deliveries with the cream cans for farm supplies, and on the mail delivery for urgent supplies such as meat, bread and groceries, as well as on kind neighbours to take us to town occasionally. But we needed a car. Cars were not readily available and were mostly pre-war vehicles. Dad was fortunate to obtain a pre-war Graham. It was a big old car of 1930s square design and we could all fit in. We were in heaven as we could now go to town, or to visit friends and relations or doctors and dentists when necessary. Unfortunately, it sometimes broke down as all cars did then and parts were not readily available. On about three occasions the crown wheel, part of the main transmission mechanism, packed up. Finding a replacement part was difficult and Dad would scour the North Island to get one. Sometimes that took several months so we were without a car again for those periods. Percy Collins, who was on the adjacent farm and had an old Ford Ten, was very good at helping us to find parts and taking Dad to have a look when a possibility was identified. I can remember one day going with Percy and Dad to Cambridge to meet a man from Taranaki coming through the Waikato on his way to Auckland, who had a part which might fit. Full of eager anticipation, we awaited his arrival. When eventually he arrived, he took a sack containing a crown wheel out of his boot. But it was a huge let-down when Dad and Percy decided that it was not the correct type. It was a sombre trip home.

There was just so much to do to get the farm ready for milking. Fencing, water supply, installing rudimentary races or tracks. I would be out on the farm at every opportunity trying to help Dad and absolutely loving it. But ragwort dominated our lives for a few years. The law required this nasty noxious weed to be controlled, in particular to not allow it to seed. Sheep are able to eat it and thus control it, so as a sheep farm there had not been a problem. But with the sheep replaced by dairy cattle which did not eat it, the ragwort just went wild. Our whole family, Dad, Mum, Michael, Denise and I would be enlisted to attack it. There were no sprays then; if it was flowering you pulled it out (usually difficult as it was well rooted), put it on the trailer and took it home to be burned so that the seed could not spread, otherwise you ground your heel into the crown and sprinkled sodium chlorate on the stems. That killed it provided you got the sodium onto every stem. Miss a stem and it regrew. Properly applied sodium was probably about 60% effective, much less if not well done. We would start at one end of the farm and work our way towards the other end. By the time we had finished six weeks later we would go back to where we had started where the dreaded weed would be flowering again. We did this for several years, although each year the work of the previous year would pay off and there would be less to deal with.

When we started milking, we supplied cream, to the Morrinsville Dairy Company The milking machines delivered the milk into an open square vat which then fed a separator. The cream came out of one spout into a ten-gallon cream can. The skim milk exited from another spout into a pump that sent the skim through an underground pipeline to the piggery, which was between the orchard and Collinses' farm boundary. The cream was taken to the gate each day using a horse-drawn sled where it was collected by the dairy company truck. Cleaning up after milking was a huge chore as the separator had to be dismantled and the seventy or so parts of it washed by hand after each milking. It was a major job which was given to me if I was not going to school.

We had six sows and a boar in the piggery. The sows each had their own pen of about 25 by 25 yards with a small shed in each, where their litters were born. The pigs were a lot of work, having to be fed twice a day by carrying skim milk in buckets from a central trough where the pump had delivered it, to each pen. Farrowing had to be supervised to ensure that the sow did not lie on her newborn piglets and suffocate them, which they were prone to do, and young males were castrated when a few weeks old. We used to put them in an old gumboot to hold them while we conducted the very elementary surgery. Piggeries always smelt and pigs squealed loudly. It was impossible to love them as you could cows. If they were let out onto pasture, they would root it up with their snouts and ruin it so we had to put rings in their nose. They would often get smart and use the sides of their snout so we usually ended up with at least three rings in their nose.

Dad was keen to supply milk rather than cream to the dairy company, but Morrinsville Dairy Company were not prepared to accept milk supply from us. Fortunately, New Zealand Dairy Company came to the rescue and offered us milk supply with on-farm tanker collection. Almost every farm on Paratu switched over to New Zealand Dairy, something we never regretted because there was widespread dissatisfaction with Morrinsville. What a joy when that happened. No more pigs, washing the separator and cream cans, and taking the cream cans down to the gate every day. Farming became easier, simpler and more profitable as milk production increased and the often-conflicting priorities between pigs and cows were eliminated.

We had no tractor but did have a pair of draught horses. We had neither a wagon nor a dray just a sled, which depending on the weight which was on it, was drawn by either one or two horses. I was able to manage the sled by myself so could do all sorts of jobs such as transporting the lighter fencing materials or feeding out hay, or taking the cans of cream down to the road to be collected, so the sledge was great fun. Hills were a problem, though, particularly going downhill. The sled was connected to the horse by chains so it tended to take off and slide into the horses' back feet, and when going sideways it would slither off line to the side by as much as 90 degrees on a steep hill.

One day I came home from school and there was a tractor parked by our house, a 14 hp Ferguson. This was a big event. Life then just got so much easier for us all, even more so when Dad got a trailer. I had been taught to drive a tractor by Jim Howes, a farmer up the road whose son Clem was, and remained, a very good friend until he died in 2022, so I drove the tractor from an early age whenever I was allowed. A few years later the 14 hp model was replaced with an 18 hp model which despite being only 4 hp greater, had so much more power.

Having a tractor opened up more and more opportunities. A buck-rake, mounted on the hydraulics at the rear of the tractor, replaced horse-pushed sweeps for silage making. This enabled the cut grass to be lifted, carried and placed right on the stack in the correct position so sileage making became much easier and could be undertaken by one or two men compared to the six or more required only a few years earlier.

Gradually, the farm was developed. Mum and Dad had little money but a huge work ethic. Mum worked on the farm, milked, cooked marvellous meals, looked after the house, made our clothes, helped us with our schoolwork and always had time for us. Dad had to build the farm from scratch and do it all by hand. He understood that the only way you got something done was by doing it, and the only thing he could get for nothing was his own labour, so he worked very hard and did virtually everything by hand. Drains, trenches to lay water pipes, filling for troughs and gateways were all dug by hand. Barberry hedges, grown from canes cut from existing hedges to save money, were planted around most paddocks and gradually the farm became a model well-kept and very productive farm.

And then there was Grandad. He was a huge support to all of us. He kept us self-sufficient in vegetables by maintaining a large and highly productive vegetable garden, meaning Mum never had to buy vegetables. He looked after the chooks and slaughtered and dressed those destined for the pot when their laying days were over. He peeled potatoes, shelled peas, sliced beans (I have never seen anyone slice beans as thinly as he could using his mother of pearl pocket knife), peeled apples, pears and peaches for preserving, made soap in the "copper" boiler, babysat us kids and got meals for us. He was a rock. Born in Leicestershire in 1871 and a Boer War veteran, he was always a great source of stories from different lands and a different time. I remember one day one of our best cows, Scottie, had fallen ill with pneumonia. Grandad suggested to Dad that he drench her with a bottle of beer. Dad was not impressed and called the vet. The vet duly came, informed Dad that Scottie had pneumonia and a stimulant was the only thing that would help her. Scottie got her bottle of beer and survived. "So the old man does know something," Grandad wryly commented!

Grandad had a significant influence on all of our lives till he died at home in 1954 from pneumonia at eighty-three years of age. I remember the day he passed away; he had been low for several days. That morning Mum was very scratchy and could not get us out of the house quickly enough to go to school. It was a Wednesday which was sports day at college and when that afternoon I saw Dad coming across the playground to get me, I knew that Grandad had gone. We all missed him greatly. He had always been part of our lives; it left an emptiness when he was no longer there.

I experienced sheep farming also. About half of Paratu was still run as a sheep station. Shearing was an exciting time with shepherds bringing huge mobs of sheep to the yards. Dogs barking and sheep baaing; it was all noise and action. There were six or so shearing stands and watching the skilled shearers, sweating profusely, peel the wool off a sheep was amazing. With three or four fleecos and a cook serving smokos and lunch for about twenty people, shearing was a big event and quite an experience. I also went and helped with docking (removal of tails and testicles) where there always seemed to be a useful job I could do, usually bringing sheep up to the dockers, which made me feel very important.

Dryden the shepherd

But what I enjoyed most was lambing time. I had silver pony called Jo. I used to accompany Lloyd Booth, who was the son of the station manager and a few years older than me, on the lambing beat. Mum would prepare some sandwiches or a piece of bacon and egg pie for me. I would saddle up Jo, put on leggings and oilskin coat and go round the station where the ewes were lambing. We would help those who were having difficulty lambing, get those which had become cast on their backs up onto their feet and pluck the wool off any ewe which had died, saving it into a bag. The wool was much easier to pluck when the ewe had been dead for three or four days, but it was also much more smelly and unpleasant.

We had to ford the creek in a few places, which was usually pretty easy, but one day the creek was in flood. It looked very dangerous and I was pretty apprehensive, but Lloyd counselled me that the horses would swim: "Trust Jo, she will get you through. Let her do that and don't try to control her. If you fall off, grab her tail and hold on till she gets you out." He was right. She always got me across safely.

In those days there was a lot of scrub on the station land. This made great places to explore, build huts, undertake expeditions, go bird nesting, play hide and seek, and climb trees. With my friend Clem Howes, we climbed the cliffs which gave Paratu (Lofty Heights) its name, on what became Pennys' farm. There was an old Māori pā, the earthworks of which were very well preserved, on top of the cliff. It was a wonderful defensive position and the one side from which it could be attacked had very skilfully positioned and erected palisades.

It looked as though it would have been impregnable in the days before artillery as most pā were.

It was a real disappointment to me when the rest of the station was settled into dairy farms. All of these exciting events were no longer occurring, and we could not roam far and wide doing the things we had been accustomed to doing.

SIX
WALTON SCHOOL

I started school at Walton in Standard Two. By this time Michael had started school. At that time Paratu Road had a temporary wooden bridge over the creek. A new bridge was under construction, but the wooden bridge was considered unsafe for a school bus, even though every other vehicle went over it, including trucks with loads of cream and farming supplies. This meant that we had to walk down to the bridge to catch the bus and walk home from there. We were also the first pick-up in the morning at 7.30 am and the last drop off at night at about 5 pm. We had to leave home at 7 am to walk to the bridge and got back home at 5.30 pm. In the winter we left home in the dark and it was again dark when we got home in the evening, so it was a very long day. When Denise started school, the poor wee girl was so tired that she usually went to sleep on the bus after school and I carried her the rest of the way home, often still asleep, on my back. That came to an abrupt end one evening when after carrying her all the way from the bridge, just as we came through our house gate and for no understandable reason, she bit me in the back. I dropped her to the ground, she howled and ran up the path complaining to Mum who gave me a good telling off, but apologised when I showed her the bite mark on my back. Denise walked home after that.

In due course the new bridge was completed and the bus then came across it to the Paratu Link Road corner, which was a much shorter walk for us. Then, the Paratu settlers got together and block voted Dad and another Paratu father onto the Walton School Board to get the bus routes rearranged to more reasonable times. As Paratu was settled and more children started school, the bus went right around the loop and stopped at our gate.

On my first day at Walton School the bus seemed to take forever to get there. On the way to Walton, it detoured up Hutchinson Road almost to the railway line and then, just when the village was in sight, it detoured again up Landsdowne Road. In the end, though, it arrived at the school, which in those days had three classrooms: the old two-classroom block which housed Standards One and Two in one room and Standards Three to Six in the other. There was a newer room for the primers. Walton School had a swimming pool (not many schools did then), a bike shed, a large full-sized rugby field playground, and a horse paddock and saddle shed. Some children rode horses to school at that time.

Walton was quite a community then. In addition to the school, there was a hall where films were screened every month, and dances and other functions were frequently held. There was a railway station with a large goods shed. A railway gang of about six men together with a station master and a porter were located there. Several passenger trains stopped at Walton daily and it was possible to catch trains to Matamata, Morrinsville, Rotorua, Taneatua, Hamilton and Auckland and places in between. There was a blacksmiths shop; a saddler's shop owned by an Irishman, Jim Shanahan, which also sold and repaired sporting goods such as footballs and tennis racquets; a general store which supplied almost everything – groceries, haberdashery and clothing, wire, staples, nails, nuts and bolts, paint, crockery, newspapers, books, petrol and much more. There was a scout hall, tennis courts, bowling green and croquet lawn. Walton had its own rugby club with a senior team, cricket club, table tennis and badminton clubs, bowling, indoor bowls and croquet clubs.

I was in Standard Two. Standard One was in the same room and shared our teacher, Miss Simmons, who married a local farmer, Bruce Fawcett, a few weeks after we arrived. She was tough and demanding but an excellent teacher. I had been about an average student, but she lifted me so that I was top of the class in our final exams at the end of the year. I got on very well with her and was sometimes described as "Mrs Fawcett's pet". Betty Fawcett taught at Walton for many years, and we were delighted to have her teaching some of our children before we moved to Elstow in 1977. Her son Kit became an All Black.

The following year I was in Standard Three. Four classes, Standards Three to Six, were in the same room sharing the same teacher, Jackie Melville, who was a long-serving and popular headmaster. But part way through the year, and to everyone's disappointment, he moved to the larger Bethlehem School in Tauranga.

The new headmaster, Harold Honnor, was different. A dour personality, he was a committed Seventh Day Adventist who had rather different views on many things, especially diet, than most of us had been brought up with. At first, he was a stern disciplinarian who was not very popular, but he was a very good teacher and after we had all lifted our standards to where he wanted them to be, which was rather higher than they were when he arrived, he was not too bad after all. He certainly lifted our performance, particularly in maths. He would write a list of random numbers on the blackboard, call someone out and require them to run down the list adding up the numbers or perhaps answering rapid-fire multiplication. Most of us became very quick at arithmetic, something which has been most valuable to me throughout my life.

Dryden, Denise and Michael

When I started at Walton School it had a hand-operated water pump in the playground, but this was soon replaced by an electric pump housed near the swimming pool, and water was reticulated around the school. It was the days of milk in schools. There was a small milk shed and each day we had to carry the crates of milk up the hill to the classrooms and distribute them to each class. Each child received one half-pint bottle of milk per day. I learned to make butter by sucking out the milk by straw from the bottom of the bottle, leaving the cream behind, then gently shaking the bottle until butter formed. It tasted a bit different but Grandad told me that was because it did not have any salt so I took salt to school and added it, and sure enough Grandad was right.

For heating each classroom had a large iron stove. In the winter mornings the earliest-arriving older boys were responsible for lighting the fire in the stove in each room and keeping it stoked. We would pile the wood in and it would get very hot indeed. By the time lessons started the room would be nice and warm. The school had a large copper urn and we would fill it with milk from bottles and place the urn on the stove. By morning break the milk would be hot and we would add cocoa and sugar and stir it with a big paddle. A couple of the bigger boys would then carry the urn around the different classrooms distributing a mug of hot cocoa to every child who wanted it. Today Health & Safety would have a fit if kids did any of those things, but we loved it.

We played rugby in the winter and cricket in the summer but did not get any coaching in either sport. There were no children's organised rugby games as there are now. There were only three rugby grades, Senior, Junior and Third Grade (under 18). Competitive opportunities were limited to school games against Richmond Downs, which given their small roll were pretty one sided. There was an annual seven-a-side tournament each year in Matamata in which all of the schools in the Matamata District participated. Because I was fast, I usually played on the wing. We also had one fifteen-a-side game, usually against Tirau, when some of the local men would coach us. These were great fun and it was in one of those games that I moved to breakaway, played well and that became my preferred position.

There was also an annual Sports Day in Matamata for the district's schools. I usually won the sprint race for my age group. It was here that I first met Howard Marston from Tirau who usually pushed me pretty close.

At playtimes we usually played Bullrush. Marbles also was very popular, and we often played for "keepsies", when you kept the other person's marble if you won. As new marbles were difficult to obtain, keepsies could keep you well supplied if you were good enough.

In 1950 the Empire (as the Commonwealth was then) Games were held in Auckland. By this time radio was widely available and sporting events were being broadcast live. The Empire Games received extensive radio coverage and exposed us all to a wider range of sports. The rowing was held as it is today, at Karapiro, so Dad took our family there to watch the finals. The highlight was when the New Zealand Four defeated the Australians to take the gold medal. Mum prepared a huge picnic lunch with my favourite, bacon and egg pie. We had a wonderful day.

I had become very interested in sport and listened to every sporting broadcast I could. There was weekly professional boxing and wrestling then, so I would plead to be allowed to stay up to listen to the boxing and even to the wrestling! I would read every sports article I could get my hands on. I can recall organising a range of sporting events mimicking the Empire Games at school during play and lunchtimes. Of course, I was New Zealand and we usually won.

We used to play outside almost every minute of the day, exploring, making huts, bird nesting, roaming the farm and the Paratu area. We played just about every game which existed at that time, tennis, table tennis, badminton (with tennis racquets), rugby, soccer, running, long jump and hop step and jump, high jump, cricket and we made a few games up as well. We were active, fit and had huge appetites. Mum was a marvellous cook and we had seconds of everything, mains and desserts.

By now our family had grown. Paul was born in 1951 when I was just twelve. He was a big baby (12 lbs; 5.4 kg) which Mum credited to me, as when she was expecting him, I used to make her a big thick delicious Horlicks milkshake every night. Dad had gone overseas to war when I was four, Michael was only one year old and Denise had not been born. He had not had the pleasure which comes from experiencing babies as they grow up, so Paul was the apple of his eye. We all thought that he was pretty neat too.

By this time our transport had been upgraded. The Graham was gone but new cars were in short supply and very difficult to obtain. Dad had bought a small Bradford van, brand new and with a two-cylinder motor. At the lower end of the price range, Bradfords were very popular. It served our family very well for a number of years.

There was a strong Scout group in Walton which I wanted to join, but Mum and Dad would not allow me to do so. They were concerned that I would have to attend the occasional church parade held in a Protestant church. In those days the Catholic Church frowned on attending services of any other denomination Eventually, they relented and I was allowed to become a Scout. Ian Wills and subsequently Derek Wills were the leaders. I learned so much at Scouts, including ropes and knots, first aid, bushcraft and many other useful things. We had an annual camp, usually at Labour weekend, and sometimes overnight camps in the bush. They were great fun and we learned so much. I progressed to become a First Class Scout. Scouts was a very positive and enjoyable experience.

SEVEN
COLLEGE

Mum and Dad wanted us all to have a Catholic education. When we lived at Waitara it was their plan that I would go to St Pat's Silverstream, Wellington, which took boarders. They had been paying into an insurance policy which would mature when I went to college and contribute to the cost. When we moved to the Waikato it seemed logical that I go to Sacred Heart College in Auckland which was closer to home, so that became the plan. I accepted that would happen, although I was not at all enthusiastic as I used to get homesick whenever I was away from home.

One Sunday Father Eugene, a Passionist priest, came and spoke at Mass in Matamata. He told us that the Passionist Order was establishing its first community in New Zealand. They were setting up a Retreat House at Insoll Avenue, Hamilton. Retreats would be held at weekends but during the week they would board boys who could attend Marist High School at Hamilton East. This seemed to me, and to Mum and Dad, to be ideal for me. I would receive a Catholic education but would be home on Friday night for the weekend until

Monday morning, so we agreed that I should go there. That decision was to have unforeseen, but adverse, consequences for my education.

I would catch a bus from the end of Paratu Road on Monday morning and would arrive at school around 9 to 9.30 am. After school we would bike to Insoll Avenue about six miles away. We would bike back to school each morning. One of the teaching Marist brothers would ride with us and stay overnight at the hostel and then ride back to school with us in the morning. But there was a catch. In the morning, we had to leave the hostel with the brother at 7 am, arriving at school at 7.30, then amuse ourselves until school started at 8.45. After school we would have to hang around the school amusing ourselves until after 5 pm for him to accompany us back to the hostel. This was most unsatisfactory.

It was even worse. Marist was a small high school with almost no sporting facilities or organised sport. It was not a boarding school so was not organised for boarders. Boarding schools know that they need to keep the boys' lives organised every minute of the day, but we were left to fend for ourselves at school for about four hours every day and there was also nothing to do outside of dinner and prayers in the evening. Given those circumstances, it was inevitable that I should become terribly homesick and miserable. As a consequence, I was severely distracted, was not focussed on my school work and fell behind. I had always loved maths, social studies, geography, history and science. In the third form you are introduced to the new maths of algebra and geometry and that becomes the basis for undertaking more complex calculations. Unfortunately, my distraction was such that I failed to grasp those concepts. That has been a hindrance to me all of my life. I am very numerate but have always had to carry out a lengthy series of simple arithmetical exercises to complete more complex calculations. I hated going back to school on Monday mornings and frequently phoned Mum and Dad in tears. A couple of times Dad had to come over to the hostel to settle me down. I pleaded to be allowed to come home and go to Matamata College. At the end of the first term, Mum and Dad relented.

I was delighted to be home and going to Matamata College, but the effects of my unhappy time at Marist lingered. I was given the option of taking either Professional, Technical or Agriculture courses. I wanted to be a farmer so opted for Agriculture. Unlike at the start of the year when starting college students were given advice on what would be the most suitable course for them, and most were talked out of Agriculture, no such advice was given to me. Had I been at Matamata at the start of the year and given my good scholastic record I would have been pushed into Professional with the top students. I found that very little Agriculture was actually taught, but the class was largely a repository for the least academic students who were not at all interested in school.

In our agricultural class most of the boys were not interested in learning and were filling in time before reaching the age of fifteen when they could leave school. There were quite a few apprentice jockeys, most of whom were not at all scholastic. They would get up at 4 am each day for ride work, then come to school and after school go back to the stables for other work such as mucking out the stables. Those poor kids were so tired that they often fell asleep in class. This environment was certainly not conducive to learning and acting the goat was common behaviour. With little effort I had no difficulty being first or second in the class while being disruptive at the same time. My school record, therefore, was pretty dismal.

My thirst for knowledge, however, only increased and I continued to be a voracious reader, devouring every book I could get hold of and on a wide range of subjects. In the fifth form we were introduced to accounting and commercial practice. Our teacher was Mr Scott.

Initially, accounting seemed to be the same boring stuff until we began to apply what we had been taught and construct a list of transactions into a set of accounts and a trial balance. All of a sudden, the light switched on. I found accounting to be extremely interesting and became enthusiastic about it. Had I not become a farmer, I almost certainly would have become an accountant.

One of my strengths which began to show out at college was public speaking. I reached the final of the fourth form speaking contest, coming runner up. Edmund Hillary and Sherpa, Tenzing Norgay, had a short time earlier become the first people to climb Mt Everest and that was my subject. I learned much from that experience and the following year won the fifth form speech contest. My subject was an obscure topic, "Freedom is Truth", or something like that. That research led me to the Greek statesman and philosopher Pericles, whose leadership and writings on democracy were central to Greece becoming the world's first democracy, which I drew on and quoted. My ability to communicate effectively to large audiences was critical to my later career and leadership roles.

Matamata College was a good school. It was co-ed but had a very strict senior mistress, Miss Tompkins. She would not allow the girls to even talk to boys. The masters were rather more tolerant with us boys, but of course it was a rule made to be broken, which we did at every opportunity. Each year the college put on a concert for parents, families and supporters. It had been the practice for the fifth and sixth forms to be allowed to have a dance during the time they were waiting for their item on the programme. This encouraged most of us to audition and get selected for the item our class was putting on. We were horrified to learn a few days before the concert that there would be no dance and that we would be confined to our classroom for the whole time we were not performing. This was most annoying, as we felt that we had been inveigled to participate in the concert on false pretences as the prospect of a dance was the only reason we were there. So, four of us arranged to meet with our girlfriends in the playground after our item was over. Inevitably, our absence was noted, we were caught, and there was hell to pay when we arrived at school next day. The girls of course copped it far worse than we boys did.

At one time in our science class, we studied Magnetism and Electricity and learned how to make a telephone. Boys being boys, we looked for ways to put this knowledge into practice. We noticed a hole in the floor at the back of the classroom and had an idea. A recce discovered a similar hole in the girls' classroom next door so we rigged up telephones in a desk in our room and another in the girls' classroom. We then climbed under the school and laid a wire connecting the two telephones. This was great; we were able to chat with the girls on the telephone, initially only outside of class times. Then we got more audacious and began to have chats during class, which was dangerous but even more fun. But we could only do so by making arrangements with the girls in advance. To be able to contact the girls at any time we wanted to, we rigged up a buzzer. That worked well until one day the girls did not answer promptly (their teacher was nearby) so we kept buzzing and gave the whole game away.

We also used to have Cadets where we had military training and drills. We were taught to shoot; the school had its own rifle range. A sergeant from the regular army was our instructor, but he was not the brightest penny. Most of us were farm boys and quite good shots. We would deliberately put all of our shots into someone else's target, which of course meant that our own target was untouched. The instructor would then painstakingly coach those of us who had clear targets and we would respond by working our shots closer to our own target as he coached us. He would be thrilled that he had taught us to shoot straight and we were thrilled to have fooled him. I don't think that he ever woke up to what was going on.

I had my heart set on farming and the school, and Mum and Dad, finally agreed that it would be better if I left school and went home to the farm. School Certificate was only about two months away, but I did not sit it. Had I done so I am sure I would have passed. So apart from public speaking and sport, my college record was undistinguished, to say the least.

EIGHT
FARMING CALLS

At last, I was farming but if I thought that I would have complete freedom I still had a lot to learn. Being the excellent parents they were, Mum and Dad continued to exercise the control on my life necessary to keep me on the right path and out of trouble. For example, I was not allowed to go to dances without their permission, which was not easily obtainable. I broke the rules and went anyhow a few times, but they always found out and then I was in trouble.

But I was farming and loving the life, the open air, the freedom and the wide range of activities involved, even if I did not really like the twice-daily chore of milking which was a real tie. We had a six-bail walk-through cowshed, but with the help of Joe Colbran, a friend of Mum and Dad's, Dad and I extended it to eight bails which helped speed up milking. At that time, we did not have a chiller unit on the vat. Instead, we had an ice bank chiller which built up a bank of ice between milkings. Water was then circulated through the ice bank into a bar cooler to chill the milk before it went into the vat. The ice bank was large, about 2 m by 1.2 m by 1.6 m high, so it took up a fair amount of space in the dairy.

At that time the power supply was not very reliable and power cuts were frequent. If the power was off at milking time, we would position the tractor at the back of the dairy and hook the tractor power-take-off pulley up with the vacuum pump, using a wide belt about 8 metres long to run the milking machines. In the house a cut-off switch prevented both the stove and hot water being operated at the same time. The hot water cylinder only had a small 750-watt element and for several years the power went off at 10 pm and did not come on again till 5 am. We had a bath but no shower, so hot water was always in short supply and had to be carefully husbanded.

Dad was a good farmer with a very strong work ethic which he instilled into me and also into Michael and Denise. Like all young boys, I enjoyed working the tractor. By now Dad had upgraded to an 18 hp Ferguson which had a lot more grunt than the 14 hp. We had a sickle bar mower, a buckrake, a hay tedder, a Cambridge roller which we used to lend to everyone on Paratu, a set of tine harrows, a trailer and a Gallagher spinner top dresser, which bolted onto the trailer and was driven by a chain from a cog welded onto one of the trailer wheels. Any other implements we required we had to borrow from other Paratu farmers who were very generous at sharing what they had.

Top dressing was a job I did not like. Fertiliser came in heavy 50 kg bags and was not always available when required, so Dad tried to keep about six months' supply in our shed. At that time, it was superphosphate which when stored set hard in the bags. We would have to smash the bags with a maul, empty the bags onto the floor of the shed, smash up all of the lumps and re-bag the fertiliser. We then loaded the trailer and Dad drove the tractor while I staggered around on a moving trailer lifting the heavy bags and pouring fertiliser out of them into the spreader hopper. It was even worse for the lucerne paddock at the top of the farm. Lucerne requires a lot of potash and would be fertilised every three months. Potash would set even harder than super so we would have to carry out the same process as well as mixing the super and potash together before re-bagging. It played hell with your hands, especially if you had any cuts or abrasions. Oh, the joy when serpentine super and potassic serpentine super became available, both of which could be used straight from the bag. Many years later even greater joy came when bulk spreading eliminated the need for bags, and we no longer had to spread fertiliser manually at all.

The land at Paratu was initially quite low in fertility and the farm was very susceptible to summer drought, so Dad planted a large paddock in lucerne which grew well during the summer. It was used for sileage. We had a large silage pit cut into the side of the hill and harvested several cuts of hay. It provided virtually all of our supplementary feed and was grazed only once each season during the winter. Haymaking for me was not a pleasant experience. The lucerne was baled very green to retain the leaf, which contained most of the nutrition and was lost as powdery dust when really dry. Dad always had the contractor bale into larger bales to reduce the cost, and it was very stalky. So, we had very heavy stalky bales, which sometimes required two people to lift onto the trailer and stack in the barn. The hard stalks played havoc with your hands, thighs and long trousers, if you wore them to protect your thighs. I was to do away with the lucerne when I took over the farm, but that brought a different problem as bloat became an issue every time the cows were in that paddock.

As a fifteen-year-old farm hand my wages were a modest £4-5-0 a week plus, of course, free board. I was paid monthly and saved £12 each month. After a couple of years, I had saved sufficient to buy a car and purchased a 1951 Ford Prefect for £340. I continued to save every penny I could because my goal was now to go sharemilking as soon as possible. Of course, now having a car to run I could no longer save three-quarters of my wages each month, but I relished the freedom of being able to get out and about without having to ask Mum and Dad for their car. They still exercised discipline on where I went and what I did though.

Like Dad, Mum was good at most sports. They both took up playing bowls. In her first year Mum reached the finals of the Walton Women's Junior Singles. She was beaten by Elsie Wilkie who went on to become both New Zealand and Commonwealth Games Women's Singles Champion. She also played in a four which beat most teams around the region and which went on to win the National Women's Fours title a couple of years after she had moved to Rotorua. Grandad had played bowls so there were many discussions around the dinner table with the pepper and salt pots being moved around to demonstrate the layout of the bowls on the green. Mum and Dad continued to play bowls until they were both close to ninety. They also played indoor bowls in the winter.

When I was eighteen, I was asked to become an artificial insemination technician. We were trained in Hamilton on town milk herds which calved all the year round. The training lasted two weeks and we stayed at the old Central Private Hotel in Hood Street. Staying in a hotel was a new experience for me as was living in a city. Most of those in the same training course were of a similar age to me and we soon found our way to the Starlight Ballroom in Anglesea Street, which held dances most nights. In those days it was illegal to be in possession of alcohol within, I think, one mile of a dance. I did not drink anyhow so that was not a problem. We soon learned how to set up a blind date with nurses from the nurses home at Waikato Hospital.

Artificial breeding (AB) technicians were very well paid for the ten-week season, receiving £23 a week, a huge sum which helped my savings. I enjoyed the job and visiting my forty farmers each day. I seemed to have an aptitude for it and most years my group was in the top three for conception rate in the South Auckland Herd Improvement Association. Mum and Dad allowed me to also supplement my income by picking up hay and doing casual farm work around the district. This was most valuable experience as I learned how to do a much wider range of tasks, and how to do them in different ways, than I would have learned just by working with Dad. My knowledge and experience grew enormously during this time, and I enjoyed the company and working with others rather than working by myself as I often did at home. My bank balance benefitted also.

Mum and Dad made a large sacrifice to ensure that we received a Catholic secondary education. It did not work out for me, but Michael was sent to board at Sacred Heart and Denise to Baradene, both in Auckland. The downside of that sacrifice was that when they finished School Certificate, they were both taken out of school. Michael came home to the farm and a year later Denise started work at the Walton Store. After a few months she managed to get a job at BNZ in Morrinsville. Michael did not want to leave school. He had set his sights on joining the air force and wanted to be a pilot or alternatively a navigator. Both of those roles required University Entrance so Michael was not able to qualify. But he was determined, and I can recall him buying books on advanced maths, and trying to educate himself to UE standard, to give himself a chance of joining the air force.

So, when I was eighteen Michael came home to the farm. I found a job as a builder's labourer at the Kiwi Fertiliser Works at Morrinsville which was then under construction. It was heavy work and I had to lie about my age to get the job. We worked nine hours a day, six days a week, but the pay was very good as I received £17 a week. The work was physical and often boring, much of it associated with concreting, digging foundation holes and trenches, shovelling metal into concrete mixers, or laying large areas of concrete. Every couple of weeks a train would arrive with 100 tonnes of cement in hundredweight (about 45 kg) bags. Three of us would have to unload the cement onto a truck, then unload the fertiliser off the truck and stack it in the store. It took all day and we were absolutely exhausted by the time we were finished. I was then fortunate to be assigned as a fitter's mate, so worked with the engineers erecting steel structures, installing conveyor belts and bucket elevators, and a lot of plumbing work connecting piping and vessels for air, water and acid. I learned to use an oxy-acetylene torch and to weld.

During my time at Kiwi, I learned so much which was to be so useful to me in my farming career, especially about construction and engineering, knowledge which would have taken me years to accumulate on the farm. But I learned much more than that. I discovered just how hard people at the less qualified end of the labour force work. How boring the work often is, how often they have no idea of the purpose of the job they are doing. How demoralising it is after digging a hole, for instance, being told to fill it in because someone has made a mistake and it is in the wrong place. It was also a new experience for me to be in an industrial environment of mostly Labour voters and strong union supporters and seeing the union rep come to the site every fortnight looking for grievances and taking them up with management. I observed that usually the only help or support a worker ever received came from the union. This social and industrial experience shaped my understanding and approach to people in my later commercial leadership roles.

After about a year at Kiwi I left to do an AB round. I received a very good reference from Mick Conroy, the engineer and works manager. I still have it and is the only job reference I ever sought or received.

After the AB season was over, I did casual farm work, sileage, hay, fencing, relief milking, drain cleaning and scrub cutting. It was hard work which physically matured me. I made good money and gained a huge amount of knowledge, learning many different ways of doing things. Then with winter approaching I applied for a job at Waharoa Dairy Factory. At that time of the year with milk supply declining, dairy factories were usually not hiring, but by now I was playing senior rugby and the butter factory manager, Mr Willcocks, who was a strong United supporter, gave me a job in the lactalbumin plant. It was a good place to work especially in the winter, and when the milk flow ceased, we did maintenance work on the buildings and plant. The money was good, although the payment structure was very complicated, reflecting the round-the-clock operation for most of the year.

NINE
SPORT

I was always mad about sport. In my early teens I played tennis in the summer and was runner up in the Walton Tennis Club Junior Championship.

Michael and I used to play "test match" cricket on the lawn. We were England and Australia; New Zealand did not count at cricket at that time. Australia was the best side in the world so we took it in turns to be Australia. I made a bat from a willow branch, shaped it to have a handle and blade and oiled it with linseed oil. It jarred badly, but the ball went like a rocket if you hit it in the sweet spot. A truck coming onto the section had left double wheel indentations in the lawn. We used to put the stumps in the middle of these indentations and bowl down them. We could bring the ball in from either the leg, or the off, by landing the ball on the ridges on either side. We would argue like mad as to whether a shot was caught or it had gone for four. We had plenty of miraculous catches as well as dropped sitters. We both understood we had to agree to a fair number of each.

At college I graduated from sprinting to middle-distance running and won the Matamata College Junior Athletic Championship. I won the mile, 880 yards and high jump, coming third in the 440-yard race to clinch the title. I was selected to represent Matamata College in the Junior mile at the Waikato Interschool Athletics Championship. I had very little experience in competitive racing and was amazed how quickly the field took off. Before I knew it, I was near the tail of the field about 100 metres behind the leaders. I picked the pace up and worked my way up through the field to finish a creditable fourth. The following year, though, I was ready for the opening stampede. I knew who the top competitor was (a guy who would go on to win several national titles) and resolved to follow him closely and hope to outsprint him at the finish. I stuck with him and was tucked just behind him at the top of the final straight, but I did not have the legs to match his sprint. Two others passed me in the straight and I blacked out at the finish line. I had given it everything I had but was not quite fit enough and came fourth again. I decided athletics was not for me and never ran again.

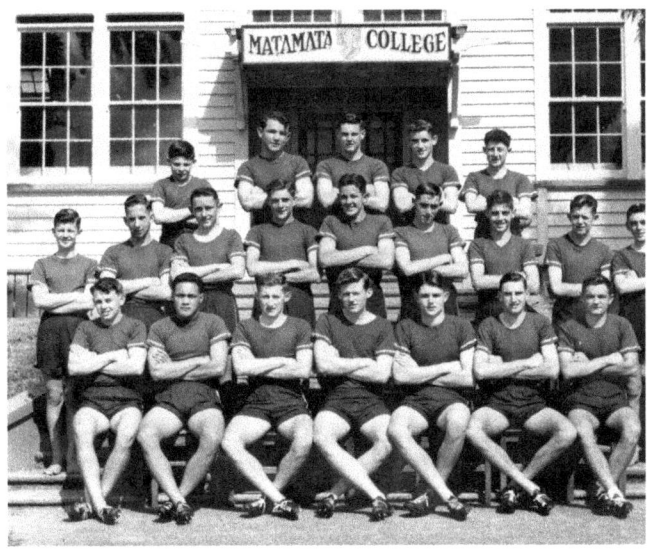

Matamata College Athletic Team, 1952

I had been introduced to table tennis by Mum who was one of the top women at Walton Table Tennis Club. By the time I was in the fourth form, I was in the Walton A Team and playing in interclub competition.

But rugby was my first love. In my second year I was chosen for the Third XV. This was the team the more promising players were placed in, and it regularly defeated the Second XV. We played other colleges in the Waikato and Bay of Plenty regions and went for several years undefeated. Our coach, Mr Fisher, had played halfback for Wellington. He was an outstanding coach. At our first training session he had invited the prominent Waikato No. 8 George Nola to show us how to scrum. We put the first scrum down and George made us stay down while he showed each of us what our job was and how to do it. We were allowed up only once during our one hour, twenty minutes session. By then we were exhausted, stiff and sore, but we really knew how to scrum and that was the basis of our forward effort that took us through the season undefeated. I was later to play senior-grade rugby, against George Nola, and with him in the Matamata reps. The following year our coach was Mr Scott and I was vice-captain. Again, we had a well-drilled team which won every game including against Tauranga, Rotorua and Hamilton Boys, all much larger schools than Matamata.

Sport continued to be a major interest for me. Waharoa, Walton and Wardville Rugby Clubs had amalgamated into United, which had its home ground, and in due course a clubhouse, at the Waharoa Domain. I captained the United Third Grade team and made the Matamata Reps. We defeated Te Awamutu to win the Cucksey Cup for the top Waikato Third Grade Sub Union. I continued to play table tennis usually twice a week, in tournaments and interclub matches.

I played cricket for Walton Cricket Club, which was very strong, while I was still at school. There were nine cricket clubs in Matamata, and we used to play on the two rugby fields at Bedford Park. Four games were played on that relatively small area at the same time. The fields were overlapping and sometimes when fielding at long off on one field, you were almost in the slips on another. I was a Walton Club selector and served on the Matamata Cricket Association Management Committee. I took a few wickets and made a limited number of runs so was a pretty ordinary cricketer, but I enjoyed it enormously. I was also enjoying the company of some very fine men who gave me every encouragement and help.

In 1956 the Springbok rugby team visited New Zealand. The All Blacks had never won a series against them, while they had defeated us in New Zealand in 1937 and demolished us 4–nil in South Africa in 1949, so national pride was at stake. I attended their first match at Hamilton in front of a crowd of 31,000. Waikato kicked off and the Springbok who took the ball was hit by seven Waikato forwards and then the eighth, George Nola. The sound of those forwards hitting reverberated around the ground. Waikato won the ball, first-five Jack Bullick kicked high and last man into the ruck, George Nola, was first man out. He collared the catcher. Again, Waikato won the ball, halfback Ponty Reid went to the blindside and Malcolm McDonald scored right in front of me in the first minute. The Springboks never really recovered from that experience for the rest of the tour. Waikato continued to dominate and won 14–10 despite playing much of the game with fourteen men, as no replacements were allowed in those days. They had lost first-five Jack Bullick with a broken cheekbone about 30 minutes in. George Nola played an outstanding game but was a passenger for the last fifteen minutes after being punched in the testicles by Jan Pickard.

By the time of the fourth test in Auckland a couple of months later, the All Blacks were up 2–1 and poised for a series win. Dad and I left home about 10 pm on Friday night to attend my first All Black test. There was no television in those days so like most people I had never actually seen the All Blacks play. We arrived about half-past midnight and queued all night outside Eden Park along with several thousand others. In those days there were very few seats and reservations; it was mostly standing room. The gates opened at 8.30 am and we sprinted into the ground to get a good possie. The crowd was huge, over 61,000, and we stayed jammed in like sardines until the game started at 2.30. It was a brutal match at a time when boots and fists were often used. The All Blacks won 11–5 with Peter Jones playing an outstanding game. National honour was redeemed! It was at this time that Winston McCarthy was at his peak as a commentator. He was a household name at a time when there was no television and we relied on radio commentaries. His piercing call on goal kicks, "Listen … It's a goal", was legendary. He was the greatest rugby radio commentator there has ever been.

As I worked on Saturdays at the Kiwi Fertiliser Works, I stopped playing rugby and cricket. However, I met up with Bill Anderson who had played lock in the great Waikato Ranfurly Shield-winning team of the 1950s. He was a typical lock of those times, hard as nails and believed in "getting retaliation in beforehand". He had bought a farm by the railway line on Hutchinson Road. I had worked in a hay gang with him and we had become good friends, even though he was about twelve years older than me. He was now player coach of the United senior team. He asked why I was not playing rugby. I told him that I was working but that I intended to play the following year. It was towards the end of the season, and he suggested that I come to training with the Senior team, believing that it would prepare me for the following season. I agreed and started training with the senior squad. Even though I was only eighteen, I found that I was enjoying being with all of these adult men, some of whom had been my idols when I was at primary school only six years before. United had won the Matamata Sub Union Club Competition and were now playing for the Binnie Cup to determine the top club team in the Waikato. To my surprise, at training one evening Bill told me that I was playing flanker on Saturday.

At this time Dad took me aside and told me that he had played first-class rugby even though he was only ten and a half stone. The only reason he was able to do it was because he was always fitter than anyone else. He said, "Dryden, during your rugby career you will come up against many players who will be more talented than you and there will be nothing that you can do about it. But you can be fitter than everyone else; that is totally within your control and if you are, you will be as good as any of them and better than most." He was right. I was later to apply the same principle to my business career.

I was thrilled and so proud to be playing in the senior team. I resolved to give it everything that I had and started like a rocket. However, after only three weeks of training I was not at all fit and by halftime I was completely spent. But we managed to win. I was encouraged, though, that when reviewing our performance at training the following week, Bill said that I had "played very well until you ran out of steam but you will come again". Next week I was in the team again, playing lock. At 12 stone dripping wet, I was far too light for lock but was good in the lineout and quick around the field. "I have put you at lock because you need to learn to play tighter," said Bill. "Don't worry, Johnny will look after you." Johnny was Johnny Gillett, a giant of a man and very good rugby player. He did look after me, we won that game and were into the final against Athletic from South Waikato. We scored a try almost on full-time to beat them and were the Waikato club champions. It had been a pretty eventful introduction to senior rugby for a lightweight and rather unfit eighteen-year-old.

The following year most of our best players had retired, but our young team improved through the year. We had a wonderful team spirit and were very close; even during the summer we got together. The next year I made the Matamata Sub Union Reps. I began to be frequently selected for the Corinthians. The Corinthian Rugby Club was a Matamata club similar in concept to the Barbarians and Harlequins. Players from all over the Waikato, Bay of Plenty, Thames Valley and Auckland were invited to play for it. Each team usually brought together experienced "name" players, including a few All Blacks, some local stalwarts and promising young players. Games were played on Sundays against a range of teams; for example, we played Auckland Marist, NZ Police and Auckland Armed Services. These games attracted good crowds as an open style of rugby was played and it was a good opportunity to see well-known players. For a young player like me, each game was a wonderful experience to play with and against some outstanding first-class players including some All Blacks.

In 1961 Matamata Sub Union had a new coach, Tom Guy. He made it known that he was looking for size in his forwards so I thought that I would struggle to make the team. One day he asked me what my weight was, and when I told him 13 stone (I was almost 12 with my gear on), that seemed to satisfy him and I was selected. But when I arrived for our first training, there he was with a set of scales and a measuring ruler. He was clearly going to weigh us, and measure the height of every player, so I thought that it was all over for me. I was going to be found out and would never get a game. I was first to training and Tom said to me, "Springy, come over here and I will measure your height then I want you to weigh every player as they come in and record their weight in this notebook for me. I have got your weight as 13 stone, isn't it?" A narrow escape but I am sure he had worked out that I weighed a lot less than 13 stone!

MATAMATA SENIOR RUGBY REPRESENTATIVE TEAM
WINNERS PEACE CUP 1961

Matamata, the Peace Cup winners, 1961

We had a very good team and were winning our games. We had a Peace Cup elimination game scheduled against Waitomo. They had Colin and Stan Meads who were then at the peak of their form, and another All Black, flanker Tom Coughlan. Tom Guy went to watch them play. At the following training he told us about a move they used often and to great effect, in which Coughlan took the ball at six in the lineout and fed it to either Colin or Stan Meads as they came round the end of the lineout. I was told that I would play at seven and my job was to tackle the Meads boys as they came around the lineout. We practised doing that all night at training. Tom had the biggest guys in the team peeling around the lineout for me to tackle.

By the end of the night I was bruised, stiff and sore. I was not looking forward to the game against Waitomo. However, I was saved. To our great relief, Lower Waikato beat Waitomo so we had to play our elimination match against Lower Waikato. In the mud at Huntly, we won 6–3 when a penalty from my best friend Arthur Cochrane just sneaked over the bar. That qualified us for a Peace Cup challenge.

The Peace Cup was in those days played for on a challenge basis by the sub unions from Counties, Waikato, Thames Valley, Bay of Plenty and King Country. It was a very popular competition and was well attended with crowds numbering up to 10,000 in cities such as Hamilton or Rotorua and 3000 to 5000 in the rural towns such as Matamata.

Rotorua had a star-studded team and had dominated the Peace Cup for many years. So off we went to Rotorua to challenge them. It was a tough and bruising game and quite dirty too, but we scored a couple of tries and managed to beat them. We were thrilled for this was a major achievement. We arrived back in Matamata that night to a large cheering crowd and a mayoral reception. We defeated the remaining challengers that season to hold the Peace Cup at the end of the season.

At the start of the following season the Corinthians sponsored a team comprising our Peace Cup team to tour to Manawatu and Wanganui to help prepare our team to defend the Cup. Touring was a new experience for most of us, but we won all of our games and developed an amazing team spirit.

Our first defence of the 1962 season was against Rotorua. It was a big day for Matamata: a civic parade through the town before the game, lunch in the dining room of the Matamata Hotel for the team; Winston McCarthy doing a live radio commentary in front of a crowd of close to 5000. We had home advantage but were defeated

10–6, with the All Black second five-eight Bill Gray scoring two tries under the posts, both of which originated inside their own 25!

I continued playing for United and Matamata reps for the next two or three years but retired at the ripe old age of twenty-five as I was now sharemilking and our young family was growing. I stopped playing cricket at about the same time.

TEN
WORK EXPERIENCE

In the spring I left Waharoa factory to do an AB round again. I was also doing casual farm work, making good money and continuing to save. By this time, I had 50/50 sharemilking set firmly in my sights.

My social life was expanding and I was active in the Catholic Youth Movement which, at that time, was very strong in the Auckland Diocese. We had a young Assistant Priest, Father Ewen Derrick, who was involving young people in the church, something which had not previously been the case. I respected him enormously and he had an influence on shaping my character. We organised a lot of events, some spiritual and some social. We had a Sunday night dance in Matamata every month, and most Sunday evenings there were dances in neighbouring parishes. These were both popular and potential match-making events.

One Sunday night there was a new girl. My enquiries revealed that her name was Christine McCarthy who had just moved to Matamata with her family. I asked her for a dance and we got on well together. By the end of the evening, we were having every dance together and enjoying doing so. It seemed to me that I should offer her a ride home which she accepted without hesitation. Before long we were an item.

My nana used to come and stay with us for about three weeks every year. She was a small lady who never stopped doing things. The silver would all be cleaned till it was sparkling and the house would be spring cleaned. Any ironing or darning would be completed, and she never stopped knitting. She was loving and caring and we all loved her deeply. Reflecting the formality of those days, she and Grandad always addressed one another as "Mr Edge" and "Mrs Spring", even though they had known one another for many years, such were the times. She lived by herself in a small cottage at Eketahuna and seemed to keep good health. But one evening while staying with us she experienced severe abdominal pains and was taken to the hospital in the middle of the night. I seem to recall that she was diagnosed with gallstones or kidney stones and underwent surgery. The surgery was successful, but her mind seemed affected, something which was not unusual with the anaesthetics used in those days. She never came home from hospital.

After a few weeks she was admitted to Tokanui Mental Hospital. I went to see her there, but I don't think that she knew me. The poor dear had fallen and broken her arm which was in plaster. I was so sad seeing this loving, vibrant and active woman now in a world of her own. She passed away after several months at the age of seventy-five in 1956.

My romance with Christine continued to blossom; we became engaged and planned our wedding for August 1960. We had intended that I would work for Mum and Dad on the farm for a modest income and supplement my income through casual farm work. We were looking for a cottage nearby to rent. However, Dad was beginning to suffer severely from arthritis, both osteo and rheumatoid. He and Mum decided that he could not continue to farm so he applied for a job in the timber treatment plant at Waipa Mill in Rotorua, which had a house attached to the job. Of course, the real reason for their decision to move off the farm was to give Christine and me the opportunity to buy the herd and sharemilk on the farm.

So, in June 1960 Mum and Dad shifted into their tiny house on the Waipa Mill site in Rotorua. I did not feel great as I left Rotorua after shifting them in. I knew they were leaving their nice and comfortable family home in Walton to make way for Christine and me. However, it was only a starting point for them and within a few months they had purchased a nice house in Rotorua where they stayed until Dad passed away on 6 May 2004. Dad's arthritis continued to get worse and he suffered severely for the rest of his life, having a total of six hip replacements. One of the reasons they had chosen Rotorua was that Queen Elizabeth Hospital was the leading facility for the treatment of arthritis, and the availability of warm mineral baths was helpful in the management of the disease. Mum and Dad loved living in Rotorua and soon had a wide circle of good friends. They were very active and played bowls for many years. It was also a city which many people visited so they had a constant stream of relations and friends visit them which they greatly enjoyed.

I applied for a loan from State Advances Corporation. There was still a gap between my savings, the amount State Advances would lend to me and the cost of the herd and machinery. Mum and Dad agreed to lend that sum to me and I was to pay them back after repaying the State Advances loan. The loan appraiser, a senior and very experienced lender called Robin Wallace, duly arrived at the farm. I did not have a clue about the financial situation I would be in. No budget; I did not even know how to prepare one. He went through his work discussing many issues with me and then began to summarise the numbers. To my shock he ended with a deficit. I thought that was it, I cannot make it pay, I will not get a loan, my sharemilking career is over before it has even started. But then, to my surprise, he said, "That's okay, in August you will get the dairy company bonus and show a reasonable surplus." Whew!

I was only twenty years of age, at that time legally still a minor, and was going into business sharemilking. As a minor, I was not allowed to sign any legal documents. So, to complete a sharemilking agreement and the loan documents from State Advances, I had to go before a judge, satisfy him that I knew what I was doing, was not being taken advantage of, and receive his approval to sign the documents. As minors, Christine and I also had to get our parents' written permission to get married and then get approval from the Matamata Postmaster (the Postmaster was a senior government official in those days).

Just at the time Mum and Dad were leaving the farm, the tractor packed up and needed major repair. Dad decided after a discussion with Laurie Maber, the owner of Maber Motors, that I should get a new tractor so a Massey Ferguson 35 arrived on the farm on 1 June 1960. It cost £715 plus £35 pounds for a PTO drive (a total of around $1500). It was to be the only tractor I ever owned. My son-in-law Graham Hallett sold it forty-seven years later in 2007 and gave me a cheque for $1500. What great value!

It was exciting being my own boss and running my own business. It was hard work running the farm by myself and living alone, but Mum had taught us all to cook and look after ourselves, so I ate pretty well. In August when Christine and I were married, we had two weeks off and went to Hawke's Bay and East Coast for our honeymoon. It was a busy time on the farm; calving was just about over but spring had not yet arrived. I was fortunate that my cousin, Toby Robinson, and Mum came and milked for me while Christine and I were away.

The young sharemilker (on the farm at Paratu)

I had inherited my parents' strong work ethic and belief that if a job was worth doing it was worth doing properly. So, I worked hard to be a good farmer and improve the farm. I subdivided all of the eleven paddocks into a total of twenty-five, using single-wire, mains-powered electric fences. I cleared the area of manuka that was growing in a swampy paddock, dug drains to drain a number of small swampy areas and installed tile drains in wet spots below hillsides. I cleared rushes growing in some of the paddocks and replaced some boundary fences which were in poor shape. I installed races, carting sand dug by hand with a shovel, to surface them. Gradually, the farm became more productive and I lifted the stocking rate from the seventy cows I started with to 120. I prided myself on having the tidiest and best farm on Paratu.

Christine was marvellous. A girl brought up in Wellington, until her family moved to Matamata where Winston McCarthy, her father, was manager of the TAB, she gave up her job as a legal secretary when we got married. She adjusted well to farm life and helped with milking, calf feeding and other farming chores. She soon became pregnant and in June 1961 she had a difficult birth and was taken by ambulance to Waikato Hospital where Mark arrived. What a wonderful experience it was to be the proud parents of a bonny little boy!

It was to be the start of what, for a while, became almost an annual event. Julie-Ann was born in August 1962, Greg in July 1963, Kevin on New Year's Day 1965, Lisa-Jane in October 1967 and Annemarie in June 1970. Christine was later to comment to Peter Freeth, who was writing an article on her for the *New Zealand Herald*, "that she came in with the cows every year for a few years". Amazingly, she continued to help milk for much of the time through those busy years, as well as being a top-class mother and excellent housekeeper. She loved music and singing and after Anna was born, she also found time to participate in the annual productions of the Matamata Operatic Society, taking some significant roles.

We were fortunate to be bringing up our large family on a farm. Julie-Ann and Mark were later to comment at the time of Julie-Ann's wedding, when by that time we were living in Elstow, that they "were so lucky to have grown up in Walton; it was such a lovely place". With a large family we need to be pretty strict and while that was not always easy for them or us, they all grew up to have great character, good values and a very strong work ethic. Christine and I received many compliments about how well behaved our kids were, which made us pretty proud of them.

PART THREE
A FARMER POLITICIAN

ELEVEN
FEDERATED FARMERS

I CONTINUED TO READ VORACIOUSLY AND HAD A VERY broad interest in the world beyond the farm. My time in the Catholic Youth Movement and particularly the guidance I had received from Father Derrick had developed my social conscience, while working as a labourer on industrial sites had made me aware that life for working families was often difficult. The Catholic Youth Movement also stressed leadership and the obligation we all had to use our talents to help others. I was conscious that I was doing nothing beyond the farm gate other than play sport.

One day our neighbour Percy Collins asked me if I would like to accompany him that evening to a meeting of the Walton Branch of Federated Farmers. I was very happy to accept. I found the meeting to be most interesting, but even better was that when the meeting concluded the chairman, Harry Watson, shouted drinks as he had been chairman for ten years. It was a great night and I got home about midnight!

The following month I eagerly attended the next meeting hoping for another shout but was disappointed. However, I found the discussions to be even more interesting as I was beginning to understand the issues. I continued to attend each month. One evening it happened to be the annual meeting at which the officers were elected. I was nominated to be the sharemilker delegate to Morrinsville Sub-Province. With an excess of modesty, I demurred, but Ian Wills persuaded me to accept when he said, "Dryden, I advise you to accept. You will find that it is very interesting and the further you go in Federated Farmers the more interesting you will find it." His advice proved to be spot on.

The Sub-Province meetings were held in the Morrinsville Veterinary Club Boardroom. They were most interesting and before long I was an active participant, looking forward to each month's meeting. A year later at the annual meeting of the sub-province, I was chosen to be the delegate to the Waikato Provincial Sharemilkers Sub Section. Recalling Ian Wills' advice, there was no demurring this time. I had become an enthusiastic participant and was delighted to have the opportunity to become more involved.

I set out to promote more activity by sharemilkers within Federated Farmers and organised a meeting in Morrinsville with a local accountant, Gary Barnett, as guest speaker, on farm accounting and record keeping. It attracted a huge crowd of close to 300 sharemilkers. There was soon a request from other districts to help them arrange similar events. All of this was very positive encouragement to sharemilkers to join Federated Farmers as they could see it was doing something for them.

The Provincial Sharemilkers Executive met four times a year, in a relatively new building which Federated Farmers had built next to the New Zealand Dairy Company Building in London Street, Hamilton. Its role was narrower, dealing with issues exclusive to sharemilkers such as contracts and finance for sharemilkers to buy their own farm. The Sharemilking Contracts Order, which dealt with 29% and 39% sharemilking agreements, was a statutory agreement. It had not been updated for many years and sharemilkers were keen for it to be brought into line with current farming practice and made more beneficial for sharemilkers. We agreed with the sharemilker employers to negotiate an updated agreement.

The chairman of the Sharemilker Employers was Doug Carter, MP for Raglan and later Minister of Agriculture. He was a very fine man whom we respected sufficiently to ask to chair the negotiations, which he did with scrupulous fairness. The negotiations took two days and ended with an agreement which, while not giving us all we wanted, met several of our concerns. This was my first experience of negotiating in detail and required intense concentration for two full days. I was exhausted and mentally drained. Having reached agreement with employers, it required intensive lobbying by me and would take another three years or so, before the government finally amended the agreement by Order in Council. This was my first but not my last experience of how slowly the wheels of bureaucracy moved.

I was soon the Waikato Provincial Sharemilkers chairman and national vice president of the Sharemilkers Association, the official body recognised to negotiate contracts on behalf of sharemilkers. The president was Bert King from Normanby in Taranaki. He was an older gentleman who was in his sixties but was a fine and experienced man. I was to learn a lot from him and admired him greatly. In June 1965, he asked me to take over as president of the Sharemilkers Association and the Sharemilkers Sub-Section of Federated Farmers. The latter position entitled me to a seat on Federated Farmers Dominion Dairy Section Council as it was then called.

So here I was, only three years after attending my first Federated Farmers meeting, holding national office at the age of twenty-six. I can recall the morning after my election, as I loaded my trailer with silage, realising that I had just made a major commitment which was going to change my life. I was most apprehensive about how I would handle it all. Would I be any good at it? How could I do the job while continuing to farm to a high standard? I had a wife and four young children (later to become six); how could I ensure that they did not suffer? How could I continue to progress towards farm ownership and secure my family's economic wellbeing? These were daunting questions and for a while I was quite depressed about my ability to cope and having second thoughts about whether I should be doing it at all. However, after a few days, and with some wonderful support from Christine, I had begun to work out how I could do it all and regained my enthusiasm. But to fit everything in I had to give up sport and most other recreational activities.

As sharemilkers chairman I was often called upon to assist sharemilkers who were having a dispute with their employer. These were mostly 50/50 sharemilkers and covered a wide range of issues. The most common categories, though, were disputes about farm maintenance, with individual sharemilkers and employers having widely differing views on what was expected, and over the amount of supplementary feed left on the property. Very often the first notice a sharemilker received that there was a problem was when the final dairy company payment was withheld, after they had completed their contract and left the property. I would visit the farm, inspect it and have a discussion with both the employer and sharemilker and try to get them to resolve the matters in dispute. Sometimes that was achieved but if agreement could not be reached, my advice would be to refer the matter to arbitration as provided for in the sharemilking agreement. I would then work with the sharemilker and their solicitor to prepare the case for arbitration. Often, I would then be requested to act as arbitrator for the sharemilker, the employer would appoint an arbitrator and the two of us would then agree on the appointment of an umpire. A hearing would then be held, evidence submitted and the arbitrators would then try to resolve the issues, with the umpire making a binding decision where the arbitrators were unable to agree. Invariably, there was fault on both sides and the arbitration decision reflected a common-sense approach to what was reasonable. As a consequence, it was rare for either side to be completely satisfied. Each case usually involved several days' work, but a reasonable fee was paid to each arbitrator.

In each arbitration the appointment of umpire was critical. This was a particularly difficult area for me. I was inexperienced, my network was very limited and suitable people were usually farm owners. I was acutely aware that if I agreed to appoint the wrong person, my sharemilker could be disadvantaged. I found that often the employer would appoint a man called Russell Davis to represent them. He was chairman of Sharemilker Employers and managed a large number of sharemilker-operated farms. He was very experienced and had a fearsome reputation as a very hard man. He had a very smart mind. I felt intimidated by him but always stood up to him. To my surprise I found that although he was tough, he was fair and consistent and did not hesitate to come down hard on employers he considered to be in the wrong. Gradually, I earned his respect as he earned mine. I was thrilled when he asked me to act as an umpire in a case in which he was representing an employer. I came to respect him greatly and he was to become a most valued colleague, mentor and friend.

Usually, the arbitration hearing was held with only the arbitrators, umpire and the sharemilker and employer present, but occasionally the parties wished to be represented by their lawyers. These hearings often took place in the local courthouse. On a couple of occasions, including once when I was umpire, the parties were each represented by queen's counsel. David Tompkins and Bill Dillon were two of the brightest young lawyers in Hamilton and both went on to become judges, Tompkins became a High Court judge and Dillon a judge of the High Court of Samoa. It was quite an experience sitting on the bench in the courtroom with these two talented QCs scoring points off one another and from time to time asking me as umpire for rulings on points they raised!

A new experience for me was the interest taken by the media (newspapers and radio only in those days) in what I thought or said. I found that I was regularly contacted for comment on all sorts of matters. I tried very hard to be a straight shooter, to say what I thought, but to do so in a balanced, respectful and non-controversial manner. In those days reporters would ring back after they had written their story to check that it was accurate. That helped greatly. I put much thought into every public statement I made and as I gained experience, I found that I was naturally a very effective public communicator, something which was essential as most communication with farmers was through the press.

A matter of great importance to every sharemilker and young farmer was farm finance. The availability of finance to purchase a herd to start sharemilking, buy more cows to increase herd size and particularly to purchase that first farm was a big issue. For farm owners, finance to fund development was a critical need not very well served by existing lenders. Bank lending was tightly regulated and strictly controlled by the government. State Advances Corporation was the main provider of first farm purchase loans but its funding was limited. The main function of State Advances Corporation was housing, on which its board, management and staff were mostly focussed. Its rural lending function was of low priority. We gave a lot of thought to how a better farm finance system could be developed and reached the view that a separate rural finance organisation or rural bank, with clearly identified funding and dedicated to meeting the specialised funding needs of agriculture, was justified. Our research identified that most countries had a specialised agricultural lending organisation. We set out to advocate the establishment of an independent rural bank.

Like young people in town who wish to purchase their first home, young farmers and sharemilkers had to be able to contribute cash as well as borrow heavily to be able to purchase their first farm. The sums required to purchase a farm were of course much greater than required to purchase a house. The quickest way for a sharemilker to build equity was to increase the size of their herd; sometimes this required moving to a larger farm. The increase in the value of the herd was taxable but it was only a book entry, no cash had been received, although cash had to be paid for the tax. This severely impaired the ability of sharemilkers to save. We developed a concept which we called Farm Ownership Savings Account. Young farmers would open such an account with State Advances Corporation. Deposits would not be taxable but would not earn interest. Funds withdrawn from the account and used in the purchase of a farm would not be taxed, but funds withdrawn from the account and used for other purposes would be taxed at the normal rate. This scheme had widespread support among young farmers. We believed that it would be a major incentive to young people to go farming and encourage saving.

The then President of Waikato Federated Farmers, Ralph Woolerton, suggested that I convey sharemilkers farm finance needs directly to the government through the Minister of State Advances, John Rae, and set up an appointment for me. I did not know how I should go about presenting the case but the Vice President, Max Hewitt, advised me to prepare a written submission detailing what we wanted and the rationale supporting the case for improved access to farm finance for sharemilkers and young farmers. I had about three weeks to prepare this and wanted it to be as factual and evidence based as possible. I consulted many people and then began to consolidate the picture I had received into a written submission. It was July and calving was well under way so I was flat out on the farm. After dinner at night and when the children had been put to bed, I would draft a section. About 10 pm I would be ready to dictate the text to Christine and we would then call it a day. We would be up at 5 am to milk and Christine would then type up a draft during the day. I would work on the farm all day and then repeat the process at night. When the meeting date arrived, I had a comprehensive fifteen-page document which contained closely argued recommendations, some administrative and some policy, which I was rather pleased with. Christine's contribution was huge; I could not have done it without her input. But we were both exhausted.

The meeting with Minister Rae went well enough and he was complimentary about my submission and how I had presented the case. He had the General Manager of State Advances, Ron Millard, present and I followed up in more detail with him next morning which was useful. I had mixed success in obtaining the support of Federated Farmers for improved finance for young farmers and the Farm Ownership Savings Scheme. Waikato Province was strongly supportive as were the dairying provinces and the Dairy Council. But Federated Farmers Dominion Council was dominated by sheep farmers who were very conservative and reluctant to support what they regarded as special pleading. However, I did have very strong public support from sharemilkers and young farmers.

I continued to push our case publicly, to government and within the National Party. A breakthrough came when I went to see the Leader of the Opposition, Norman Kirk, who quickly grasped the problem and saw merit in what we were after. He introduced me to the Labour finance spokesman and later prime minister, Bill Rowling, and asked him to work on it with me. Labour then included both the greater availability of State Advances funding to young farmers and the Farm Ownership Savings Scheme, as well as an independent rural bank, in their election manifesto. That was a major breakthrough.

TWELVE
HIGHER OFFICE BECKONS

BY 1967 I WAS MARKED DOWN AS A RISING YOUNG TALENT and while still Sharemilkers chairman was elected as junior vice chairman of Waikato Dairy Section of Federated Farmers. Terry Fitzsimmons was chairman and John Kneebone senior vice chairman. John had been a prefect at Matamata College when I was in the third form. The following year Terry became Dominion Dairy Section chairman and John and I each moved up a slot. These were very senior and responsible positions and had never been held by any one in their thirties, as John was, let alone in their twenties as I was. We were inexperienced but keen and enthusiastic although apprehensive about the task ahead of us. I can recall John and I musing about how successful we might be as we flew to Wellington one day.

In 1969 I was asked to accept increased responsibility and was elected junior vice president of Waikato Federated Farmers which was a big step up. Christine and I had just purchased the farm from Mum and Dad who had helped us do so. We were now farm owners and had a significant debt. I was determined to ensure that I maintained our family's economic progress despite the significant amount of time I was expending on farming industry affairs. Federated Farmers was now paying me a modest honorarium which enabled me to employ full-time labour on the farm and I worked long hours and weekends on the farm to make certain that the farm was well run and high levels of production were achieved. I retired as Sharemilkers chairman.

The President, Colin Gordge, asked me to look after the administration and commercial activities of Waikato Federated Farmers. These were quite considerable. Waikato had an insurance agency for Primary Industries Insurance Company (now Farmers Mutual Group) which yielded a significant commission income; operated a farm cadet scheme with over 200 cadets; and employed fifteen staff. It also owned a large six-storeyed commercial building in London Street, Hamilton, which had just been completed. It was not fully tenanted so was not paying its way. My priority was to get it fully tenanted as soon as possible, something I managed to achieve within two years. This was wonderful experience for me as I was exposed to a commercial environment which was so different from farming. I had to learn a lot of new skills and learn them quickly.

During this time, we were faced with the need to recruit a new provincial secretary, as the top staff role was then called (today it would be titled CEO). It was suggested to me that I consider applying for the position. We enjoyed farming and living in the country, and Walton was a lovely place to bring up our family. But by now I had realised that I enjoyed the professional roles I had and was confident that I could have a very successful professional career. The sale of our herd would have funded a very nice new home for us in Hamilton and the salary package was attractive, being rather more than we earned sharemilking. So, after a lot of consideration and discussion, and not without reservations, Christine and I decided that I should apply.

I was shortlisted and it appeared that I would be offered the position; however, then the President, Colin Gordge, advised me that the Executive believed that, while I would be an outstanding appointment to the position, they considered that I had the ability to go to the very top of Federated Farmers and that it would be in the best interests of both the Federation and myself for me to continue in an elected role. He suggested that I withdraw my application, which would allow me to participate in the selection process. I was very happy to do so because I was not sure that I wanted to give up farming and Christine and I preferred to bring our family up in the country. Had I been appointed to the position my career, and our lives, would have been quite different.

Earlier I had been asked to serve on Waikato Federated Farmers Political & Economic Committee, tasked with finding a solution to the increasingly difficult set of circumstances farming was having to operate within. Farm production was expanding in Europe and the USA and surpluses of livestock products were building up. These were being dumped into world markets, depressing returns. The New Zealand economy was closely regulated to protect New Zealand manufacturers; compulsory union membership created a closed shop for labour and inflation was increasing. This was pushing farmers' costs up so they were caught in a squeeze between falling returns and rising costs, causing farm profitability to decline.

As we looked at the problem, we realised that there was little in the short term that we could do about product returns. We could and should push for trade reform, but the problem would continue to get worse before it got better. We could and should continue to push the government to open up the New Zealand economy to competition by removing protection from both manufacturing and compulsory unionism to lower farm costs, but there was little political appetite to do that. We therefore concluded that until protection of the non-farm sectors was removed, Government should compensate farming for the additional costs it was bearing to support protection for New Zealand industry and labour.

We devised an objective scheme to measure how much compensation was required and how farmers should be compensated. Paying compensation on product prices was simple and efficient but would be production distorting. It was also unlikely to be politically acceptable so we settled on paying on-farm inputs such as fertiliser. We called our proposal the Farming Cost Compensation Scheme. We believed that as the cost of compensating farmers was measured, the true cost of protecting New Zealand industry and labour would become obvious and would eventually force the government to reduce protection and open up the New Zealand economy.

Waikato Federated Farmers Executive supported our proposal and asked us to undertake the selling of it to the farming community. And so began the great "farm subsidies debate". We soon had the support of Waikato farmers, but there was strong opposition from other parts of the country because it involved the dreaded subsidies. This was an absolute anathema to many, particularly to sheep farmers and farming leadership so opposition was quite entrenched. But a widespread public debate commenced, further increasing my profile.

In 1970 Conference elected me senior vice president. In 1971, partly in response to the representations I had continued to make on farm finance, the government established a Committee of Inquiry Into lending to Farmers. By now increasing farm output was a government objective. Existing farm lending structures and institutions were inadequate in achieving that objective. In part response, State Advances Corporation was now lending to farmers to develop their land and increase production. On behalf of Federated Farmers, I appeared before the committee and made a comprehensive submission which made some twenty-two recommendations, each of which was closely argued with supporting evidence. Most were supported by the committee when it handed down its report to Government, including the most important of all, that an independent rural banking and finance corporation be established. What we had been advocating for several years was now likely to become a reality.

THIRTEEN
THE PRESIDENT

In 1972 Colin Gordge decided to stand down, so at the tender age of thirty-two I was elected president of Waikato Federated Farmers. I was fortunate to have two extremely talented vice presidents in Rob Storey and Jim Bolger. Although older than me, both were still in their thirties so we had a young, enthusiastic and talented team full of fresh ideas. We needed all of those qualities because farming was entering an almost perfect storm. Given the youth of our team, I wanted a more mature and experienced person as treasurer. John Kneebone suggested my old sharemilking adversary Russell Davis. I knew immediately that he was exactly the person I wanted. He accepted the appointment and proved to be an inspired choice. His experience, wisdom and sage judgement rounded out our team. He became a very good mentor to me and I relied on him a great deal. We developed a close friendship which continued until he passed away about fifteen years later.

The seventies were a very tough time for farming. Several consecutive years of severe drought curtailed production; product prices for dairy, meat and wool were low; inflation was beginning to take off and costs were increasing rapidly; large wage increases of 20–30% were being demanded and obtained; strikes were widespread, especially in the meat industry. This was particularly distressing to farmers who during times of drought saw their stock starve and were unable to get them slaughtered. Not surprisingly, farmers were hurt and angry and were lashing out, most often at those who were trying to help them. Federated Farmers was facing severe criticism for not doing enough, membership was declining and Action Committees were springing up all over the country demanding all sorts of direct action, some of it rather wild and counterproductive.

I gave considerable thought to what I would try to achieve during my term as president and set myself the following objectives:

1. Farmers needed to feel that their organisation was fighting for them and advancing strategies which were in their interest. Our leadership would never compromise on fighting for what was in farmers' best interests; we would do it without fear or favour, but we would do so in a balanced and responsible way.
2. New Zealanders needed to understand that farming was a winner for New Zealand. We would promote farming as a successful, progressive and dynamic industry. That it was the engine, generating the foreign exchange needed to keep our economy going and New Zealanders prosperous.
3. We would increase the professionalism of Federated Farmers. Research the issues and base our policies and advocacy on fact and logic, rather than emotion and anecdote.

President of Waikato Federated Farmers

As worldwide inflation gathered pace, the Kirk Labour Government attempted to insulate New Zealand from it by revaluing the New Zealand dollar. They also attempted to reduce the effect on New Zealand consumers of high international meat prices by introducing a Meat Reference Price under which farmers would get less for meat sold on the domestic market than for meat which was exported. It was an ill-considered proposal which almost certainly would have resulted in a shortfall in domestic meat supply, especially during the winter and summer months when finishing stock for local trade was more difficult and expensive. There was little that farmers could do about revaluation, which caused a significant drop in farmers' income, but they were outraged over Meat Reference Pricing. I called a public meeting held in the Ruakura Farmers Hall which was attended by a huge crowd of over 1500 angry farmers. They demanded action to stop the scheme and pledged their support for any action Federated Farmers took. Federated Farmers Head Office under President Bill (later Sir William) Dunlop, as wily a character as you will ever meet, was engaged and making some progress with Government. Our job was to marshal the troops and carry the public debate. I had a very high public profile and credibility, with farmers but also more broadly. I took a leading role in the public debate, addressing many meetings of farmers and townspeople who wanted to know what farmers were so riled up about. I also appeared on the prime-time TV current affairs programme *Gallery*. We began to make progress with public opinion while Bill Dunlop was getting traction with Government.

One day I received a phone call from a very successful man whom I knew well and greatly respected. He asked if I could meet later that morning "with a few of us". When I arrived there were about twenty people present, most of whom I knew. All were very successful farmers of large farms who were widely respected throughout the Waikato. All were year-round suppliers of stock to the local trade and thus would be adversely affected by Meat Reference Prices. They were direct and to the point. They wanted Meat Reference Prices stopped. They looked to Federated Farmers to do it. If it did not, they would take matters into their own hands. They had no confidence in Federated Farmers' National Office and in Bill Dunlop whom they considered not strong enough. However, they had great confidence in me and would give me their unequivocal support. They all took out their cheque books and offered me whatever sum I required. I explained that they were a bit harsh on Bill. He was a wily negotiator who was trying to find a way out for Government which did not lose it too much face. My job was much simpler: to carry the debate with farmers and non-farmers. I have never seen an issue on which farmers were so united, and in due course Government was persuaded to let the idea die a quiet death.

Our efforts to make Federated Farmers more effective continued to resonate with farmers, membership was growing again and we were getting huge support from the rural community. I continued to maintain a very active public speaking role both to farmer meetings as well as to urban groups all over the North Island. On several occasions, I was invited to address the Auckland Rotary Club luncheon before very large crowds of up to 400 business people. These were great opportunities to get across the contribution of farming to the prosperity of every New Zealander.

Part way through my first year of presidency in 1972, I lost Jim Bolger as vice president when he was elected to Parliament. At that time, I thought that I would enter Parliament in due course. Jim and I were very close and had actually agreed that we should go into politics together, as we would be able to support one another. I was not ready at that time. I did not want to give up my farming career and I felt an obligation to give Federated Farmers a reasonable term. I also had a very young family of six children all under the age of twelve. While Christine would have supported me had I decided to go into politics, I knew it was not right for our family at that time. As time passed it did not seem any more right for our family. Over the years I was approached many times to stand for electorates all over the Waikato. On one occasion after press speculation and a delegation had visited me, I was touched to have all of my children, led by Mark, together come and tell me that they thought I should stand for Parliament because they thought that I would be good at it; they would support me; they understood that it would take me away even more but they would all help Mum. As time went on and my business career developed, I realised that business was where my interest was, and I decided to give politics a miss. I am so glad I did.

FOURTEEN
WAIKATO FARMERS TRADERS

Within a few weeks of becoming president, I was facing the challenge of Waikato Farmers Traders, and it was major. Waikato Farmers Traders had been established by Federated Farmers about eight years previously to provide farmers with lower cost inputs. It operated out of a small building owned by Federated Farmers on the back of the London Street, Hamilton site. It had its own board, was independent of Federated Farmers, operated mostly through merchants orders and thus was a low-cost, low-capital operation which realised worthwhile discounts for farmers. It was regarded as a very successful initiative. However, the board, led by former President Ralph Woolerton, succumbed to the persuasion of a developer to build a much larger four-storey building further along London Street and lease it to "Traders". Some of us had serious reservations about this as it completely changed the nature of the business to a high-overhead, capital-intensive business which was undercapitalised, but the directors went ahead regardless.

Inevitably, the next year's accounts showed a large loss. The new premises had been occupied for only a few months so the annualised loss was likely several hundred thousand dollars. The board proposed to cover this by requiring farmers to each contribute a significant amount of capital. Times were tough and there was concern that with the same board and management in place, injecting more capital might only be throwing good money after bad with no guarantee that the problems would be solved, so farmers were most reluctant to contribute more capital.

I called a special meeting of my executive. Their view was that farmers should not be required to contribute more capital unless it was certain that it would be safe. With that caveat, they wanted the Federation to do what it could to save Traders and restore it to profitability. I undertook to come back to them with a plan. To do that I needed expert assistance. I identified two highly regarded businessmen: Gordon Brown who was general manager of The Manawatu Co-op, a consumer cooperative in Palmerston North, and David Muir, who was GM of a department store in Hawke's Bay. They very generously agreed to help.

In simple terms the plan which I put to my executive was.

- Replace the board and management. Three of the farmer directors were actually managing the business and were neither qualified nor capable of managing it successfully.
- Suspend the capital raising until the viability of the business could be determined. Any capital contributed should be held in escrow until the viability of the business was established and refunded to shareholders if the business could not be saved.
- Federated Farmers to provide a temporary bank guarantee until the future of the business was decided.

The executive supported my recommendations. Two of my executive members were actually directors of Traders. I asked them to resign, which they agreed to do. The executive then agreed that Russell Davis and I should be appointed to replace them. I went to the branch managers of National Bank and Marac Finance who were funding Traders, advised them of my plan and asked that they continue to support the business while we ascertained its viability. They agreed. My executive members also undertook to convey our plan to their farmers and collect proxies. Farmer support for what we were proposing was strong.

Then I had to undertake a most personally difficult task. On the morning of the shareholders meeting, as a raw young thirty-two-year-old, I had to walk into the office of Traders Chairman Ralph Woolerton, a man more than twice my age and a respected former president of Waikato Federated Farmers who had supported me when I was Sharemilkers chairman, and ask him to resign. He was most unhappy and refused point blank. He asked, "Why should I?" I replied, "A very good reason is that there will be about three hundred and fifty people at the shareholders meeting this afternoon. I have five hundred proxies in my pocket!" He agreed that was a good reason and accepted the inevitable. The meeting that afternoon gave me overwhelming support.

I asked Russell Davis to chair the new board, and he proved to be an absolute rock. Our advisors Gordon Brown and David Muir agreed to become directors so I knew that I had the right business expertise and judgement on the board. We set in motion the process of finding a suitable manager but knew that would take some time. The preliminary view of our advisors was that the business was probably losing $10,000 to $15,000 a month. When those losses for the four months since the end of the previous financial year were added to the published loss for the previous financial year, the business was insolvent. However, we had anticipated this, had taken immediate steps to reduce overheads to eliminate the monthly losses, and with the guarantee from Federated Farmers the National Bank and Marac were prepared to extend us further credit. We immediately commenced a full financial balance to ascertain what the actual position was. That would take about three months.

As expected, the shaky financial position of the business created difficulties with suppliers withdrawing credit and withholding supply. Gordon Brown and David Muir were invaluable in enabling us to negotiate our way through what was becoming a legal minefield and ensuring that we did not breach any of our obligations (many of which I was previously unaware of) to the company's creditors. We were receiving a continuous stream of lawyer's letters and had our own lawyers present at each board meeting. Unfortunately, when the financial balance was completed we found to our dismay that the ongoing losses had been closer to $30,000 per month rather than the $10,000 to $15,000 our advisors had estimated. While the actions we had taken had saved about $15,000 a month, we had continued to lose $15,000 every month and thus the company was insolvent. The only action available to us was to put Traders into receivership, which we did immediately.

I felt very badly about this. I had failed to save Traders for my farmers. I felt for all of the unsecured creditors, many of whom were small businesses who supplied us with favourable deals. I was concerned about my reputation. But what was literally terrifying to me was the realisation that I was now in a very litigious situation where I could be personally liable for any mistakes I may have made, even inadvertently, which caused loss to others. I was quite depressed and berated myself for my foolishness in placing my family's very modest wealth and wellbeing at risk. Fortunately, we had done everything correctly and no action was taken against the directors who had acted in good faith and done everything reasonably possible to save the business and avoid loss. The creditors' meeting, though, was quite an experience, albeit a most unpleasant one, but I learned much which was to guide me in future years, not the least of which was the absolute need for sufficient capital to cover the exigencies of tough times. Inadequate capital was a common weakness in cooperative companies.

I was keen that my farmers should continue to have access to cheaper inputs, so I went to Ivan Blackmore, chairman of Auckland Farmers Union Trading Society, which operated in Auckland and Northland in a manner similar to how Waikato Farmers Traders was originally set up and should have continued to operate. They were relatively small but very well run. I asked them to open a branch in Hamilton. I offered them attractive initial terms to rent the building which Federated Farmers had originally rented to Traders and which was now empty. I also encouraged them to negotiate with the receiver of Waikato Farmers Traders to purchase stock. They saw this as a very attractive opportunity, agreed to open in Hamilton but insisted that I join their board.

This enabled me to salvage something from the debacle of Waikato Farmers Traders:

- My farmers continued to enjoy the benefit of a low-cost farm trading society.
- Unsecured creditors of Traders got better recovery of their debt from the purchase of its stock by AFU.
- Federated Farmers had a secure tenant in what was previously an empty building.

Waikato Farmers Traders was my first role as a director. It was not a success, but I learned in a few months what would otherwise have taken years. The lessons were to influence me throughout my subsequent commercial career.

I learned that:

- A bad situation will usually be worse than it initially appears.
- Temper your optimism. Be sceptical about predictions and forecasts.
- Be cautious, things do go wrong, sometimes several at the same time. The business must be able to survive such circumstances.
- Be conservative with capital. Particularly, ensure that the business has sufficient capital to operate with decent headroom. This is often a major issue with cooperatives, which, due to their focus on short-term returns to farmers, often operate with less capital than they should.
- A director is exposed to personal liability. Recognise that and be careful. Do not put yourself and your own assets at risk. Stay clear of risky situations. Take out directors indemnity insurance cover. It is expensive but you cannot afford to not have it.

FIFTEEN
A BIG YEAR

THE YEAR 1973 WAS TO BE AN EVENTFUL ONE FOR ME. NEW Zealand Jaycees had organised a search for New Zealand's Outstanding Young Man of The Year. Each region was to call for nominations for the award, hold a selection process and choose a finalist. I was nominated by Chartwell Jaycees. Shortly after I accepted their nomination, I was approached by both Matamata and Morrinsville Jaycee Clubs but was already committed to Chartwell. Nominees were interviewed by a panel which included Dorothy Jelicich, the Labour Member of Parliament for Hamilton West, and Dr Edgar, the director of Ruakura Agricultural Research Centre. At a function in Hamilton, I was chosen as Waikato Outstanding Young Man of The Year.

The national final was held in Rotorua where the nine regional winners met for two days with the judges. For me Rotorua was a great location as Mum and Dad lived there and were able to attend the gala dinner where the winner was announced by Governor-General Sir Denis Blundell. I knew that I had interviewed very well, but there were some outstanding young men among the finalists, including a future prime minister of New Zealand, David Lange. It was a bit of a shock to hear my name announced as New Zealand's Outstanding Young Man of the Year by the governor-general. The award was sponsored by the tobacco company WD & HO Wills and carried a grant of $2500, a significant sum in 1973, to be used to further my development.

New Zealand's Outstanding Young Man, 1974

I continued to have a very high public profile and was readily able to attract headlines. The Outstanding Young Man of The Year accolade further increased my profile and initiated a significant increase in speaking requests from right around the country. I tried to accept as many of them as possible for the opportunities they created for me to present the value of farming to New Zealand to a broad audience of New Zealanders.

A young family celebrates

At each monthly meeting of my executive, I tried to have a new initiative to table. The subsidies debate continued and we were getting traction as more people began to realise that despite the inherent dislike most farmers had for subsidies, something had to be done to help farmers remain productive. One argument we advanced was that successive governments were quite happy to maintain a protected cost-plus economy, provided that exporters (mostly farmers) were willing and able to absorb the end cost. But when farmers were no longer willing or able to absorb that cost, Government would be forced to remove protection and free up the economy. A decade later events would prove our arguments correct. Government began to provide input subsidies on a modest scale, principally on fertiliser and then development costs. These increased each year until they became an increasing burden on the economy. But it took until 1984 before the Lange Labour Government boldly deregulated the economy by removing protection, floating the New Zealand dollar, and removing all subsidies. As the initial consequence was that the NZ$ strengthened, this created an even more difficult period for farming, but it responded strongly and became more efficient and profitable as competition forced costs down.

The government was working hard to mitigate the damage caused to the economy by Britain's entry into the EEC by bringing leading European politicians, journalists, farming leaders and other thought leaders to New Zealand. Most of them visited the Waikato and I was usually called upon to host and show them New Zealand farming. Sir Henry Plumb (later Lord Plumb) of the National Farmers Union, Baron von Herreman of the German Farmers' Association, Dr Diana of the Italian farmers organisation and Andre Herlitska, executive director of COPA (*Comité des organisations professionnelles agricoles*), the EEC farmers' body, were only some of those I was fortunate to host, a number of them in our home. I developed good relationships with most of them, which was valuable later when I was chairman of the Dairy Board and lobbying hard for our dairy farmers, as most of them still held very influential positions.

It was becoming obvious to me that it was agri-business which would most influence the future prosperity of farmers. Dairy farmers were fortunate to own the supply chain from cow to customer through the cooperative dairy companies and the Dairy Board. I was also finding that I most enjoyed the commercial side of my work for Federated Farmers so my ambitions were beginning to gravitate towards a future in the cooperative dairy industry. One evening I received a call from Jack Cookson, a director of both New Zealand Cooperative Dairy Co. and the Dairy Board, whom I knew but not well. He told me that he had just returned from a New Zealand Dairy Co-op meeting that day which had created a new ward based on Morrinsville which would be ideal for me if I were interested. He hoped I would be. Over the next four days I was to receive similar calls from five other directors, including Chairman Reg Bates.

The timing was not ideal, as I was only in my second year as provincial president of Waikato Federated Farmers, and I felt I owed the Federation a reasonable period of time. But it was as good an opportunity as I was ever likely to receive to enter a governance role in the cooperative dairy industry. I did not hesitate. With Christine's ready support I canvassed my farmers to ascertain the support I would have, and their response encouraged me to put my name forward. I realised that if I was fortunate enough to be elected a director of New Zealand Dairy Company. I would need to make a long-term commitment to the cooperative dairy industry; it would have to become my priority. I was happy to do that.

Being a director of New Zealand Cooperative Dairy Company was a most sought-after and prestigious role. There were three other highly regarded nominees, all older and more experienced than me. The choice would be made by the 426 suppliers of the Morrinsville Ward which stretched from Orini to Walton, and from the eastern edge of Hamilton to State Highway 27. I posted a circular, announcing my candidature and setting out my credentials, to every farmer in the ward. It was printed on yellow paper to stand out from the circulars of the other candidates. I also visited every farmer seeking their views on the Dairy Company and their support in the election. It was a wonderful experience which I knew would never be repeated, but by the time of the election I knew every farmer in the ward. I found that farmers greatly respected New Zealand Dairy Co-op and were very strongly supportive of it, but there was an underlying concern that its performance might not be as strong as it had traditionally been. Events were to prove that to be a perceptive view. I was elected by a comfortable margin and a new chapter of my career commenced.

PART FOUR
THE BUSINESSMAN

SIXTEEN
A COMPANY DIRECTOR

I took my seat in the New Zealand Dairy Co. boardroom at the tender age of thirty-three. I was the youngest director by more than ten years and twenty years younger than most. I was one of the youngest directors, if not the youngest, in its history. It was one of the largest companies in the country, and turnover in 1974 was $164,784,808, while payout was $1.35 per kg butterfat. I was entering a new world. I found a company strong on tradition, which had huge scale and financial strength, but which did not challenge itself or readily accept new ideas. It was flabby, relying on its reputation, scale, size and financial strength. My farmers were right: there was trouble ahead.

There were a myriad of new terms, concepts, processes and measurements to learn and understand the significance of: man hours per tonne of product; kilograms of milk powder per 1000 litres of milk; kilograms of steam per tonne of milk powder; kilowatts of electricity per tonne of coal, and hundreds more. It was bewildering and I was totally ignorant. I kept my head down and applied myself to learning to understand it all. I prided myself on being a quick learner, but it took much longer than I expected to understand it all. But as I got my mind around it all I realised that something was missing. It was all detail but no picture. It was impossible to understand how the company was performing. More worryingly, nobody knew. I was not very experienced, but I knew that the financial reporting was less than adequate. After a couple of meetings, I plucked up enough courage to ask, "Don't we have a profit and loss account each month?" I was told: "We have quarterly cost reports." I crawled back into my hole! I was to raise the issue from time to time, usually to deafening silence.

At the commencement of each meeting, the minutes of the previous meeting were read and confirmed. This took thirty to forty minutes and was a complete waste of time. I asked why they could not be circulated with the board papers and taken as read. I was told that was not allowed. I asked why and was told that it was against the law. I did not know anything about the law, but I went to the Matamata Library and looked up the Companies Act. I could find no prohibition on circulating the minutes and no requirement for them to be formally read before confirmation. Next month I asked for the specific relevant clause, or clauses, of the Companies Act. Nobody could quote them, but management agreed to look it up and let me know. Of course, they never did as there was no such prohibition. I raised the matter again and began to get support from my colleagues. Ultimately, the board agreed to circulate the minutes and refrain from reading them. I was to have exactly the same experience in every company I was a director of for most of the 1970s.

My new role as a director, together with my work in Federated Farmers, was clearly going to occupy me full time. Christine and I agreed that we needed to employ a farm manager. I was fortunate to find Charlie and Linda Manning who were first class. Our farm had only our home on it, but I was able to rent Mark Crowder's cottage just across the road. With Charlie and Linda milking and running the farm day to day, I was able to handle what was a significant workload quite comfortably. I milked during their weekend off each month and was able to put a reasonable amount of time, mostly during weekends, into farm maintenance and improvement. The fees I received from the Dairy Company and the honorarium from Federated Farmers meant that we were not out of pocket from replacing most of my own labour on the farm.

The Dairy Company had investments in quite a wide range of associated activities which included coal mining, milk-processing equipment, cold storage, local market butter and cheese distribution and speciality cheese manufacture. The most important of all was the New Zealand Dairy Board which purchased and marketed all of the company's export production. The governance responsibilities for these activities were allocated among directors with the more experienced and capable directors being allocated the more important roles. The prime appointments of course were the three appointments as directors of the Dairy Board, one of whom was usually the chairman.

At my first meeting Reg Bates retired and a senior director, Ron Greenough, elected chairman. Jim Graham was elected deputy chairman. As a new director, in line with normal practice, I was appointed a director of Glen Afton Collieries. It was also decided that the deputy chairman should chair Glen Afton, which I thought was sensible as it gave the deputy chairman experience as a chairman and strengthened succession. I was happy; Glen Afton was important to the company, and it would give me good experience. However, I soon recognised that it was markets and marketing which would most influence farmers' economic wellbeing, so it was the New Zealand Dairy Board where my medium-term aspirations soon lay.

In 1976 I was appointed to the AFFCO Board. This was considered a most desirable role as AFFCO was one of the largest meat companies in the country and importantly was a cooperative. With dairy farmers earning up to 20% of their income from meat, AFFCO was important to dairy farmers who gave it strong support. It operated in a very competitive environment. Competition for stock was fierce, particularly in the eight off-peak months of the year. AFFCO was well managed and quite efficient but was constrained in its ability to compete for stock off peak by its cooperative nature under which all farmers expected to be treated equally, a constraint which its competitors did not experience. I remained an AFFCO director until 1980 when I resigned on becoming deputy chairman of New Zealand Dairy Co. My experience as an AFFCO director was another important component of my development and skill base. I learned much, particularly about competing effectively for business on a day-to-day basis and the importance of flexibility and quick reactions.

With world butter production exceeding consumption, surplus butter stocks worldwide were huge and increasing. The Soviet Union entered the market for the first time, buying very large quantities for a few hundred dollars per tonne. They needed to export to earn foreign exchange and the Dairy Board wished to encourage them. Belarus tractors, Lada cars and potash were imported into New Zealand from Russia. CEO Rex Haggie canvassed a proposal to invest in importing and selling Belarus tractors with the New Zealand Dairy directors. I was opposed as I believed that the company needed to focus on its core business; however, the directors were supportive. I was surprised a few weeks later when Jim Graham advised me that he and the chairman, Ron Greenhough, would like me to be involved with Haggie in the project. The proposal was that Fletcher Challenge, Moller Motor Group, and New Zealand Dairy Company form a company, to be called New Zealand Tractor Marketing, to import and sell Belarus tractors. Both Fletcher Challenge and Moller Motors were significant and reputable companies and brought skills that such a business would require. Mollers were importing the small Hinomoto tractors and had agreed to put that franchise into the business. Jim told me that if I did not think it was a goer, to say no. I realised later that I had been asked to be involved because I had been against a proposal that Jim was also not keen on. He considered that I would probably recommend against the investment. However, that would prove to be easier said than done. I was to find that Haggie had given a firm indication that New Zealand Dairy would take a certain number of tractors annually. On that basis, our partners had placed an order and the tractors were on their way to New Zealand. While legally we may have had an arguable case that our commitment was not binding, at the very least New Zealand Dairy would have been acting in really bad faith if it had reneged. All three companies were very honest and reputable, regarding their word as their bond.

So New Zealand Tractor Marketing was born and I was asked to chair it. We hired as chief executive Tony Dowling, who had taken Kubota tractors into a leading market position. He was a good salesman and we did well with building sales numbers, but he proved to be less well equipped with some of the other qualities a CEO requires. Although sales numbers were reasonable, we had difficulty in making money. The principal reason was that under the price-control regulations existing at the time, we could only charge a margin which was about average in the industry. We had a tractor which was by far the lowest priced on the market. But it also had much higher costs, particularly for warranty costs which were about ten times higher than industry standard. We could have charged a much higher price, sufficient to cover our higher costs, and still have the cheapest product on the market by a substantial amount, but under the regulations were unable to do so. Eventually, the partners decided that we should exit the business. That was not easy to do but, in the end, we managed to do so. New Zealand Dairy, and the other partners, took a loss on the venture, although it was not huge. Still, it was a pretty dismal outcome for which I felt responsible to a large degree. It did, however, teach me to be sceptical about entering into new businesses, particularly those where the organisation had no experience.

In 1976 I retired as president of Waikato Federated Farmers. I had served four years and the organisation was in good shape. By now I saw my future in the dairy industry, and I wanted to concentrate on that. The constitution provided for the immediate past president to continue to be a member of the executive and the Dominion Council, as it was then called. However, I told my successor, Rob Storey, I would attend executive meetings for three months only, and thereafter I would then only be available at his request. I felt that Rob as my successor was entitled to operate as he wanted to without me looking over his shoulder. That is a practice I was to follow throughout my business career. Whenever I retired or resigned from a board, I finished completely and never went back. The Annual Conference of Federated Farmers unanimously elected me a Co-opted Member of Dominion Council which I accepted as I felt that I could help improve the sometimes testy relationship between Federated Farmers and dairy companies. I remained a member of Dominion Council until 1979. In 1977 Allan Wright, later Sir Allan, became national president of Federated Farmers. He invited me to become his senior vice president, which would have led to me becoming president three years later. I declined as I had other intentions.

In 1976 Frank Onion, who was chairman of the Dairy Board and a director of New Zealand Dairy Company, was retiring, thus creating a vacancy on the Dairy Board to be filled by an appointment from among the New Zealand Dairy Co. directors. I was by now making an impact on the New Zealand Dairy Co. board deliberations and was seen as a rising star. I was really keen to become a member of the New Zealand Dairy Board as it was obvious that marketing was the most critical influence on farmers' incomes. I had good reason to be confident of being chosen as a majority of the directors, including the chairman and other senior directors, had told me that I was the obvious choice and that I had their support. A couple of days before the election, Frank Onion gave me a hint that it might not be so clear cut when he told me that "some think that an older man might be more suited for the job; you are young and have plenty of time ahead of you". But given the commitments I had, I continued to be confident. Frank was a shrewd politician who proved to be spot on.

Nevertheless, it was a shock to me when the result was announced to learn that I had come second. Still a little bewildered, I went into the chairman's office at the conclusion of the board meeting for the normal after-meeting drinks. Alvin Woolven came up to me and said, "You get the message from that result?" I shook my head. "The company wants you. They see you as the next deputy chairman and a future chairman." I was not particularly consoled by that as it was expected to be another three years before the chairman retired. Jim Graham who would succeed him was young and could do ten years as chairman. A wait of thirteen years or more seemed an eternity to me.

SEVENTEEN
OVERSEAS EXPERIENCE

Britain, which took 74% of our dairy exports and most of our lamb, had just entered the European Economic Community and was required to phase out access for New Zealand dairy and lamb. This was a daunting prospect for New Zealand farmers. But it was even more serious because in its quest for self-sufficiency in food production, the EEC was beginning to produce beyond its own needs and dump the excess production at low prices into the very markets we were trying to diversify into. New Zealand farmers rightly saw the EEC as a threat to their livelihood, but did not have much of an understanding of what the EEC was all about, what was driving its actions and what were the future implications for New Zealand farming. It was obvious to me that for some time ahead the EEC was going to be the single biggest influence on New Zealand dairying.

I decided that I would use my $2500 grant from the Outstanding Young Man of The Year Award to spend some time in Europe to try to gain an understanding of the EEC, how it might develop and the likely implications for New Zealand. I also wanted to spend some time with the National Farmers Union of England and Wales, which appeared to be a very professional and well-run organisation, to learn what we might do to make Federated Farmers more effective.

So, in 1974 I set off on my first overseas trip. I was planning to be away for three months. Unfortunately, with a young family it was not possible for Christine to accompany me, but we agreed that she should meet me in Melbourne on my way home where we would spend two weeks. Although not a huge sum, the Award grant was sufficient for me to purchase a round-the-world air ticket and make a significant contribution towards my other expenses. Very generously, the Dairy Company helped towards my costs, believing that it would benefit in the future from my development.

Federated Farmers was active in the Pacific Basin Economic Cooperation Conference (PBEC), which was a business organisation set up to promote economic activity and business in the Pacific Basin. In a sense it was the forerunner of today's APEC. PBEC was holding its annual conference in Washington DC. The Dominion Council agreed that I could attend and represent the Federation. I flew through Honolulu and Chicago, arriving in Washington early one morning in May. Charles Patrick, deputy general manager of the Dairy Board, had described PBEC to me as "a group of ruthless businessmen grinding personal axes with a false Rotary veneer of good fellowship". He was not wrong. I was surprised to see the sparse attendance at the formal sessions but noted that there were heaps of one-on-one meetings going on all over the venue. PBEC was fulfilling its purpose of facilitating business relationships. I made many contacts, among them some prominent New Zealanders, but also a number from other countries. The gala dinner on the final evening was held at George Washington's family home of Woodlawn Plantation in Virginia, a magnificent old mansion where we sipped mint juleps on the veranda – tasted like gin with mint sauce!

After five days in Washington I departed for Baden, Austria where I was to represent Federated Farmers at the International Federation of Agricultural Producers (IFAP). This was a rather leisurely event which was scheduled for two weeks, although most of the senior leaders only arrived for the second week. The first-week attendees were largely staffers and as they were mostly about my age, I became very friendly with some of them. By the time I was visiting Europe as chairman of the Dairy Board twenty-five years later, some of them held very influential positions.

Here I first began to first experience the EEC as it then was and gain a sense of what it was all about. Throughout history, European nations had fought one another and the people had suffered. Led by the two main protagonists, France and Germany, Europe had resolved to work closely together, indeed, to become as one, to eliminate war between them. When they had fought in the past, food production had suffered and the people had starved. It was therefore not surprising that the spearhead of their cooperation was food production, where they aimed for food security or self-sufficiency. At that time the Common Agriculture Policy consumed nearly 70% of the EEC budget.

The European farmers organisations were very professional, well-resourced organisations. A very high proportion of their staffers had doctorates, were extremely competent, and many were intellectually brilliant. They were completely focussed on the Common Agricultural Policy and ensuring that its regulations covered every aspect of farming. For example, while the EEC produced only very small quantities of sheep meats, they were determined to ensure that a sheep meats regulatory regime was established to protect their very small number of sheep meat producers. They had little or no interest in agricultural trade, liberalisation of trade in agricultural products, or in the circumstances of countries like New Zealand which earned a living from exporting agricultural products. For them, there could be no such thing as "free trade", but they were all in favour of "fair trade". Fair trade to them meant keeping out more efficient competitors through high tariffs, the higher the better, and the prohibition on entry of agricultural products into their markets. Britain had just entered the EEC and they saw our large UK butter and cheese markets as being rightfully theirs. I observed that farmers from most of the other IFAP participants, including to my surprise USA, were predominantly domestic producers, had little interest in exporting, and held similar protectionist views.

After the IFAP Conference was over, I boarded an overnight train for Rome. I had a wait in Vienna of about five hours during which I intended to explore that beautiful city. Unfortunately, it was a cold, rainy, rather depressing day which meant that I was unable to leave the railway station. I had now been away from home for three weeks, but I had been with New Zealand friends for that period. Now I had left their company and was all alone to find my way around Europe and England for the next ten weeks. I was missing my family and became quite homesick. I thought seriously about curtailing my trip and heading home. I think that Christine was quite alarmed when she received the letter that I wrote her from the Vienna Sudbahnhof (south-bound train station).

The next morning, I awoke just as the train was travelling down the Italian side of the Alps, which were a spectacular sight. I only had Austrian schillings, having not thought to obtain Italian lira in Vienna. I found that the food vendors in Italy would not accept schillings, so I was unable to buy anything to eat until the train arrived in Rome late in the afternoon and I found a money changer, who of course ripped me off, but at least I was able to hire a taxi to my hotel. The weather in Rome was balmy, I had cheered up and was enjoying that eternal and fascinating city. I met with Dr Diana of the Confederazione Agricoltura whom I had hosted in Hamilton. His office was in a beautiful old building adorned with fresco paintings.

One of his staff spent a day taking me out into the country to see Italian agriculture and meet farmers.

After an enjoyable three days I again boarded a train heading for Brussels where I was to meet a New Zealand friend, Rowland Woods, who was the New Zealand Meat Board European director. His wife and family were in New Zealand so he very kindly invited me to stay with him. His staff also assisted me to plan and book the remainder of my European tour and make appointments with the people and organisations I wished to visit. This was of huge help as there was no internet or cellphones and the cheaper hotels I was staying at often did not have a telephone in the room. I had a very full programme of meetings, as Brussels was the Headquarters of the EEC and virtually every agriculture business or organisation was represented there. My friend Andre Herlitzka, Secretary General of the European farmers organisation COPA, was very good to me. He took me to stay with him and his family at their holiday cottage in the Ardennes in Luxembourg and spent a day taking me around visiting Luxembourg farmers. One evening he took me out to dinner in an old inn at Waterloo which had been Napoleon's headquarters during the battle of Waterloo. I kept pressing him on trade protectionism and why the EEC would not liberalise trade. In the end, he said, "I will show you something." He turned off the main road and headed in a different direction. We finally arrived at an area where there was nothing but empty derelict glasshouses, thousands of them. It was a most eerie and depressing sight. The cause, he explained, was that the EEC had allowed a range of warm-climate fruits, berries, melons and the like from some of the poorer southern Mediterranean countries to enter. That had put all of the producers, thousands of them, of those products out of business. "Now, you know," he said.

My next visit, this time a train journey of only an hour, was Bonn. There I was looked after by Dr Jan Lotz who later visited and stayed with us at Walton. He took me to his home for a meal. I caught up with Baron von Herreman, president of the Bauernverband, the German farmers' organisation, for dinner. I had a useful series of meetings and Dr Meuws, the secretary general of the Bauernverband, took me to his home for dinner and then to catch the overnight train to Copenhagen.

My visit to Copenhagen was to focus on Dairy Company interests. I was hosted by Niro who were the principal providers of spray drying equipment to New Zealand Dairy Company. They were the world milk-drying technology leaders and I spent some time viewing both their R&D activities and their manufacturing workshop. I got to know Poul Nordham very well. He was to become Niro CEO. I learned much about milk-drying technology and the developments Niro were working on. They were a most impressive organisation.

I then caught the ferry to Malmo, just across Oresund in Sweden, where I was met by Ovind Hoel, New Zealand Dairy Company account manager for Alfa Laval. He took me to their Lund plant which was manufacturing centrifuges. There I met two extremely bright younger Alfa Laval executives, Harry Faulkner and Lars Haldane. Each of them went on to become CEO of Alfa Laval. Then it was off by train to Stockholm where again I was hosted by Alfa Laval and visited their Head Office, R&D centre, and manufacturing plant. Alfa Laval was a high-quality organisation with a strong commitment to R&D and an amazing ability to engineer technological advances.

I then flew from Stockholm to Amsterdam to visit the three Dutch farmers' organisations. There seemed to be three of most organisations in Holland, split largely along religious lines, Catholic, Protestant and Royal. However, they did have an umbrella organisation over the top of them to ensure coordination. I also visited several farms. As you would expect, they had deep, fertile alluvial soils, and the farms were extremely productive. Much of the country was close to, or below, sea level, so control of water was critical and the Dutch controlled it to the centimetre. Everywhere I went it was possible to see a church spire in every direction, such was the density of the population. It was amazing that an affluent population of about 15 million people was able to be supported on a land area about one third that of the North Island. It was springtime and the tulips were blooming. To see acres and acres of tulips in full flower was a stunning sight.

Then it was a short train journey to Brussels to meet up with Rowland Woods. The next day another train journey to Paris where in three hours connecting between trains, we walked down the Champs-Élysées, visited the Eiffel Tower, walked through the Tuileries Garden to the Louvre and attended Mass (it was Sunday) in Notre Dame. Then we caught a train to Lyon where we were hosted by Baron Henri De La Celle in his thirteenth-century chateau. The chateau was magnificent but in poor condition as were most chateaux in those days. I had a huge bedroom with a large four-poster bed on a raised dais. It had a very basic en suite. Henri's wife Annie had put out a cake of nice scented soap, still wrapped in the cellophane, for me. Next morning, I found that mice had gnawed at it! We then set off by car to Millau in the south of France, a journey of 400 kilometres. We spent a fascinating three days as guests of the Roquefort Cheese industry. Roquefort is a blue vein cheese made from sheep's milk. It is matured in huge natural limestone caves. It was a fascinating few days, during which we saw the industry in some detail: from modern rotary milking sheds to old, small traditional barns making their own cheese and where DDT powder was sprinkled about by hand to kill vermin; to the domestic and international marketing operations all undertaken by a single cooperative.

I then flew to Paris and on to London. The following day the National Farmers Union (NFU) were having a special meeting of their council. There was a crisis in beef prices and UK beef farmers were critical of a lack of action by the National Farmers Union. I was privileged to attend the council meeting and watched the very polished performance of the president, Henry Plumb, later to be Sir Henry and then Lord Plumb. At the outset he faced severe criticism but ended the meeting with the farmers eating out of his hand. It was a masterly performance by a skilled operator. Christine and I subsequently hosted Henry at our home and later in my career he was to become a good friend and colleague.

I had five weeks in the UK, with two weeks in London where I spent time with the National Farmers Union gaining an understanding of how they worked and setting up a programme of visits to some of their county operations. I also spent time with Empire Dairies which was the Dairy Board operating business in the UK. Dudley Hodson, the managing director, was very generous with his time and took me to lunch at the Savoy Grill on a number of occasions. That was quite an experience for a raw young farmer. I spent a day with the Milk Marketing Board which gave me a good understanding of the UK dairy industry. I was hosted on an early-morning visit to the Smithfield meat market by the Affco agent Ted Curzon, which concluded at 10 am in a pub for breakfast of beer, bacon and eggs. Vaseys, which was the New Zealand Meat Board's market and promotion adviser, gave me a great insight into the marketing strategy for New Zealand lamb. I also caught up with Keith Dexter, who I'd met in New Zealand; he was director of Meat in the UK Ministry of Agriculture. He became a good friend. Christine and I subsequently hosted him and his wife at our home in Elstow.

Then it was off to several counties where the NFU very generously hosted me. This gave me a good understanding of how the NFU operated on the ground and took me on numerous visits to farms including to some farmhouse dairies where the milk produced was made into cheese on the farm. I visited the Scottish Farmers Union in

Edinburgh who organised some farm visits for me. I usually spent the weekend with either one of my old school and rugby mates Lawrence Shephard and Jan or with Carole, who had stayed with us when she was in New Zealand a few years previously, and her husband Ian. Lawrence and Jan and Carole and Ian lived about 20 kilometres away from one another in Surrey. All of this meant that I travelled widely throughout the UK and experienced a broad cross section of UK agriculture. Britain had entered the EEC the previous year and I was able to gain an understanding of what that might mean for our dairy industry.

I also spent a week in Ireland where I was hosted by the Irish Farmers Association. Their vice president, Dony Cashman, and his wife Peggy, hosted me at their home in Cork and I visited many farms and dairy factories. Give my Irish heritage, I felt very much at home in Ireland but was surprised at how backward it was. The dairy industry was quite different from that of the UK, which was entirely domestic with protected high prices and based on feeding concentrates. Ireland was very much like New Zealand. They exported a significant proportion of their production and received lower prices similar to us. Milk production was pasture based like New Zealand and much more efficient than the UK or Europe. But Ireland had entered the EEC the previous year and as a consequence was moving towards EEC milk prices which were more than double what Irish farmers had traditionally received. Not surprisingly, farmers were beginning to feed concentrates and so milk production was taking off. It was expected to double over the next five years. I spent some time with the Irish Dairy Board, or An Bord Bainne, an organisation I was very impressed with. The great Irish rugby wing Tony O'Reilly had been CEO until a few years previously and had built it into a vibrant and progressive organisation. His influence was still evident and they had some outstanding young executives. It was clear to me that Irish farmers saw the UK market as now rightfully theirs and expected us to vacate it for them. Clearly, a battle to retain our UK entry quota for butter lay ahead.

After what seemed an eternity to me it was time to head home. I was missing Christine and my family and was lonely. Even though I had met and been with a lot of people I had essentially been by myself for three months. But the knowledge I had gained and the contacts I had made were priceless. I had gained a good feel for the EEC, what motivated it, what drove the individual member states, how they thought and where the EEC might go. It was clear to me that there was a very strong European commitment to greater integration and that food self-sufficiency was an overriding objective; that the Common Agricultural Policy of price support for farmers was the essential foundation on which closer integration would be built; that the EEC was inherently bureaucratic and interventionist and would inevitably become more so; that self-sufficiency would inevitably overrun into surpluses which they would seek to export. It was clear to me that difficult days lay ahead for New Zealand dairy and sheep farmers.

EIGHTEEN
ELSTOW

CHRISTINE AND I HAD FOR SOME TIME BEEN LOOKING FOR a larger farm. We had Paratu in first-class condition with high production but had little scope for further improvement. It was also a little small to profitably employ a sharemilker, which I would at some time need to do, given that I was now engaged almost full time in the dairy industry. It would have been ideal if we could have purchased Percy Collins' farm next door, but we knew that it would be a long time before Percy and Jess gave up farming. In fact, it turned out to be twenty years before they retired. Expecting that I would be appointed to the Dairy Board, we had been looking for a fully developed farm in the Matamata district which was in supply to New Zealand Dairy Co. or was able to supply it. That ruled out about half of the farms in Matamata which were zoned to supply Sunny Park Dairy Company. Matamata was a most desirable area so land was expensive and although we had looked at many farms, we had not managed to find a suitable property which we could afford.

But my circumstances changed when I failed to be appointed to the Dairy Board. I had just retired from Federated Farmers and was now going to have more time available. It was now possible for us to consider a property which required development. That meant we could afford a larger farm. I had always enjoyed developing land and making it highly productive, so was attracted by the prospect of undertaking a development project. So, we changed our instruction to the land agents and began to look for development propositions. We needed to find a property in, or close to, my Dairy Co. ward, which restricted us to the Matamata-Morrinsville-Te Aroha triangle.

My three girls (Lisa–Jane, Annemarie, Julie-Ann)

We found a 78-hectare property in Elstow which was badly run down. It required a lot of work: fences, races, water supply, drains and buildings were all in poor condition. Significant capital investment would be required to develop the property. But the land was very good, capital for development was readily available from the Rural Bank, we could afford it and were confident that we could turn it into a highly productive farm. Paratu was a desirable, high-quality property which was readily saleable at a good price, so Elstow became ours.

One of the problems with Elstow, when we purchased it, was that virtually everything needed attention at the same time. We intended to employ a 50/50 sharemilker. The cottage, which had not been lived in for some time, needed to be renovated and brought up to standard, a new cowshed built, a central race upgraded and metalled, subdivision fencing erected, and a new water supply installed and reticulated. Although a network of underground field drainage tiles had been laid many years previously, and most of the paddocks had 'hump and hollow' drains, neither had been maintained and were basically useless. The property was therefore wet, and a basic drainage network had to be dug. There had been little or no fertiliser applied for many years so we put on a heavy application of capital fertiliser (to overcome nutrient deficiencies). There was rubbish everywhere and lots of fallen trees which blocked drains and were a great home for blackberry. The homestead was old and required major renovation, but that would have to wait for a year or two as getting the farm producing had to be the priority, so our own living conditions during that period would be substandard. However, we were warm and dry, and Christine and our family made a home of it.

My three boys (Mark, Gregory, Kevin)

That first year was especially difficult and production was rather less than I had anticipated. I worked extremely hard and enjoyed it. Gradually, we were getting the property cleaned up and into shape. With heavy fertiliser applications, fertility was improving, although pasture species were not ideal but undersowing and cropping were progressively rectifying that. Our first sharemilker did not work out. For the second year we were thrilled to have Charlie and Linda come to sharemilk for us. Unfortunately, they came from lighter, free-draining land and their cows were calving nearly six weeks earlier than we wanted for our heavier land. That season happened to have exceptionally heavy and prolonged rainfall, so with that and early calving we suffered extensive pasture damage and a severe feed shortage. In September we had to send half the herd off the farm for six weeks. That season was a disaster for both Charlie and Linda and ourselves, with production down sharply.

As soon as we were able, we undertook major renovations on our house. We looked into building a new house, but that would have cost three times as much as our renovation plans. We were able to completely renovate the interior while leaving the exterior weatherboard cladding, which was generally in good condition, largely intact. A new roof and aluminium joinery were installed. When the renovations were completed, we had a large, comfortable family home which served us well.

We continued to improve the farm, cleaning up the rubbish and fallen trees and stumps. Fertility was responding to the application of adequate fertiliser; more grass was being grown and production improving. Progressively, as we cropped each paddock, we were able to level out the surface and sow better pasture species. The farm was still wet, but a major step forward was the installation of underground drainage, initially clay field tiles, then plastic Novaflow, with mole drains pulled at right angles over the top. A block at a time, we progressively covered most of the farm. This significantly improved drainage and increased pasture production. Gradually, the farm became tidy and fully productive.

In 1986 Jul and Graham came onto the farm to sharemilk. This was an opportunity for them to get ahead but was also great as far as the family were concerned, and when Adam and Mel came along Christine and I got huge pleasure out of having our first grandchildren just across the paddock. I missed a great opportunity in the early 1990s when Hornes' farm next door came on to the market. It was an opportunity that a farmer would always jump at as it would have doubled the size of our farm. However, at the time I was fully extended as chairman of the Dairy Board and had neither the time nor the emotional energy required to complete the purchase and the projects needed to consolidate the two properties into one. I have always regretted not grasping that opportunity.

In 1998 with my time at the Dairy Board nearing an end, Christine and I purchased a very nice home on a 3685-square-metre section at 124 Burwood Road, Matamata. I had always intended to retire to Matamata, which was a town I liked and which had been good to me. This also enabled Jul and Graham and their growing family to move into our house on the farm. The large section at Burwood Road eased my transition from the open space of the countryside into the confines of town.

Grandad, Adam and Melanie on the farm

NINETEEN
THE RURAL BANK

From almost the beginning of my career as chairman of the Sharemilkers Sub-Section of Federated Farmers, I had pushed for the establishment of a rural bank. At that time the State Advances Corporation was the government lender for housing and farming. Initially, it lent only for the purchase of a first home or farm and had done a wonderful job, particularly with the Rehabilitation Schemes settling returned soldiers with farms or houses following the Second World War. But the capital requirements of farming had changed, as the emphasis moved from soldier settlement to developing the productive capability of agriculture. The investment needs of farming were not being adequately met. The lending of trading banks was controlled directly by the Minister of Finance, who imposed tight restrictions and micro-managed their lending, which was mostly directed to providing short-term working capital. They also lacked skilled agricultural staff. The medium and longer-term investment needs of farmers for development funding were being inadequately provided. In response State Advances had begun to lend for farm development. It had a high-quality team of farm appraisers who were very skilled at farm lending. But the Rural Division was a rather small part in the much larger State Advances Corporation whose primary business was financing home ownership. Its board and management were largely engaged in housing settlement. As its funding was provided by Government in one single vote it was hard to understand just how much capital was being allocated to farming. A clearly identified sum allocated to a rural bank would provide much more assured funding for farming and eliminate the surreptitious practice of reducing farm lending to support greater housing investment.

My research showed that at the time most countries had specialised agricultural lending institutions. I believed that New Zealand would benefit if it were to have a rural bank as it would be better able to provide more reliable funding and better meet the specialised needs of farming. In this I was supported by Waikato Federated Farmers. The Dominion Dairy Section Council, after initially being hesitant, came aboard, but Dominion Council for rather obscure reasons continued to resist the concept. As Sharemilkers chairman I had advanced the concept directly with both political parties. I had met Norman Kirk, then Leader of the Opposition, in 1969, who was obviously keen on my "Farm Ownership Savings Scheme" but was also receptive to my call for a rural bank. Labour clearly were keen to pursue both concepts and included them in their Election Manifesto for the 1972 election when they became government. When Bill Dunlop, later Sir William, became President of Federated farmers in 1972, he soon persuaded the Dominion Council to push for the establishment of a rural bank.

The Rural Banking and Finance Corporation of New Zealand, or Rural Bank as it became known, was established under its own Act of Parliament in 1974. The retired general manager of State Advances, Ron Millard, was appointed chairman. I was appointed a director, along with my mentor Sir William Dunlop, Laurie Pickering (a former National Cabinet minister), and George Evans who ran the large Māori farming trust, Whakatu. Ron Millard retired at the completion of his first term, having done a great job in getting the bank established. He was succeeded as chairman by my good friend Allan Wright. State Advances continued to manage the Rural Bank with Ted Babe, one of New Zealand's most competent civil servants, as general manager. We pushed hard for the Rural Bank to employ its own management and staff. Despite strong opposition from State Advances, Government acquiesced a few years later.

As New Zealand looked to the future, it had become obvious that our country needed to increase farm production for it to prosper. Farming needed significant investment and now Government had a vehicle to facilitate investment of the sector. For the next decade investment in farm development increased each year and despite volatile prices farm production continued to increase. In the first year of existence Rural Bank lending totalled $103 million. By 1980 we were lending $305 million. This grew to $466 million by 1982. Our team of highly experienced farm lenders handled this with great skill and minimal loan losses. They were particularly adept at understanding the risks and tailoring loans to suit the economics of each project. For the first time in New Zealand's history, farmers had good access to capital and despite weak prices farm production surged. Farming productivity and efficiency gains were massive.

When my term expired, I was reappointed. I was reappointed again by a National Government a couple of times and then again by the Lange Labour Government. Each year we visited two regions and over three days were able to have a close look at agriculture there. This gave us an excellent understanding of the needs of each region and farming type. Over the next ten years we visited every region of New Zealand at least twice. I consider myself extremely fortunate to have visited almost every town in the country. There was a huge difference in the funding needs of a sharemilker in the Waikato and a large-scale apple farmer in Nelson or Hawke's Bay. Investment needs also varied greatly among farming types. Lending to a Waikato dairy farmer was usually for stock, fencing, water, cowsheds and fertiliser. A cropping farmer in South Canterbury required irrigation and expensive machinery and grain siloes. An apple farmer required capital to set up an orchard and plant trees, but also needed large sums to erect buildings and install complex packing equipment as well as cool storage. Our people intimately understood the needs of each region and farming type. One need which had traditionally been poorly serviced was rural housing. Difficulties with title often meant that farmers just could not borrow to upgrade their housing or that of their employees. We believed that housing was a farm asset just as much as a cowshed or shearing shed and decided to lend to renovate existing houses or build new accommodation. This facilitated a significant upgrade of rural housing stock.

With traditional farm products such as meat, wool, dairy or apples, processing facilities were usually adequate to accommodate the production of new entrants. Processing and storage facilities for new products, however, were usually inadequate or even non-existent. We resolved that for emerging agricultural products the bank should consider the whole value chain from farm to market. In appraising on-farm funding applications for new products, we should also consider the adequacy of processing and storage facilities for the production those projects would create, as well as the ability of markets to absorb increased volume. We decided that while we would not fund marketing investment, we should be prepared to fund processing and storage facilities. These were likely to be provided in different ways. Large farmers might install packing and storage facilities on farm. The private sector was also likely to invest. In some cases, farmers wished to establish shared or cooperative processing and storage facilities. We should be prepared to consider applications from, and lend to, them all.

At that time the kiwifruit industry was growing rapidly. The original entrants were mostly existing dairy farmers in the Te Puke area, who progressively converted all or some of their farms to growing kiwifruit. But there was soon an influx of growers, many of them sharemilkers from the Waikato, who purchased small blocks of 4 hectares or so which they developed progressively over a period of four or five years to grow kiwifruit. Initially, the availability of processing and storage facilities was far from their minds, but as their orchards began to produce fruit it soon became obvious that the industry had a serious problem with the lack of processing and storage facilities. Most new agricultural products have relatively small volumes which are often directed mainly at the domestic market. But kiwifruit was the reverse. Production was growing exponentially; domestic sales were small, with most production going to export. It looked to us as though kiwifruit had the potential to become a decent-sized export industry, one of the top five alongside dairy, meat, wool and apples. We believed that we should be prepared to back it. As I lived close to the Bay of Plenty, my director colleagues tasked me with obtaining a good understanding of the emerging needs of the kiwifruit industry and liaising with growers and processors.

The Rural Bank was soon the largest funder of kiwifruit orchard development. When lending to farmers, we encouraged them to think about the availability of processing and storage for their crops when their orchards began producing, and we insisted that they plan ahead and make provision for investment to ensure that facilities would be available. We also lent to private-sector operators, establishing or expanding processing and storage capacity, and facilitated the establishment of several processing cooperatives which we insisted be properly capitalised. This created a problem for many growers who had put everything they owned into developing their orchards and just did not have the cash to invest in their cooperative.

In some cases, the bank was prepared to lend growers the capital contribution to their cooperative, securing the sum against their property. The Rural Bank's investment in the kiwifruit industry was a winner for New Zealand. This relatively new industry is now New Zealand's fourth largest export earner after dairy, meat and forestry, earning more than twice as much as apples and wool combined.

In addition to its core role of funding investment in agriculture, the bank was tasked with operating two other significant government policies. In 1977 the Muldoon Government introduced a package of measures designed to increase farm production. Under the Livestock Incentive Scheme, farmers received a per stock unit payment for increases in stock numbers over the base period. In 1978 Land Development Encouragement Loans provided for interest and 50% of the principal to be written off if increased production targets were reached and sustained. The Rural Bank was well equipped to operate these two substantial programmes which injected significant sums into the rural economy. These schemes, however, were of mixed blessing. They did result in increased production, but unfortunately some land was developed which would never be economically viable and soon reverted. The Livestock Incentive Scheme initiated a large increase in livestock numbers but with a decline in per head performance. It became colloquially known as the "Skinny Sheep Scheme"!

In 1984 New Zealand farming was facing a crisis. The economic restructuring undertaken by the Lange Labour Government, while undeniably the correct policy, had withdrawn all forms of government support from farming. The New Zealand currency was floated, again the correct thing to do. It had been expected to fall but unexpectedly it had risen, sharply reducing farm prices. Most farmers were running deficits and many were in dire financial straits. Farmland prices plunged and some farmers had negative equity. Government had to step in with a debt-restructuring programme to save those farmers who could be saved and assist those who could not to leave the industry with dignity and a small amount of equity to enable them to purchase a home. The Rural Bank was asked to operate the Farm Debt Mediation Scheme and did so most effectively. By restructuring the debts of financially distressed farmers, most farmers were saved and the number who had to exit farming was very small.

In 1984 Government decided to sell all of the banks it owned, Rural Bank, Post Office Savings Bank, BNZ, and the Development Finance Corporation. As part of the reforms, Government had freed up the private financial sector and removed the restrictions on lending. Banks and other financial institutions quickly grasped the opportunity and met the needs of farming and other sectors. There was now no need for the Rural Bank. The Rural Banking and Finance Corporation was disestablished and converted into a company to prepare it for subsequent sale, so my term as a director ended. I was pleased with what the Rural Bank had achieved during its ten-year life. For the first time significant capital had been made available for farm investment. By 1983, 36% of farmers' total debt had been provided by the Rural Bank compared to only 12% by the trading banks. Farm production had grown sharply, increasing export income for New Zealand. I was proud to have contributed to that.

TWENTY
FERTILISER

In my second year on the New Zealand Dairy Company Board, I was appointed a director of New Zealand Farmers Fertiliser Co. Ltd. It was to be a most valuable and amazing journey. Many years previously, when Sir Walter Goodfellow was managing director of the New Zealand Dairy Co., it had joined forces with Wright Stephenson to establish the Challenge Fertiliser Works. At that time fertiliser was in short supply and this investment assured the company's farmers of adequate fertiliser supplies. Challenge subsequently merged with New Zealand Farmers Fertiliser Co., under that name, but the Dairy Company continued to have a large shareholding in the merged company which enabled it to nominate a director to New Zealand Farmers Fertiliser. This was a lucky break for me. In 1975 I was most fortunate to be appointed a director. As a publicly listed company, it exposed me to a much wider range of commercial practices and broadened my experience enormously. I was able to use that experience to benefit the Dairy Company, and subsequently the Dairy Board, in so many different ways.

New Zealand Farmers Fertiliser Ltd operated fertiliser works in Auckland, New Plymouth, Whangarei and Morrinsville, where in my teens I had worked as a builder's labourer during its construction. It was a small company. In prosperous farming years when fertiliser use was heavy it would make $6 to $7 million profit, while in a bad year when less fertiliser was applied the number could be as low as $2 million. It had a low profile, was seen as a solid and reliable company, but was certainly not a share market darling. The Goodfellow family continued to hold a large shareholding as did Kempthorne Prosser, a South Island fertiliser manufacturer and pharmaceutical company. Together with New Zealand Dairy Company, these three large shareholders gave it a stable share register. Douglas Goodfellow, the son of Sir William, ran the extensive Goodfellow family interests and was also a director. He was a wise and canny businessman who became a good friend. I was to learn much from him.

Peter Riddell was appointed general manager (no such thing as a CEO in those days) shortly after I became a director. I rated Peter Riddell who was a young general manager with new ideas and a desire to not only grow the company but to make it less dependent on fertiliser sales which were highly cyclical, varying year to year by 50% or more according to the prosperity of farming. At that time New Zealand had a very protected economy with import licences being required for all imports. New import licences were impossible for competitors to existing licence holders to obtain. As he looked for opportunities to expand, Peter resolved to avoid any business which required protection.

He soon built a useful chemicals business based on the company's acid production. Those products were used in water treatment so had stable and reliable sales. There was little competition so they were very profitable. He then moved into agricultural chemicals, 2,4-D and 2,4,5-T weedkillers, bloat drenches and dairy hygiene. This was a very competitive business dominated by large multinational companies. The strategy was to use the existing network of sales reps and storage facilities to provide a top-class distribution service. Progress was steady but slow, but brand recognition and market share were growing.

In addition to its fertiliser works in Wanganui and in the South Island, Kempthorne Prosser (whose chairman Peter Fels was a New Zealand Farmers Fertiliser director) owned 20% of Dominion Fertiliser located at Timaru. Dominion was a highly profitable company, which unlike Kempthorne Prosser had a good reputation among farmers. In 1977 Kempthorne decided to take over the 80% of Dominion Fertiliser it did not own. Farmers held a significant shareholding in Dominion. Kempthorne decided to "sup with the devil" by engaging the assistance of Brierley Investments Ltd, then at its peak as a corporate raider. Peter Ridell considered that Kempthorne was making a mistake. He knew that farmers were unhappy with Kempthorne's service and tried to dissuade Kempthorne from going ahead with its attempt to take over Dominion, believing it would destabilise the industry. To safeguard its position, New Zealand Farmers Fertiliser decided to "stand in the market" and buy Dominion shares, offering $3.60 per share.

As expected, Kempthorne's bid was most unpopular with farmers who were concerned that Dominion's high standard of customer service would be replaced by Kempthorne's poor service. They were quickly galvanised into action. Led by my very good friend Peter Elworthy, and with the support of Federated Farmers, Ravensdown Fertiliser Cooperative was formed and also began to buy Dominion shares. Ravensdown had the support of almost every farmer in the region but had one major problem, it could not fund the purchase of Dominion. However, they managed to persuade Brierley to change sides, to hold the Dominion shares it had purchased for Kempthorne Prosser, and fund the takeover of Dominion by Ravensdown. With the support of Brierley, Ravensdown then launched an audacious bid to take over Kempthorne, offering $4.25 per share. They were soon in sight of 50%. Kempthorne then upped its bid with cash and Kempthorne scrip to $4.60. This prevented Ravensdown from gaining the 60% holding it needed to qualify as a cooperative, and the taxation and other benefits cooperative status enabled.

New Zealand Farmers Fertiliser had also been buying Kempthorne shares. It sold some assets to Kempthorne, receiving 2.2 million Kempthorne shares in consideration. That blocked Ravensdown but attracted writs from both Ravensdown and Brierley. There was a prolonged standoff with both Ravensdown and New Zealand Farmers Fertiliser buying any Kempthorne stock available but neither had any chance of prevailing. Given my involvement in the farming community, I had become a member of the NZFF four-man strategy and negotiating team, along with the chairman and a young executive who was about my age, Kerry Hoggard.

It was an unusual experience for me with my cooperative background to be a protagonist for private enterprise, against several of my farmer friends who were supporting a cooperative. I was able to act as a conduit for back-door negotiations and worked to look for a solution that both parties could live with. We kept meeting with Peter Elworthy and his Ravensdown colleagues with whom we were able to maintain a good relationship. Brierley was running the Ravensdown bid. This was where I first met Paul Collins, later to become Sir Paul, who was then a very bright young man in his twenties. The standoff continued for some time with neither side gaining any ground. After some torrid negotiations a compromise was finally reached. Ravensdown and Brierley sold their Kempthorne shares to Farmers Fertiliser. Kempthorne's fertiliser assets were placed in a cooperative fertiliser company owned 60% by Ravensdown and 40% by New Zealand Farmers Fertiliser.

NZFF emerged from this saga with a significantly enlarged fertiliser business holding 40% of the combined Kempthorne and Dominion business. It also ended up with both the pharmaceutical assets of Kempthorne and Brierley-controlled Medical Supplies. The quality of Kempthorne's pharmaceutical business was mixed. It had some very good businesses and some rather mediocre units. As much of it was agency business for foreign drug manufacturers, it was always vulnerable to the brand principal establishing their own New Zealand company when sales became large enough to support that. It was a difficult business from which to make satisfactory returns. New Zealand Farmers Fertiliser sold it when a more enticing opportunity came along.

I was appointed a director of the new Ravensdown Fertiliser Company and continued in that role for a couple of years until resigning when I became deputy chairman of the New Zealand Dairy Company. By then Ravensdown had been successfully established and was providing farmers with improved service and achieving satisfactory profit. NZFF did not see it as a long-term investment. We believed that sooner or later the farmer shareholders would want to move to 100% shareholding. However, in the meantime it was providing a useful profit stream to NZFF and was materially assisting the growth of our agricultural chemicals business in the South Island. Today, Ravensdown is a much larger business which is highly efficient and profitable.

Kerry Hoggard quickly developed into an outstanding executive. He was clever, innovative, extremely good with people, a first-class manager and adept at spotting opportunities. He soon established himself as the logical successor to Peter Riddell as CEO. In 1982 he spotted an Australian agricultural chemicals company, Nufarm, which was located in Melbourne. It had been founded by a guy called Max Fremder who owned about 90% with the balance being owned by Nufarm's three senior executives. Kerry established a close friendship with the general manager, Doug Rathbone. Fremder wanted to sell and had a binding sale and purchase agreement with a multinational chemical company; I cannot remember if it was Monsanto or DuPont. But the sale to a foreign buyer required Overseas Investment Commission regulatory approval. Our advice was that if there was an Australian buyer, regulatory approval for a foreign purchase would be declined. Kerry engineered a bid which Fremder was prepared to accept that involved 30% of the shares being owned by Doug Rathbone and the other top two Nufarm executives. To make the proposal work, NZFF had to fund the purchase of 30% of the company by the three Nufarm executives with Doug Rathbone receiving the major share of about 19%. The plan worked. Approval for the sale to the foreign buyer was declined. Fremder accepted our bid and regulatory approval was obtained. Nufarm became a NZFF subsidiary. This was to be game changing for NZFF.

When I became deputy chairman of New Zealand Dairy Company in 1982, I retired as a director of NZFF. As Jim and I set about our task of turning the Dairy Company around we reviewed all its investments. We decided that the investment in New Zealand Farmers Fertiliser was not core; we could employ that capital elsewhere to greater benefit, so we decided to sell the Dairy Company's holding in NZFF. We worked with Waikato Federated Farmers President Bruce Smith to explore the possibility of a farmer-owned entity purchasing our stake as a first move towards establishing a farmer-owned fertiliser cooperative. A farmer-owned company, Fertiliser Holdings, was incorporated to which we sold our shareholding.

When I retired as a director of NZFF, they asked me to return if my workload eased sufficiently at some time in the future. They kept in touch with me and on several occasions asked if I was able to return yet. By 1985 I felt able to do so and was again appointed a director. At about the same time as I rejoined, New Zealand Farmers Fertiliser decided to change its name to FERNZ, an abbreviation of Fertiliser

New Zealand. As around half of the profit was being earned from activities other than fertiliser which would continue to decline in importance, it wanted to move away from being seen as a fertiliser company and project a more modern image as an innovative agri-chemicals company with good growth prospects.

During the Ravensdown saga Brierley took a shareholding position in NZFF. It subsequently increased that position to, I think from memory, around 16%. No company wanted Brierley on its share register. In those days Brierley Investments was a very successful and feared corporate raider. It was skilled at recognising undervalued companies, taking a position in them and developing a strategy which made money for Brierley. That often involved breaking a company up and selling it or merging it with another company. It pushed for a position on the FERNZ Board which was hard to deny. It was soon clear that Brierley's appointee was primarily there to gather detailed information about FERNZ and its activities. FERNZ began to consider how to get Brierley out.

Bill Wilson was the chairman of FERNZ. He was a fine man and was very well respected within the business community. Among his many other board roles, he was chairman of Unity Group. Unity Group had been founded by two Te Aroha men, David Muller, brother of Peter Muller, and Mark Wyborn. They were smart opportunists who had started out in property but had purchased some other assets and broadened their activities. Bill Wilson suggested that Unity might be a suitable partner to purchase Brierley's shareholding in FERNZ. After much consideration, and not without some misgivings, the board agreed. Eventually, in October 1987, Unity reached agreement to buy Brierley's shareholding for a little over $2 per share, which returned a tidy profit for Brierley. But it missed out on a much bigger prize.

David Muller came onto the FERNZ Board. He made a good contribution but obviously had his own interests in mind with another agenda. By now Peter Riddell had retired and Kerry Hoggard had been appointed CEO with Doug Rathbone as managing director of Nufarm. They were a formidable team who complemented one another. Doug was a chemical engineer. He had great vision, was very entrepreneurial and was not afraid to take risks. He was great with people, adept at doing deals and forging strong partnerships with suppliers to Nufarm. Kerry was across the detail of the business, was measured, reliable and strong at managing and reducing risk. He had great strategic vision. They had a strong friendship and worked well together. While NZFF still retained its traditional fertiliser business, strategy was now focused on chemicals where much greater opportunities existed. Led by Nufarm, agricultural chemicals were contributing an increased share of FERNZ profit. The sharemarket was beginning to notice FERNZ and its share price was moving upwards.

Then it came. Unity Group launched a takeover bid for FERNZ. We considered the offer inadequate, but it was not too far away either. It came immediately before the FERNZ Annual Meeting so the pressure was on. We were going to have to make a recommendation to shareholders and explain our reasoning to them at the Annual Meeting. Bill Wilson, however, was in an invidious position. He was chairman of FERNZ, but he was chairman of Unity Group also. He would have to retire from one. Which one would it be? Would he chair the Annual Meeting? Would he even attend? None of us knew, but Bill opened the meeting that morning, referred to the Unity bid and announced that he had resigned that morning as chairman and a director of Unity Group. There was a storm of applause from the FERNZ shareholders who clearly welcomed his decision, seeing it as a massive vote of confidence in FERNZ. Kerry and Doug then gave an excellent presentation explaining why the directors were going to recommend against the takeover offer. The market responded positively with the FERNZ share price rising above the takeover offer price. Unity Group were stymied. They then made a big mistake. They folded. Had they stayed in the fight and upped their bid, they would have made a lot of money.

Unity Group had demonstrated that they were opportunistic shareholders rather than the long-term committed shareholder FERNZ wanted. We wanted them out; they wanted to exit. Assisted by Douglas Goodfellow, Kerry and Doug negotiated to buy Unity's shareholding at a price which realised a tidy profit for Unity. But Nufarm was by now performing very well. In two years, the share price soared from a little over $2 per share to over $7. Brierley and Unity Group were both ruing a missed opportunity; the stock they had previously owned was now in the hands of long-term stable shareholders and Kerry and Doug had become very wealthy.

In 1988 FERNZ turnover was $211 million. Its future clearly lay in agricultural chemicals. It was obvious that it should exit fertiliser and deploy the capital freed up as a result into Nufarm's higher returning agrichemicals business. But there was really only one natural buyer for each of the fertiliser works so an exit strategy needed to be carefully crafted if reasonable prices were to be obtained for the fertiliser assets. FERNZ Kiwi Fertiliser plant in Morrinsville faced fierce competition from Bay of Plenty Cooperative, while in South Taranaki the Ravensdown Whanganui plant was a strong competitor. In 1987 FERNZ sold its 40% share in Ravensdown Fertiliser Company to Ravensdown Cooperative. In the same year FERNZ lodged a takeover bid for Bay of Plenty Cooperative Fertiliser Co. This was against my advice as I did not believe it had a chance of succeeding. But it would be very much to FERNZ's benefit if it were to succeed, so as a director of FERNZ I could not oppose it. However, as expected it received little traction among Bay of Plenty farmers. In the end, we agreed to sell Kiwi to Bay of Plenty in exchange for 40% of Bay of Plenty Fertiliser Co. We believed that it was better to have 40% of a very good business than 100% of a less profitable one.

By 1992 FERNZ turnover had reached $610 million, and its share price had reached $9.95, it was on a strong growth path as it expanded into a significant global agrichemicals company. Doug Rathbone was particularly skilled at taking older chemicals such as 2,4-D and glyphosate as they came off patent, negotiating exclusive distribution deals with the large chemical companies which formerly held the patent, and selling them through highly effective distribution channels to build leading market shares.

In 1998 New Plymouth fertiliser works was sold to Ravensdown. In 1998 Whangarei was sold to Bay of Plenty. In 2001 FERNZ sold its 40% share in Bay of Plenty Fertiliser to Bay of Plenty Cooperative and the Norwegian company Norsk Hydro. Exit from fertiliser had now been completed at satisfactory prices.

With little business remaining in New Zealand, FERNZ was relocated to Melbourne and renamed Nufarm. Kerry retired as CEO and became chairman, with Doug as CEO. Nufarm continued to expand around the world, delivering increasing profit. I retired in 2003 when Nufarm returned a profit of $77 million, an increase over five years of 48%, and a stunning return on equity of 15%. It was in good shape and its share price was on an upswing which continued for several more years. I had been a director for twenty-five years. I could reflect on my time with satisfaction, as the company had grown from a small fertiliser company making a couple of million dollars of profit to a leading global agrichemicals company, in the process having created significant shareholder value.

PART FIVE
DAIRY BUSINESS

TWENTY-ONE
EARLY DAYS AT NEW ZEALAND COOPERATIVE DAIRY CO

One reason why I enjoyed commerce is that performance can always be measured. The annual profit number tells it all. There is no place to hide. For a cooperative dairy company this was expressed as "payout", which was the profit after providing for the financial needs of the company, distributed to farmers.

When I became a director of New Zealand Dairy Company in 1974, its turnover was $164 million. With its great scale efficiencies and huge financial strength, New Zealand Dairy had traditionally more than matched its much smaller cooperative dairy company competitors in the Waikato. But times were changing. The other Waikato co-ops had to compete fiercely to survive. Without our advantages they had to be efficient, lean and mean. New Zealand Dairy Company suffered a huge loss when its highly regarded and extremely competent general manager, Alvin Woolven, suffered ill health and had to step aside. He continued in a largely advisory role as managing director, but his successor Rex Haggie was fully responsible for managing the company. He was untested and certainly not up to Alvin Woolven's exceptional standard. The company had grown complacent and flabby. A management restructure created several empires, with wrong people in the wrong places, all vying for supremacy. Capital was wasted on inefficient plant. Quality diminished, staffing and costs increased. I was overseas at the end of that first financial year. The payout of $1.35 per kilogram of milkfat was disappointing, being below average, and our farmers became unsettled. Although payout the following year was down to $1.30 per kilo, we were a little more competitive.

That was the year that testing for butterfat was changed from the manual Babcock test undertaken at each factory to the automatic Milko machine at one central site. This gave much more reliable and consistent results across the whole company. It also credited slightly higher butterfat content to farmers which depressed payout by about three cents per kilogram. We were thus at a disadvantage compared to our competitors who were all still using the less accurate Babcock system. The Milko testing system also allowed testing for protein with the results made available to farmers but not used for payment.

But worse was to come the following year. Management reports through the year suggested things were going along well but quality and yields continued to slip and costs increased. With no monthly profit and loss reporting, the directors were unaware of that until the end of the year, when we had to set a payout which, although higher than the previous year at $1.48 per kilo, was below our competitors. By now our famers were becoming agitated and vociferous. I initiated a series of twenty or more cowshed meetings in my ward where I took farmers through the results and what we were doing to fix them. We had an excellent turnout of about 80%. My farmers continued to have faith in me, but their faith was being tested. The problem we faced was that with inadequate reporting systems, we had no real-time information and just did not know what the results actually were. As is usually the case, an unsatisfactory situation is usually worse than it initially appears, so in trying to fix it you are usually doing too little too late. That was the position we were in.

New Zealand Dairy Co. payout from 1976 until 1980 continued to slip below the average of Waikato dairy companies. We were not making any progress in improving the company's performance; in fact we were failing to deal with the real issues, so continued to lose ground. Our farmers were quite dissatisfied and each year the number defecting to our competitors was growing. That was serious because lost milk throughput is costly to high fixed-cost businesses such as milk processing. At every farmer meeting, directors and management were on the back foot defending our performance. Our farmers expected us to fix the problems, not explain them, a view they were entitled to.

Part, but only part, of the problem was that we had lost scale in our factories. While the company had huge scale, the actual milk-processing factories which had once been the largest in the industry were now below average size and were thus below average efficiency. We had failed to upscale our plants and had fallen behind in utilising the new technologies which were emerging as a result of the huge growth in milk production in Europe. This was despite the very large technical and engineering resource we had compared to our competitors. In fact, that resource was itself largely the problem as it had outdated knowledge but an inflated opinion of its own capability. It had fallen some way behind the technologies now available from the European milk-processing equipment manufacturers.

In 1977 the building of a new town-milk processing and bottling plant at Takanini was approved. In 1978 construction of a new infant formula plant at Waitoa was signed off. Management and directors were now beginning to understand the need to invest in modern, efficient milk-processing plant. In 1979 we developed plans to build three new factories, a butter factory at Paerata and cheese factories at Kerepehi and Waitoa. We hoped they would help improve our performance. But our planning ability was very poor; one cheese factory twice the size would have been more efficient and both Kerepehi and Paerata sites were closed down within twenty years.

One most innovative development occurred in 1979. Carberry Dairy in Cork, Ireland had developed the technology to make ethanol from whey. Brewing and distillation science is thousands of years old, but whey is an acidic liquid which contains only about 4.5% lactose (milk sugar) compared to, say, molasses at over 50% sugar. The economics of producing alcohol from whey are therefore poor. But Carberry had discovered a yeast which significantly improved yields. Rex Haggie had negotiated a technology agreement with Carberry which gave us access to their technology. But knowing how to produce alcohol was not sufficient. There had to be a good plan for marketing it. New Zealand's industrial alcohol was supplied by Australian sugar company CSR who were able to extract a price well above the world market price. Haggie negotiated an arrangement with CSR and their New Zealand distributors, in which they vacated the New Zealand market in return for a royalty payment. This made installation of an alcohol refinery viable. It also eased what was becoming an increasing problem for the company in disposing of whey. It was a smart move by Haggie.

The chairman, Ron Greenhough, was retiring in 1979 and Deputy Jim Graham was to succeed him. Since missing out on the Dairy Board appointment in 1976, it was expected that I would become deputy chairman. However, a month or so before the annual general meeting I became aware that Jim was pushing for Rex Byles to be his deputy. We had different views over what needed to be done to turn the company around. Jim believed that building a couple of new plants and picking the low-hanging fruit would be sufficient.

I held the view that the problems were much deeper seated. We needed management change; an infusion of more highly qualified new people across the whole company; a significant reduction in the head count which meant fewer but larger plants; better technology; and much better information which meant better information systems. These would not be quick fixes and it might actually cost more in the short term. Jim's opposition to me could have proved fatal to my chances of promotion. But I worked hard to maintain my support among my colleagues and with the help of a couple of good friends managed to do so. When I was announced as winner of the ballot, Jim looked most uncomfortable. After the meeting he asked if we could meet at 9 am the following day.

Jim started our meeting next morning by asking what responsibilities I would like. I told him that there was something we had to sort out first. I got up, shut the door, told him that I did not appreciate him lobbying against me. I asked him what the problem was and told him that it would be difficult for us to work effectively together if he continued to hold reservations about working with me. He responded that some of our views differed, and he knew that I would challenge him on issues. He was concerned that I would challenge him for chairman and felt he would be better off with somebody who was less of a threat. I responded that I agreed that we would have different views on issues from time to time. But he should regard that as an advantage because we were more likely to consider all of the alternatives and arrive at better decisions. That I reserved the absolute right to express my views and I expected him to carefully consider them. But I acknowledged that he was the boss; in the event of a difference of opinion I would support his decision and he would have my full and active support. I gave him an undertaking that I would not seek the chairmanship during the next two terms (six years). Clearly hugely relieved, he got up, came around the desk with a smile on his face and his large hand out to shake my hand.

That was the beginning of what became an extremely close working partnership. We were very tight and almost inseparable, as Jim insisted that I accompany him on virtually all appointments or activities in which he was involved. We often had different views, debated them vigorously, considered carefully the other's opinion, agreed the way forward and then acted as one. Jim made it clear to management and staff that in his absence I had his full authority and backing. Our trust in one another deepened as did our friendship.

We agreed that I would retire from both Affco and New Zealand Farmers Fertiliser boards to apply myself full time to Dairy Company affairs. Jim asked me to take the chair of Glen Afton Collieries. I had a strong view that we needed to improve our systems and reporting. Jim agreed and asked me to take responsibility for establishing a monthly profit and loss reporting system, on both a company and individual factory basis. I was delighted to do so. I believed that we needed to make a management change and make it immediately. Jim's view was that we did not have the time that would take and that he and I taking a hands-on role would bring quicker results.

Jim was a great communicator and he and I were both trusted by farmers. The company performance was poor, but farmers wanted to believe in the company. As we outlined our plans for improving performance, farmers trusted us and gave us huge support. An article in the *NZ Dairy Exporter* referred *to* "NZCDC winching itself out of the mud". We tightened up things in a few areas quickly where improvement was readily attainable. The three new factories under construction were expected to bring significant benefits when they came on line in two or three years' time and our farmers were anticipating an improvement in our payout. We had improved morale throughout the company both among the staff and our farmers. Quality was better but still not great. We decided to consolidate butter manufacture onto three sites and close down a number of smaller butter factories. Paerata would manufacture consumer packs for the domestic retail market and two large bulk factories of massive scale at Waharoa and Te Awamutu. Very significant efficiencies could be expected from that reorganisation which would ultimately be largely realised. But our planning and ability to think long term had not improved, and both the Waharoa and Paerata sites were closed within twenty years.

While the new plants brought benefits when they came on line and we had taken the easy wins to improve performance, we had not actually dealt with the real issues of inadequate management and inefficiency which were causing our performance to be unsatisfactory. In addition, our competitors were not standing still; they were all improving their performance so we were finding it difficult to close the gap. The New Zealand Dairy Company was a "for-life" employer, a little like the government. People rarely left and outside recruitment was even more rare. It was largely living on its past, which was glorious but was well past its best. It was an insular organisation and lagging behind modern commercial practice.

Rex Haggie had started as a mail boy and progressed to become general manager. Promoting from within was the normal company practice and until now had generally turned up good leaders. However, he had not been properly trained for the job and was not up to date with current commercial and management practices. I did not rate him. I pushed for him to be replaced, but Jim's view was that we did not have time. "You and I can fix this place in short order," was his reply. Oh, that it would be so simple. Yes, there was low-hanging fruit and we did quickly harvest it, but as is always the case, for every issue we fixed many more arose.

The company was arrogant, with the whole organisation believing that it had the best people in New Zealand. Although limited, my experience outside of New Zealand Dairy had convinced me that was far from being the case and that we needed better people. I pushed for Haggie to identify high-potential younger people from right across the company and send them on executive training courses. I had in mind the New Zealand Staff College and overseas universities such as Harvard or INSEAD business school for the most promising. Jim agreed with me as did Haggie. When pushed, Haggie identified Jeff Jackson as the executive most likely to succeed him. We had not seen anything in Jeff to rate him as potential CEO material but suggested that he undertake the Advanced Management Programme at Harvard University. He did so and came back a changed man. The participants in the Harvard programme were very senior people, CEOs or potential CEOs of many of the world's best and largest companies. Living and working with those sorts of people, in an environment where they were expected to find solutions to difficult problems and get things done, brought out the potential and talent of Jeff which had hitherto been hidden. Other senior executives attended management courses in New Zealand and overseas, with lesser but still worthwhile results.

However, we did make one external senior hire. A few years previously, the then chairman, Ron Greenhough, had taken several of us on a market visit to Asia. In Hong Kong we met Simon Caughey who was a senior marketing executive for the large conglomerate Hong Kong Land, which itself was owned by the legendary British/Hong Kong company Jardine Matheson. He had previously been marketing manager for Fisher and Paykel. He was smart, polished and clearly a leader. All of us were most taken with him and agreed that it would be worth considering hiring him in a senior executive role when his contract in Hong Kong concluded. A few years later he approached Haggie, they got along well and he joined us as assistant general manager (Commercial). I hoped that he would give us another option to succeed Haggie as general manager in due course.

Then after only three years something completely unexpected occurred. The chairman of the Dairy Board Ken Mehrtens was retiring in June 1982. My close friend Graham Calvert was deputy chairman and the logical choice for chairman. The chairmanship was Graham's to lose and lose it he did. Graham was a smart and capable individual, but he had some serious flaws which he could not control. He was prone to drama and overstatement which impaired his judgement, and often did not display the maturity the position demanded, particularly outside of the boardroom. Also, his social skills often left much to be desired. I, and others, had counselled him on several occasions to rein himself in, improve his behaviour and show better judgement, but sadly he was unable to do so. Eventually, the directors of the Dairy Board reached the view that Graham could not be entrusted with the chairmanship. They turned instead to Jim Graham and appointed him chairman elect.

This was all most unexpected. I had anticipated serving as deputy chairman to Jim for some time, and in fact I thought that it would be nine or ten years before he would retire and I would have the opportunity of becoming chairman. But the opportunity had presented itself much sooner. The Dairy Board announced Jim as chairman elect in February 1982. At its next meeting in March 1982, I was appointed chairman elect by the New Zealand Cooperative Dairy Company Board.

TWENTY-TWO
A COAL MINER

Traditionally the energy for most dairy factories had been provided by coal. New Zealand Dairy Company had gone a step further than any other dairy company in configuring its energy plants. The high-pressure steam from the coal-fired boilers was used to generate electricity and the residual low-pressure steam was used in the milk-processing plant. More than fifty years previously the company's mining subsidiary, Glen Afton Collieries, had acquired coal reserves sufficient for several hundred years and operated three coal mines. Although originally two of them were underground mines, they were now all opencast. The largest, at Maramarua, also supplied large volumes of coal to the Meremere Power Station on the banks of the Waikato River on State Highway 1. The coal was transported across the Whangamarino Swamp, from the mine to the power station, along a twelve-kilometre aerial ropeway. The coal field owned by Glen Afton lay adjacent to a similar reserve owned by the Crown. When Meremere was established, Glen Afton and the Crown agreed that it would be more efficient to jointly mine the two reserves and had established a joint venture company to do so, Maramarua Coal Fields, which contracted to supply coal to the power station. Glen Afton was contracted by Maramarua to undertake the actual coal extraction activities.

As chairman of Glen Afton Collieries, I had to supervise the largest coal-mining activity in New Zealand. Opencast coal mining is essentially a quarrying or earthmoving activity. It involves removing, or stripping, large quantities of earth or overburden, and depositing it elsewhere to expose the coal which is then extracted. In a large mine it may take several years to remove the overburden and expose the coal so it requires the ability to plan, think ahead and deal with the unexpected. It is normal to have about one year's coal with very little overburden cover at the end of each winter; any less and the risk of having no coal to meet our factory needs during the following spring is unacceptable. But if too much coal is exposed in advance of it being required, more capital is unnecessarily outlaid for no return. The key economic parameters are the cost per metre of overburden; the ratio of overburden to coal; and the cost per metre of removing overburden; depending on the price of coal and the cost of removing overburden, a ratio of above 10 metres of overburden to 1 metre of coal may be uneconomic; the price of coal must reflect the sum of those parameters.

Glen Afton had significant issues. For some years insufficient volumes of coal had been exposed, so we were having to mine in a less than optimal manner to supply our factories and the Meremere Power Station. We were at serious risk of being unable to supply coal if an adverse event occurred. For example, with the mine being over 80 metres deep, there was always a risk of a slip bringing earth down onto the coal which would then have to be removed. A large slip might take a year or so to clear away. We directed management to increase our stripped reserves of coal. The cost of that meant that we had to raise several million dollars to finance it and it would take more than a year to complete.

The next issue was the contract to supply coal to Meremere Power Station. New Zealand had an energy crisis. Government was establishing two huge new underground mines in Huntly and wanted to use coal from those mines to supply Meremere, so it intended to abrogate Maramarua's coal supply contract with the Crown. We had outlaid tens of millions of dollars on stripping coal which we would not be able to sell. We would have a claim for compensation but that was not of much comfort to us, as we preferred to have the contract honoured and to sell coal to the Crown. Negotiations with the Crown were difficult and protracted. State Coal, the Electricity Department, Crown Law and at one stage Government Supplies Board all represented the government. None of them wanted to own the responsibility; each wanted to pass the buck to one of the other Crown agencies. Government Supplies Board intended to follow their usual procurement practice and call for tenders for the supply of coal to Meremere. They went away when we very firmly told them that while we were happy to deal with them administratively, we had a contract with the Crown to supply coal to Meremere for the life of the power station, at a price determined according to the formula specified in that contract; that if they departed from that they would be responsible for triggering a Crown liability which could reach nine figures. Negotiations with officials were particularly difficult but we kept escalating the dispute to the government, in which, fortunately, the Minister of Energy was Bill Birch, a minister with a good record of solving problems, who was helpful. We kept emphasising that in nearly thirty years of supplying Meremere, we had not once failed to meet its requirements for coal. After more than two and a half years of negotiation, we obtained a contract for a reduced amount of coal but a volume which we could live with. Ironically, the government-owned Huntly underground mines never performed and minimal quantities of coal were extracted before they were permanently closed. Therefore, we actually continued to supply quantities of coal in excess of the contract.

The other major issue was the cost of stripping. When the Kopuku field was developed in the early 1950s it was by far the largest earthmoving job in New Zealand and there was insufficient suitable equipment available in the country. A contract was entered into with WA Stevenson & Sons Ltd which undertook to purchase and import the large fleet of earthmoving equipment necessary to do the job. In return, a contract term of "the life of the field" was agreed. In line with most contracts at that time, the price was based on cost plus a margin. Every penny spent by Stevensons, whether capital or operating cost, went into the cost base. The price charged went up every year and the contract became increasingly favourable to Stevensons. Twenty-five years later circumstances had changed. There was an ample supply of equipment and many contractors. Competition for tenders was intense. Our other mines were letting stripping contracts for around $1.40 per cubic metre of dirt moved, while we were paying Stevensons close to $3.50 per metre. That price was increasing each year and the coal field still had sufficient coal for at least another twenty-five years. However, the ratio of overburden to coal was increasing and it would become uneconomic to extract that coal if the stripping cost continued to increase. We decided that we needed to bite the bullet and bring the Stevenson contract back to a finite term to enable more competitive costs to be obtained.

Australia, of course, undertakes more opencast mining than any other country in the world. Max Walker, our mining superintendent, and I travelled to Australia to look at the mining methods employed there. We were most impressed with the bucket-wheel excavators which loaded overburden directly onto a conveyor belt that carried it to where it was to be deposited. Our economic analysis showed huge benefit if we could successfully use that method at Kopuku. However, we were concerned that the conveyors might not satisfactorily handle the more sticky material in our wetter climate. We decided to run a trial using some of our existing equipment to load overburden onto a relatively short conveyor system.

We then set out to renegotiate our contract with Stevensons for a finite term after which we would be free to tender the work. Bill Stevenson was the person we were dealing with. He was a good guy and Stevensons were actually reliable contractors who had done a good job for us, albeit at significant cost. We did not wish to get rid of them, but we did have to get the cost down through a competitive contract. Not surprisingly, they stuck to their life-of-the-field contract and refused to budge. We worked to convince them that we were determined to obtain a finite and competitive contract. The conveyor trial we were undertaking helped show that we were serious. Eventually, we decided to advise Stevensons that their contract would be terminated and a new contract tendered. We hoped that they would tender. We knew that we would be sued to try to enforce the existing contract, but our advice was that courts were reluctant to enforce perpetual contracts. Also, the economics of continuing under the existing contract were poor, making the litigation risk acceptable. When we called for tenders for a three-year term, we received several from contractors whom we would be happy to let the contract to, including Stevensons. Each of them, including Stevensons, were at a much lower price than we were currently paying, although Stevensons was the highest-priced tenderer.

As we evaluated the tenders, Stevensons lodged a High Court application for an injunction to prevent us letting a new tender. We strenuously challenged the injunction which was nevertheless granted. This was not unexpected as it was a temporary injunction until the main claim could be heard. Our QC Alan Houston was of the opinion that the Court would not enforce the existing perpetual contract. We prepared for trial, but as Stevensons had tendered, believed this indicated that they were prepared to negotiate a new contract on more favourable terms. I felt it was time to reopen negotiations and asked Jim Graham to intervene directly with Stevensons. I wanted him to be the "good cop" wanting a settlement, with me the "bad cop" seeking a change in contractor.

Jim and Bill Stevenson agreed to meet one Saturday morning in Auckland. There were two QCs and other senior lawyers in attendance. Stevensons restated their existing contract rights. We insisted that we would only accept a new contract for a three-year term at a competitive price. We argued well into the afternoon and finally agreed that we should recommence negotiations. This was actually a significant win for us as we were now talking about a new contract. Over several meetings we narrowed the differences. It was clear a new contract was achievable: we were offering three years, they wanted five. On price they wanted their tender price, while we wanted a price no greater than the lowest tenderer. We were making progress and agreed to meet at the Maramarua mine. We argued all morning and then adjourned to the Red Fox tavern in Maramarua for lunch. We argued over lunch and into the afternoon and later Bill and I decided to go to the bar for a beer together. We were there for more than an hour and had several beers, much to the consternation of our respective teams who were watching from the other side of the room and trying to gauge what was happening from our body language. I was prepared to agree to a five-year term but wanted a competitive price. Bill wanted the price at which he had tendered. We finally settled on a price which was lower than his tender price, being about half of what we had been paying. We shook hands and I shouted drinks for all of his, and my, team members to celebrate. We had retained our preferred contractor Stevensons, but at a much lower price, while Glen Afton Collieries would be free to competitively tender the contract after five years. It was now on a much sounder economic footing.

TWENTY-THREE
THE CHAIRMAN

I OFFICIALLY BECAME CHAIRMAN OF NEW ZEALAND Cooperative Dairy Company in June 1982. That year company turnover was $605,086,127. I had effectively taken up the role a couple of months earlier as Jim became increasingly involved in Dairy Board affairs. During that period, I began to plan what needed to be done to turn the company around. It was by now clear that our performance was still lagging that of our competitors. Tinkering would not cut it; there needed to be major change and we had run out of time. Our payout that year would not be good enough and our farmers were again growing restive. In fact, the shareholders in my Morrinsville Ward had passed a "vote of no confidence in the directors". I managed to reach an agreement with Alan Faulkner, the chairman of Morrinsville, that they would pay their farmers no more than three cents per kilogram above our payout. That eased the reaction from our farmers, but we were on borrowed time.

For years, annual payout would be reduced by the "clean-up" or finalisation of the previous year. There will always be a small difference, either positive or negative. The problem was that it had become always negative, with the sum increasing each year. This meant that we started each year from behind. This was the consequence of excessive optimism in valuing stocks and debtors to enable a competitive payout. I immediately took the decision to bite the bullet, only taking into the year's results recoveries which were absolutely certain. The hit to payout that year was about 4 cents per kilo. From then on clean-up was always positive by a relatively small amount.

But the real problem I had was that we had run out of short-term fixes. I had a fair idea of what needed to be done, but it would take time to translate into results. Half of the year's production would be processed in the next four months which meant that our result for the year would be largely determined by the end of October. I was determined to deal with the real issues the company had and not be sidetracked by short-term considerations.

The first requirement was that we had to have better people, particularly a new leader. I knew that hiring a CEO took time, if we had to go outside: a minimum of six months if we were lucky, but more realistically twelve to eighteen months. We did not have that time. Then there was always a risk that bringing someone in from outside might not work out and an external appointment would take time to become familiar with the company and work out what needed to be done. Sending Jeff Jackson to Harvard Business School had been a master stroke. He had learned to think analytically and strategically and to get things done. I had worked very closely with Jeff for a couple of years as he drove the upgrading of our systems and accounting. While there was still much to do, at least we now had monthly P&L results, and were identifying heaps of issues for improvement. Jeff was largely responsible for executing that. I had seen him grow enormously over the previous couple of years. We had had many discussions on what the issues were and what needed to change, and as a result I had become confident that Jeff was capable of handling the chief executive job. I resolved to make a change, but I had to have a strategy for handling Haggie.

I engineered the opportunity over dinner one evening in July at the White Heron Hotel in Auckland. I suggested an enlarged role for Jeff, of which Haggie was strongly supportive. I then suggested that Rex should assume the role of managing director, as his predecessor Alvin Woolven had done when his health deteriorated, focussing on strategy, industry policy and industry affairs, while Jeff should become general manager handling the day-to-day management. In the end, Haggie warmed to the idea and agreed. First thing next morning I rang Graham Calvert, whom the directors had given another chance, after he had blown his opportunity to be Dairy Board chairman, by electing him my deputy chairman, and advised him. He was delighted but warned me that Haggie would probably change his mind and gave me very good advice. He suggested that I get Haggie to suggest it to the board, which was meeting that day. This was to be my first board meeting as chairman. When I arrived at the office, Haggie was waiting to see me. Forewarned, I pre-empted his attempt to walk back our agreement of the previous evening and so defer any change, by thanking him for selflessly putting the company ahead of himself and suggested that his standing with the board would be greatly enhanced were he to suggest to the board that Jeff should be promoted to general manager. I had outmanoeuvred him and he had little option other than to agree to do so.

At 5 pm that afternoon I asked the executive team to leave the boardroom and advised the directors that the general manager had a matter he wanted to raise with them. He told them that he thought it was time for him to take a less hands-on role and for Jeff to be promoted to general manager responsible for the day-to-day management of the company. Rex then withdrew, leaving the directors to consider his suggestion. The directors wholeheartedly supported the promotion of Jeff to run the company. They were less enthusiastic about the proposed role for Haggie. He was no Alvin Woolven and they were particularly anxious that Jeff must be given a free hand, reporting directly to the board and not be managed, or appear to be managed, by Haggie. However, the directors readily accepted that it was an elegant way of effecting an immediate change of management. I then rang Jeff at home and told him that I urgently needed to see him and his wife Rosemary. Graham Calvert and I went to his home at Te Kowhai, advised him of Rex Haggie's new role, and offered him the position of chief executive officer. Until now the role had always been designated general manager, but I wanted it to be obvious that Jeff was completely in charge. Jeff was surprised but delighted and readily accepted. We agreed that he should commence on 1 August which was about a week or so away. By midday the following day an announcement to staff had been dispatched. It was just three weeks since I had assumed the chairmanship and I overheard one of my directors remark to a colleague, "The new chairman is not wasting any time, is he?"

Before we could start to develop a plan to turn the company around, we had a pressing issue to deal with. The new season's milk flow was now under way and was increasing rapidly towards the peak which would be reached in the second week of October. During the previous year we had agreed to consolidate butter manufacture onto three sites: a smaller volume plant at Paerata, patting butter for the local market, and two very large export butter plants at Waharoa and Te Awamutu. At each of those two plants, the two existing six tonnes per hour butter makers would be replaced by two ten tonne per hour machines. The economics were very attractive as a number of smaller plants would be closed. It was originally intended that one plant would be done first and the other the following year, but our engineering staff became overexcited and believed that they could do both at the same time. Jim and I had been sceptical about this as our experience was that it always took longer than expected to complete and commission a new plant, but the payback was attractive so we accepted the assurances that the projects could be completed on time and gave the go-ahead.

Inevitably, there were delays in completing the work and commissioning was not going well. A dairy processing line is purpose built for the particular job and brings together complex pieces of equipment which must all function together in perfect harmony. It is not like a car where the key is turned and the vehicle is operational. Commissioning is often a very difficult process with many malfunctions as each component is set up and fine-tuned. With each line turning out a tonne of butter worth $2500 every six minutes, it can also be very expensive if there are difficulties. Worryingly, the projects had run over time and commissioning was not going well. As the milk flow increased, we could not process all of our cream, a backlog was building up and we were having to send cream to our competitors for processing. They were happy to help us out while they had spare capacity but would have little spare capacity at the flush so, unless we could get our plants up to design performance by early October, there was a serious risk that cream might have to be dumped. We just scraped through, but it was a near-run thing.

By mid-November the flush had passed and almost half of the season's milk had been processed. Jeff and I could now turn our attention to a plan to turn the company around. We knew that the most urgent needs were:

1. Significantly upgrade the quality of our executive team.
2. Reorganise the company's management structure to reduce layers and improve accountability.
3. Reduce staffing to lower operating costs.
4. Significantly improve quality.
5. Improve the use of capital.

In the restructured executive team, Simon Caughey would become Group General Manager Commercial and would take on some additional responsibilities to support Jeff. John Bell, the company secretary, was a long-term employee with great institutional knowledge. He was quite suitable to continue as company secretary. The most critical task, though, was to find a person to run the dairy-processing operations. This was a massive role as it involved running the total dairy processing, storage and logistics operations. We knew that this would not be an easy role to fill. Most dairy companies were single-site operations so there was no obvious candidate in the entire New Zealand dairy industry who had experience in a job of this scale. A long-term existing employee, Vince Pooch, had been superintendent of factories and in charge of operations for many years. He was very experienced, had great technical knowledge, an extensive network both in New Zealand and overseas and was a forceful driving personality who got things done. His industry knowledge in New Zealand and around the world was unparalleled. We rated him highly but felt that this was a position which urgently needed new blood from outside. We had a long discussion with him which culminated in Jeff appointing Vince to be his technical advisor. It was to be an inspired decision; Vince came on board with great enthusiasm. Once he knew what we wanted he used his knowledge to give Jeff and me sound advice and great support.

Mac Calvert was the younger brother of Graham. He was CEO of the small but well-performing Opunake Cheese Company and was a rising star among dairy company managers. His chairman, Lawrence Barrett, a man I greatly respected, rated him but commented that he had to be managed. Jeff and I met him at a motel in Te Kuiti. I asked him for his assessment of each of our senior factory managers. He gave us an amazingly perceptive analysis and it was obvious that he had the ability to motivate a team of individuals. He was keen to join us so we appointed him Group General Manager, Operations.

We needed to significantly upgrade our finance capability so commissioned an external search for a senior executive who had CFO experience. I wanted a well-seasoned senior finance person from outside of the dairy industry, a person who had seen it all. We were fortunate to recruit Brian Haskell who had been chief financial officer for some significant companies. He was very experienced, had a good track record and was a little more mature than the rest of us. He proved to be a great appointment.

We had now chosen a senior executive team of high-quality individuals which Jeff and I were satisfied had the ability to change the company's fortunes. The two most important roles, operations and finance, where most of the problems lay, were filled by people from outside, while Simon Caughey also had only been with us a short time. However, it was into the autumn of 1983 before they were all in place. As the new team progressively came aboard, we were able to start planning. To free ourselves of the normal day-to-day distractions I took them away on retreat for a couple of days. Graham Calvert was keen to focus on issues which might give us a few cents' better result for the year. But I expected the executives to deal with those in the normal course of business and was determined to address those big institutional issues which would need to be fixed if we were to significantly lift our performance. Chief among these was structure.

Our existing structure was hopeless. It was multi-layered, fragmented, siloed, cumbersome and bureaucratic. It was product based, with a senior executive in charge of each of the cheese factories, butter factories, casein factories and milk powder factories. All were located in head office. Each of the support service departments in each factory – engineering, electrical, laboratory, powerhouse, storage, and transport – also reported to different executives located in head office. The milk-processing factories were the heart of the company's activity, it was what the business was all about, yet the factory managers had no control over the support services which were essential to the factory's operation and comprised a large proportion of their costs. As most of our sites produced at least two products, each site reported to at least eight executives in head office.

It was much worse than that. Factory managers, most of whom were highly qualified technically, were responsible for processing the milk each day into products of specified composition and quality, but they were not responsible for making money. Nor were they expected to know anything about doing so. That was not unreasonable as they had little control over services which comprised a significant part of their cost base and which would largely determine how effectively their factories operated. But it was a structure guaranteed to produce poor results.

I was keen to decentralise management of the company and create profit centres rather than cost centres. We decided upon a "site"-based structure in which each site would be managed by a site manager. Every factory manager and services manager located on the site would report directly to the site manager, who would have profit responsibility for the whole site. There would also be a suitably qualified site accounting manager located on site to provide financial information in real time to the site manager. Site managers would be accountable for the profit results of their site. There would initially be seven sites, the managers of which would report to the Group General Manager Operations.

Appointments to the site manager positions were decided, then Jeff and I visited each site to explain the new structure and what we wanted to achieve to all of the managers on site. The reaction was extremely positive. They all welcomed the changes and enthusiastically committed themselves to supporting what we were doing. We also advised them that we would be back shortly with more specific advice on targets, including profit targets, which we expected them to achieve.

We had believed that the company was about 10% cent overstaffed, but as Jeff and his team analysed our operations, they reached the conclusion that the true number was over 15%. We set a target of reducing staffing by 20%. This was a most difficult decision for me as it meant that we would be laying off a large number of people. Most had families and were good, honest people who worked hard. Many had given long service and were very loyal to the company. We decided to offer voluntary redundancy to every employee. We hoped to get sufficient acceptances to avoid having to lay people off against their will. It meant that we may lose people we would rather retain, but we considered that preferrable to compulsorily making people redundant.

When the offer of voluntary redundancy was made to staff there was a flood of acceptances. It was soon obvious that at least 15% of our staff would accept redundancy, but the acceptances kept coming. We decided to accept every application we received. Finally, 30% of our staff opted for redundancy and we accepted every application. As this process was under way morale fell and continued to decline until the day in November when the redundant staff actually left. On that date I went around the factories to support the managers and staff who were losing so many valued colleagues and friends. At Waitoa, Site Manager Earl Greaney was particularly gloomy as he spoke of the 570 years of experience which that day was walking out the door.

But once the redundant people had departed morale quickly recovered. As redundancy pay was related to length of service, and departing employees could withdraw their superannuation funds, there was a strong incentive, particularly among our long-service employees, to take early retirement. Many of our older and longer service staff did just that. That brought with it a major benefit which we had not foreseen. A lot of those departing were managers, or in leadership or supervisory positions. Their departure unexpectedly created opportunities for younger people to be promoted or advance their careers. Opportunities they had not expected to arise for many years now became available. They were to wholeheartedly grab the chance and subsequently perform beyond our expectations. We were not sure that we could get by permanently at the lower staffing level, but our remaining younger and more enthusiastic staff made it happen. This gave us a huge improvement in productivity which increased sharply. The whole exercise had been hugely successful. In three months, we had reduced our staffing to the lowest level in the industry and improved the quality of our workforce as well.

The issue which bothered me most was whether we would be able to maintain quality at the lower staffing level. I need not have worried. Quality improved significantly as a result of improved performance of our younger workforce under new leadership, and with no spare people to fix up mistakes our people were getting it right the first time. Morale continued to climb and our people became proud of performing well. At Christmas I suggested to Jeff that we should give a turkey to every staff member to recognise their efforts. This was extremely well received and as I moved around head office on Christmas Eve, meeting individual staff to wish them a Happy Christmas, each of them thanked me for the gift.

In the new year I got the executive team together. Although I knew that the result for the year had been largely determined by now and would show an improvement, I asked them to try to find a further six cents per kilogram over the next four months. This they did. At year end we decided to expense the redundancy cost of $7 million to reserves, on the basis that it was effectively an investment which was giving us huge ongoing savings. That year our payout was fully competitive, which surprised our competitors who were aware of our redundancies and the disruption they caused and expected that to impair our result. However, they had no idea of the huge improvement in productivity we had made. With that benefit available for twelve months in the new season, rather than six months in the current year, I knew that we would deliver a very good performance in the new season. I also knew that there was more to come as we worked on other initiatives.

Jeff and I were not satisfied with our engineering, project planning and technology capability, while our ability to plan, control and execute capital expenditure left much to be desired. We had huge engineering resource, which was a carryover from earlier years when imports were restricted and import licences were not available if an item could be made in New Zealand. Of course, virtually every component could be made in New Zealand as it was only a matter of cost and quality. Thus, the company had developed an engineering resource which could do almost anything. We also had a powerful technical capability. Between them the two designed much of our plant configuration. But in the mid-seventies there had been huge growth in European milk production which required heavy investment in milk processing. Food-processing equipment manufacturers responded by investing heavily in technology and more efficient milk-processing plant was developed. As a consequence, New Zealand plants had fallen behind modern best practice. While the Te Rapa plant, opened in 1968, had world-leading technology, and at that time its three tonne per hour dryers were the largest in the world, technology had advanced and dryers of twice that size had been built in Europe. The use of information technology in processing control was progressing apace. It was clear that we no longer had world-leading engineering and technical capability; on the contrary, we were lagging and falling further behind each year.

In 1982 Jeff and I decided to visit Europe to look at the latest milk-processing technology; where it was going; who were the technologically most advanced equipment suppliers; which suppliers were investing in R&D most heavily; what equipment was available; what suitable product opportunities existed. It was a fascinating experience and our view that we were now lagging behind was confirmed. We concluded that we had to significantly upgrade our skills and capability, particularly in processing-control technology where computerisation was delivering huge benefits. It was an area in which we were light years behind. But we had gained a good understanding of what technologies were available and from whom.

It was obvious that our traditional fitters' skills were no longer suitable for the complexity of modern processing equipment which made extensive use of microprocessors. Specialist technicians with rather different skills were needed and they should be located on the processing line and not in a workshop located elsewhere. When designing a new plant or a plant upgrade our people had developed a habit of selecting different plant items from different suppliers and incorporating them into a process line. They believed that they were selecting the best individual component in each category. For example, in consolidating and upgrading our butter factories we had purchased pasteurisers from one supplier, the butter makers and packers from another, but the silo in between those two was provided by yet another supplier! This practice had a major flaw as different items of plant were therefore not synchronised to plant items either side of them and, most importantly, equipment suppliers could not be held to account for performance. We found that equipment manufacturers were now providing complete processing systems, from milk in to product out, which were designed to work together. All of them had embraced information technology and most had developed process-control systems which were integrated into the complete processing system. Most importantly, the supplier could be held to account for performance. It was clear that we needed to shift our plant design and planning to the purchase of complete systems. When we conveyed this policy shift to equipment suppliers, they were delighted but expressed surprise that it had taken us so long to realise that this made sense.

Jeff and I agreed that we should undertake a European visit each year to keep in touch with the latest developments in technology. Each year we would consider what projects were likely to come up in the next five years or so and focus our trip on getting a good understanding of technologies available and the capability of potential equipment suppliers. We looked closely at the manufacturing facilities, research and development capability and the investment potential equipment suppliers were making in their business. We also wanted to understand the direction in which technology was heading and what developments were in the pipeline.

Topping off Anchor House

I spent a good deal of time in the factories which was where the money was made (or lost). Each year when I received the first drafts of the maintenance and capital budgets, I would visit each factory and look at what was being considered. This was most valuable in enabling me to understand each project, its benefits and risks, and to ensure that capital was used wisely. We also introduced a requirement for each project to undergo an independent "return-on-capital" analysis. We set a demanding return target of 30% return on investment which needed to be achieved if a project was to gain approval.

Planning was rudimentary to say the least, not much more than back of the envelope. It needed to be elevated in importance to be a critical piece of annual work. As soon as most of the short-term problems were more or less under control, I asked Jeff and his team to get a planning process under way. I suggested that they get some outside help. Simon Caughey had worked with Bruce Hinchcliffe, an experienced planner, in Hong Kong and he came aboard to guide us. Our first effort was fairly basic and for a relatively short term of three years. However, it provided a framework for us to develop a more comprehensive and satisfactory plan. We subsequently developed a ten-year plan to handle the increasing milk flow; balance our product mix capability; increase product mix flexibility; upgrade our technology to position the company as a technology leader; retire aged or inefficient plants and replace them with the latest technology and of greater scale, all the time grinding costs down. We identified the cost of doing this and the economic benefits which would result. The capital required to do all this was considerable. To be satisfied that the plan was the best option and to ensure that our board had an alternative to the very large investment required, I asked Jeff to develop an alternative plan in which capital expenditure would be limited to replacing facilities which were reaching the end of their life. We called this the "Do Nothing" strategy, although in reality that was a misnomer as significant investment was still required to do little more than maintain the status quo. This option, although less profitable, still improved performance and payout but resulted in much lower debt and therefore had lower interest costs. We put both options before the directors and were thrilled when they completely rejected the "Do Nothing" strategy in favour of the riskier, more capital-intensive and more profitable plan. With the plan in place, we had a clear view on where we wanted to take the company.

When I became chairman, quality was definitely not a company strength. I was anxious to ensure that we did what was necessary to improve our quality performance and earn a reputation as a reliable top-quality producer. Poor quality results in dissatisfied customers but is also a huge financial cost. The New Zealand Manufacturers Federation had sponsored a visit by W. Edwards Deming to New Zealand. He was an American who had been the brains behind the emergence of Japanese industry after the Second World War. His approach was based on statistical analysis in which each step of a process was measured, cost, waste and weaknesses identified, and then rectified. Jeff wanted to apply his methodology and had committed New Zealand Dairy to be a founder of the Deming Institute which was being established in New Zealand. This was an inspired move which gave us huge benefits and helped us to achieve our objective of being a reliable high-quality manufacturer.

I was fortunate that in my teens I had worked on a large construction site and as a factory hand in the Waharoa Dairy Factory. This had given me a unique understanding of how soul-destroying large industrial sites could be for many employees. They often were not told what was expected of them, hard work and helpful suggestions were rarely acknowledged, and the work was often boring. I had determined that every one of our employees was entitled to know what was expected of them and to be properly trained for the tasks we expected them to undertake. They should also be informed about how the company was tracking and what resulted from their work. I expected the CEO and his group general managers to regularly visit each site and communicate directly with staff. This was extremely well received by our staff. Each year on Christmas Eve, I would go through head office and wish each staff member and their family a happy Christmas. On Christmas Day, our factory staff had to work; the cows did not stop producing milk on that day. I commenced the practice of visiting the milk-processing factories. One year I would start at Reporoa at 5 am, go through the factory and wish every person working that day a happy Christmas and thank them for working on Christmas Day for us. I would then move to Tirau, Waharoa, and finish at Waitoa, arriving home in time for Christmas lunch. The next year I would start at Te Awamutu followed by Te Rapa, Paerata and finish at Kerepehi. The first year I did this I arrived at Waharoa factory and one of the first people I met was my old rugby mate Johnny Gillett. He was surprised to see me and exclaimed, "What are you doing here, Boss?" I replied, "If it is good enough for you to work for me on Christmas Day, Johnny, it is good enough for me to come and wish you a happy Christmas." "Put it here, Boss," he said, holding out his huge hand. The feedback I received was that these visits were well received by staff. They appreciated that I was interested in them and that their contribution was noted and valued. Morale progressively improved as people regained their pride in belonging to New Zealand Dairy. My practice of frequent factory visits was hugely beneficial to me. I learned much from them which helped me to make good decisions.

With the company's cost problem rectified, our performance improved and payout became competitive. I began to focus on revenue and searched for opportunities to increase our income. Most of our revenue came from sales to New Zealand Dairy Board. Quality and flexibility of product mix provided some opportunities, but they were also available to all of our competitors. New product development was another but was something that we were not very good at, and we needed to substantially lift our game. While these opportunities were worthwhile and we needed to pursue them, collectively they were not a game changer and were all available to our competitors. We needed some new initiatives.

The most obvious opportunities were in the domestic market. Most were not large, but margins could be worthwhile if done well. We had few marketing skills and no distribution capability. Distribution was the key and in New Zealand has always been horrendously costly. We owned almost 50% of Auckland Farm Products (AFP), our competitors, the other Auckland Province Cooperative Dairy Companies, were the other shareholders. Auckland Farm Products had no marketing capability and provided a low-cost, bare-bones distribution service for butter and cheese, but it was simply not good enough for other products. Butter and cheese, though, were the two volume products which could provide a baseload to build an effective distribution network to get other products to market, but we were contracted to distribute all of our butter and cheese through AFP. That left us with the need to establish a distribution chain for a small volume of mostly dry products, which was always going to be expensive. We established a company called NZ Dairy as a separate profit centre, and geared up its marketing and distribution capability, but the small scale of this gave poor economics. We set out to gain control of Auckland Farm Products using our intention to market our own butter and cheese as a lever. This did not make us any friends with the other dairy companies and took some time but eventually it became Anchor Farm Products. Then in September 1987 we purchased the shares in Anchor Farm Products owned by the other dairy companies and integrated our local sales business into it to create Anchor Foods.

A company called Frosty Boy was selling an ice-cream powder which we supplied to make soft-serve ice cream in Australia and New Zealand. It also had the agency in both countries for the Taylor Soft Serve machines which were the industry leader. We purchased Frosty Boy from the founders with a target of making an annual profit of at least $1 million. In New Zealand we were able to put the ice-cream mix product through our existing blending and packing plant, but in Australia we had to operate a separate plant in Brisbane. It was a tough business, especially in Australia where there was stiff competition from local liquid products.

Frosty Boy made a useful contribution but never quite reached our target.

New Zealand Dairy Company supplied half of the liquid milk to the Auckland market. The milk was supplied by a separate group of farmers who produced milk 365 days a year. They received a year-round milk price which was about 160% of the price for manufacturing milk. The company made a useful margin bottling the milk through a plant at Takanini which I had the privilege of opening in 1979. The surplus town milk was processed in our manufacturing plants, but its year-round availability made it a resource which Jeff and I wanted to better utilise.

UHT technology for liquid milk was progressing rapidly around the world and we believed that sooner or later much of the world's liquid milk would be aseptically packed. High freight costs currently precluded the export of any significant quantity of UHT milk. Nonetheless, we believed that we needed to have the technology even though the initial market opportunities were small. The Dairy Board had established a UHT line in our Takanini factory, principally for export. We established another, mainly for the domestic market, alongside it. Not surprisingly, that ownership structure created operational problems. Ultimately, we joined both facilities into a single joint venture called Ultrapack with the Dairy Board and ourselves each owning 50%. It became a very good earner when we were able to purchase the ZAP flavoured milk brand and put the product through our marketing and distribution network.

But the big opportunity was cultured foods. Around the world large and increasing volumes of milk were consumed in fresh cultured foods, predominantly yoghurt. The New Zealand market for these products was immature but growing, and it was dominated by our Auckland competitor Auckland Cooperative Milk Producers with its Swiss Maid and Fresh 'n Fruity brands. It was a market we believed we should be in, but as second cab off the rank in a relatively small market, being able to enter and make money was a real challenge.

The French cooperative Sodiaal owned the Yoplait brand and franchised it around the world. They had been very successful and Yoplait was the world's leading cultured foods brand. The multinational giant pharmaceutical company Glaxo (which actually had its origin as a dairy company in Palmerston North) had purchased the franchise for New Zealand and established a plant on their site in Palmerston North. Not surprisingly, it had not been a success for them, and the business was for sale. Our analysis had clearly shown that we would not be able to make a start-up cultured food business work. Buying an existing business with the product technology, marketing knowledge and the technical and marketing support of the world's leading brand was a better option, provided the price was right. We negotiated an acceptable price and became the owners of the Yoplait brand in New Zealand. A disadvantage was that the plant was in Palmerston North, but we intended to relocate it to Auckland in due course. We were now beginning to have a domestic-market business of reasonable size which was making a reasonable contribution and had the potential to do much more. But Yoplait struggled. The remote location proved to be a greater disadvantage than we had expected, and Auckland Milk were formidable competitors who did everything they could to prevent Yoplait getting a foothold. After a couple of years, we were making little progress with market share and were still not earning any return on capital, so it was difficult to justify the cost of relocating the plant to Auckland. A long and tough road appeared ahead of us.

TWENTY-FOUR
TOWN MILK: A BIG OPPORTUNITY

While these investments and a few others were making a reasonable contribution, it remained tiny in relation to our overall business. As I pondered what we could do to develop a larger scale opportunity, or opportunities, I could not go past the domestic liquid milk market. It was the largest and most valuable domestic category and with our Ambury's group of town milk producers and our Takanini bottling factory, we were already the largest player in it. The largest market (Auckland) was within our operating territory, our cooperative competitors were not in town milk and it would be extremely difficult for them to enter. It therefore offered us an opportunity which could be a game changer.

The domestic liquid milk industry, or town milk, was quite separate from manufacturing milk. Every aspect of it – farm production, processing and distribution – was tightly regulated under an Act of Parliament and administered by a government-appointed Milk Board. They controlled who could process milk, who could distribute it and sell it (home delivery vendors only), even the packaging which could be used (glass bottles only) was controlled by the

Milk Board. Payment margins at every stage of the value chain were controlled by the board. The industry was protected and extremely inefficient. Milk production was contracted to a small group of farmers who each agreed to produce a specified quota volume of milk each day for 365 days a year. Obviously, it cost more to produce milk through the winter and for this they received a premium over manufacturing milk. But the premium of 60% of the manufacturing price for the whole year on every litre was grossly excessive. Town milk production was very profitable, and farms with quota had a much higher value than farms supplying manufacturing milk on a seasonal basis. Every litre of available quota was eagerly sought and we had a waiting list of farmers who had applied to supply town milk should we have any vacancies for new suppliers. While a margin was justified to produce milk through the winter months, I believed that there were better alternatives available. Distribution was hugely expensive; vendors received almost as much per litre to distribute milk as manufacturing farmers received for producing it. There were many small processing plants which were totally uneconomic and which only survived because the system guaranteed them throughput and a profit and protected them from competition.

I could see a great opportunity for New Zealand Dairy if the industry could be deregulated. I had also become convinced that there were other reasons why the milk market should be deregulated. Milk consumption was steadily declining. We needed to get milk into modern packaging, as bottles were expensive; quality was an issue as bottles were not aseptic and provided no protection against light which degrades quality; the use of milk vendors was not only an inefficient and expensive way to distribute milk but did nothing to promote consumption, which was declining. As consumption went down, vendors were paid more per litre to compensate for their loss of earnings. We needed to lower the cost of producing winter milk, slash the cost of distributing it, improve quality, and make a wider range of products available to consumers (there were then only two products available: full cream and reduced fat milk); aggressively market milk and get it into supermarkets where most food was purchased. I also believed that deregulation would provide opportunities for New Zealand Dairy to build a very profitable business of considerable size.

In 1983 I began to politically agitate for deregulation of the New Zealand liquid milk market. I was pretty much on my own. Every entity involved in the industry, farmers, vendors and processors, benefited from the existing structure so wanted it to continue. The whole regulatory structure was built around daily home delivery, something which no other industry had been able to sustain. It was horrendously expensive and economically completely unsustainable. Glass bottles were the shield which protected this regulatory dinosaur. The only way milk in bottles could realistically be distributed was through vendors, so glass bottles were exclusively mandated ostensibly to protect vendors. Those privileged to be part of this highly protected and profitable market understood that if other types of packaging were allowed, competition would occur and then industry deregulation would follow. So, the debate was all about protecting glass bottles and home delivery, for which there was a strong political constituency.

Tetra Pak, the Swedish company which had developed aseptic packaging and the UHT process, supplied UHT machines and specialised aseptic packaging materials, making most of their money from the latter. The regulations prevented their process from being used for milk, restricting their New Zealand business mostly to fruit juices, so it was small and would remain so as long as they could not access the milk market. They too were keen to see deregulation and were prepared to take action to make it happen. Their NZ CEO was Rodney Hoare. He had offered to put a Tetra Pak aseptic line into Takanini which we would not pay for until we started to use it, even though that could be years away. Jeff was resisting this as he favoured Combibloc because of its more flexible packaging sizes and its ability to process high-viscosity liquids, and had installed one of their machines in Takanini. We decided to visit Tetra Pak in Lund, southern Sweden during our European visit that year. I was amazed when we disembarked from the ferry in Malmo to see Rodney Hoare waiting with a car and driver to take us to Lund. He said he happened to be visiting HQ at the time of our visit. I suspected, and later confirmed, that he had flown to Sweden specifically to accompany us. Jeff and I were staggered by what we saw at Tetra Pak. What stood out was their focus on supplying a complete system, from milk into the plant to finished product out. Their materials handling was amazing and they were quite superior to their competitors, who produced some reasonable individual plant items, but none of them could supply a complete integrated system. Their R&D was equally impressive, and it was obvious that the gap between them and their competitors would increase. It was clear to us that we needed to rethink our strategy.

That evening Rodney took us to dinner. We drove for about ninety minutes across southern Sweden and up the east coast to a lovely restaurant on a golf course where we had an excellent meal. Over dinner and the three hours we spent in the car that evening, we developed a strategy to bring about deregulation and exploit the opportunities that would create. It appeared to us that New Zealand Dairy should, without delay, purchase some of the smaller town milk entities. This would both remove potential competition and create national coverage. We agreed to work together on deregulation. Rodney offered to buy our Combibloc machine and install a Tetra Pak line in Takanini on the basis of pay as you use it. Tetra Pak had much deeper pockets than us and had spent hugely on market research, brand development and communications support. They offered all of that to us, including the brands they had developed, at no cost other than we use their equipment.

I began to strongly lobby Government, meeting many individual Members of Parliament, consumer groups and milk vendors. I had a suitcase full of sample products to show them what would be possible under deregulation. The Tetra Pak research was comprehensive and I had little difficulty in demolishing the many myths advanced to perpetuate regulation. In 1984 the then Labour Government agreed to ask the Industries Development Commission to "review all aspects of the Town Milk Industry". The Commission called for submissions and then held a public hearing. I appeared at the hearing and presented a submission pushing for deregulation, being almost the only party to do so. I had a great tussle with Brian Kimpton, chairman of the Town Milk Producers Federation, and their legal counsel John Beattie, who, as expected, vigorously defended the status quo. In October 1985 the Commission recommended to Government the repeal of the 1967 Milk Act and deregulation of the industry.

There was much opposition to the recommendations so the government vacillated. Responsibility for the matter was then moved from the Minister of Agriculture to David Caygill, Minister of Commerce, who was reform minded. Government began to move slowly and announced that from October 1986 the restrictions on packaging would be removed and from September 1987, regulation of milk production would cease. Complete deregulation was now inevitable, although resistance from the industry did not lessen. A new Milk Act became law in 1988 which mandated almost complete removal of restrictive regulation. The Town Milk Producers Federation and the Milk Board fought a vigorous rear-guard action, but with the removal of the restrictions on packaging, change was inevitable, and they were powerless to stop it. With removal of packaging restrictions, there was soon major change in the liquid milk market.

The Industries Development Commission Report in October 1985 recommending deregulation was a clear sign that deregulation was inevitable. It was only a question of when. This gave us confidence to commence implementing our strategy. Within eight weeks we had purchased Rotorua Milk Company at a cost of $1.7 million. We closed the Rotorua plant down and recovered a fair amount of our purchase price out of the sale of their assets. Their shareholders received a windfall gain but that milk going through our system was extremely profitable. On 1 June 1986 we took over Hamilton Milk Producers Ltd at an initial cost of $7.8 million, some of which would be recovered when we later closed their plant, but it was a windfall for their suppliers also. In 1987 we purchased the small Waitomo Milk Station, closing it down and putting the milk through our existing plant. We made an offer to purchase Thames Valley Milk Producers but missed out when they choose to go with Morrinsville Thames Valley Dairy Co. That did not bother us as it was a tiny volume and with deregulation imminent, we expected to be able to compete for and win some of that business. Morrinsville had no knowledge of the industry and would find it difficult to operate profitably. We had the cities covered with strong national brands, and with deregulation imminent we were confident of being able to compete for and take volume from them.

Many of our suppliers were not happy with the significant sums we paid to purchase these town milk companies from the farmers who owned them. But we were buying a processing and marketing monopoly in those regions, at least for a period of time. When that volume was put through our existing system it was extremely profitable and our return on capital was very high. But we were also effectively buying town milk farmers out of their town milk quotas. Town milk quotas had traditionally been allocated on proximity to cities, regardless of whether the soil type or climate were suitable for the production of milk during the winter. The milk price they received was then engineered to cover their higher costs. We believed that by drawing on the wide range of soil types and climatic conditions across our very large number of farms, we would be able to source milk year-round for little more than the manufacturing price. For ten months of the year, we had plenty of milk to supply the town milk market; the problem was with the two winter months of June and July. We believed that by contracting with farmers who wished to produce "winter milk" and paying them a premium for it, we could source sufficient milk to cover our requirements at a cost which was substantially below what was being paid to town milk farmers to produce milk 365 days a year. We believed that together with a more efficient processing and distribution system, a very large price differential would be available to our manufacturing suppliers.

With deregulation came the need for marketing and sales skills. I had met Dr John Bryden when he was general manager of the very successful "Big M" and "Moove" marketing campaigns run by Victorian Milk Producers. I suggested to Jeff that he have a look at him as he could bring us skills we were going to need in a competitive market. He was able to bring him aboard. I had thought that we would use Anchor as our liquid milk brand but the significant market research provided to us by Tetra Pak was not complimentary about how consumers perceived Anchor, which came as an unwelcome shock. The research showed the need to differentiate brands, particularly as a wider range of products was introduced, so the marketing team were persuaded to go with "Springtime" for standard full cream milk, "Active" for low fat, and "Paradise" for cream. It was obvious that eventually most milk would be purchased in supermarkets, so to be able to give national coverage to the two supermarket chains we set out to franchise these brands throughout New Zealand. For a small royalty, we provided to several milk producer groups the right to use what were national brands and strong sales and marketing support. We had a network of seven of the larger milk companies right across the country. We did not see the royalty as being a significant earner, the value to us lay in being able to offer national brands, without having to freight milk around the country when it was uneconomic to do so.

We were now in a strong position: the domestic liquid milk market was deregulating, the opportunities we had identified were being captured. We had consolidated our regional domination with half of Auckland, and all of Rotorua and Waikato. We could offer national brands and distribution and soon had all the major cities covered. We had introduced a small trial winter milk scheme which we intended to roll out in short order. Our competitors and potential competitors were all far behind us. We now had a very profitable business which was going to become a lot more profitable.

The only potential threat was Auckland Cooperative Milk Producers (ACMP) who were very smart and well managed. They had a very strong cultured-foods business which dominated the market. We were not making money with Yoplait and would not do so until we wrestled lead position from them. We were making little headway doing that. The reality was they were much better at cultured-foods marketing than we were. I could see a long, hard and costly fight ahead. As Jeff and I wracked our brains about what to do, the solution finally occurred to me. Buy ACMP. It would be costly but would be a game breaker. If we could pull it off, we would be dominant in liquid milk and dominant also in cultured foods in which we would own a very profitable business in a rapidly growing market. We would also be able to convert from year-round milk-supply contracts to winter milk-only contracts, much more quickly and with less difficulty. This had the potential to be extremely profitable. Equally as importantly, we would gain skills, experience and capability in fast-moving consumer goods which we did not have. The pay-off could be huge. But would they sell?

A few years earlier the Dairy Board had purchased 40% of ACMP. It wished to draw on the Auckland Milk expertise to assist them enter cultured foods markets internationally. We were not happy with this. The Dairy Board, which we effectively owned one third of, already controlled the domestic butter and cheese market. If they were to participate in liquid milk, in the three largest domestic product markets we would have to compete with the Dairy Board, effectively competing with ourselves. But I reasoned that if ACMP farmers had been prepared to sell 40% of their company for a large sum of money, there was at least a chance that they might sell their remaining interest for an even larger sum. Also, most of their farms were close to Auckland City and would at some stage be subdivided for housing or industrial development. This gave their farms a value which was much greater than could be supported by farming, so many of their farmers were awaiting the eventual development of their land for housing and industrial use. A bid from us would be an opportunity for them to realise value for the town milk quotas, which would in due course be lost as development occurred.

When I shared my thoughts with Jeff, he at first thought I was dreaming. We had never even considered anything as significant as this. We would require Commerce Commission approval and that might not be forthcoming. But as we talked about it, we agreed that it was worth considering and we should explore the concept. Confidentiality was imperative so we wanted the people involved kept to a minimum. Rick Bettle had replaced Simon Caughey, and this fell within his area of responsibility so he was brought into the loop and tasked with analysing and preparing a business case which confirmed my view that if we could pull it off the benefits to New Zealand Dairy were potentially huge. Our legal advice was that Commerce Commission approval would not be easy because we could be creating a monopoly in the Auckland liquid milk market. But the imminence of deregulation which would allow competition and relatively low barriers to entry would ultimately allow a clearance. We would also need to deal with the Dairy Board and ideally buy their shares, but that could wait for another day. The Dairy Board was hugely respected, and we thought their 40% ownership might help us a little with the Commerce Commission.

Our investigation was comprehensive and thorough. We took it to our board, who after subjecting the proposition to critical scrutiny, authorised us to proceed. A key decision was the price we should offer. Obviously, we did not want to pay more than necessary, but our price needed to be sufficiently attractive for ACMP to engage. Whatever price we offered would give each ACMP supplier a large sum of money. We decided to go in at around $13 million, expecting to have to lift it during negotiation. We were far too optimistic.

In September 1987 we sought an urgent meeting with Chairman Ian Montgomerie and CEO Alec Brown. Jeff, Rick Bettle and I arrived at Rockfield Road and met Ian and Alec in a small room off their smoko room. Bill Walker, an old school friend of mine who was their GM Marketing, was with them. After exchanging the usual pleasantries, I launched into my pitch, covering what we believed to be some very significant benefits for their suppliers. I put our $13 million figure on the table to feel them out. They were completely blindsided and when I concluded, there was a long silence, broken when Ian Montgomerie said, "Shit, I need to have a smoke!" We then had a constructive discussion on details and issues which needed consideration, but I was struggling to maintain the dialogue at the number we had suggested. It was obvious that we had to significantly lift our offer price to be able to even continue discussions. But we ended on a positive note, agreeing that, subject to ACMP board agreement, our executives should continue discussions.

Auckland Milk were tough negotiators but by 21 October we had an agreement with their directors at a price around $22.4 million, to purchase their suppliers' 60% of the company, with a recommendation to accept from their directors who had agreed to accept the offer in respect of their individual shares. It was a higher price than we had initially expected but was within a normal commercial price range for similar transactions, although at the upper level. But the potential benefits to us were huge. We would consolidate milk processing onto our Takanini site, thus doubling its throughput. In time cultured foods would also be relocated to Takanini and the Auckland Milk site at Rockfield Road sold, thus recovering some of our purchase price. Some distribution depots would be closed and the sites sold. Investment required to switch from bottles to cartons and plastic bottles would be reduced. Importantly, we would have the ability to control milk production and pricing, introduce our winter milk scheme and convert supply over to it, without risking farmer defection and milk supply. We would also have a very good cultured and fresh dairy foods business with market shares of around 85%. We would have to sell Yoplait, perhaps at a loss, but overall the deal would be a game breaker for us. There were still some hurdles to jump, however, including one we had not expected.

After advice of our offer became public on 21 October, a consortium of cooperative dairy companies, Waikato, Morrinsville-Thames Valley, Tatua and East Tamaki, moved to lodge a counter offer. With the exception of Tatua, they were all struggling to match our payout and could see that with the huge benefits we would obtain from taking over Auckland Milk, it would be game over for them if we succeeded. They moved quickly, which indicated that they had done little analysis, and lodged an offer which was identical to ours both in price and other conditions. The fact that they had not overbid our offer indicated that they were at their limit and could go no higher. It was a desperate move which I am sure they had not properly thought through. They had no knowledge or expertise and gained no synergies through rationalisation of facilities. They would face vigorous competition from us, both for liquid milk and cultured foods, which would have cost them lost sales, volume and margin. It would have been costly for us too, but a disaster for them and would have been a drag on their payout to their existing suppliers for years.

I presented our offer to a special general meeting of Auckland Milk suppliers on 4 November, as did Don Sadler on behalf of the South Auckland consortium. The Auckland chairman and directors came out very strongly in favour of our offer. The Dairy Board remained neutral. Then it was over to the Auckland Milk suppliers. Next morning the race was on to collect acceptances from Auckland Milk suppliers before the offer closing date of 30 November. Together with some of my directors, I spent several days in the field canvassing Auckland Milk shareholders for acceptances. But we had done our homework, acceptances rolled in, and the South Auckland consortium decided not to proceed with their offer. Before long we were holding acceptances totalling 100% of Auckland Milk's issued shares. But there remained one more hurdle ahead.

South Auckland Dairies Consortium was not yet finished. The takeover of Auckland Milk required a clearance from the Commerce Commission. We knew that this could not be taken for granted and had investigated the matter very thoroughly before launching our bid. We had retained Russell McVeagh partner David Williams, who had succeeded on appeal in gaining clearance for the Goodman Group takeover of Wattie's. Russell McVeagh's advice was that we would receive Commerce Commission clearance.

On 4 March 1988 the Commission released a not unexpected but most unwelcome draft determination, which concluded that the takeover would create a dominant position in the Auckland liquid milk market and the national cultured foods market (not a surprise to us) but that the public benefits arising from the merger would not outweigh the public detriment of such dominance. The Commerce

Commission decided to hold a public hearing in the first week of April. David Williams had been appointed a High Court judge, so was no longer available to us. Our solicitor Frank Quinn of Russell McVeagh became our counsel and it was agreed that I would be our lead advocate. Jeff Jackson had left to head up Fletcher Fishing and Mac Calvert was now CEO, but Rick Bettle continued to have executive responsibility. South Auckland Dairies, however, brought in the big guns. They retained Alan Bollard, one of New Zealand's leading economists who was then director of The New Zealand Institute of Economic Research and was later a distinguished Secretary of Treasury and then Reserve Bank governor. He was a very competent and respected individual. Their counsel was QC Douglas White. It was a very formidable team, against whom we had Frank Quinn, economist Brian Easton and me.

It would be difficult for us to successfully argue that the merger did not create dominance, even though we had a strong case that it did not. We thought that we could prove "public benefit" and obtain clearance. I was able to persuade one of the largest supermarket operators, Foodtown, to support us, which demonstrated to the Commission that the retail trade did not have a problem. Rick Bettle saw clearly that the greatest public benefit would arise from our winter milk scheme, which would significantly lower the economic cost of producing milk year-round for liquid consumption. He urged me to focus our case on that. I was a bit reticent. It would be tricky to make that a key pillar of our case, without alarming our own town milk farmers who stood to lose from a winter milk scheme. They were already apprehensive about our plans and the last thing we needed was for them to oppose our application. In the end, I got it and agreed with that strategy, but I would need to handle the point delicately. We were fortunate that the hearing was to be chaired by the Commerce Commission Deputy Chair Kerrin Vautier, who was a respected economist, rather than the chairman who was a civil servant, so a "sound economic benefit" case was likely to find sympathetic ground. Kerrin was later to become a colleague and good friend.

At the hearing the issues were vigorously contested by Bollard and White. I quote from Alec Brown, former CEO of Auckland Milk, in his book *Town Milk*.

> "The undisputed star of the show was NZCDC Chairman Dryden Spring who, in an all-day virtuoso performance, made light of opposing viewpoints and concentrated on the lack of dominance in foods and the potential public benefit from an enlarged town milk operation. There were he said plenty of yoghurt manufactures and chilled food distributors. There were cost efficiencies of $2m annually from milk station rationalisation with even greater milk price savings from his company's Winter Milk Scheme. In any case said Mr Spring if public benefit was the nub of the matter, the public included the thousands of NZCDC shareholders and their dependants."

At the end of a long day, the hearing adjourned to continue next morning with each party to sum up their case and rebut the opposition. After a discussion with our team lasting about 45 minutes, I excused myself, went to my room, ordered dinner to be sent up and set about preparing my presentation. I worked through the night and by 4 am felt well prepared and comfortable with my summation and rebuttal. I managed to get three hours of sleep. I was happy with how the final presentation went. Kerrin was very interested in the Winter Milk Scheme which obviously resonated with her. Through the hearing she had made several rulings in my favour which helped me explain the benefits, without too much detail being made public which would have created commercial difficulties for us.

When the hearing concluded, I felt satisfied with how it had gone and believed that we were in with a good chance. Rick Bettle was confident that we had done enough, while our counsel Frank Quinn was confident that if the Commission went against us, we would obtain clearance on appeal to the High Court. He believed that the merger did not legally *create* dominance. At the moment there was dominance, by the Milk Board, which was also a very prescriptive regulator. Our takeover of Auckland Milk did not change that dominance. With deregulation imminent, any party would be able to enter the liquid milk market. There was plenty of milk within one hour of Auckland, enough to supply the market many times over. With packaging in cartons or plastic bottles permitted, a processing plant could be erected for as little as $2 million so the barriers to entry were low. The High Court had a record of reversing Commerce Commission clearance declines on appeal. But I was not keen to have to go through an appeal.

I was at a Dairy Board meeting on 26 April when a note came in to me advising that the Commission had authorised the takeover. There was a nervous wait to see if the decision was appealed, which fortunately it was not. That was a huge relief to me and a real breakthrough in our competitive strategy as I knew that in the medium term as we realised the benefits of the takeover our competitors, with the exception of Tatua, would not be able to match our payout.

Our task now was to harvest all of the potential benefits. Auckland Milk had great expertise in marketing, chilled distribution and fresh products which we did not have. I was anxious to retain their key management personnel for as long as we could. I knew that when we had made our takeover offer the Auckland Milk directors had decided to give their five top management individuals a pair of "golden handcuffs", a large payment if they stayed for two years. This made it inevitable that they would leave at that time, but I wanted them to set the new company up and impart as much of their expertise to our people as possible before they departed.

Mac Calvert was very much hands-on. Rick Bettle had left and been replaced by Gary Langford who was responsible for our commercial domestic market activities. He had no experience in this market and as a new executive he would be keen to prove himself. The more hands-on approach of these two executives would be difficult to accept for Auckland Milk's management team which was used to a large degree of freedom, reporting directly to their own board. We also had a 40% minority shareholder, the New Zealand Dairy Board. I decided to continue to operate Auckland Milk as a separate company with its own board which I would chair, as I felt that I could best manage what I foresaw as being difficult relationships, through the ownership transition and the integration of Auckland Milk and our Amburys Town Milk operations into one entity.

A further challenge now had to be dealt with. The Dairy Board owned 40% of Auckland Milk. We could not execute our plans to rationalise activities and integrate our plants without their approval on most major decisions. Their interests would not always align with ours. To capture the full benefit of our investment and fully implement our plans, we needed to buy them out. I did not believe that they would want to continue as a minority shareholder in a business with us holding the majority of the company. Generally, a premium of 10% to 15% could be expected for a controlling interest, so our starting point was 15% below what we had paid to Auckland Milk shareholders for their 60% interest. However, Dairy Board CEO Murray Gough was a shrewd and tough negotiator who was in a strong negotiating position. We ultimately settled for the same price per share that we had paid to Auckland Milk shareholders. This took our total purchase price to around $40 million, but we were now free to integrate the two companies. We had also given the Commerce Commission an undertaking to divest the Yoplait franchise. This was not easy as given the market share of Auckland Milk's Fresh 'n Fruity and Swiss Maid brands which we now owned, buying Yoplait to compete with us was a daunting prospect for any potential buyer. However, we were fortunate to sell Yoplait to Plumrose, a Danish worldwide smallgoods business, although we had to take a small loss on the sale.

Alec Brown, the outstanding CEO of Auckland Milk, resigned, as did all of his executive team, when they qualified for their retention payments. This was expected but I was still sorry to lose Alec and his marketing people. Alec had already identified his potential successor, Richard Punter. We were satisfied that he was a quality executive and were fortunate to obtain his services. In March 1989 Auckland Milk was amalgamated with Amburys Milk Company and renamed New Zealand Milk Corporation, a wholly owned subsidiary of New Zealand Dairy Group. It was now time to disestablish the separate board and bring New Zealand Milk Corporation directly under the control of New Zealand Dairy Company management.

Deregulation played out pretty much as we expected it. Once alternative packaging was allowed, wholesale change occurred rapidly. Plastic bottles quickly eclipsed cartons. Vendors were offered the opportunity to carry glass bottles, cartons and plastic bottles. Supermarkets began to carry milk but refused to handle glass bottles, opting only for cartons and plastic bottles. Customers quickly preferred plastic; the use of glass bottles plummeted and soon ceased. Vendors simply could not compete and distribute milk at an economic cost and soon exited the industry. Milk sales rapidly shifted to supermarkets who played milk suppliers off against one another, in the process grabbing an increase in margin for themselves. A wider range of products became available and the steady decline in milk consumption was arrested.

For New Zealand Dairy all of this was a game changer. We still had a lot of work and significant investment to capture the potential benefits. Auckland Milk liquid-processing operations would be shifted and integrated with our operations at Takanini. Cultured foods would continue at Rockfield Road while we constructed a new factory on our Takanini site. The valuable Rockfield Road site could then be sold. It would take three years to get the Winter Milk scheme to the level required to securely provide the volumes of winter milk we required. The benefits would progressively become available as those projects were completed. As always, it took longer to complete those actions, but five or six years later the annual surplus from our liquid and fresh foods business was huge, equivalent to around 50% to 60% annual return on capital, giving us a massive advantage over our competitors.

New Zealand Dairy Company payout was now more than fully competitive with other dairy companies in the Waikato and was becoming more so as we lifted our performance. Tatua was an exception. They were smart, understood what was needed to occupy a sustainable niche, and had avoided the one big mistake which sooner or later caused most smaller dairy companies to fail. Our domestic market and liquid milk operations were now large scale and were providing a significant profit contribution. It was an edge that our competitors could not replicate and would in due course lead to their demise.

TWENTY-FIVE
UNION ISSUES

THE DAIRY INDUSTRY HAD TRADITIONALLY HAD A VERY good industrial relations record. It needed to as it was a very vulnerable industry. Given the perishable nature of milk, stoppages of only a few hours could result in large volumes of milk having to be dumped. The industry was widely dispersed throughout rural areas. Most dairy factories were small, usually employing fewer than 200 people. Most staff lived in the local community, they belonged to the same football or Lions club as farmers did, their children went to the same school as the children of farmers. This created some strong bonds. This environment did not provide fertile ground for militant union activism, and the dairy industry was a caring employer which provided good working conditions. Although basic wage rates were only about average, with roster and shift payments, actual pay received was more than competitive.

But those conditions by themselves do not guarantee industrial peace if there is a militant union. From 1951 the Dairy Workers Union had been led by Sid Wheatley. They could have had no stronger advocate for their remuneration, working conditions and rights. But he was also constructive, understanding that there was no real winner from stoppages and strikes. He had been able to achieve wage rates for his members which were above most comparable industries and did that entirely by negotiation. He had ensured that the Dairy Workers Union was not swallowed up by larger more militant unions. At a time when communist influence in unions was widespread, he successfully kept communist agitators out of the Dairy Workers Union. He retired in 1978.

As is often the case with a strong long-serving leader, he did not leave a strong successor. It was not too long before a Socialist Unity Party cell was established in our largest factory, Te Rapa. The Socialist Unity Party was the pro-Soviet Union faction which in 1966 had split from the New Zealand Communist Party which was pro-China. It controlled most of the major trade unions in New Zealand and certainly all of the most disruptive and militant. By about 1983 a Te Rapa Socialist Unity Party cell was in control of the Dairy Workers Union.

As we considered how to make our factories more efficient, milk powder packing stood out. A factory like Te Rapa processed 25,000 bags each day. More people were employed in the powder-packing room than in the rest of the factory combined. The work was repetitive and boring. We had been looking to automate packing for years, but no suitable plant was available. No other country packed powder on anything like our scale so powder packing had not been a priority for R&D expenditure. However, as Jeff and I visited Europe each year, powder-packing automation was top of our list. We finally identified a potentially suitable plant. Our technical people carefully evaluated it and prepared a business case which the directors approved. The automated packing plant would significantly reduce the number of people employed in the packing room. The jobs which remained, though, would have better working conditions and be less boring. They would also be more skilled and thus be higher paid. We knew that we would have to negotiate a deal with the Dairy Workers Union. In the past with Sid Wheatley that would not have been too difficult. Common sense would have prevailed and agreement to share the benefits soon reached. It would have been a win-win for both workers and the company. But Sid Wheatley was no longer there and his communist successors had other ideas. Their position was simple. If we agreed to pay the same total amount as was currently being paid to all of the staff in the packing room, to the much-reduced number of staff who would be employed to operate the new automated packing equipment, then we would be allowed to operate the new system. Until then, the new packing room would not be used.

This was industrial blackmail which we could never accept. Negotiations ground on for months without progress. From time to time the union would try to put pressure on with work to rule and stop-work meetings which would go on for hours. Our intelligence told us that most of the Te Rapa staff considered our offer to be a fair one so we tried to appeal directly to them. We set up with the union a meeting with all Te Rapa staff at which Mac Calvert and I and the union leadership would speak to the workers. The union officials did not turn up. The dispute dragged on for months. Not only were we losing the savings the new equipment would provide, but factory operations were being disrupted and relations with the remainder of our staff were being poisoned. It was becoming impossible for us to operate the whole Te Rapa site effectively. Our farmers too were becoming restive and questioning our handling of the dispute. I decided to call a meeting of our farmers. There was standing room only in Hamilton's Founders Theatre so we must have had about 2000 present. The Dairy Workers Union was outside handing out flyers setting out their side of the story. I was under pressure when the meeting commenced but by the time it ended the farmers were solidly behind us. I had shown charts which explained to farmers:

- What the benefit to farmers would be from operating automated equipment at Te Rapa.
- The benefit from automating packing at our other factories.
- What the workers employed in the Te Rapa packing room had actually earned in the previous financial year.
- What our actual offer was.
- What the workers would earn if our offer was accepted.

There was a loud gasp when farmers saw just how well paid the workers were. By the time I had finished my presentation it was "game, set and match". The farmers were right behind us.

But the dispute ground on. I began to observe signs of stress among our executive team. It was wearing them down. My concern deepened as the weeks passed with no progress. If this continued, we could easily lose people to nervous breakdowns. That was the last thing we needed. I told management that we had to find a circuit breaker. They came back with a recommendation that we close Te Rapa factory permanently, declare all of the staff redundant and pay them off. By now milk flow had declined to a level where we could do without the factory. But this was a nuclear option which had some significant risks: a retaliatory strike across the whole company, perhaps the whole industry, which would force us to dump milk; load-out bans which would prevent product from being sold; we would need the factory to process next season's peak milk, but the union might blacklist it and prevent it from reopening. It also left unresolved the issue under dispute, manning scales and wage rates in automated packing rooms, thus preventing us from obtaining the huge potential savings from automating the packing rooms in our other powder factories.

Sometime previously the industry had agreed to share losses from industrial disputes of "national importance". This was to ensure that the union did not target one company and force it to agree unfavourable conditions which it could then leverage across the whole industry. This gave us confidence that our competitive position against other dairy companies would not be weakened. We also knew that most of our workers, including those at Te Rapa, were pretty fair and loyal to the company and did not agree with the attitude of the union in the packing room dispute. Packing milk powder manually was not great work and most packing room staff were actually looking forward to their workplace being automated. We considered that if long-serving good people began to lose their well-paid and secure jobs they would push back against the union and force it to negotiate a realistic agreement. Closing the factory was risky, no one knew how it would play out, but we could not go on as we were. The dispute had to be brought to a head. We did not have any better options.

But there were some actions which had to be taken first to protect the company and improve the likelihood of success. First, we had to secure the support of the dairy industry. Some time ago we had gained industry agreement that the dispute was of "national importance". We had to get them to sign off on our strategy to close the plant and agree to indemnify us from any consequential losses which occurred. Then we wanted the support of the Employers Federation of which we were members. Their Hamilton advocate, Graeme Perfect, had been of great assistance to us throughout the dispute. We needed a commitment from the Employers Federation National Office. I arranged a meeting in my office with Max Bradford, the executive director of the Employers Federation. He had a very high profile on employment matters and later entered Parliament and became a Cabinet minister. I soon learned that while he could pontificate elegantly about theoretical employment issues, when it came to practical hands-on measures, he was a bag of air.

While all of this highly confidential activity was going on, we had to ensure that the union, and particularly all of our Te Rapa staff, became aware that closure of the factory was now a serious possibility. Our staff became very concerned for their future as they learned of this. The union now began to negotiate seriously. Negotiations were not easy, but eventually an agreement was reached which we could live with, and we had set the basis for automation in our other factories which we wanted to undertake as soon as possible. Would we have closed the factory? One thing which you must never do is make a threat which you are not prepared to carry out. So, yes, we would have. But we were all mightily relieved that we did not have to do so.

TWENTY-SIX
PERSONNEL

A YEAR AFTER JEFF HAD BEEN APPOINTED CEO, AND REX Haggie became managing director, I called Rex to my office and suggested that it was time for him to consider taking early retirement. He had not seen it coming and his reaction was as though I had hit him in the solar plexus; he was staggered. He had enjoyed the last twelve months, received the same remuneration as when he was CEO but with a minimal workload, had no stress and no accountability. He hoped to continue in the role for several years yet. From the company's perspective it was a position which added little and which we did not need. I also wanted Jeff to be free from any influence or obligation to his previous mentor. Rex told me he needed to take advice, which was reasonable enough, and came back a few days later with a very optimistic severance wish list. While I was anxious to treat a long-serving and senior officer with compassion and allow him to exit with dignity, I felt no obligation to be generous and offered him a very modest exit package which he accepted, although when approving my recommendations, my directors told me that I was too generous. Rex was later to tell me that he recognised that I had done the right thing for the company and thanked me for allowing him to leave with respect and dignity.

We had a large board with thirteen directors elected on a ward basis. They were of course all farmers and were very sound, but this did mean that we had little diversity and a narrow skill base at director level. In 1986 I persuaded my directors to increase the size of the board by appointing two directors chosen for their business acumen. It was a step which the shareholders had to approve and they did so cautiously. I was fortunate to recruit two leading businessmen, Bill Wilson, a leading tax accountant and chairman or a director of some of New Zealand's largest companies, and Don Clark who had a background in finance and banking, and was one of the country's most experienced and astute businessmen. It was a measure of the reputation which New Zealand Dairy now had that we could attract such experienced, talented and sought-after individuals. Don was a director of New Zealand Insurance Group. When that company got into trouble during the 1987 recession, he was appointed CEO and had to resign from our board. He was replaced by Brian Allison, a business consultant who was well regarded and an experienced company chairman and director whom I had worked with and rated highly. The appointment of such quality businessmen brought much to our deliberations as a board, to the extent that even the doubters soon became enthusiastic supporters of having a couple of commercial outside directors.

The management team which Jeff and I had pulled together had performed extremely well. Brian Haskell had completely transformed our finance and accounting function. He had built a talented team of high-performing financial people who provided high-quality real-time information. Every activity was now either a profit or cost centre, which was able to accurately measure its performance. We had introduced return-on-capital measures to all activities, so were using capital more efficiently and gaining good returns on it. We set stretching return-on-capital benchmarks for new projects. Despite that, our people kept coming up with a steady list of projects which could meet the high threshold of 30% *internal rate of return* on capital we had set. We had traditionally financed our business with bank funding, with some recourse to the Dairy Industry Loans Council. I had encouraged the obtaining of a credit rating, believing that it would strengthen disciplines around the use of capital and open up a wider range of funding options. Standard & Poor's rated us at AA– (very strong capacity to repay debt) which was an excellent outcome. We were then able to access new capital sources, including the commercial paper market, which gave us increased funding flexibility and lower funding costs.

John Bell was the first change in the executive team. He had made a very good contribution and with a lot of new people in senior positions his encyclopaedic knowledge of the company was invaluable. He retired when he reached the mandatory retirement age of 65. We were later to lower the retirement age to 60 as the baby boomers arrived on the job market. The company had a very good lump-sum superannuation scheme, membership of which was compulsory, so most of our staff were happy to retire upon reaching retirement age. Jeff and I had agreed that our hiring strategy should be that every new hire should be better than the person they replaced. That way we would continuously upgrade the quality of our people. John was replaced as company secretary by Barry O'Donnell who was much younger but had very broad commercial experience, in New Zealand and overseas. He was soon a major contributor, and his wide experience and new perspectives added considerable value.

Our London Street office was old and cramped with very basic conditions. It was certainly not helpful in hiring the quality of personnel we desired to attract. I was always reluctant to spend money on head offices. The productive assets of the company are always my priority. But we had prioritised investment in our income-earning factory assets and by 1986 the company was performing to a high standard, so we felt justified in doing something about head office. We looked at options including upgrading the existing London Street building. We concluded that the best course was to erect a new building on our site, on the other side of London Street, which was occupied by our retail trading store Anchormart. There was an existing building on the side of the site which Jeff had converted into a very functional conference centre. We wished to retain that in any new development. Our architects presented us with a most attractive design concept incorporating the conference centre, the indicative price of which was reasonable. Eventually, we took the proposal to our directors who authorised us to go ahead. In July 1987 we opened the new Anchor House. It was a most attractive building which won a national design award, but which more importantly provided a quality working environment for our staff, one which would help us attract the high-quality people we needed to keep improving our performance. The cost was relatively modest, around $12.7 million.

Mac Calvert was larger than life with very high energy. He was the typical operations leader, hard driving and got the job done regardless of the difficulties. These were important qualities in milk processing where the milk was coming in every day and had to be processed within twenty-four hours, because the same volume was coming in again tomorrow. He was smart with a good mind and was unquestionably the best manager I have ever worked with at reading people and getting the best out of them (although only for a period). He was able to handle a huge span of control and a very high number of direct reports. He was adept at finding ways around problems. He built high morale among our operations people, introducing many talented technical and operations people to our workforce. He willingly accepted stretching targets and invariably achieved them. He continued to identify improvements, reduce overall staff numbers and improve operational efficiency. He worked with the Dairy

Workers Union to improve our industrial relations and the relationship with our factory staff. Our factory performance had reached a high standard and continued to improve. He was a simply outstanding performer. We were delighted with his performance.

But it was not all plain sailing. He shared some of brother Graham's weaknesses: flamboyance, basic insecurity, a need to be recognised and loved, with a high level of drama always present. He also was prone to social excess. He was impetuous, and I soon learned not to think out aloud in his presence as he would rush off and do what he thought I wanted even if it was not a good idea. He would bypass Jeff and lobby the directors directly. His moral compass was not always strong, with the end often used to justify the means, which meant that some of his methods and actions were questionable. He liberally used both the stick and the carrot to motivate people. The carrot was money and he was no respecter of the disciplines which large organisations have to apply to remuneration to keep the wage bill under control. The stick was heavy threats to staff and suppliers of services who did not do as he wished. While he was a great motivator of staff, he demanded that they be personally loyal to him. The drama which surrounded most of his activities pushed staff to breaking point, and sometimes beyond. He also pushed to take control of more and more activities. As Lawrence Barrett had warned me, he had to be managed and that was not always easy, particularly for Jeff who had to try to constrain his excesses and constant flouting of policies.

Jeff was an outstanding CEO. He was not intuitively commercial, but he had a good mind, was disciplined and established good processes. He drew on his learnings from Harvard to work through issues in a methodical way. He was a straight shooter whose integrity was beyond reproach. He was a really good guy who was well liked and respected by staff. His approach was gentle, but he was tough underneath and always courteous and gentlemanly. He selected and hired good people and got the best out of them. People performed for him because they respected him. He was the person responsible for turning the New Zealand Dairy Company around and winching it out of the mud. While he hired good people who all contributed, he was the leader who set the direction and standards and ensured their achievement. No other executive had the executive leadership skills of Jeff, nor could they have achieved what was achieved under his leadership. As the turnaround of New Zealand Dairy Company became more widely known across New Zealand business, the "head hunters" came looking. I became aware that he had been approached for the position of CEO of New Zealand Steel. I headed that off by asking the board to finance him into a lifestyle block at Horsham Downs which he wished to purchase. But we were on notice that he had been observed by others and was an attractive candidate for companies looking for a proven CEO. We would need to look after him.

Simon Caughey was well bred; his family was the Caughey of Smith and Caughey, and he was very well connected having been to school and university with many of New Zealand's business leaders. He had extensive experience in New Zealand and overseas. He had an outgoing personality, was loyal and great fun to work with. He, Jeff and I had a wonderful and most enjoyable working relationship. His weakness was that he tended to be distracted by all of the politics and intrigue. But when we spelled out clearly what we wanted from him he got on and developed our domestic business. He was a great team player, always prepared to take one for the team and became a key contributor. He was good in group dynamics and would take on the difficult issues which lacked an owner. He was fiercely supportive of Jeff, often acting as his enforcer, doing stuff that Jeff found personally difficult, such as firing people close to him. He was a staunch ally of Jeff in the ongoing and exhausting struggle to keep Mac on track and operating in line with policy and company rules, which Jeff found emotionally exhausting. Jeff became increasingly reliant on him, which worried me.

In 1986 Simon was approached to take up the position as CEO of the Kiwifruit Marketing Board. We tried very hard to keep him but the opportunity of a senior CEO role was too good to turn down so he accepted it, albeit reluctantly, as he was enjoying his role with us. Jeff was particularly downcast at Simon's departure. He knew that without his "enforcer" Simon's loyal support, managing Mac Calvert was going to get a lot more difficult. I saw it as an opportunity to get someone who was better than Simon. We were fortunate to find such a person in Rick Bettle, CEO of the New Zealand Rennet Company. He was a first-class executive who would be a very good contributor and play a major role in our town milk expansion. But he was never going to be an enforcer for Jeff.

Her Royal Highness Princess Anne – Anchor Centenary, 1986

Nineteen-eighty-six saw a milestone achieved: 100 years of the Anchor Brand. We wanted to celebrate the occasion but to do so inexpensively. I also wanted our shareholders to be involved. We held a black-tie dinner in Auckland for our customers and partners which was very well received. We gave each of our suppliers a silver butter knife. Jeff and I then travelled to London where in conjunction with the Dairy Board subsidiary Anchor Foods, we sponsored a dinner for our customers and partners at the Barbican which was attended by senior executives of all of the supermarket chains, followed by a performance by the London Philharmonic Orchestra attended by Her Royal Highness Princess Anne. The proceeds went to Save the Children Fund of which she was patron. I had the privilege of sitting next to her through the concert and a charming companion she was. She told me that the Royal Family had been brought up on Anchor butter.

In 1988 Jeff advised me that he had been offered the position as CEO of Fletcher Fishing and intended to accept it. He had been CEO for six years and the burden of managing a large and complex business was beginning to weigh heavily on him, compounded by the constant challenge and difficulties in managing Mac. I understood that his decision to leave was probably best for him personally, but it was most unwelcome. He had been an outstanding CEO whom I would always admire and who would remain a good friend. After a term at Fletcher Fishing, he was to become CEO of AFFCO.

We commenced a search for his replacement. There were two internal candidates shortlisted, Mac Calvert and Rick Bettle, both of whom I felt could do the job. They stacked up well against external candidates. Rick Bettle pulled out, I never knew for certain why, but suspected that Mac had persuaded him to withdraw. Mac had performed superbly as Group General Manager Operations. He had huge strengths and some significant weaknesses. But he had earned the right to be appointed CEO. I was confident he would continue to improve the company's performance. I also knew that life would become more challenging for me as he would be difficult to manage.

Rick Bettle was never going to work for Mac, so soon resigned to become CEO of Wrightsons Ltd. He was replaced by Gary Langford, a well-qualified executive. Mac's job as Group General Manager Operations was taken by Rod McLeod who had experience managing processing operations for Interstate Milk Producers of Pennsylvania, and with the New Zealand Dairy Board. He too was a quality appointment.

Mac took off at ninety miles an hour and kept coming up with new initiatives to improve our performance. He was very hands-on and had difficulty retaining more independently minded people, so tended to surround himself with "yes men" However, he was skilled at getting the best out of people. He rocked a lot of boats, although not always constructively. He built great morale among the troops, but in doing that a high level of social activity became the norm. Murray Gough, CEO of the Dairy Board, was soon advising me that his staff were having difficulty dealing with Mac who was often bullying. I watched these behaviours closely and, on several occasions, remonstrated with Mac. In fairness to him he was always receptive to my counsel and was mortified when told that he was upsetting people who were important to the company, and he responded positively to modify his approach. However, that was his natural style which he had difficulty reining in, so it was an ongoing challenge for me to get the best out of him while at the same time curbing his tendency to excess. Mac's heart was always in the right place. He was a strong supporter of the cooperative structure and of the New Zealand Dairy Board single seller.

TWENTY-SEVEN
A STRONG FINISH

Planning had not been a company strength but that had been largely rectified and New Zealand Dairy Company had made considerable progress in its ability to think and plan. The initial three-year strategic plan had been successfully executed. We were now operating new cheese factories at Waitoa and Kerepehi; a new infant formula plant at Waitoa; a new milk bottling plant at Takanini; upgraded butter plants at Waharoa and Te Awamutu, and a new butter factory at Paerata making consumer packs for the local market. All were employing state-of-the-art technologies. There had also been significant upgrades to other plants to utilise modern technology to increase throughput and improve efficiency. Costs had been significantly reduced and our payout was now fully competitive. In 1986 we began to implement a five-year strategic plan which focussed on increasing revenue and utilising technology to further reduce operating costs. We needed to ensure that our plant configuration provided product flexibility with optimal efficiency.

A new milk powder dryer at Te Awamutu was planned. Costing around $70 million, it would be the largest dryer in the world. My greatest concern with this project was energy. Glen Afton Collieries had provided New Zealand Dairy with cheap coal fuel. But we did not use energy efficiently, thus losing much of that fuel cost advantage. I was determined that we did not repeat that mistake in the new Te Awamutu plant. I pushed management to design the plant to be as energy efficient as modern technology allowed. With a significant part of the total cost being the energy plant, I wanted to be satisfied that optimum economics were gained by using coal to generate high-pressure steam to generate electricity with the low-pressure steam then being utilised in milk processing. A huge amount of work was undertaken, including outside advice, to ensure that the energy plant was configured to be energy efficient and to deliver optimum economic results.

By now my Dairy Board role was occupying more of my time. I knew that I was making a solid contribution to Dairy Board activities and was confident that when Jim Graham retired, I would be well placed to succeed him as chairman, but I did not expect that to occur for some time. Approaching sixty years of age, he was relatively young, and Dairy Board chairmen usually held the role well into their seventies. I knew that Jim would not continue that long as he tended to make his contribution and then get out. I also knew that he had no desire for a lengthy commercial career, that he had decided upon a time when he would retire and go back to the farm. Nevertheless, I believed that he would continue as chairman for several more years.

I was comfortable with that and with what I was doing. I was enjoying the role as chairman of New Zealand Dairy Company. It was performing well and its performance was improving each year. It was on a pathway to earning a significant contribution to payout, from the substantial liquid milk and domestic market business which we had built. They provided earnings which I knew that our competitors could not match. The writing was on the wall for them, and they knew it. As they had seen our performance improve,

Morrinsville, Te Aroha-Thames Valley, Sunny Park-Hinuera and Te Awamutu Dairy Companies had progressively amalgamated into Waikato Dairy Company and consolidated onto Morrinsville and Hautapu sites. Kaipara had joined New Zealand Dairy, Tatua and East Tamaki remained independent. Tatua remained very strong but East Tamaki would in due course go out of business as Auckland city absorbed their farms. Their remaining supply came to us.

I was also enjoying my role on the Dairy Board. My workload was very heavy, but I was adequately handling that. In November 1988 Jim Graham advised me that his Deputy Chairman Gordon Mackenzie, a Southland farmer and a solid director, had just advised him that he intended to retire next June. This was most unwelcome news for both of us as Jim had intended to retire the following year. The board would need to elect another deputy chairman. That person should not come from the same company as the chairman so I could not be a contender. Someone else would be chosen which would give that person a head start on the chairmanship when Jim retired the following year. Jim was adamant that I was the best choice for chairman. After discussing all of the ramifications, Jim concluded that the risk that someone else may become chairman should not be taken and rather selflessly decided that he would retire the following year at the same time as Gordon Mackenzie, a year earlier than he had intended.

At the December board meeting Jim announced that he would retire at the end of the financial year, the end of June 1989. He suggested, and the board agreed, that a chairman designate and his deputy chairman should be elected at the next board meeting in February. Over the holiday period I talked with each of the directors. The only other candidate was likely to be my friend Peter Jensen from Tauranga. At the conclusion of my consultations, I was confident that I had the support of all other directors. I then had a discussion with Peter, advised him that I had the numbers, that I would like him to be my deputy and asked him to withdraw from contention for chairman. He agreed to do so. In February 1989 the board formally elected me chairman designate to take office at the conclusion of the Dairy Industry Conference in June.

I had one final task as chairman of New Zealand Dairy Company, to oversee the transition to my successor. The board of that company agreed that a chairman designate and his deputy should be chosen at the April meeting. My resignation was to take effect at the end of the financial year, 31 May. I had a problem. My deputy chairman was Graham Calvert. He and I were close friends. He had given me loyal service and been a very capable deputy. But I knew that he had serious flaws which made him unsuited to be chairman. Socially he was a problem. For some time, I had purposely avoided his company after 5 pm. After he had disgraced us at dinner one evening by offending some very important customers with whom we were trying to engineer a major deal, I ceased involving him in any entertainment of customers and partners. The fact that his brother was CEO by itself should have been enough to disqualify him, as there could be no circumstances under which it would be a good idea to have brothers as chairman and CEO. Graham and Mac were also too much alike and had the same serious character defects.

I had been considering for some time how I could create some other succession options for my fellow directors. I had worked hard to develop the capability of my directors. I had always encouraged my directors to undertake ongoing education to better equip themselves for their role. In my annual reviews of directors' performance, I had identified for each of them various courses and activities that would help develop their ability. I had also worked to strengthen lines of succession to be able to give the board some choices when I stood down. I had worked hard to promote a few of the younger directors including Tony Wilding, Murray McNaughten and Ian McGillivray, but none of them had stepped up. Rex Byles was a safe pair of hands, but John Storey was the best of them. He was ambitious and reasonably commercial but was not clever enough. He also was not popular with his fellow directors. However, time had run out on me. Graham was really the only option to succeed me. John Storey became his deputy.

I retired as chairman in 1989 well pleased with what had been achieved under my leadership. My early belief that everything depended on good management had been confirmed. Appointing a new CEO in Jeff Jackson had been the single most important action I had taken. He had then turned the company around. It was now well managed, efficient and performing well. My plans to increase revenue were now paying off, the commercial group sales had reached $434 million, making a significant $25 million profit contribution to our payout, which was now better than any of our competitors other than Tatua. I knew that there was more to come. Company turnover had reached $1.4 billion. For the first time we had received a Standard and Poor's credit rating of AA– which gave us access to a range of competitive new funding options. But I was deeply disappointed with myself for not leaving my directors with better leadership succession options. Graham had some ability, but I knew that he would blow it sooner or later. With him and Mac having the same serious flaws, I was sure that big trouble lay ahead.

TWENTY-EIGHT
PORT REFORM

UNTIL 1988 NEW ZEALAND PORTS WERE OPERATED BY harbour boards which were politically elected from within the catchment area of each port. Waterfront workers employed on the traditional wharves were employed by stevedoring (labour hire) companies, under terms and conditions set by a central Waterfront Industry Commission. Waterfront workers were militant, and there was no accountability so the Commission always gave in to them, usually sooner rather than later. Not surprisingly, port operations were grossly inefficient. Wage rates on the waterfront were extremely high, being more than 60% higher for some trades than for similar work outside the wharf. Even worse were the restrictive practices and overmanning which resulted in appallingly low productivity. Rorts were commonplace. One frequently experienced example was: a ship would be close to completing loading on a Friday. If loading was not completed that day and the ship wished to be worked on a Saturday, notice had to be given to the union by 2 pm on Friday. Once notice was given, a full day's pay at penal rates had to be paid to each worker, even though the loading may be completed in a shorter period. During Friday loading would slow down, until by 2 pm it would be obvious that loading would not be completed by the normal knock-off time of 4 pm, so notice to work Saturday would be given to the union. Loading would then speed up, be completed by 4 pm and each worker would receive a full day's pay at penal rates but not need to work at all on Saturday. There were many other such rorts.

The whole operation was a mess, productivity was low, among the lowest in the world, and port costs exorbitant. Even worse were costs arising from excessive ship time in port. Ships only earn revenue when they are sailing. When they are in port, they earn nothing. Shipping charges to New Zealand exporters were among the highest in the world because of the longer time ships took to load in New Zealand ports.

In 1988 the Labour Government implemented the Port Companies Act. It was a courageous move which was certain to create major conflict with the powerful waterfront unions. But it was to result in New Zealand ports becoming some of the most efficient in the world. It required each harbour board to appoint an Establishment Unit, which was required to:

- Establish a commercial entity to conduct the commercial business of the port.
- Identify the commercial assets of the port.
- Value the commercial assets of the port.
- Negotiate the purchase of the commercial assets of the port from the Harbour Board.

This provided a unique, one-time opportunity to effect major improvement to New Zealand ports. I was asked to join the Auckland Port Establishment Unit which had six members. New Zealand Dairy Company was by this time performing well, so given the importance of ports and shipping to New Zealand dairy farmers I felt that I should make the time available and accept. It proved to take rather more time than I had expected.

Labour was clearly going to be the major issue. The wharves were effectively controlled by the unions. We decided to concentrate on removing restrictive practices and eliminate overmanning and rorts. We decided that for the time being we would not tackle wage rates, as eliminating overmanning and restrictive practices would give us huge productivity gains and substantial cost reductions. Rates could wait for another day.

We met with each of the unions, about thirteen of them, advised them of our task and told them what we expected to achieve. We made it clear that we were intending to significantly improve efficiency. We also made it clear that the port would have to operate round the clock for seven days each week; that restrictive work practices and feather bedding would have to go; that manning scales would be significantly reduced. We told them that we wanted their help to achieve those things, sought their input and undertook to consult further with them as we worked through the process. While as expected there was some huffing and puffing from some of the unions, the overall response was better than we expected. A few even proffered that they were surprised that it had taken the employers "so long to wake up". They knew that what was happening on the wharves could not continue. They understood that the Port Companies Act had given us an ace in our hand which they would not be able to combat. They were also probably relieved that we were not going to reduce wage rates. Nevertheless, we expected a tough battle with the unions.

The new Port Company was to begin operating on 1 October 1988 so we had only about six months to complete what was a major exercise. We met on two or three days each week from 7.30 am usually until about 5 pm. Auckland Harbour Board owned large areas of land in downtown Auckland. We identified what we needed for "commercial port operations" and commissioned a valuation of the port. At $250 million the valuation was higher than we expected and we would have to borrow 100% of the value to purchase the commercial port assets. We had to consider how we could make the port profitable with that debt, negotiate a purchase price with the Harbour Board, arrange funding and then complete the purchase of the port's "commercial assets" from the Harbour Board. Without any prior notice we were served with a writ from Auckland City Council disputing our assessment of what was "port-related" land and claiming that much of such land should be given to them. We successfully defended that. As our view of how we would run the port and the work practices and manning scales we would require developed, we undertook several rounds of consultation with each of the unions. They were mostly reasonably constructive, some unions more so than others, but they all provided valuable input which we listened to carefully. Then we began to negotiate the actual contracts with each of the unions.

The legislation provided us with a real advantage when we came to negotiate labour awards with each of the unions. The new entity, Ports of Auckland (there were two ports, Auckland and Onehunga), was required to start operating on 1 October 1988. The legislation imposed no obligation on it to employ any of the existing Harbour Board or wharf staff, although it was free to do so if it wished. Any existing staff not required by Ports of Auckland would become redundant on 1 October and redundancy compensation would be paid by the Harbour Board out of the funds they received from the sale of the port. By 1 October we had reached agreement with a number of the unions, but some unions dug in. We decided that we would not open the port until every union had accepted the contract we were offering to the individuals we chose to offer it to. On 1 October the whole workforce was declared redundant by the Harbour Board. That quickly focussed the minds of individual workers who then took their destiny into their own hands. More and more individuals began accepting the jobs, wages and conditions we were offering. The port remained closed until 11 October but the hold-out unions had no option other than to reach agreement with us as most of their members had already accepted jobs with the new company. By 11 October 1988 all unions had accepted and Ports of Auckland commenced operations.

The Establishment Unit had completed its task on 1 October and was dissolved. A new board of directors took over from that date. I was one of only two Establishment Unit members asked to accept appointment to the Ports of Auckland Board and was appointed deputy chairman. The reform generated huge benefits. We were selective in who we employed and with the total number of staff being reduced by 40% it was possible to significantly upgrade the calibre of the workforce. Productivity gains were huge. After two years, in the conventional port, the average ship turnaround time improved from more than three days to thirty-six hours; ship waiting time reduced from eighteen hours to thirty minutes; in the container terminal the ship turnround time reduced from thirty-six hours to twelve hours.

Over the next few years continuing improvements in productivity further lowered ship turnaround time. Staffing numbers were further reduced despite increases in cargo volume. We tackled the difficult issue of wage rates, obtaining significant reductions. Within two years port charges had been reduced by between 15% and 30% and shipping rates reduced as ships were being turned around in much shorter times. Ports of Auckland was listed on the NZ Stock Exchange. The business had been purchased for $250 million, all of it borrowed. It then had to pay interest and tax, yet within four years it was worth $879 million. Productivity and financial performance continued to improve each year while shipping rates were further reduced.

I retired from Ports of Auckland in 2003. I was by now chairman of the Dairy Board and my workload had increased, but the job was done. Ports of Auckland was now an efficient operation and costs to shippers had been significantly reduced. The whole port reform exercise had been an outstanding success and brought huge benefits to New Zealand exporters and importers. A great deal of credit was due to the Labour Government and Minister Bill Jeffries. I am proud to have been involved in such a successful programme.

TWENTY-NINE
USA FOREIGN LEADER GRANT

In 1984 the United States Government offered me a Foreign Leader Grant. This offered me the opportunity to visit the USA for one month, as a guest of the US Government. I could go anywhere in the country, visiting whomever I wished, with the government meeting all of the cost. They expected that a reasonable amount of time would be spent on cultural or recreational activities. I decided to focus my trip on having a good look at the four largest US dairy cooperatives.

I flew to Washington DC where I spent the first week. An agency had been contracted to organise and manage my visit. On the first morning we worked out a programme for that first week in the nation's capital, which the agency arranged for me. They then prepared a programme for the remainder of my visit.

I had a fascinating week in Washington. A bill to restrict New Zealand casein imports was before Congress so I was able to observe the New Zealand Ambassador Lance Adams-Schneider and his team in their efforts to ensure its defeat. I was fortunate to meet the long-serving and powerful chairman of the House Agriculture Committee, Congressman Eligio De la Garza from Texas, and the sponsor of the Bill, Congressman James Jeffords from Vermont. I met with the largest farmers organisation, the American Farm Bureau, the National Milk Producers Federation and the US Dept of Agriculture where I caught up with a friend, Bud Anderson, who had previously been the US Agricultural Attaché in New Zealand. I had a great meeting with Randall Torgerson, the director of the Cooperatives Division whom I had previously met. I also spent a day with the Agricultural faculty at College Park University in Maryland where I received a great insight into US agriculture. On Friday afternoon it was back to the agency to receive a confirmed schedule of appointments for the remainder of my visit, travel tickets and accommodation vouchers.

I boarded an Amtrak train for Philadelphia where I met with the management of Interstate Milk Producers, a Pennsylvania cooperative. I found that there were huge differences between how New Zealand and US cooperatives operated. I was driven to their plant at Holly Springs, about two and a half hours' drive away in central Pennsylvania, by Rod McLeod, a New Zealander who had worked for the Dairy Board and was to later join New Zealand Dairy Company.

I then flew to Boston where I visited DEC (Digital Equipment Corporation) who were supplying the computer equipment for the systems Jeff was installing in the New Zealand Dairy Company. Their headquarters building was an old woollen mill, complete with a stream running through the building, driving water wheels which had been used to power the mill machinery. The wooden floors and panelling reeked of lanolin. Massachusetts used to have hundreds of such mills, but they had all closed down and shifted south where labour was cheaper. This was a most valuable visit. I knew little about IT but knew that it offered huge potential benefits which would revolutionise how businesses operated. Capturing the information once, and in real time, seemed to be a no brainer. If that could be done as part of the production process, the benefits would be huge. For example, rather than test finished product for compliance with specification and quality after the product had been made and was in the store, why not use the data from the production process itself in real time. My visit enabled me to get an understanding of where the technology was headed, giving me an idea of potential benefits. At the conclusion of my visit, DEC helicoptered me back to my hotel.

I then flew to Minneapolis, Minnesota. At each place I visited, the agency which organised my trip had organised someone to look after me, take me where I wanted to go and show me the sights. Often these were volunteers, sometimes they were as in this case, from the state government or the city administration. There was also usually a volunteer couple who would take me out to dinner during my stay. They were all very hospitable and generous. The whole programme was very well organised, enabling me to meet lots of ordinary Americans. State Governor Rudy Perpich made me an "Honorary Minnesotan", presenting me with an Honorary Citizen of Minnesota Certificate. At the weekend I was hosted by a Minnesota State Congressman, Rick Krueger, at his home in Brainerd, a small town about one hour's flight north of Minneapolis. It was graduation weekend so we spent all day Sunday visiting graduating students at their family home.

I visited Land O'Lakes Dairy Cooperative which I had heard a lot about. It had been a very large company when most dairy cooperatives were very small. Liquid milk drove most dairy cooperatives which usually had no manufacturing activity, being effectively milk brokers selling liquid milk to distributors. Land O'Lakes was different. It was much more like New Zealand Dairy, with a significant manufacturing operation, strong marketing capability and well-established brands. It was much more a full-service cooperative, retaining ownership through to the retailer and seeking to add value for its shareholders. Twenty years earlier Land O'Lakes had been a world-leading dairy cooperative but had rather lost its way as it extended into beef, hogs and grain. It carried a lot of overhead and its dairy performance had suffered as a consequence.

Then it was off to Burlington, Vermont, where I visited a whey-processing plant owned by Carbery, the Irish dairy business located in Cork with whom we had an ethanol technology agreement. Vermont was a dairying state. Like much of north-eastern USA it was formerly glacial country and the granite rock was never far from the surface. It was a pretty place, but farms were small with soil types which were often very poor.

I spent a weekend in Buffalo, New York, visiting the spectacular Niagara Falls. Then it was off to Louisville, Kentucky, the birthplace of Cassius Clay. Here the soil was rich and deep so farming was more prosperous. I visited the third largest cooperative, Dairymen Inc. Then it was on to Springfield, Missouri to visit Mid-American Dairy Cooperative. Their hospitality was extremely generous and I spent three full days with various members of their executive team including the CEO Gary Hanman. With a large supply and smaller population than in the east, much more of their milk went into manufacturing so they were rather more like New Zealand Dairy than any of the cooperatives I had visited previously. I had heard that US dairy surpluses were being stored in caves as they had run out of storage capacity. I was taken to a "cave" storage facility in Carthage, Missouri. It was anything but a cave. A large underground site had been quarried for marble. When marble extraction was completed, the underground workings had been developed into an impressive high-quality commercial storage facility, which had great recreational facilities, including tennis courts, for the staff. I also visited a cheese factory at Mt Vernon where the cheese curd went straight off the cheese belt through a "hole in the wall", to a processed cheese plant owned by Schreiber Foods who made processed cheese for McDonald's. This was an impressive plant, by far the most efficient I had seen.

Then it was down to San Antonio, Texas to visit American Milk Producers Inc. (AMPI), which was the largest American dairy cooperative. Again, it was largely a milk-brokering business, but I was impressed by its IT systems which were more advanced than any I had seen. I was invited to a meeting of the San Antonio City Council where I was publicly introduced and welcomed by Mayor Henry Cisneros who subsequently became a Cabinet Secretary (Minister) in Bill Clinton's administration.

My last week was allotted to recreation. A night in Las Vegas. A flight in a small plane to Grand Canyon where we flew below the outer rim of the canyon for over an hour. It was an amazing experience. Then a day travelling around the canyon enjoying the spectacular sights. Then off to LA, a day at Disneyland followed by dinner at their home with friends Gene and Barbara Huber. Then off next day to London to meet up with Jeff for our annual European visit.

I had a great experience and enjoyed generous American hospitality. I had a useful introduction to the US political system in Washington, visited twelve states and spent much of my time in rural areas. Surprisingly, I found that many of the small rural towns were backward and looked rather less prosperous than most New Zealand rural towns. I had seen two of the natural wonders of the world, Niagara Falls and Grand Canyon, and what I regarded as a man-made wonder, Disneyland. I had gained a good working knowledge of the US dairy industry which was to be most valuable when I became chairman of the Dairy Board.

While the New Zealand dairy industry had to export and live on market returns and our cooperatives evolved to ensure the wellbeing of New Zealand dairy farmers, US Dairy farmers on the other hand relied on politics to guarantee their incomes. As a result, cooperatives were not essential to their wellbeing, so farmers did not seriously invest in their cooperatives which were all undercapitalised, having little permanent capital. The capital of most cooperatives was really only sufficient to provide working capital. They had insufficient capital to invest in more capital-intensive assets such as processing plant.

I found that:

- In the populous east and west most milk went to the domestic market. Cooperatives were mostly just milk brokers who did little but contract to liquid milk distributors and retailers. Of course, that required little capital.
- In the less populated rich lands of the Midwest, while liquid market was still the largest use of milk, cooperatives had to undertake processing into other products to dispose of their milk. Cheese was the second largest use of milk.
- Butter consumption was relatively low, largely a consequence of high butter support prices. Butter and skim milk powder were the default products for any milk which could not be sold, and the US Government purchased any surpluses of those products at a guaranteed price.
- Any processing undertaken by cooperatives was usually only to the primary stage. Very little tertiary processing or value adding was undertaken. That was usually left to the private sector. Land O'Lakes and Mid-American were exceptions to a limited extent only.
- Most processing facilities were a generation behind Europe and New Zealand.
- R&D and innovation were largely absent.

- All cooperatives lacked capital. The law allowed funds to be "retained" but they had to be held in individual accounts. Depending on the circumstances of each individual company, it was usually repaid on a revolving basis anywhere between seven to fifteen years later. As a consequence, "shareholder funds" were small and the company starved of permanent capital.
- Cooperative boards of directors were large, usually having between twenty and thirty-five directors.
- They were completely run by management, and input from elected directors seemed minimal. All of my visits were hosted by management. Not once was I introduced to a chairman or director.
- All had comprehensive and well-developed directors' manuals.

I did not learn much of value about US cooperatives other than the need for them to build strong capital structures if they are to make a meaningful difference to returns for their members. But I did learn much about America, American dairying and the American political system. I greatly increased my store of knowledge and gained many contacts who were later to hold senior positions.

PART SIX
NEW ZEALAND DAIRY BOARD

THIRTY
INTERNATIONAL BUSINESS

It was customary for the chairman of the New Zealand Dairy Company to occupy one of the company's three seats on the New Zealand Dairy Board. When I became company. chairman in June 1982, I decided not to take up the Dairy Board position until the beginning of 1983. New Zealand Dairy was not in good shape and the task of turning it around was both formidable and urgent. I had a new CEO to whom I needed to be available at all times. My priority was New Zealand Dairy and for a period I needed to exclusively devote all of my time and effort to it, so I deferred joining the Dairy Board for six months.

I became a director of the New Zealand Dairy Board on 1 January 1983. The demands of New Zealand Dairy were still onerous and demanding. Chairman Jim Graham initially allocated me a relatively light workload. It was the practice for directors to be allocated responsibility for various activities. Jim agreed to put me into the South East Asian region as it would involve less travelling. It was also our best-performing region to which a lot of New Zealand Dairy Company product was supplied, so that suited me ideally. I was soon enjoying the marketing function of the business and the interaction with markets and customers. I looked closely for opportunities which the industry could take advantage of. I soon reached the view that there was a need to get the manufacturing dairy companies more directly involved with customers.

Prior to joining the board, I had not fully appreciated the critical role of the Dairy Board in R&D, logistics and particularly external policy where the subsidising policies of EEC and USA were the dominant influence on dairy prices. The directors were required to deal with many issues directly affecting New Zealand Dairy which I was not particularly familiar with. The then CEO, Bernie Knowles, was an amazing individual who did an incredible job in equipping the Dairy Board, and the dairy industry, to handle the challenges they faced. He tended to have the Dairy Board take over many functions, which while it suited most dairy companies, was a policy I did not agree with. I believed that superior results would be achieved with a partnership approach, in which most New Zealand-based activities were undertaken by the manufacturing dairy companies in close collaboration with the Dairy Board, while the board focussed its efforts on marketing and offshore activities. I was the first director to question the direction on these matters and my continued questioning created some tension.

When I received the board papers each month, I identified agenda items which affected New Zealand Dairy, and sought comments from the appropriate company executive. This meant that I was always much better briefed than most of my colleagues and frequently challenged recommendations. But my New Zealand Dairy executives were usually taking a narrow, and often limited, view, and I fell into the trap of being parochial and thus inevitably sometimes negative. When Murray Gough, whom I respected enormously, succeeded Bernie Knowles as CEO, he raised the matter with me. He bluntly told me that I was too parochial and needed to focus on the wider picture. I told him that I was not there to win any popularity stakes. I had a job to do which was to look after the interests of New Zealand Dairy. It was not part of my game plan to become chairman of the Dairy Board. He amazed me by urging me to reconsider that, as in his view I was clearly by far the best equipped to succeed Jim as chairman in due course. His comments stimulated me to have a deep think about my approach. I realised that I had become negative, which mortified me because I always prided myself on being constructive. I soon realised that challenging conventional thinking was not the issue, failing to do it constructively was. I resolved to up my game, focus more on the wider picture and become more constructive.

The 1980s was a difficult time for the dairy industry. The subsidising policies of the EEC and USA were producing more milk internationally than was being consumed. Large surplus stocks of butter and skim milk powder were building up. EEC surplus butter stocks, for example, reached over 1.2 million tonnes, or four times the total accessible world markets of only around 300,000 tonnes annually. New Zealand exported around 200,000 tonnes so we had to capture around two thirds of available markets. Prices were depressed, sustained at US$1350 per tonne only by a "minimum price" agreement within GATT, designed to protect New Zealand. From time to time the Soviet Union entered the market, purchasing large volumes at prices as low as US$300 per tonne, under deals approved by GATT. This helped to take some pressure off the market by reducing surplus stocks, without really solving the problem, as each year further surpluses were still being produced. Still, it was often the only home for some of our production.

In 1984 the Lange Labour Government was elected. They inherited a serious financial crisis to which they unexpectedly responded with an inspired decision to deregulate much of the economy. The New Zealand currency was floated. Contrary to expectations the New

Zealand dollar soared, driven by high interest rates. This lowered payout and further reduced farm income. While these steps were long overdue, and should have been undertaken by National years earlier, the strong currency and abrupt removal of farming subsidies slashed farm income. The New Zealand Dairy Board had always been funded by the Reserve Bank at an interest rate of 1%. This enabled the board to pay farmers for their milk on the twentieth of the following month, when the products into which their milk was processed would not be sold and the cash received by the Dairy Board for six months or more. It was a wonderful arrangement for dairy farmers but over the years the amount advanced to the board had steadily increased to a total of $750 million. The Muldoon Government had decided that this facility should no longer be available to the board. The board would have to arrange sufficient finance to fund its operations on normal financial markets. This had the potential, at least in the short term, to severely disrupt dairy farmers' cashflow. However, Jim Graham and Bernie Knowles persuaded the government to convert the outstanding sum of $750 million into a 40-year loan at 1% interest. With that loan secured and Finance Minister Roger Douglas deregulating the economy, they then adroitly negotiated with the government to purchase the loan for its current commercial value. This was a very smart move as a forty-year loan at 1% interest will always be valued at a heavy discount. Very clever negotiations with Government by Jim and Murray Gough enabled the $750 million loan to be purchased from Government for $100 million. It was agreed with Government that the difference between the face value and the purchase price of the loan could not be paid to farmers but would be transferred to reserves. This would create equity of $650 million for the Dairy Board. This gave the board a very strong balance sheet and enabled it to arrange adequate alternative credit facilities from commercial lenders. It also enabled the board to invest in marketing and offshore marketing facilities. It was the deal of the century.

In 1986 the opportunity arose for the board to invest in Chile, where over the years New Zealand had sold worthwhile quantities of milk powder. But a boycott by the New Zealand Federation of Labour, when the socialist Allende Government was overthrown by a military coup, had prevented trade for many years. Under the coup leader General Pinochet, Chile was starting to emerge from years of political and economic upheaval and international isolation. He had engaged the "Chicago Boys", a group of University of Chicago-educated economists who were reforming the economy along market lines. In those days almost all of Latin America was ruled by autocratic governments, many of them military, following highly interventionist policies, often designed to protect the wealthy. They were mostly economic basket cases. Chile, though, in adopting market economics, was making significant economic progress, being virtually alone among Latin American countries in doing so.

There was an opportunity to buy Anagra, which was an agricultural company with interests in fertiliser, agricultural chemicals, soya beans, vegetable oils and rice, none of which were of interest to us. But it also owned a controlling share in Soprole, which was Chile's largest consumer marketer of milk and fresh dairy foods. Its brand recognition in Chile was impressive, being second only to Coca-Cola. But to gain ownership of Soprole, we had to purchase Anagra. We did so intending to divest the rest of the Anagra activities, which was a risk for us as businesses are always easier to buy "high" than sell "well". In the meantime, we would have a large agricultural company in Chile to run.

Although the economy was liberalising, it was still tightly controlled. Reversion to dictatorship or socialism remained a possibility. Foreign exchange movements were tightly controlled, so if we invested in Chile we might not be able to get our money out again. But Soprole fitted into our strategy to develop branded consumer capability. Chile was a "high sovereign risk" country with many unknowns. We met the Chilean Minister of the Economy, a very bright young man called Hernan Buchi. He told us that he could not give any assurance that Chilean laws would not change in the future, but he did give us an assurance that they would not be changed retrospectively. Opportunities to buy an established branded business, with dominant market shares, in established economies were very rare. The board decided to go ahead and so completed the deal.

To attract foreign investment the Chilean Government allowed a discount of 25% on the exchange rate on the funds we invested to buy Anagra. That investment could not be repatriated for ten years but the discount made it a very attractive deal as it effectively reduced our purchase price by 25%. The Chilean Government used the discount to attract inward direct investment which Chile desperately needed. It varied the discount rate from time to time, increasing it when capital inflows slowed and decreasing it if sufficient capital was being invested in Chile. When we needed to increase our investment to buy out some of the Soprole minorities and to upgrade Soprole facilities, the discount had increased to 40%. Given Chile's high "sovereign risk", banks had low individual client limits of around US$2.5 million, which meant that we had to deal with a banking consortium which included virtually every bank in Chile. Selling off the parts of Anagra we did not want took rather longer than we had anticipated, and yielded less than we had hoped, but when it was completed, we had acquired a controlling interest in Soprole for less than US$20 million. It proved to be a wonderful investment, leveraging its dominant market share to earn good profits. Twenty years later the business was worth over US$500 million. As the Chilean economy improved and living standards increased, dairy consumption increased faster than domestic milk production and imports were required. We were in the box seat to provide these and were soon supplying around 10% of their total dairy consumption with imports of New Zealand milk.

I was appointed to the Anagra Board. Our long-term Chile agents, O'Shea, were allocated a small shareholding and were to manage Anagra, while Soprole would have to be managed as a separate company because of its minority shareholders which included a couple of small cooperatives and a charitable trust, the beneficiary of which was the Catholic Church which was very influential in Chile. As the name indicates the O'Shea family were of Irish origin. Their business was a trading house and their people traders so, not surprisingly, O'Shea was quite unsuited to managing a business like Anagra. At one board meeting Pancho O'Shea told us that Anagra had made a small investment in berries and other fruit. On enquiry we were told the sum involved was only US$1.5 million. We were told that the investment was to fund farmers into buying seed and fertiliser to plant the canes and fruit trees. We asked if there were any other liabilities. The answer was no. But as we probed, we found that there was also an obligation to buy the fruit when it was harvested. That would require processing and storage facilities which would have to be built to handle the crop. Where would it be sold? Nobody had a clue. A few calculations showed that the investment we were in the hole for was over $30 million, all of it at high risk. Then markets needed to be found for the production. Pancho O'Shea slapped his face and said, "I do wish I had talked to you first." It was obvious that we needed to make other management arrangements and were fortunate to persuade the previous CEO of Anagra, Javier Poblete, to rejoin us. He was a very good manager.

The O'Shea family were very well connected, though, and enabled very good access to ministers and government officials. The Minister of Agriculture Jorge Prado became a regular lunch guest whenever we visited Santiago. We visited all of the Soprole and Anagra locations, travelling from Puerto Montt in the south to Santiago by bus, which gave us a good understanding of the company's operations and a fascinating insight into Chile, which in those days was a poor country with very high levels of poverty.

Soprole plant Chile opening. Author with Fernando Lenitz, Agriculture Minister Mladic, President Frei

For the next three years I continued to visit Chile every three months. When we first established in Chile, the military junta was in control and inflation was around 40% per annum. It had peaked at over 500% in the 1970s before the military coup. By 1986 the Pinochet Government had stabilised Chile politically and got the economy growing. To cope with hyperinflation, accounting regulations required "current cost" accounting, under which company accounts had to be adjusted for inflation. This effectively indexed inflation. Each month an adjustment equal to the amount of inflation in the period and termed "monetary compensation" had to be made. Profit was adjusted down by the amount of inflation and both assets and liabilities increased by the same amount. Each month the sales would be higher, as would be profit. A monetary compensation adjustment for inflation was then deducted from the profit. It was always a large number which often wiped out all of the profit increase. The monetary compensation system did nothing to contain inflation but merely passed it on. The ultimate losers of course were the poor people, as they always are with inflation.

General Pinochet had laid down a pathway for return to democracy over the next three years. This was most unusual as military dictatorships rarely voluntarily give up power. I was to experience this transition during the period during which I visited Chile regularly. By the time democracy had returned the economy was growing strongly and living standards were increasing. After Pinochet surrendered power, Chile has had mostly socialist presidents, but they have all continued the "market" economy established by Pinochet. Today Chile has a modern, progressive and vibrant economy with the highest living standards in Latin America.

In 1985 Bernie Knowles had advised the Dairy Board that he was resigning as CEO to take up the position of chief executive of the New Zealand Wool Board. He was an interesting character. He had an outstanding intellect, was extremely entrepreneurial and understood that a major upgrading of the New Zealand dairy industry was required, as too was the marketing capability of the Dairy Board. He was frugal and paid little respect to convention, his focus being on doing what had to be done. He often took the view that "it needs to be done and no one else is doing it, so the Dairy Board will make sure it gets done". He increasingly centralised decision making and ownership of facilities in the Dairy Board. That attitude was supported by smaller dairy companies who usually did not have the resources required to do things themselves. It often brought him into conflict with New Zealand Dairy Company, during both Jim Graham's term as chairman and during mine. New Zealand Dairy had the resources to do what was needed and felt that the resource advantages it had were being neutralised by Bernie's policy of Dairy Board centralisation. Bernie's management style was light on process but strong on achievement. He picked good people who were encouraged and empowered to get on with it and get the job done. His instruction to his staff was along the lines of: "This is what I want achieved, you are authorised to do what you have to do to achieve it, unless I have specifically advised you that you may not do it." During his ten years as CEO, he had done an outstanding job of modernising the industry and improving the capability of the Dairy Board. The board had much to thank him for, but different skills were becoming required.

The board was fortunate to have some suitable internal candidates. Murray Gough, John Parker, Phil Lough, Alan Pollock and Peter Benjes were all outstanding executives and a wide search failed to turn up any better candidates. Murray Gough was selected by the directors. He was an accountant who had worked for IBM when it was the world's leading IT company before joining the Dairy Board. He had then had several years running our largest and most important subsidiary, Anchor Foods, in the United Kingdom. He was an experienced and well-rounded executive with exactly the skill base the Dairy Board required for the future. Murray appointed John Parker and Phil Lough as deputy chief executives with John taking responsibility for cream, milk powders and consumer while Phil would look after cheese, protein and speciality ingredients.

In 1986 the GATT Uruguay Round got under way at Punta del Este in Uruguay. For the first time agriculture was to be included. The American Trade Representative Bill Block had urged the food-exporting countries to get together to push the case for liberalisation of trade in agricultural products. This led to the formation of an alliance of food-exporting countries which came to be known as the "Cairns Group". It was to be led by Australia and included New Zealand. Mike Moore, the New Zealand trade minister, was to have a large influence within that group. There was at last some hope for an international agreement which liberalised trade in dairy products. However, the average length of time taken to conclude GATT rounds was seven years; that was without agriculture included. With agriculture in, this one would take even longer. Meantime, we would have to cope with continuing increases in milk production in the EEC, with surpluses of butter and milk powder in Europe and the USA, depressing prices.

With economic reform in New Zealand proceeding apace, every convention or arrangement was being challenged. Treasury began to argue that the "single seller" Dairy Board was in neither New Zealand's nor farmers' interests. It was to be the start of a fifteen-year debate which ultimately led to the removal of single-seller legislation and the formation of Fonterra. While arguing that the single seller was in both dairy farmers' and New Zealand's interests and should thus be continued, as always the board wished to be proactive and have a plan of what to do if the "single seller" was abolished. Murray Gough prepared a paper suggesting that a joint stock company be formed into which all of the assets and liabilities of the Dairy Board would be transferred. Dairy companies would be allocated shareholding based on their individual share of New Zealand's milk production. Any dairy company which did not want to be involved would be paid out their respective share of the net assets of the company and be free to go their own way. The concept was supported by the Dairy Board directors and also by all cooperative dairy companies including New Zealand Dairy.

Because of the need for large volumes of butter to be sold to the Soviet Union, which was chronically short of foreign exchange, John Parker advocated the establishment of a trading company to facilitate two-way trade with the Soviet Union. Sovenz, as it was called, facilitated the import of Russian Lada cars and Belarus tractors as well as the sale of New Zealand mutton and a range of other products. Some of New Zealand's leading companies such as Fletcher Challenge and Amalgamated Marketing were involved in various aspects of Sovenz activities.

The Latin American region was a large importer of dairy products so was an important area for us. The economies of the countries in the region were weak, many of them basket cases. Most were ruled by autocratic governments which were often dictatorships, a number of them military regimes. Incomes were low and most people extremely poor. Much of what we sold was to government agencies for welfare or semi-welfare uses. Currencies had often been "dollarised" into US dollars. Their ability to buy dairy products was restricted by the availability of foreign exchange, namely US dollars. The board established a trading company, LATENZ (Latin America New Zealand) which exported goods from Latin America countries. It was a relatively small operation but helped provide South American countries with limited amounts of foreign exchange. It also importantly gave New Zealand Dairy Board great credibility with governments in the region.

THIRTY-ONE
CHAIRMAN OF THE NEW ZEALAND DAIRY BOARD

At the age of forty-nine, I was the youngest chairman in the history of the New Zealand Dairy Board. My first day on the job was a wet and miserable one. I walked into Pastoral House on Wellington's Lambton Quay to find that the chairman's office was undergoing renovation and I had been allocated a small office on the sixteenth floor, three levels up. My secretary remained on the thirteenth floor, which was less than ideal. I walked into my office to find a huge floral arrangement, a gift from Katsuya Shono, chief executive of Snow Brand, the board's most valuable Japanese customer. It was a very kind gesture and an indication of the respect of Snow Brand for my office.

One evening a month later, I was in my office preparing my remarks to farewell Gordon Mackenzie, Jim Graham's deputy, at a valedictory dinner in his honour that evening. Murray came in to tell me that two of the senior executives would not be attending. They were on their way to Hamilton where "irregularities" had been found in Dairy Containers Ltd, which was a Dairy Board subsidiary making cans for milk powder. A large sum of money appeared to be missing.

This was most unwelcome news as I had been chairman for only a few weeks. Fortunately, Murray said the executive team had recently gamed how to handle a significant defalcation. They knew exactly what to do and had already commenced the process to deal with it. We were holding insurance to cover such an eventuality. In cases of significant fraud, as with physical disasters such as earthquake or fire, gathering the evidence to support an insurance claim becomes the major objective in order to recover any loss. With large sums involved, insurers will challenge everything to reduce their loss, so a watertight case has to be built. That was what our team were concentrating on.

The top three executives of Dairy Containers had conspired to defraud the company. They had started by diverting proceeds from the sale of used plant to themselves. Then, masterminded by the CFO, a brilliant young man who had been top of his year at Waikato University, Dairy Containers cash had been deposited under false names with a finance company, First City Finance, located in Auckland. The cash then just disappeared. Our team did a great job unravelling what had occurred and finally succeeded in recovering all of our losses, which was a good outcome from a bad event. Dairy Containers' duplicitous CFO was very helpful in providing detailed information on how the fraud had been carried out. All three executives were charged and ultimately convicted. Charges against two well-known Auckland businessmen who were the major shareholders in the finance company were thrown out when it was revealed in court that the board had paid the wife of Dairy Containers' CFO a sum to facilitate the sale of their house to recover some of the board's losses. There were to be other consequences.

While the overall outcome was satisfactory, the perpetrators had been convicted and the board had recovered over $12 million, farmers (and others) were disturbed that the case against the finance company executives had collapsed due to the board "paying a thief's wife". It was hard to defend but I needed to answer to farmers and explain to them the need to unravel what were some very complicated transactions, in order to gain full recovery from our insurers. We also needed the cooperation of the wife, to be able to sell their house to recover stolen funds. I sent a letter to every farmer explaining the matter and the board's actions. It was a difficult letter to write. In this highly public matter, I had to be honest with farmers but not expose the board or its executives to any further risks, so it was very carefully written. That was just as well, as the Auditor General (who had legislative oversight of the Dairy Board) decided to investigate.

The Auditor General wished to examine:

1. Whether the Dairy board had acted with propriety regarding the payments made to the CFO's wife, and that the payments made sound economic sense for the dairy farmers of New Zealand.
2. Whether the statements made by the board (in my letter) accurately reflect the basis for the decisions and actions taken since the recovery of the defalcation.

The Auditor General concluded that the board did act with propriety and the payments did make sound economic sense for the dairy farmers of New Zealand. He also believed that the communication by the board could have been more complete by acknowledging that the payments to the wife could have increased the chances of cooperation by the CFO in order to expedite and maximise recovery action.

A secondary consequence, however, was most beneficial to the board, although it took until 1993 to play out. Under the Dairy Board Act the Government Audit Office, which came under the jurisdiction of the Auditor General, was the board's auditor. From my experience with other companies, I knew that the Audit Office provided us with a service which, although cheap, was not up to the standard a complex international business like the Dairy Board required. I had asked the Minister of Agriculture to have the board released from being required to use the Audit Office. But to the Audit Office, the board was their most prestigious client, one that they wished to keep. I could get no support from anywhere within Government.

However, the Dairy Containers fiasco confirmed my belief that they were not up to it. The previous year, as part of the audit process, the Audit Office had written to First City Finance seeking verification that the amount showing in Dairy Containers' books as invested with them was correct. This is a normal audit practice. In due course they received confirmation, accepted it and moved on. But the confirmation was on Dairy Containers' letterhead and signed by the Dairy Containers' CFO, not as it should have been on First City Finance letterhead and signed by one of First City's personnel! Red lights should have been flashing and bells ringing, but the Audit Office had not even noticed this very obvious discrepancy. This was basic audit stuff. The Audit Office was just not sufficiently competent for the job.

I was sure that we could successfully sue the Audit Office but knew that this gave us a lever which would enable us to pry the audit away from them. However, a few weeks later Wayne Cameron, the deputy government auditor, sought a meeting with me. I intended to raise the matter with him, but to my surprise he told me that the Audit Office wanted to withdraw from our audit as soon as could be arranged. They had taken a decision to withdraw from all their commercial audits. Although our auditor by law, they were able to delegate the conduct of our audit to another provider, without the need for a law change. They intended to do that. Although not stated, it was clear that the Dairy Containers debacle had made them realise that they just did not have the capability to audit a complex business such as the Dairy Board. I was delighted.

We had to move quite quickly as they did not wish to undertake the 1994 audit. That suited the board as we wanted immediate change. We issued a Request for Proposal to the "big four" accounting firms. They had to be able to service us in every country in which the Dairy Board operated, and be able to commit rates, partners and personnel anywhere in the world. Each was very keen to obtain our account which was large and prestigious. Usually, when these firms audited international companies' New Zealand business, they were the "tail of the dog", wagging in response to their parent company in another country. Here the New Zealand auditing firms had a rare opportunity to be the "dog", wagging the "tails" of their parent all over the rest of the world. They all made their very best people available. After an exhaustive process, the audit was placed with KPMG whose partners Michael Morris and Don Scott were very highly rated. It was soon obvious that what they were able to provide to us was a world ahead of the Audit Office.

Unlike New Zealand Dairy Company, when I became chairman, the Dairy Board was in good shape and performing well. It had an outstanding CEO in Murray Gough who was an experienced and well-rounded executive with a formidable intellect. However, there was no shortage of challenges. As I pondered my major objectives, five areas seemed especially critical to success.

First, the world was awash with milk. There were huge surplus stocks of butter and skim milk powder (at peak 1.2 million tonnes of each) held by the EEC as it was then, and surpluses of both held in USA. The "world market price", which is what New Zealand farmers received, was less than half of what was paid for milk in the United States and less than one third that of Europe, a consequence of their policies of subsidising farmers. Each year world milk production exceeded consumption and the surplus was getting worse. Apart from a few mainly small volume quotas, both the EEC and USA prevented our product from entering their markets. At the same time, they were competing with us in those limited markets to which we did have access, by exporting their surpluses there, with their taxpayers paying export subsidies, typically 200% to 300% of the world market price. Put another way, for every $1 the EEC earned by exporting skim milk powder or butter, it paid another $2 to farmers from the EEC budget. That depressed world market prices, thus lowering our returns. Trade reform was vital to our future. Nothing else had the potential to increase returns to farmers as much as trade reform. Negotiations inside GATT (General Agreement on Tariffs and Trade) had commenced in Punta del Este, Uruguay, in 1986. For the first time agriculture was included in a GATT negotiating round. This was the first opportunity to establish international dairy trading rules and change trade practices which were so damaging to New Zealand dairy farmers and to our country. It was an opportunity we certainly had to take. But New Zealand was the only country whose dairy farmers earned their living by exporting, so no other country apart from Australia was interested in liberalising dairy trade and particularly imports. There were many, however, including most of the large and powerful countries like the EEC and USA, which were keen to protect their dairy farmers by keeping imports out. We needed to ensure that any agreement included significant dairy trade liberalisation of benefit to New Zealand. As the virtual sole voice for dairy trade liberalisation, if *we* did not fight to have dairy included in GATT Uruguay negotiations, nearly every other of the 107 country participants would be happy to exclude it and we would miss out. Until significant trade reform occurred, we needed to ensure that surplus disposals were responsibly managed to limit damage to New Zealand. I needed to ensure that we had the resources and strategies to influence trade reform. Trade policy was an area of which I had little experience and only limited knowledge. However, trade policy was a core skill of the board with Murray Gough and External Policy Manager Nigel Mitchell being highly regarded. But with the GATT Uruguay Round due to conclude in 1993 I needed to quickly get up to speed on trade policy and devote a significant effort to it. Getting close to New Zealand's Trade Department and Minister Mike Moore and our senior trade officials was an urgent priority.

Secondly, we did have an entitlement to enter 70,000 tonnes of butter into our traditional market, the United Kingdom. The price we received for this was three times what we would earn if the product was sold anywhere else in the world, but there was continuous pressure for it to be abolished. It had been scheduled to progressively reduce to 55,000 tonnes by 1992 with no guarantee of any access at all beyond then. We simply had to retain the highest volume possible, for as long as possible, as that "quota" was so valuable and was vital to our ability to sell our annual production of butter. There were no alternative markets anywhere in the world.

Thirdly, Murray Gough had done much to improve the operating effectiveness of the Dairy Board but more needed to be done. I had always been a strong advocate for continuous improvement and wanted to ensure that principle was fully embraced by Dairy Board directors and management. Performance measurement and transparency were vital tools in that process which needed to be strengthened.

Fourthly, I wanted to see a big improvement in the board's ability to add value. The majority of our sales were commodities, often to single buyers. For example, Latin America, Middle East, North Africa and Eastern Europe mostly had single buying agencies. Commodities can be profitable but required a very low-cost operation. The food ingredients market was growing rapidly but changing and becoming more specialised. We needed to get close to customers and design products to meet the specific needs of individual customers. This meant more people, with greater authority, located offshore, but would give us the chance to have less volatile and more secure sales at higher margins. This would require close collaboration with our scientists at the Dairy Research Institute. They tended to see themselves as an independent and autonomous organisation, but the board paid most of their bills and they needed to see themselves as part of our sales and marketing operation.

Branded, fast-moving consumer products was where the highest margins and return on capital existed. Apart from Anchor in the UK, and small volumes in places where the passenger liners used to call in the days of sea travel such as Mauritius and Trinidad, the board had never succeeded in breaking into branded markets. But that had begun to change with success in Sri Lanka where Anchor had become brand leader. But our total branded sales, including the very successful Anchor Foods in the UK, were still only $400 million in a turnover of $2.94 billion. I wanted a strategy, and a sustained effort, to lift that substantially and make us a major world player in branded products. Succeeding in both specialised food ingredients and branded products required getting closer to customers and consumers and having a comprehensive understanding of their needs. Our structure needed to be looked at to ensure that it could deliver these more profitable but complex needs. I was also keen to implement my belief in decentralisation by putting more authority in the hands of those closest to customers. This would mean more people offshore and fewer people in head office.

Finally, there was communication both with farmers and with New Zealanders. I believed that to justify allowing the dairy industry to have the single selling statutory powers, the government and the people of New Zealand had to be satisfied that it was beneficial, not only to farmers but to New Zealand. Above all, the Dairy Board needed to perform well, but it also needed to effectively communicate with politicians and the New Zealand public, to satisfy them that the New Zealand Dairy Board was doing a good job and that the dairy industry was a winner for New Zealand. Farmers wanted to be confident that the board was performing efficiently and doing everything possible to increase their incomes. They also deserved to be kept well informed of the issues. This would require increased disclosure and transparency as well as a high level of communication with them.

Communication was one of my most effective skills, while the board had in Neville Martin an outstanding communications executive who was highly trusted by media and public. Transparency, though, needed to be improved. The use of commercial confidentiality to avoid giving away sensitive information was too often the easy option. While avoiding disclosing sensitive information, we needed to be much more open.

Later that first day as Murray gave me my first briefing, I was blindsided when he told me that he would give me one more year then would retire as CEO. I rated him highly, so was devasted as my first thought was that Murray did not wish to work with me. He quickly allayed my concerns by assuring me that on the contrary he greatly respected me and what he knew I would bring to the role and was looking forward to working with me. But he had been CEO for five years, and he believed five or six years was a reasonable term for a CEO; that he would have finished this year had Jim not retired. He would stay for another year because he believed there should not be a change in both the chairman and the CEO in the same year. I was relieved but mentally resolved to do everything I could to motivate Murray and keep him for a longer period. In the end, he stayed for three years. They were three of the better years of my chairmanship.

THIRTY-TWO
ANNUAL CHAIRMAN'S EUROPEAN TRIP

For many years it had been the practice for the chairman and CEO to travel to Europe and the USA in May or June. This was a major and important activity. In the EEC the major dairying countries were visited each year, while the smaller dairy-producing countries like Greece, Spain and Portugal were visited occasionally. Usually, one other director accompanied the chairman and CEO. I had accompanied Jim and Murray in 1987 and as chairman-elect in 1989 on Jim's final visit.

These trips had a number of objectives:

First, there were the board's commercial activities. In Europe, board subsidiary companies Anchor Foods in London and NZMP (Europe) in Hamburg were visited and their activities reviewed. Customers were visited, as were partners or potential partners and customers. While most of the engagement with the latter was undertaken by local executives, the presence of the chairman, and/or the CEO, at such meetings was helpful to them. I remember meeting Tom Vyner, CEO of Sainsbury's, the largest supermarket chain in the UK. Our local executives were always complaining about how difficult Sainsbury's were to deal with and how modest their purchases of our products were. We had a great meeting. Our local team were amazed when he asked me, "Dryden, is there anything we can do for you?" That gave me the opportunity to advise him that we were rather disappointed by their very modest purchases, which were below their competitors'. Anchor was one of the largest brands in the grocery market, so I said we would like to see Sainsbury's buy more from us. Vyner was surprised and undertook to look at the matter. He obviously did, as eventually their orders increased. My relationship with him was later to be very valuable when we had a major problem with British Customs. We also engaged with the European trading houses where we picked up valuable market information. We had a very close relationship with the Belgian Van Waeyenberge family, the very respected Baron Piet and his brothers Jozef and Luk. Sadly, Luk died at an early age while on a plane home after a visit to New Zealand. They were very well informed, were usually ahead of our competitors and we worked closely with them, particularly when from time to time large-volume butter disposals to the USSR were being contemplated.

In 1973 when Britain entered the EEC, New Zealand was exporting 178,000 tonnes of butter to the UK. Most of the EEC member countries were committed to our access being progressively eliminated and by 1988 the volume had been reduced to 74,500 tonnes. That access was vital to us, as despite our efforts to find alternative markets, without it we would have been unable to sell all of our butter production anywhere in the world, at any price. Our volume entitlement was renegotiated, always down, every four years. We had to fight for every tonne to maintain the volume, against ongoing EEC pressure to eliminate it over the next four-year period. France and Ireland were the strongest proponents of elimination while the UK fought hard for us, usually at cost to themselves. Denmark always supported us. Germany was key, usually coming down on our side. But inevitably our volume entitlements were always reduced in each four-year negotiation. But it was not all bad, though, as we managed to effect a trade-off, in which we received a higher price for the lower volume. In fact, by 1995 when our volume was down to around 55,000 tonnes, we were still receiving the same amount of money as we had received for 178,000 tonnes in 1973.

Every year as we visited the EEC Member States, we were either preparing for a negotiation, were currently negotiating, or had just completed negotiating a new agreement and were finalising the details of it. In each country we would visit government. Ministers, usually Agriculture, Economics and Foreign Affairs, as well as senior government officials from the same departments. We would meet with the Farmer Organisations and some of the large cooperatives, government trading entities and often groups of MPs. Next morning, we would jump on a plane or train, travel to another country and do it all over again. It was exhausting but necessary to retain our valuable butter quota.

During our visits to both EEC and Washington we were given great support by our Ministry of Foreign Affairs and Trade. They set up our meetings and organised the "trade" activities of our trip. As chairman of the New Zealand Dairy Board, I had close to ambassador status. On arrival in each country, we were usually met at the airport by the New Zealand Ambassador who often took us through the diplomatic entry lanes; we were briefed by embassy officials and provided with the use of the ambassador's vehicle. Other embassy resources were made available to us and lunches and dinners with influential people were hosted for us. My visit provided an opportunity for each embassy to obtain access to ministers and senior influential people that they would otherwise find difficult to obtain.

We worked hard to build relationships and had many good friends among European senior officials and ministers. Much of our overseas marketing network had originated as joint ventures, often with family-owned companies. The New Zealand Dairy Board had a reputation for being a good partner. This was brought home to me when, while chairman designate, Jim asked me to meet with Haagen-Dazs, the successful American premium ice-cream company who were looking at locating in New Zealand. Murray Gough and I had a good meeting with their president, operations director and commercial director over dinner at Boulcott Street Bistro, Wellington. Murray asked them why they wished to come to New Zealand. Their operations director, Rod Heine, replied that there were two reasons:

- They knew that New Zealand would always be competitive in milk prices.
- The New Zealand Dairy Board had an enviable reputation around the world as a good partner and a good company to do business with.

The UK was central to our battle to retain the right of entry for our butter and would fight strongly for us even at some cost to themselves. We worked closely with the New Zealand High Commission in London to strengthen our support among politicians and civil servants and to neutralise our opponents, mostly in the National Farmers Union where we maintained excellent relationships despite our opposing views. The Anzac Group in the House of Commons was large and could be relied upon for strong support, so keeping them enthused was a priority. However, my biggest concern was that they were mostly of an older age group which time would eventually whittle away.

The key meetings were in Brussels with the EEC Agriculture Commissioner and other Commission officials as they had the greatest influence and the decisions were ultimately theirs. They were also responsible for the purchase of surplus skim milk powder and butter and its disposal through the export subsidy scheme. High per tonne export subsidies meant low market prices and low returns for us. We worked hard to cooperate with the Commission in the market and persuade them to keep export subsidies low, pointing out to them that in a fixed-volume market high "restitutions", which was their term for export subsidies, forced market prices down, which not only meant low returns for us but low returns for them also. But I stressed that with high export subsidies and at high cost to their budget, they would not sell a single tonne more as we could never afford to give up market share. They pretty much understood that and we were moderately successful much of the time provided they were in a reasonable stock position. However, their restraint reduced as their surplus stocks rose.

The author with Warren Larsen

In Washington we usually met with the Secretary of Agriculture, the Chairmen of the Senate and House Agriculture Committees, other senators and congressman who were members of those committees or their trade committees. We met Agriculture and State Department senior officials, the US trade representative and senior trade officials, national milk producers and other USA regulatory bodies. The issues here were a little different. The USA was less principled. They were strongly for trade liberalisation but protected their farmers from "unfair competition" which really meant from lower cost producers such as New Zealand by limiting access to their market! However, despite the considerable support given by the US Government to US dairy farmers, their milk-pricing system was much more market related than that of the EU. When surpluses did arise from time to time, milk prices were adjusted so their surpluses were mostly kept under control. The US Department of Agriculture usually attempted to avoid disrupting "commercial markets" when disposing of any surpluses. But any surplus sales, by them or any other country, inevitably meant lower prices for us. However, we put a great deal of effort into encouraging the US to act in a way which caused the least damage to our commercial interests.

On my first visit to Europe as chairman in 1990 the EEC Agriculture Commissioner was Ray MacSharry, a respected former Irish Minister of Finance. He was a tough and disciplined man who stood his ground but scrupulously honoured any agreement. My meeting with him went rather well. I liked him and we got on well. At lunch at our ambassador Gerry Thompson's residence, I met Peter Pooley, EEC assistant director general of agriculture. He commented that he understood that my meeting with his boss, MacSharry, had gone rather well. I replied that I also considered it had and was rather satisfied with it. He then told me that as chairman of the New Zealand Dairy Board I would have access to the commissioner whenever I wanted it, something which not more than five commercial organisations in the world would enjoy. This emphasised for me that retaining and building those strong relationships should never be far from my mind. But I was soon to experience the hard side of MacSharry.

On these visits we built some close relationships with influential ministers and officials. Denmark was always supportive and their top official Poul Ottosen was a good friend. Ireland had a contrary position. They wanted us out of European markets which they regarded as rightfully theirs, but they were strongly supportive of lowering the tariff we paid so that we received the same amount of money, albeit for a lower volume. Their agriculture secretary, Michael Dowling, was always constructive. As a trading nation the Dutch were in favour of trade liberalisation, understood our position and were generally supportive but were quick to exploit every commercial opportunity which the EEC support system created, and there were many. Their long-serving Minister of Agriculture Gerrit Braks was always helpful; he had two brothers farming in New Zealand. Italy and the smaller members of the EEC would use any opportunity to leverage off us for something which was important to them. On one occasion when a hard-fought negotiation to allow us to enter butter for another four years had been concluded, Greece vetoed our agreement. They were not actually against entry of our butter to the UK but wanted a better deal on sheep meats which had nothing to do with us, being an internal EEC matter. So, we needed to be vigilant and selectively visit the smaller countries, particularly any of them which were scheduled to hold the presidency during the next year or so.

Murray Gough, EU Agriculture Commissioner MacSharry, and the author

France was the driving force behind the EEC. They provided much of the vision and the intellectual horsepower which has shaped how it has developed. Their position was based on a very strong relationship with their historical arch-enemy Germany, anchored in the belief that it was better to work together to cooperate, and ultimately to integrate economically, rather than repeatedly go to war as their countries had done for centuries. Their long-term vision was of a "United States of Europe" with a high degree of political integration. France was very strongly protective of their farmers, were well organised, always advancing a unified and consistent French position which was unusual, as in most countries there were usually sharply divergent views between the agricultural, economic and foreign affairs ministries. Agriculture was always highly protective, while economic ministries wished to curtail the rising cost of agriculture, which in those days absorbed 70% of the EU budget. Economic ministries in most countries were usually keen to liberalise trade in farm goods. Foreign Affairs took a more principled approach and were keen to have good relationships with New Zealand whom they regarded as a reliable friend. We tried to exploit those differences. At the same time France was always the most far sighted of European countries, had superior long-term objectives and was making more progress than most other EEC members in structurally changing their own farming to improve its efficiency. They were very tough negotiators who gave nothing away.

They also thought differently. On one occasion over lunch in the New Zealand Ambassador's residence, the most senior French official present was a man called Jean Claude Nestor who was Chef de Cabinet (chief of staff) to France's Minister of Agriculture, Henri Nallet. He was unfailingly courteous, spoke excellent English, had a lovely pointed waxed moustache and was always impeccably dressed in a dark pin-striped three-piece suit. We were debating subsidies. He commented that while he agreed in principle that subsidies were not desirable, French farmers could not survive without them so any change could only occur over a very long time. I challenged that view, commenting that subsidy dependence made farming less efficient. I outlined the New Zealand experience for him, how by the early 1980s New Zealand farmers had become very dependent on subsidies and the budgetary cost was blowing out. Subsidies were removed overnight; farm incomes took a hit but only a very few farmers did not survive. But within five years farming had recovered, had become much more efficient, farm profitability was up and today few farmers would want to go back to subsidies. His response was classic French. With great dignity he courteously exclaimed. "Thank you for explaining the New Zealand experience, monsieur. You can do without subsidies monsieur, good for you. New Zealand can do without subsidies, good for New Zealand. But France cannot do without subsidies. We are different. We are French!"

On another occasion, the Uruguay Round Agreement had been reached and was proceeding to implementation. The very nature of such complex and wide-ranging agreements left plenty of loopholes and opportunities for individual countries to weasel out of parts they did not like. So, we needed to be vigilant to ensure that the potential benefits were not eroded by such activities. The French were proposing something which would make it less painful for them to implement but would severely erode benefits to us. I was fortunate to score a meeting with a man called Yves-Thibault de Silguy who was the top economic adviser to the French Prime Minister and later became economics minister. I outlined our objections to what they were proposing, explained the impact it would have on us and that we considered it did not comply with France's obligations under the Uruguay Round Agreement. His response was clear cut and typical. "Thank you for explaining New Zealand's position to me, monsieur." He then said, "I will now explain to you my prime minister's position on the Uruguay Round Agreement. France will honour its obligations under the agreement but will do no more, not one centime more, not a centime!"

The other EEC "major" was Germany. The richest country in the EEC, its farms were smaller and less efficient than many others. It had a very large farming population, many of whom were part time, also having other jobs. It wanted to look after those people and could afford to. But its wealth came from its industrial and commercial industries which relied upon trade and access to markets around the world. It needed access to the markets of the world so was pro free trade. It was by far the largest contributor to the EEC budget. It was as strongly committed as France was to the axis with France but was much more aware of the influence of EEC actions on the rest of the world. It was more supportive of trade reform but would never do anything which would fracture the France–Germany relationship. Our meeting with their agriculture minister was always pivotal as we fought for continuation of our butter quota. It was always a huge relief when he committed to supporting us, as they usually did.

THIRTY-THREE
EARLY TIMES

When I took over from Jim as chairman in 1989 things were looking pretty rosy. The EEC had introduced "milk quotas" in 1984. This had stabilised their milk production which, although still greater than their consumption, was at least no longer rising. A one-off sale of several hundred thousand tonnes of butter to the Soviet Union had reduced their butter surplus to manageable levels. Much of their skim milk powder surplus had been consumed in a large-scale animal feed programme. Prices had risen as a result, enabling the board to make a farm payout of $5.30 per kg of milk solids for 1989, well above the $3.60 payout of the previous year. In the board's annual report, Jim described the favourable conditions as "sustainable". As we met with farmers around the country, his optimism increased as he told farmers that he was relying on me for his superannuation, and he was expecting $6! Farmers did not observe that his tongue was firmly in his cheek as he made these comments. He made similar comments as we toured Europe and USA immediately prior to his retirement.

Murray and I talked about how we could best structure the board to ensure that it was capable of delivering what we wanted. He had appointed two highly capable executives, John Parker and Phil Lough, as deputy CEOs. Each had a significant commodity trading role. John was to be responsible for the two largest products, butter and milk powder. Those two products also comprised most of our branded consumer business which I was determined to build into a market-leading business. He was well suited to each of those tasks which was unusual as good traders rarely made good consumer marketers. Phil took control of cheese and casein, which were both mainly used as food ingredients. Tailor making specific products to the needs of individual customers was the requirement if we were to improve margins and add value. With his science background, Phil was ideal for this role.

Offshore operations were structured into "regional holding companies", South East Asia head quartered in Singapore, East Asia in Tokyo, North America in Santa Rosa, California. Central and South America was to be located in Fort Lauderdale, Florida where there was a large Latin American population, principally because air services around the region were far superior to any location in South America. Middle East was located in Bahrain, Europe in Hamburg and the jewel in our branded business, Anchor Foods, at Swindon in the UK. Pacific Dairy Products to look after our small but valuable Pacific islands business was located in Aukland. Each regional holding company was to be responsible for the performance, including full profit and loss accountability, of individual countries within their own region. A high level of authority was delegated to them. They were to be fully resourced with strong financial capability and detailed financial reporting obligations. They would be mostly staffed by local employees. Locals would fill most executive positions but there would be judicious use of New Zealanders especially in senior finance, technical and managing director roles. But branded consumer marketing especially required knowledge that only skilled and experienced locals could bring. This was big step towards my commitment to decentralisation. As we put this structure in place, we were intending to employ more highly skilled local executives, who would bring knowledge and skills we did not have. I felt comfortable that we were now well structured to push our value-adding strategies ahead at pace.

During my first year in office in 1989/1990 the world milk supply and demand remained in reasonable balance, resulting in good prices which enabled a 9.4% increase in payout to $5.80 per kilogram. However, in the second half of 1990, consumption had eased back and surplus skim milk powder and butter stocks purchased by the EEC Commission began to increase. Butter, in particular, was again becoming a problem. But in July 1990, under pressure the EU panicked and increased "restitutions" (export subsidies) for skim milk powder by a savage US$550 per tonne. Inevitably, market prices immediately fell by that amount. We and other sellers had no option but to match them if we were to sell our season's production. It was a crazy decision because we knew that the EEC would not sell one extra tonne. What could we do about it? The answer of course was really not much, but I was concerned that when it found that there had been no increase in sales, the EEC might (probably would) be tempted to increase export subsidies again. I immediately sought a meeting with the Minister of Trade Mike Moore with whom I had developed a good relationship. After we both had a good moan, Mike asked me, "What can we do?" I said, "We need to dramatise it. I want you to immediately fly to Brussels with me and ask them not to go ahead with the subsidy increase." Mike's officials who were there immediately advised him not to go. They stated, correctly, that he would be refused. Officials hate their minister going to bat if they think he will fail. They think that he should only intervene if there would be a favourable response and their minister can get some kudos for it. Of course, they were right. There was no way the EEC was going to reverse the increase, I knew that. But my greater concern was that we had no choice but to match their lower prices, they would sell no more and when the EEC realised that their sales had not increased, they could well raise export subsidies again and further drive market prices down. That would bankrupt many farmers. We simply had to prevent that. Mike agreed to consider my request, despite the contrary advice of his officials.

Two days later I received a call from the minister's office asking to see me that afternoon. When I arrived at his office reception area it was crowded with journalists and TV cameras. I immediately knew that the answer would be yes. He was hardly going to say no to me in front of TV cameras. We went into the ministerial conference room; Mike asked me to state our position. I stressed my concern that another increase in export subsidies by the same amount would force our payout down to around $2 a kilogram of milk solids which would bankrupt many of our dairy farmers. We simply had to prevent that from occurring. He then sought the views of his advisers which had not changed; they remained opposed. Mike then summed up the issues, thanked his advisers for their "professional advice" and announced that he had decided to go.

I left my Wellington flat at Herbert Gardens at 8 pm on a Monday evening to fly to Brussels with Mike and Murray Gough. The European holiday period was just starting, MacSharry was scheduled to go on leave and was most reluctant to see us. But Mike had secured a meeting with Frans Andriessen, the EEC foreign affairs commissioner and former agriculture commissioner with whom he had a very good relationship. Andriessen was a smart, urbane Dutchman, who had preceded MacSharry as agriculture commissioner.

They did not get on with one another personally and had different perspectives. MacSharry saw himself as the defender of European farmers and was thus basically opposed to significant trade reform, while Andriessen was supportive of trade liberalisation. With Andriessen agreeing to meet with us, MacSharry had little option but to delay his leave and take a meeting with the New Zealand trade minister.

In the thirty hours or so that it took us to fly to Brussels, New Zealand's Ministry of Foreign Affairs ran a major lobbying campaign. Every EEC member country ambassador in New Zealand was called in and advised of the damage that the EEC action was causing New Zealand. New Zealand ambassadors located in the EEC member states sought meetings with the Minister of Foreign Affairs to convey the same message. When we arrived in Brussels, Murray and I were briefed by the New Zealand ambassador and his officials (this was the first time I met Tim Groser) who reported that it was clear that most European states were embarrassed by the move. We were getting some traction. We had a great meeting with Andriessen, but MacSharry was a different story. Most of his staff had gone on leave so his normally busy office was quiet and almost empty. He had been scheduled to be on leave also but had to stay back to meet us and was dressed in sports clothes. He was anything but quiet and relaxed, however, immediately going straight onto the attack, vigorously laying into the New Zealand Dairy Board, trying to put a wedge between the board and New Zealand Government. I am sure that his voice could be heard down the corridor. He was being told by his traders that they could not match our prices and berated us for capturing most of the market. He accused us of undercutting the market price. He did not seem to understand that while his farmers received a "guaranteed" milk price, supported by EEC taxpayers even if their product was not sold, our farmers got nothing at all for product that we could not sell. We simply had to meet the market and sell, whatever the price. He could not understand what the fuss was all about, believing that he had taken a simple administrative decision to even up the playing field. He was highly annoyed at having to have to stay back from his leave, and I think was embarrassed at the position that he was now in with his fellow commissioners. So, for him, attack was the best form of defence. Twenty minutes into the meeting it was an absolute slug fest and I was wracking my brains trying to think of how I could get us out of what had degenerated into a verbal brawl and back to a rational discussion. Although he calmed down as the meeting progressed, he did not give an inch and refused to assure us that there would not be further subsidy increases. After the meeting when Mike and I climbed into the back seat of his ministerial car in the basement of the Berlaymont, the EEC Commission headquarters, Mike put his head in his hands and said, "F**k, in all my life I have never experienced anything like that!"

We were in Brussels a little over twenty-four hours. I kept both my watch and my body cycle on New Zealand time while we were there. We departed straight after our meetings and I was home on the farm for lunch on Friday. A whirlwind trip but ultimately successful, as further increases in EEC export subsidies disappeared off the radar screen. We had simply made it politically too difficult for the Agriculture Commission to take that route, so job done. But MacSharry was certainly the toughest person I ever dealt with in my career.

The damage had been done, however. In 1991 we largely sold our production, although butter was difficult; the EEC sold no more but we both received much lower prices. In October 1990 we had to reduce our advance payout by 40 cents and our payout for the 1991 year was reduced to $3.70. We took a thirty-minute slot on TV1 at 10 am when I explained to farmers what had caused such a disastrous fall on the previous year. It helped them to understand what had happened even if it did not make them happy. A couple of weeks later I held a cowshed meeting with some of the farmers in my ward. I explained what had happened. They listened carefully to what I had to say, then I took questions. One guy who would often challenge me cleared his throat. I thought, "Here it comes." To my surprise he said, "Dryden, you just have to stay chairman for ten years." I thought, wow, and asked why. He replied, "When Jim Graham became chairman, the payout fell, now you have become chairman and there has been an even bigger drop, you just have to stay as chairman for ten years; we cannot afford another change!"

In the second half of 1990 butter was again a problem. EEC stocks had built up to over 300,000 tonnes. USA also had about 100,000-tonne surplus stock which they wished to sell. We had a carryover of stock from the previous year of about 50,000 tonnes which looked likely to increase to close to 100,000 by year end. There was no home for those volumes anywhere in the world unless a sale to Russia could be engineered. Our intelligence suggested that they wanted to buy around 350,000 tonnes at very low prices. We simply had to clinch a sale at the best price we could get. First, we had to obtain a derogation (exemption) from the GATT minimum price for butter of US$1300 per tonne.

We had done that by October 1990 when Murray and I were in Brussels for what was supposed to be the final Uruguay Round negotiations. The problem we had was that there was a lot more butter available than the Russians wanted to buy. If they were really smart, they could play the various suppliers off against one another and keep driving the price down. We wanted to prevent that which meant we somehow had to reduce both the tonnage being offered and the number of offerors. While in Brussels we met with Guy Legras, EEC director general of agriculture. Small in stature, he had a big mind, was smart and very tough. On this occasion, however, he was much more accommodating. We understood that Russia wanted about

350,000 tonnes. He agreed to let us carry out initial negotiations with Russia to set the price; he knew that we would obtain a much better price than EEC traders. He was happy to restrict the volume from the EEC to 200,000 tonnes. We needed to sell close to 100,000 tonnes to clear our stock. Smaller surpluses available from other countries including Sweden, and a few other non-EEC European countries, had the potential to sell at even lower prices so we decided to cover their requirements to eliminate their disruptive influence. I got in touch with them and undertook to cover their requirements. I was also on the phone to my friend Pat Rowley, chairman of Australian Dairy Farmers Federation whom I greatly respected. I offered to cover their requirements if they refrained from negotiations until we had concluded. While all this was going on, John Parker was in Moscow negotiating a deal.

That left USA, who were our biggest concern. They had a significant surplus of 100,000 tonnes which they wished to dispose of. They had no dairy trading experience and had the potential to completely disrupt any reasonable deal if they offered. We were fortunate to obtain a short notice meeting with the US Secretary of Agriculture Clayton Yeutter who subsequently was to become a good friend. I needed to get to Washington in a hurry so flew from Brussels on Concorde. It was a fascinating experience. Concorde flew at a much higher altitude than normal airliners and you could see the curvature of the earth. The normally eight-and-a-half-hour journey took a little over four hours. Our meeting went well but as I expected, while assuring me that he understood our position and had no desire to disadvantage New Zealand, Clayton would not undertake to refrain from negotiations with Russia until we had completed. What I did not expect, however, was to receive a letter a week later explicitly refusing my request. I guess that he was just covering himself, as in the end they kept out of the market. John Parker concluded a contract which took care of our requirements at a price which although low was rather better than we expected and much better than we feared. That eased our immediate problem. I was on a pretty steep learning curve on trade policy and international negotiations and was learning fast. Importantly, the butter sales to Russia by ourselves and the EU, in conjunction with some other developments, resulted in a much-improved payout for 1992 of $5.20 per kilogram.

THIRTY-FOUR
TRADE REFORM

Of all the challenges and issues the New Zealand dairy industry faced in the 1980s and 1990s, trade reform was the greatest as global milk production climbed steadily through the period. Farm subsidies soared and world dairy prices were determined largely by political decisions on farmer milk prices in the EEC and to a lesser extent USA. When Britain entered the EU in 1973, New Zealand was supplying 180,000 tonnes of butter and cheese to the UK, 74% of our total production. Under "Protocol 18", the terms of Britain's entry were that New Zealand would progressively exit the UK market and the EEC would not frustrate New Zealand's efforts to diversify its markets. But that is just what they did. They did not do it deliberately to damage us; it was just a consequence of how governments inevitably underestimate the consequences of price changes on production and consumption. By 1983 when New Zealand's right of entry to UK for butter and cheese had fallen by almost half, the EEC had increased its milk production by more than three times New Zealand's annual production. Their consumption had barely increased so they were attempting to export most of that extra milk. I say "attempting" as world markets were quite unable to consume that extra supply so by the second half of the 1980s most of it was surplus, being owned by the EEC Government and stored in European warehouses and cool stores. These surplus stocks (for which there was no home) peaked at around 1.2 million tonnes of butter, at a time when the accessible world butter market totalled around 300,000 tonnes, and 1.5 million tonnes of skim milk powder. As would be expected with such oversupply, prices were severely depressed and our farmer payouts low. The EEC was also getting into a similar oversupply situation in other agricultural products and disrupting those markets. The USA had an endemic annual surplus of butter of around 100,000 tonnes while skim milk powder surpluses fluctuated. Food-exporting countries, like New Zealand, and their farmers were being severely disadvantaged and no relief was in sight.

In 1986 under the auspices of GATT, and largely led by the USA, a negotiating round was launched at Punta del Este, Uruguay. For the first time agriculture was on the negotiating agenda, having been excluded from the seven previous GATT negotiating rounds. Trade in manufactured goods had been comprehensively covered in the previous GATT rounds. Now most of the industrialised nations of the world urgently wanted agreements in the new trade areas of services and investment, which meant that agricultural exporters now had something to trade off.

Multilateral trade negotiations in the GATT involving 108 sovereign states were notoriously difficult. There was a huge risk that the most difficult areas like agriculture, particularly dairy, could again be put into the too-hard basket and completely left out of any agreement. That would be a disaster for us as any leverage food exporters now had would be lost for ever. We could not allow that to happen. Previous GATT rounds had usually been sorted out between Europe and the USA, but this time Bill Brock, the US trade representative, urged the agricultural exporting countries to work together to increase their leverage. So, the Cairns Group of nineteen agricultural exporting countries, led by Australia and including Brazil, Argentina and other South American countries as well as Canada and New Zealand, was formed. The group worked collectively and built significant influence. It resolved that there would be no agreement without agriculture being included.

The preparatory work had gone well. The negotiations were due to conclude in 1990 at a Ministerial Summit to be held in Brussels in October 1990. Its purpose was to finalise and endorse an agreement reached by their negotiators. There were three areas that the agricultural negotiators were concentrating on:

Market access. This was usually the first weapon used to protect farmers and most countries used it. Close the borders to food imports and keep out competition, or impose tariffs to prevent competitive imports. Of course, this is exactly what New Zealand did with manufactured goods until the mid-eighties. Previous GATT negotiating rounds had largely eliminated the closing of borders to industrial goods and limited tariffs to low levels of 10% or so. But not so for dairy. We regarded "low" tariffs as below 30%. Most were higher, often hundreds of per cent. On one occasion when addressing the Japan–New Zealand Business Council meeting in Auckland, I caused consternation to our Japanese friends by disclosing that Japan's tariff on New Zealand butter was 880%. This could not be correct, "Japan is a 'free trading country" our Japanese friends exclaimed. Of course, Japan is anything but. Faxes flew to and from Japan and our Japanese friends were suitably embarrassed when they found that my statement was correct.

Domestic subsidies: Most of the world's richer countries had an objective of ensuring that farm incomes matched non-farm incomes. They usually did this by setting product prices which were sufficiently high to achieve that. If markets did not support that price level, governments intervened financially, either by making up any price difference or by buying sufficient product and taking it off the market to cause prices to rise. This is what both the EEC and USA did. It was a dumb system. Farmers everywhere are smart. Their reaction to price signals is entirely logical. High prices paid to producers result in them producing more milk, while those high prices charged on to consumers lower consumption. Surpluses owned by the EEC and USA governments were created and held in store while they worked out what to do with them. Milk and sugar were the two products most affected, although other products like beef, poultry and grain inevitably experienced the same circumstances. Budgetary costs were huge. It would have cost them much less to let markets operate normally and make welfare payments to farmers to support their income. But then no farmer anywhere in the world would want that.

Subsidised exports: Having created surpluses the countries that did so had a problem. What to do with them? Disposing of them on their domestic market would create a bigger problem. For example, surplus butter released onto their own market would completely crash prices to unacceptably low levels until the surpluses were consumed. Skim milk powder could be sold for stock food, but the price would need to be subsidised to be competitive with grain. Any significant volume would disrupt the grain market, pushing grain prices down, thus requiring compensation payments to grain farmers. Oh, and with lower grain prices dairy farmers would feed more to their cows and produce more milk! There was never an easy answer on the domestic market. But a problem shared is a problem eased so the easy solution was to export it and that is just what they did. That pushed the prices we received down.

But to export surplus dairy products is costly. First, there was the sheer scale of the problem. At peak towards the end of the 1980s, EEC surplus stocks of butter reached 1.2 million tonnes. Total accessible world markets for butter were only around 300,000 tonnes, and New Zealand had about 250,000 tonnes of it, so markets simply were not available anywhere in the world at any price. Skim milk powder stocks peaked at around 1.5 million tonnes. Our skim milk powder sales totalled 180,000 tonnes. The surpluses held by the EEC had been purchased at a price which was three times or more higher than the traded world market price. So, to dispose of the surpluses they had purchased, the EEC would have to sell products at a third of the price which it had paid to purchase them. The difference or "export subsidy" (refunds or restitutions the EEC called them) had to be paid from the EEC Budget. These subsidies set the world market price. As their surpluses rose, the EEC increased the per tonne "export subsidy", which then forced international prices down. Prices were permanently depressed and throughout the 1980s trended lower. The GATT Uruguay Round had to address this area.

Something had to be done in all three areas in the Uruguay Round. We wanted greater access to markets, that was the ultimate but the most politically difficult, while the benefits were longer term. Anything which reduced profitability of milk production in Europe and the USA would also lower production so reducing domestic support was very much in our interest. Eliminating export subsidies could be easily done, however, and would provide significant and early benefit to us.

As we went around the capitals in Europe, USA and other regions of the world, we pushed the need for the Uruguay Round to reach a meaningful agreement on agriculture. We pointed out that food-exporting countries like New Zealand had to earn a living from food exports. That they had to be able to export profitably to be able to buy the goods that others wished to sell to them. We pointed out to Europeans that virtually every drop of milk we produced was processed on European-supplied processing equipment; most of our exports were carried on British, Danish, French, Dutch, German and

Italian vessels; our insurance was placed in the London market and much of our finance came from European markets. It was in their interests for dairy trading conditions to be improved. These arguments resonated with business and those ministries responsible for trade and commerce. We decided to step up our representations with those groups.

I had earlier met with representatives of the British Conference Shipping Lines when they had visited New Zealand. During the course of our discussions, I had stressed the importance of the Uruguay Round to New Zealand and thus to their business with us. Their chairman, Alan Bott, asked if they could do anything to help. I asked if he would coordinate lobbying with their own governments by a group of European companies who did significant business with the New Zealand dairy industry. He willingly agreed to do so. I then wrote to the CEOs (all of whom I knew personally) of several European industrial and services companies which did significant business with the New Zealand dairy industry and asked them to make representations to their own government in support of a good agriculture agreement in the Uruguay Round. They all agreed to do so. This was later to prove extremely important.

Our discussions around the world suggested that most countries and groups genuinely desired a successful GATT Round. As expected, this was rather stronger in the business community than it was among farmers. However, even the farming community recognised the need for some reform but were scared that their interests would be sacrificed in the interests of others. They therefore were redoubling their efforts to protect their position. The main objective of the negotiations was to improve access and reduce the total amount which each country spent subsidising agriculture. The general belief among the negotiators was that this would eliminate the problems. It would, ultimately. However, as we met our contacts around the world it was clear to us that farmers would fight hard to protect their markets against imports and to retain subsidies which directly protected their income. History suggested they would probably succeed.

Export subsidies were different. They did not directly affect farmers' incomes and had no moral justification. Farmers tended to hang their heads when we told them that while we respected their desire to protect their own domestic market, we could not live with having the markets to which we did have access destroyed by their surpluses being dumped in to those markets. We decided that we could live with minimal access improvement and a modest reduction in domestic subsidies if we could get a significant reduction in export subsidies. It would also make an agreement much more likely as powerful farmer opposition would be more muted. It was the one area we believed would most likely be accepted by European and US farmers. It would also bring greater benefit earlier to our farmers. We decided to focus on export subsidies and managed to persuade our trade officials to agree.

Murray and I decided to attend the GATT Summit in Brussels in October 1990. We wanted to be in the same building where decisions would be made, when they were made. New Zealand was seen as the most affected and knowledgeable on world dairy trade. We could not be in the "room" when decisions were made but we could be just outside the door. National had been elected a couple of weeks before and my good friend Jim Bolger was prime minister. Philip Burdon, whom I rated, was now trade minister and would attend, but I urged Jim to lead the New Zealand delegation. Mike Moore had done a great job on the preparatory work over the previous five years. He had a strong network and still had much to contribute, so I urged Jim to include Mike on the team, which he magnanimously agreed to do.

The Draft Agreement was encouraging but had some important provisions still not agreed. It was expected that the summit would resolve them, and we would leave Brussels at the end of the week with an acceptable agreement. But it was not to be that easy. The EEC dug in and strongly resisted some of the "draft" agriculture provisions, thus confirming our early belief about the sensitivity of increasing market access where the draft provided for imports comprising at least 5% of a domestic market to be allowed. We understood that the EEC was prepared to accept 3%. With the gap being only between 3% and 5% the differences seemed to be capable of solution. But Europe's MacSharry dug in and was unable to be moved. We understood that there was a huge fight going on inside the EEC delegation between Agriculture Commissioner MacSharry and Trade Commissioner Andriessen. It was a real advantage having Jim there. As the only prime minister attending, he gained access to individuals and discussions which would not normally involve New Zealand.

For a whole week we waited around the venue while the negotiators slugged it out. We were not idle, however. We talked with our farmer, business and government contacts from around the world attempting to influence them. I made a phone call to Alan Bott asking him to contact those on our commercial partners list and ask them to personally contact their prime ministers, urging them to intervene to facilitate agreement. They responded magnificently and a few weeks later Alan was to copy me with the replies that each of them had received from their prime minister. There was a huge media presence, so to keep the pressure on we held media conferences together with our Cairns Group friends to push our point of view and to expose the stupidity and downright unfairness of the EEC Common Agriculture policy. It was news to most of the world's media.

But by the end of the week, agreement had eluded the negotiators. While the EEC stood firm, the Cairns Group stayed staunch and the

EEC was learning that no longer would they get their way if they dug in and continued to refuse to move for long enough. The EEC genuinely wanted an agreement. In the past they would have cobbled together something with the USA and the rest of the world would just have had to accept it. Dairy probably would have been sacrificed as it was the most politically sensitive for Europe and of only limited interest to the USA. The Cairns Group changed that. They would not move till a reasonable agreement was reached on agriculture. Our role was to ensure that there would be no agreement unless it included a reasonable deal on dairy.

As the negotiations inexorably headed to breakdown, I sensed a change in sentiment occurring. All participants really wanted an agreement and were disappointed one had not been concluded. They were now facing the consequences for world trade of failure and did not like what they saw. The European industrial sector was frustrated that in order to protect agriculture, they were being denied the benefits an agreement would bring them. I believed that one more push over the next year or two would probably get us there. That is what I told Richard Griffin when he interviewed me for TVNZ. At the time, though, it was a view which few shared.

When Murray and I visited Europe in 1991 that view was confirmed. Work to recommence negotiations was under way. The phrase "we looked over the abyss and did not like what we saw" was often recited to us. The pressure on the European Commission was working as the member states demanded an agreement. That if giving ground on agriculture was needed, then that was what Europe must do. We continued to push hard on export subsidies. While to date the emphasis had been on reducing export subsidy *dollar* amounts, we reached the view that reducing the *volume* of subsidised exports would be better. Information on export prices was not readily available and could be manipulated with relative ease. Even with a lower dollar value it would be possible to subsidise the same volume of exports, in which case we would receive little or no relief. It was *volume* doing the damage to us, so it was *volume* we had to reduce. Shipping statistics were well kept, reliable and extremely difficult to manipulate, so volume would be much easier to monitor and administrate. We managed to convince our trade officials to push for volume restraints.

The author with World Trade Organisation Director General Arthur Dunkel

We were by now regularly visiting GATT, located in Geneva, where we met with its Director General Arthur Dunkel. We wanted to meet both him and the chairman of the Agricultural Negotiating Committee, a Dutchman named Art de Zeeuw, to push our case on export subsidy volume reductions. We tried to set up a short notice meeting with them. We would have preferred to see them together but only Dunkel was in Geneva. I had recently met with Dunkel so we split our team with my deputy chairman, Peter Jensen, and Murray going to Geneva to meet him, while Peter Robertson, our UK director, and I flew to The Hague to meet De Zeeuw whom I had not previously met. He was still thinking in dollar terms but engaged constructively with us. He was later to tell me that he had been convinced by New Zealand, against his will, to support volume-reduction commitments.

Work continued and an agreement was eventually reached at a ministerial meeting held in Marrakech, Morocco in 1994. While developing countries would have lesser obligations, developed countries would be required to:

- Provide minimum access to each market of 3% of domestic consumption, rising to 5 % over five years. This provided little immediate increase as the actual level of dairy imports at that time was probably around 2.5%. However, it amounted to a doubling in volume over five years which was really significant. Our UK butter quota was made permanent at the current volume so we would face no further reduction. It was also converted into an EU (as the EEC had by now become) quota, rather than a UK quota, which opened up new opportunities to us on mainland Europe.
- Average tariffs on imports were to be reduced over five years by 36%, or a minimum of 15% on any single product.
- Total subsidies were to be reduced by 20% over five years.
- Export subsidised volumes were to reduce by 21% and the budgetary cost by 36% over five years.
- Another important agreement was to establish a disputes resolution process with the power to make binding decisions where the World Trade Organisation (as it became known) rules were broken.

We believed that this would be a game changer. While it would take time, five years or probably longer, the volume of subsidised dairy products flooding onto world markets would be sharply reduced as the agreement was fully implemented. The total package of measures would force the subsidising countries to get their production into balance with their consumption. Murray Gough had by this time retired, but we had a good idea of the likely outcome before he left.

We had thought about its implications. It would be a game breaker for New Zealand. The EU would be supplying lower export volumes. World dairy prices would rise substantially. How high would they go? We believed they would be capped at the domestic price level of the next large-scale producer, which was the USA. If world prices rose permanently above the USA domestic price, it would be inevitable that production in the USA would expand and they would become an exporter of some scale. Our assessment proved to be correct. As we moved into the 2000s, dairy prices improved from around US$1300/$1400 per tonne for butter to the US$3000s and ultimately much higher, while skim milk powder rose from around US$1600 per tonne to over $3000, broadly in line with US domestic prices.

As expected, offending countries tried every trick in the book to weasel out of, or delay, their obligations, so much tough negotiation still lay ahead. They reached back several years to their highest subsidy years to establish the bases from which they had to reduce. They pushed back the starting year and extended the full implementation date. But in the end they had to fully comply.

There was an interesting little side play during the conclusion of the negotiations. I received a call at 3 am from our trade minister Philip Burdon from Marrakech. It was a call I was expecting to advise me of where the negotiations were settling and seeking my endorsement of the emerging agreement. Of course, I was delighted. What I was not expecting, though, was to be told that the EU had offered us a larger tariff reduction in return for agreeing to reduce the volume of our European butter quota. This seemed to me to be a good deal. We would get more money from a lower volume and we would be free to sell the foregone volume elsewhere. I cannot recall the amount but it was over $30 million plus whatever we realised from the sale elsewhere of the displaced tonnage. I immediately phoned Warren Larsen who had succeeded Murray as CEO. He consulted with Nigel

Mitchell, our external policy manager. They agreed, albeit reluctantly. I phoned Philip Burdon back and gave him the go ahead. I believed it to be a very good deal. However, when over the next few weeks the details were being formally concluded Warren got cold feet and reneged. He had appointed a new manager of our butter sales division who was an IT person with no sales experience. Butter was the most difficult product to sell anyhow and as he was finding it difficult to quit our total production, he found the prospect of deliberately selling less to the EU, even at higher total return, to be most unappealing. I was happy to take the money and back our ability to sell the displaced volume elsewhere in a market which was going to improve anyhow. Warren took the issue to the board. Having for years experienced difficulty in finding a home for butter and having fought so long and hard to maintain our butter quota volume, it was difficult for my directors with their chairman and CEO disagreeing. But they had been fixated on volume for so long that they found it difficult to understand that the market dynamics were changing. They supported Warren. Philip Burdon and Ministry of Foreign Affairs and Trade officials were astounded.

Of course, the Uruguay Round Agreement was not fully implemented by 1998 which was the deal. In fact, it took closer to ten years. While this was frustrating and kept prices at lower levels through that period, the trend was in the right direction and prices improved as the volume of subsidised exports being dumped on world markets reduced and the EU was forced to get milk supply into balance with its consumption. World dairy markets were now on a much more sustainable basis, were becoming properly commercial and the outlook for New Zealand was encouraging. It all played out pretty much as Murray and I had foreseen back in 1993. The payback for New Zealand from the Uruguay Round Agreement was ultimately in the order of $8 to $10 billion per annum. A big deal which was an exciting experience to have been involved in.

The New Zealand Ministry of Trade had a very small team working on the negotiations. They were extremely competent and highly regarded around the world. There were also a handful of New Zealanders employed in the GATT Secretariat who were of similar ilk. Through the negotiations these two groups played a critical role in achieving the dairy outcome we were seeking. New Zealand dairy farmers and their country owe them much.

THIRTY-FIVE
THE TRAVELLER

My workload was increasing. I had committed myself to visit each of the board's offshore companies in my first three years. I wanted to understand our markets, but I particularly wished to be in touch with our people. We were placing huge responsibility for the welfare of New Zealand farmers in the hands of very few people, many of whom were also very young and relatively inexperienced. I wanted our people to know that New Zealand was interested in them. Believing that would help build team spirit and performance. But I also wanted our offshore staff to be aware that back in New Zealand 14,000 farming families and their employees were depending on them. I knew that I could convey that message effectively. I also believed that it would be extremely motivating to our staff.

When I visited our offshore subsidiaries I would receive a presentation on company performance, visit each of the facilities in that country and try to meet individually every staff member from the CEO to the storeman. This gave me a pretty good understanding of the business, the quality of our people and the issues the business faced in that country or region. I was closely observing the country or regional heads and their executive teams. They would be the basis of our success. We were greatly relying on them and intended to give them even more authority and responsibility. I wanted to be satisfied that we had the right people in the right places.

My visits also facilitated valuable government and senior customer access which would not normally be available to our off shore people. Much of our sales were to countries which had government-owned "single-buying" agencies. Most countries had tariffs on imported dairy products which were often substantial. Wealthier western countries restricted access to their markets, allowing only relatively small import quotas. I frequently met with ministers and senior government officials, advancing the case of the New Zealand Dairy Board being a good reliable supplier of quality dairy products, which always delivered. I pushed hard for tariffs to be eased. Ministers often asked for our help in developing their own dairy industry. That of course was the last thing we wanted to do. There was no way we wanted milk production to increase in those countries to which we had access. But we did become skilled at appearing to help, without actually doing much of substance, and at establishing political goodwill without helping increase milk production, which was likely to reduce our sales.

I was soon spending over a hundred days each year travelling. It was exhausting but I was young and able to handle it. I was overseas each month, mostly departing on a Saturday or Sunday, usually at night. When I got to Auckland Airport, a brief would be waiting for me. I would read it on the plane into the small hours of the morning and then try to get some sleep. I usually planned to arrive at my destination on Sunday. When I reached my hotel, I would spend whatever remained of the day carefully preparing for each of my meetings for the week ahead. It was quite a task on my European trip where I could have over thirty meetings scheduled for the week.

Then a good night's sleep to be fit and fresh, ready to go on Monday morning.

Returning home was rather more difficult. I usually left on Friday evening, which meant arriving in Auckland on Sunday morning. I would drive home, have a shower and lunch, and then head into my office until about 10 pm to prepare for the board meeting. Next morning, up at 5 am to catch the 7 am flight to Wellington for a board meeting, starting at 1 pm on Monday. On arrival at my office, I would be briefed on the major issues prior to the board meeting. Then spend two or three days chairing a board meeting, handling jet lag as best I could. It was always a tough week.

Russia was an important market for our butter. Without them in the 1980s there would have been years when we would not have sold all of the butter we produced. Even more importantly, on some occasions when EEC butter surplus stocks were depressing world prices, they purchased large volumes from Europe which had eased the pressure on the international butter market. While their purchases were not regular, depending largely on the availability of foreign currency, we had established New Zealand as their supplier of "first choice". Russia was thus very important to us. As the USSR Government was the actual buyer, I needed to get close to the Soviet Ambassador, Yuri Sokolov. He was a fine man and we became friends. After he had returned home, I was subsequently to visit him at his home when visiting Moscow.

Russia was an irregular customer but as we were dependent on the sale of a significant volume of butter to them each year, the board had facilitated more regular purchases by granting them credit. The normal terms provided a five-year credit at market interest rates. Vneshneconom Bank, the Soviet foreign transactions bank, guaranteed the debt. This arrangement had been in place for many years and had always been scrupulously met on due date, by the Soviet Government. When under President Mikhael Gorbachev the Soviet Union began to break up in 1989, it failed to meet the payment of around US$100 million which was due in 1990, a few months after I became chairman. When the National Party, led by Jim Bolger, became government, I went to Trade Minister Philip Burdon and asked him to make a ministerial visit to Russia and seek payment. He readily agreed and in due course succeeded. However, by the end of 1990 a further tranche of credit had become overdue. Again, I called on Philip Burdon who firmly advised me that he had collected the last cheque for us, but he was not going to visit Moscow each year to collect our debts. It was pretty much the response I had expected, but I had another card up my sleeve.

I went to the prime minister and was able to persuade him to undertake a prime ministerial visit to Moscow. It was not just the Dairy Board who had overdue debt with the Soviets. The ANZ Bank had a large debt for wool purchases also overdue. Russia was an important market for butter, wool and mutton. The Soviet Union was gone. The new Russian Federation comprising 70% of the old Soviet Union had emerged and was looking for friends. It had elected a new President in Boris Yeltsin, so it was a timely occasion for a prime ministerial visit.

In advance of the prime minister's visit to Moscow, the Russian Vice President Alexander Rutskoy visited New Zealand accompanied by the Economics Minister Bakaev. I hosted the vice president to breakfast; he arrived an hour late and had obviously had a big night. I explained to him that we had supplied butter on credit to the Soviet Union for many years, including a period during the Cold War when few would do so. Now we were faced with a large overdue debt. I pointed out to him that it was not a debt owed to the government of New Zealand but rather to 14,000 farming families. I told him that we knew that Russia urgently needed more butter to feed its people. We were prepared to supply it, but only if their debt to us was paid. I did not tell him that we urgently needed to make a sale to them to clear our season's production. The meeting went well. Vice President Rutskoy believed that Russian honour was at stake and undertook to do all that he could to ensure the debt was paid.

I accompanied the prime minister to Moscow where I was joined by John Parker. The path had been well prepared by our government officials who as usual had done a thorough job. The night before our meetings were to be held, Russian Prime Minister Viktor Chernomyrdin told Jim over dinner that First Deputy Prime Minister Alexander Shokhin, who was responsible for finance, and whom we were to meet next day, had been authorised to settle the matter.

Off we went next morning in the prime minister's cavalcade of ZIL limousines. Police cars aplenty with motorcycle outriders accompanying us, all with sirens screaming, we raced through the streets of Moscow to the old Communist Party Headquarters where we were immediately ushered into a conference room. While not palatial, the building was more comfortably appointed than any other government office I had visited in Moscow. Our intelligence suggested that we had little chance of full repayment of our debt of US$200 million. But it also confirmed that Russia urgently wanted to purchase a large volume of butter. We badly needed to make a large sale to them. We decided to seek an immediate payment of US$30 million with commitment to a schedule for repayment of the remainder of our debt. In return we would negotiate a new agreement for the sale of butter. Shokhin was blond, young, smart and very personable. He and Jim exchanged pleasantries. "Welcome to Moscow, my dear Prime Minister." "It is a pleasure to be here, my dear Deputy Prime Minister, thank you for meeting with us," replied Jim. In due course we got to the commercial issues of the butter and wool debts. Jim asked his "technical people" to explain their issues and invited me to address Shokhin. I took him through the background: Russia a valued customer; New Zealand Dairy Board had traded with Russia for many years; we had provided butter and financial credit when few would do so; the debt was owed not to New Zealand but to 14,000 farming families; we understood the difficult situation Russia found itself in and sympathised with them; we would be prepared to settle for payment of US$30 million now and a three-year schedule for payment of the balance; in return we would sell them more butter. Peter Hawkins, CEO of ANZ New Zealand, then covered the smaller wool debt.

Shokhin replied, explaining that he was negotiating "schemes of arrangement" to reschedule Russia's debts with the "Paris Club" (government debt) and the "London Club" (private-sector debt). As is usual in those circumstances all creditors must be treated equally. While US$30 million was only a small amount, giving us priority would collapse the complex international agreements he was negotiating. Then out of the blue he staggered us: "My dear Prime Minister, I am sorry that I cannot accommodate New Zealand, US$30 million is a trifling sum, why, it is only a MiG fighter plane. Would you accept a MiG fighter, maybe two? We have plenty of those." My mind was racing at ninety miles per hour trying to calculate if we could sell them and for how much. It would not be the first time the Dairy Board had accepted assets in payment of a debt, although never military equipment. Jim was equal to the task. "My dear Deputy Prime Minister, New Zealand is a peace-loving country. We believe in peace through trade. I could not possibly go back to New Zealand with a couple of war planes." "What about a nuclear submarine then?" Shokhin replied. "We have some of those." "That would be worse; we have an anti-nuclear policy," said Jim, throwing his hands up in the air. "You would not have to fight with it, you could use it to generate electricity," retorted Shokhin. He seemed to be serious and probably was. Under communism, Russia had spent huge sums on arms but now had no money to feed their people, but it did have a large amount of surplus weaponry.

But they were still keen to get their hands on butter. Eventually Jim and Shokin agreed that the New Zealand Dairy Board and his people should have further discussions and endeavour to work "something" out. Jim was meeting President Boris Yeltsin that afternoon and indicated that he would raise our debt with him if no agreement had been reached by then. But he would much prefer to not have to. Shokhin seemed keen to avoid Jim raising it with Yeltsin.

The meeting ended and Russian officials swept me up and whisked me away through a labyrinth of corridors to a meeting room. I was by myself so insisted they find John Parker. He joined us and we got down to business. We battled away for about five hours hammering out an agreement to supply a large volume of butter at prices which we were happy with, conditional of course on receiving US$30 million and a commitment to repay the balance of our debt over a three to five-year period. We finalised a heads of agreement just before we had to leave for the airport. When the Russian minister who had led the negotiations passed the agreement across to the head of Prodintorg (the Russian buying agency) to sign rather than sign it himself, I realised that we had been played.

The US$30 million was never forthcoming so over the next two years we progressively sold the debt on the commercial debt market. As you would expect it had to be deeply discounted, but over a three-year period we recovered 48.6% of our total debt. Under the circumstances that was a reasonable recovery from a bad situation, certainly better than waiting for payment as Russia finally repaid all of its commercial debt from that period about 30 years later in 2017.

Having observed just how hard and effectively Government and the Ministry of Foreign Affairs and Trade worked for our dairy farmers, I decided very early in my term to do everything I could to help the government. I resolved to do whatever they asked of me. Of course, I would never refuse a request from Prime Minister Jim Bolger. I was often asked by the State Services Commission to join panels tasked with choosing government department heads. I was involved on three occasions in choosing the head of the Department of Prime Minister and Cabinet. In 1992 I was asked by Jim to join David Richwhite, Sir John Anderson and Hugh Fletcher to advise the prime minister on establishing a Prime Minister's Enterprise Council which I was to serve on for a number of years. We were also tasked with advising on developing a "Vision for New Zealand" which Jim wanted to take to the country at the 1993 General Election.

Given that the Dairy Board was the leading exporter in New Zealand and by far the largest business trading with our main trading partners, I was in demand to join many international business councils, agreeing to join the Advisory Board of the Japan–New Zealand Business Council and to become Patron of the Thailand–New Zealand Business Council and Honorary Chairman of the Philippines–New Zealand Business Council. After my retirement I was to become chairman and a life member of the ASEAN New Zealand Business Council. I also accepted appointment to the board of Asia 2000, now Asia New Zealand Foundation, of which I later became chairman.

I was always looking to how we could improve governance standards in the industry, particularly how we could improve the skills of individual directors. I was constantly looking for courses which I could recommend to my directors. I had been a member of the Institute of Directors in New Zealand since soon after its inception about 1978. It was an offshoot of the UK Institute and was a largely passive organisation. In the early 1990s, Geoffrey Bowes became the first full-time executive director. He began to increase the activity of the Institute, much of it in training, and lifted its profile. One day he and Dennis Griffin, who was president, came to see me. They wanted to set up a training course for directors. They intended to use the directors course run by the University of New England in New South

Wales and rewrite it to suit New Zealand governance requirements. I offered to underwrite the cost of doing so and undertook also to guarantee 50% of the places on the first course. I negotiated a reduced membership subscription for dairy company directors. I then contacted every dairy company chairman, asking them to have each of their directors join the Institute. I also sought their support by providing directors to fill the slots I had reserved on the first course. This gave the Institute a massive kick start which Geoffrey very effectively built on to make Institute membership a "must have" for directors.

I had a high profile and a very extensive network. I also maintained a punishing public-speaking schedule. I rarely declined an invitation to speak whether it was to farmers, business groups, non-farming entities, Rotary or Lions Clubs. I saw communicating with farmers and the New Zealand public as an important part of the job. I received many requests to address international groups, many of them quite prestigious, but was more selective about accepting those as they were very time-consuming and the travel exhausting.

THIRTY-SIX
A NEW CHIEF EXECUTIVE

By 1992 I felt that we were making good progress against my objectives. A strategic plan had been completed with an ambitious "mission" for the New Zealand Dairy Board to become the "world's leading dairy marketer".

A small Consumer Marketing Group had been established to drive the growth in branded consumer sales which were increasing spectacularly. With the skilled input of our partners in Sri Lanka, The Maharajah Group, Anchor had displaced Nestlé as No. 1, the first time we had ever achieved that. Dr Ong Poh Seng, who had joined the board from Wrigleys Chewing Gum, was an outstanding brand marketer. He had built a formidable team in Singapore and was achieving considerable success in rolling out branded consumer products across the South East Asian region. A training academy had been established under him and several of our most promising young people were sent there each year. In the 1993 financial year, total consumer pack sales reached an astonishing 230,000 tonnes or 25% of our export business.

Decentralisation of our marketing activities was well under way. Regional holding companies had been established and were making an impact under the leadership of some very good executives, some of whom were both new to the board and nationals of the region they were heading up. They were soon finding new opportunities. Marketing companies had been established in several new countries. R&D centres had been established in Singapore and Hamburg to provide in-market support to our value-adding activities. These were identifying new product and marketing opportunities.

We were reducing our exposure to butter and skim milk powder through rapidly increasing sales of whole milk powder which had reached a total of 255,000 tonnes. Few of our competitors could supply whole milk powder as it did not qualify for export subsidies.

An agreement in the Uruguay Round was looking highly likely, on terms which would permanently reform world dairy trade by improving market access for our products and reducing and ultimately ending export subsidy competition. The medium- and longer-term outlook for New Zealand was highly encouraging. I was feeling pretty comfortable and pleased at the progress which was being made towards achieving my strategic objectives.

I was enjoying working with Murray and we were a formidable team. The one year he had given me when I became chairman had become three. He seemed to remain enthusiastic and I was hopeful that he would continue. But in mid-1992 what I had expected, but hoped would not, happen came to pass. Murray advised me that he would like to finish at the end of the year. I was unable to talk him out of it. So, the unwelcome task of finding a new CEO was now in front of me.

Hiring a new CEO is the most important task directors ever undertake. Get it wrong and the consequences can be disastrous. It is also a potentially destabilising time for any corporation. Staff who are happy working for a CEO may not be prepared to work for a successor. Top executives who seek the job and miss out will be disappointed and some will leave. Others who do not expect to get the job may nevertheless be disappointed if they are not considered, taking it as a sign they are not valued. Inevitably, there will be losses of some key people. So, keeping losses of key personnel to a minimum is always a critical objective when hiring a new CEO.

My immediate objective was to give my directors the widest possible range of choices. First, internal candidates had to be identified; then I believed an external search should be commissioned; finally, the process to be followed needed to be developed and agreed by the directors. Murray's intention to retire had been well signalled so he and I had been preparing the organisation for it.

The board was rich in talent. Deputy CEOs John Parker and Phil Lough were top-class executives. Both were long-term executives of the board so had considerable experience in both international dairy marketing and international business. Between them they had largely run the operations of the board for the last three years, so we had plenty of opportunities to observe them. They were each capable of doing the job, making both strong front runners. To increase the options available to the directors, Murray and I had agreed during the previous year to bring Warren Larsen on board. He had a background in wool marketing before becoming CEO of Bay Milk Products, one of our more innovative dairy companies, about seven years previously. He had stand-alone CEO experience, as well as experience in dairy manufacturing, and international marketing experience outside of dairy. He thus brought different skills and experience for us to consider. He had been recruited to head up our North American operations, but Murray insisted that he spend a year at Head Office in charge of the Casein Division before going to Santa Rosa. He never made it to Santa Rosa. Then there was Peter Robertson who had been CEO of ICI New Zealand before joining the board to become director of our European operations. He then returned to New Zealand to become Group General Manager Finance. He was an experienced and highly competent executive. Two of our younger executives, Chris Moller who was running the Cheese Division and David Pilkington who was managing director North America, were clear standouts from their contemporaries. They also should be considered.

An external search, covering New Zealand and international, was instigated. We were looking for outstanding individuals who had CEO and international business experience. Internationally, there was to be particular attention paid to high-achieving New Zealand expats who might be prepared to return home for the right job. The directors agreed what skills and attributes we were looking for; established a timetable; appointed a search agency; and appointed a board committee to shortlist candidates. As the committee considered the internal candidates it was obvious that Lough, Parker and Larsen were clear front runners. There was a gap to Peter Robertson. While Chris Moller and David Pilkington were of outstanding talent, it was not yet their time. I now had to manage their expectations by signalling that while they were highly regarded and the directors saw them as future CEOs, now was not their time but I expected them to be leading candidates next time around.

The committee interviewed those turned up by the search. Most of them were high achievers, including a few from overseas who flew in to be interviewed. Finally, we reached the view that three internal candidates, Parker, Lough and Larsen, stood out and should each be interviewed by the board. For some time, I had been closely observing the three candidates. I had talked widely to staff throughout the business to understand the qualities they believed we required. It was clear to me that the organisation was looking for a more upfront style of leadership. The next CEO should be someone who could bring a change of style and "light the fire" under the organisation. The directors believed that Warren Larsen had that quality. I knew that in appointing Warren we would certainly lose John Parker who would retire. I thought that we would probably lose Phil Lough also. He would be an attractive CEO to many New Zealand companies. He later left to become CEO of Sealord. But Chris Moller and David Pilkington were ready to step up and a few other young executives were not far behind so we had plenty of talent. I was relieved at how the whole process had gone, losses had only been what I expected, and the organisation came through it in good shape.

With his experience as a Dairy Company chief executive and his time with the board, Warren had a pretty clear understanding of the challenges facing the board and how to deal with them. He soon assembled his own high-calibre executive team. His management style was more formal and hands-on than Murray's. He was strong on structures and processes, which was appropriate for the complex, geographically diverse and decentralised business the board had become. He was strongly committed to driving the high-value branded consumer and specialised food ingredients businesses forward, as well as kick starting the emerging food service business which targeted restaurants and fast-food operators. He believed that R&D would be critical to success. The industry had a great resource in the Dairy Research Institute (DRI) located at Palmerston North. It was a stand-alone organisation, a consequence of which was that its considerable scientific resources were underused. He used the opportunity created by the retirement of the incumbent to have Dr Kevin Marshall appointed director, making him also the Dairy Board's global director of R&D and a member of his senior executive team. This a was masterstroke which was to bring huge benefits by linking the Institute's research resources into market needs and opportunities. Warren required all of our offshore managers to spend some time at the DRI each year. Some, such as our South East Asian marketing star Dr Ong Poh Seng, initially thought that this was a waste of time which could be better spent in his own region. But Poh Seng and others were quick to realise the opportunities which access to the DRI resources could create for them. It was not long before he was bringing his whole marketing leadership team to the DRI twice a year. There were to be huge benefits from bringing a marketing perspective to research direction and making the marketing people aware of what our R&D team could offer them.

Warren also required each New Zealander appointed to an offshore management position to learn the language of the country they were appointed to. They did not have to become fluent, merely to have a reasonable working ability. This made a powerful statement to the staff they employed, most of whom were nationals of the country. It reduced the always present risk caused by mistranslation and importantly improved their business effectiveness. Language is an integral part of any culture and cultural understanding is an important component of marketing.

There was another major challenge not too far away. In 1989 I had begun negotiating changes to the Dairy Board Act with Agriculture Minister Jim Sutton. There were changes the board required, not the least of which was to clearly spell out who owned the assets of the board. The Act was silent on what would happen to its assets if the board ever ceased to exist. While it was inconceivable that there could be any serious argument that the assets did not belong to farmers, legally the government of the day could do what it wished with them. We wanted to amend the Dairy Board Act to make it clear that in such circumstances, the assets of the board belonged to farmers. Reaching industry agreement on how that should be done was difficult. While a conventional ownership share structure was supported by New Zealand Dairy Company, it was not that simple. The shares would have to be taken onto Dairy Company balance sheets. How then should the shares be valued? Valuation is not a precise science;

significant assumptions need to be made and the value will be a consequence of the assumptions used. Could they be sold? If so, could they be used as collateral? If used as collateral, was it possible for them to be foreclosed and move out of farmer ownership? If they could not be used as collateral, what value, if any, did they really have? Then there was the impact on dairy companies' accounts. For all dairy companies their share of the Dairy Board assets would be greater than the rest of their business, most markedly so. That investment would then dominate each company's balance sheet and in some circumstances could drive their financial results. The outcome of this was unforeseeable and could perhaps be undesirable. I finally obtained industry agreement that the board's "capital" would be owned by dairy companies proportionate to their milk supply. This protected the board's assets for farmers without creating ownership and the risks which would flow from that.

Of course, whenever our Act was before Parliament, there was always a risk that Government might wish to make some changes of its own which the industry would rather not have. The Labour Government of the eighties had done a magnificent job deregulating the economy. They had not finished. Agriculture Minister Jim Sutton was one of those determined to finish the job. He was also no fan of producer boards. He had requirements which would weaken the board and its powers which I was determined to resist. We battled it out and reached agreement. The draft legislation was introduced into Parliament on the last sitting day before the House went into recess for the 1990 election. It contained several provisions which were not what we agreed. I phoned Sutton and he replied that these could be sorted out in Select Committee after the election.

Labour was defeated in the election. Jim Bolger was the new prime minister, and I was now in a much stronger position. The new agriculture minister was another good friend, John Falloon. I renegotiated the bill with him, obtaining most of what the industry wanted.

One of the provisions which Sutton had wanted was for the board to be required to undertake a performance and efficiency audit every five years. An audit by definition is looking back; I saw little benefit in that. What farmers wanted to know was how the board is performing now and what shape it is in for the future. I was not opposed to an audit provided it was forward looking. Indeed, it had the potential to be beneficial. John Falloon quickly grasped the point and overruled his officials, agreeing that the study should be forward looking.

The first audit was to be undertaken in 1993. We had to commission it and get the board into shape for it. Time was short. A competitive "Request for Proposal" process inviting some of the top management consulting companies in the world to submit a proposal to undertake the audit was undertaken. As well as a sound understanding of the New Zealand dairy industry and international dairy markets, they were required to have extensive knowledge of best practices employed by the world's best companies. The top three management consulting firms in the world, McKinsey, Boston Consulting Group and Booz Allen Hamilton, all submitted. Boston Consulting Group were chosen. Their engineering-based approach was ideal for the board to obtain maximum benefit from the review.

They did not disappoint. Their review was both comprehensive and robust. They compared the board, on a segment-by-segment basis, against the best companies in the world. They were candid and did not pull any punches. Their overall assessment gave the board "7 out of 10 and improving". The result was creditable but indicated plenty of scope for improvement. The detail showed us where and how we had to improve. I thought that we had done rather well, but there was no reason for complacency. We had room to do much better and opportunities to do so had been identified. We sent a summary to every farmer.

THIRTY-SEVEN
CUSTOMS ISSUES

IN ALMOST EVERY COUNTRY IN THE WORLD TO WHICH WE were allowed access for our products we incurred tariffs which were usually very high. These were usually designed to keep our products out, so were often hundreds of per cent. Compliance with import regulations was something to which we always had to pay close attention. But in the ongoing battle to each year sell all that we produced, we had to be inventive and resourceful to find ways through restrictive barriers to entry. For example, Japan completely prohibited butter imports. However, we did obtain a small quota for "whey butter". It was made by separating out, as cream, the tiny amount of milkfat remaining in whey after cheese and casein manufacture. The "whey cream" was then churned into butter. It had an unpleasant acidic taste, but we were able to enter it into Japan. When it arrived there, it was reprocessed into standard butter. It was an expensive and convoluted process but perfectly legal which allowed us to enter some butterfat into the high-priced but otherwise closed Japan market.

In the mid 1980s, the board had purchased two cheese companies in the USA, Dorman and Roth, and amalgamated them into Dorman Roth. For some years prior to being owned by the Dairy Board, Dorman had imported several types of European cheese under quotas, some of which were held by others. NZMP Europe, a board subsidiary, had sold New Zealand cheese to a Dutchman, Bert Ruys, who manufactured processed cheese which he then exported to the USA under a quota he held for processed cheese. Dorman Roth purchased processed cheese from Ruys and marketed it. They were all arm's length transactions so it was a perfectly legal activity.

About the time I became chairman in 1989, the US Customs alleged that the transactions were related and thus in breach of US law, being an artifice to enable New Zealand cheese to be illegally imported into the USA. They advised of their intention to bring charges against the board, its subsidiaries and officers of the subsidiaries. This was a most serious situation and one we had to defend with everything we had. Our legal advice was that we had a very defendable case but to string it out as long as we could. Time could work for us in several ways: the customs officer handling the case could get moved off it, be promoted or resign; as time passed and costs mounted without any success, customs staff will likely be reassigned to other more recent and more promising cases; eventually it may just fade away. Meantime, we had go through our data, ensure that we had been 100% compliant and make voluntary disclosure of any noncompliance. It went on for many years, but as the gaps between any notices or requests for information grew longer, we became increasingly confident that our strategy was working and the matter would just fade away, as indeed it did.

In 1996 a very serious issues arose in the UK when the EU Court of Auditors advised UK customs that large volumes of our butter imports did not comply with the compositional specifications which applied to our annual butter quota, and therefore we were not entitled to the lower tariff which applied to our quota. The problem arose in 1995 when, as a result of the Uruguay Round agreement, our UK quota had become an EU quota. Therefore, instead of all of our quota butter entering the EU through British ports as it had traditionally, we began exporting some butter directly to the European ports of Antwerp and Rotterdam. This was a new experience for customs in Belgium and Holland.

The specification in the regulations prescribed that our butter should have less than 82% fat. To provide a safety margin, dairy companies aimed for the fat content on average to be a little under 82%. But under the best testing accuracy possible individual blocks could vary between 81% and 83%. When some of our butter began to arrive in their countries, customs officers in the Netherlands and Belgium had checked the fat content, found variations and applied different interpretations. The new interpretation was that if any part of a shipment had a fat content above 82%, even 82.1%, the whole shipment did not comply. In that case the lower tariff did not apply and the normal tariff was payable, even if, as was usually the case, the average fat content of the shipment was below 82%.

For years the UK had been critical of the many scandals which arose under the EU Common Agricultural Policy, some of which related to food imports and a number where bribery and corruption was alleged. The Brits had consistently argued that the rules should be more vigorously applied and countries which did not comply should be dealt with harshly. The boot was now on the other foot and the European Court of Auditors adopted the new interpretation and insisted that the UK recover the full tariff. In the past if any butter had been found to be out of specification, we would have received a phone call from British Customs and advised to tighten our compliance. But it was now an EU issue, there was no tolerance and they were coming after us. Then they alleged that our very popular "spreadable" butter was not "butter" in terms of the regulations, so should incur the full duty. The regulations stated that the product should be "sweet cream butter made directly from cream". Spreadable butter was made directly from cream, but after churning went through an anhydrous milk fat (AMF) stage before being churned again and the process completed. It was both *"sweet cream"* butter and made *"directly"* from cream, thus complying with the regulations. At one stage the total of all these claims was close to NZ$1.9 billion.

Warren dealt with the matter extremely well, but a huge amount of resource was required to painstakingly work through each shipment, virtually on a block-by-block basis. He had assembled a capable legal team and posted Graham Milne to London to handle the issue, attempting to ring fence the issue to allow our UK staff to get on with the job of running the remainder of the business. But shortly after Graham arrived, UK Customs escalated the issue by raiding our office in Reigate. Worse than that, they arrested six of our most senior executives and charged them with smuggling and fraud. These were serious criminal charges which carried a maximum penalty of seven years' jail and huge fines.

I was furious. I knew each of the individuals well. They were all fine honest men who would never do anything illegal or unethical. My immediate problem, though, was how to handle the publicity. It was worldwide news but huge in New Zealand. The matter had broken during the night. I had received a late-night call advising me of it, then another call advising me that New Zealand media were clamouring for a comment from me. After consultation I decided to leave any response till morning but agreed to an interview by Radio New Zealand on Morning Report next morning. After a restless night as I thought through the issues and pondered on how best to handle them, I walked down The Terrace from Herbert Gardens to Broadcasting House at 6.30 am next morning. It was to be the lead story and I expected to be interviewed by the aggressive Kim Hill.

However, I was relieved when it was Mike Hosking who came out of the studio to meet me and have a chat, as they usually did before an interview. I had reached the view that if I attempted to explain the matter or defend it, I ran the risk of being seen to be acknowledging culpability. There was also the matter of our arrested staff. They had been charged with serious crimes. I was not going to allow them to be branded as criminals. So, I went straight on to the attack, framing the issue as essentially one of trade protectionism, something which we had to battle with every day. But, I argued, this was below the belt and given the very close relationship between our two countries, a very poor way for the UK to treat a valued friend like New Zealand, which had stood by them through thick and thin throughout our history. I also expressed my disgust at the arrest of "my officers", "honest men of integrity who were doing a great job for New Zealand". Mike Hosking was sympathetic and very helpful in the way in which he framed the interview.

My strategy appeared to work, with the New Zealand media largely accepting that it was a "trade protectionism" issue. It also seemed to resonate in the UK where we had a very large group of supporters, many of them influential individuals. Indeed, a short while later I received a phone call from Tom Vyner, the CEO of Sainsbury's supermarkets. He told me that he knew all of our arrested staff personally; they were fine honest men who would never do what they were accused of; that as an Englishman he was ashamed of what his country was doing to New Zealand and he apologised to me. He told me he intended to raise the matter with Prime Minister John Major whom he was meeting the next week (I have knowledge that he did) and asked what he could do to help. I greatly appreciated his call.

Warren ring fenced the issue from the remainder of our business. We agreed that we would fully support our people. He hired separate QCs for each of them, with a separate team to handle the civil claims. We also had a legal team including a QC in New Zealand. Defending the individuals' criminal charges had to be our immediate priority. We were racking up legal fees pretty rapidly. We soon received notice from HM Customs, advising of their intention to invoke the provisions of the UK and New Zealand Customs Agreement which would allow them to send a team to New Zealand to gather evidence. Our legal people researched the agreement which had lain dormant for many years. They discovered that if the New Zealand Government agreed to allow the agreement to be invoked, UK Customs would have wide-ranging powers to raid whatever entities in New Zealand they chose, taking whatever documents they wanted, "breaking and entering if necessary". Their powers were actually greater than the New Zealand Police have. When I requested an appointment with Paul East, the attorney general, whom I knew rather well, he declined to see me, apologising through back channels but pointing out that the government was obliged under the UK–NZ Customs Agreement to grant access to UK Customs if their government invoked the provisions of the agreement. It was a judicial matter which would have to take its course. It was obvious that the government did not have any idea of the extent of the powers HM Customs would have if the government agreed to invoke the agreement. I got a back-channel message to the attorney general suggesting that they actually read the UK–NZ Customs Agreement before acquiescing to the UK request. Our lawyers wrote to the government, objecting in the most strenuous terms, setting out the provisions of the agreement and the extraordinary powers which would be conferred on HM Customs if the notice was accepted. To protect Jim Bolger from any possible accusation of interfering in a judicial process, I decided not to seek a meeting with him. However, I did unofficially get a message to him advising him both of my strenuous objection and the extraordinary powers government would be conferring on HM Customs. I requested that if Government was of a mind to grant HM Customs' request, he speak with me before Government commits itself. All of this worked. HM Customs quietly dropped the request.

As more information came to hand, there was clear evidence of bad faith by HM Customs. The customs case officer was an enthusiastic young man called Persson. When our people had been arrested and were awaiting being charged at the police station, he harangued and harassed our people to the extent that the police sergeant in charge told him to either shut up or wait outside on the street. Then there was an address he gave to a conference in which he said that "this is war with New Zealand". As the court process commenced, our staff were required to physically appear in court on each occasion. This was most unusual and clearly had only one purpose, maximum publicity. I became increasingly angry. This was a most stressful time for our staff and their families. Their reputations had been damaged and their lives affected. I wanted to sue HM Customs for malicious prosecution; at the very least I believed that it would change the behaviour of HM Customs. I was finally persuaded that would not be wise and that we should focus on the claims themselves. I have always regretted that I did not persist.

One evening I caught up with the UK High Commissioner, whom I knew, at a function. I told him that I was very angry at how my people were being treated. I gave him chapter and verse about the antics of Persson, telling him also that we had been advised that we had a strong case for malicious prosecution and were considering doing so. A month later I saw him again. He took me aside and advised me that Persson had been taken off the case, and he assured me that it was a planned move. I did not believe that for one moment. I know that our discussions would have been fully reported to London. I do not know if they had any influence on what transpired, but Persson's intemperate remarks had received wide publicity and undermined the prosecution's credibility. The more mature officer assigned to replace Persson looked at the evidence and stopped the criminal prosecutions immediately. There was simply no case to answer. When withdrawing the charges, HM Customs was forced to acknowledge that their officers had acted inappropriately.

While the legal team were building our defence to the civil claims, we lobbied extensively. The potential liability if the European interpretation held was huge, up to $1.9 billion, although we did not for one moment believe that the outcome would be anywhere near that. The New Zealand Government supported us but were more circumspect than usual. So much depended on trust and our reputation had been damaged. I know that the matter was discussed between the prime ministers of New Zealand and the UK. The UK Government was embarrassed by the position it found itself in. It was basically sympathetic to New Zealand. After all, the protocol which allowed entry of New Zealand butter to the UK had been negotiated between Britain and the EEC when the UK joined in 1973. If it were purely a matter between UK and NZ, it would have been speedily resolved. But the UK was in a difficult position. The EU Court of Auditors had become involved, they had followed the European interpretation and assessed that the proper duty had not been collected. The UK was responsible for collecting the duty on behalf of the EU. If they did not collect it from us, the EU would hold the UK to account and expect them to pay it. Their sympathy for us did not extend to paying $1.9 billion.

Warren and I took Kevin Marshall with us on our European visit. Our aim was to see if we could reach a technical agreement on how the regulation should be interpreted and particularly the degree of testing accuracy which was acceptable. There was not much disagreement between him and the EU technical people, but they would not commit themselves as it might prejudice the EU's case. That of course was precisely our objective. We visited the European Court of Auditors in Luxembourg. They were polite but unyielding. We knew that they had suffered trenchant criticism from the Brits at their failure to curtail European rorts. Now they had Britain over a barrel.

We raised the matter with every European minister we met including the EU Commissioner of Agriculture. I believe that they had a great deal of sympathy with us but, understandably, they were not prepared to enter the fray and tackle the Court of Auditors on our behalf. We won cases on spreadable butter in the High Court; HM Customs appealed on each occasion. The matter dragged on for seven years during which the board won some court cases. Years after I had retired, a settlement was agreed which involved the board making a small payment.

In retrospect I believe that we should have taken an action for malicious prosecution. I am sure that it would have crystalised a few things and brought about a settlement much earlier than 2003. It would also have more emphatically removed, and at a much earlier date, the stigma of criminality which hung over our executives and which impacted on their lives. I felt deeply for them. The whole episode was the blackest in my career.

THIRTY-EIGHT
RUCTIONS AT NEW ZEALAND DAIRY COMPANY

My ten years as chairman of New Zealand Dairy Board was a "game of two halves". The first half I enjoyed enormously, the second half rather less so. Dairy companies invariably appointed their most capable directors to the Dairy Board so I had a very good board. Most of the directors were experienced and were, or had been, chairman of their dairy company. They were completely committed to the board, were supportive of its strategy, policies and staff. They were resolutely focussed on ensuring that it performed to the highest standard. But then, as dairy companies amalgamated and became larger, the most capable individual usually became chairman of the amalgamated company and another director was appointed to the Dairy Board. While many were competent enough, the best people in the industry were no longer being appointed directors of the Dairy Board, which needed the very best minds in the industry. This had two other most undesirable consequences:

- Turnover of directors shot up. From 1989 to 1993 there was good continuity with the same eleven directors. But

from 1993 to 1998 the Dairy Board had a total of twenty-one directors. A number had very limited experience.
- The directors became more parochial. Increasingly, some directors saw their primary responsibility being not to the Dairy Board but to the dairy company which appointed them. It became increasingly difficult to find consensus and get all directors pulling in the same direction.
- As companies amalgamated and voting weight changed, I had several changes of deputy chairman. Peter Jensen had been an effective and supportive deputy. He was replaced by Doug Bull, an outstanding Dairy Company chairman whom I really rated. When Bay Milk was taken over by New Zealand Dairy, Graham Fraser became deputy.

Graham Calvert and I were very good friends. When I became chairman of New Zealand Dairy Company and later of the Dairy Board, he had told me, "I will always support you, Chief," and he did. Despite his flaws, his heart was always in the right place. He fervently believed in farmer cooperatives. His judgement on big issues was often poor, but he was pragmatic and when he and I disagreed, we could usually arrive at a position which was acceptable to both of us. Although well disguised, he continued to carry a grudge over his failure to make Dairy Board chairman, erroneously believing he had been "shafted" by Dairy Board staff and unable to accept that it had been his own behaviour and lack of judgement which was the cause. As New Zealand Dairy chairman he now had a chance to redeem himself.

The foundations for performance had been well laid at New Zealand Dairy Company during my time as chairman and it continued to perform well, putting real pressure on our Waikato competitors. But without a cool head to guide and where necessary restrain him, Mac

Calvert was soon getting out of hand and upsetting almost everybody outside of the company. Dairy Board staff felt bullied and threatened when they stood up to him. There was usually a threat on the table early in every discussion, but he would also use the "carrot", liberally throwing money around. Drama surrounded everything he was involved in. This burned staff out. Traditionally having had a very good reputation, New Zealand Dairy Company was rapidly becoming seen in unfavourable terms. Graham did little to constrain Mac's many excesses. On the contrary, when I spoke to him about the matter and sought his help to slow Mac down and moderate his behaviour, he slammed his hand onto his desk as was his wont, and said, "I am trying to speed him up!" I knew then that it would end in tears. The two of them were like tops, spinning faster and faster, and would eventually get out of control and crash.

I was in my Wellington office one Friday in 1992. I received a call from John Storey who was acting chairman of New Zealand Dairy while Graham was overseas, as was Mac. He asked if I could call and see him that afternoon as he had a serious matter to discuss with me. I caught an early flight to Hamilton and headed to Anchor House. Storey told me that he had received information from one of our fellow directors of alleged improper payments by the company. He had made some enquiries and was worried by what he had found. I was disappointed but not surprised. We discussed what should be done to fully investigate the matter, agreed that we needed forensic accountancy help and agreed that Bill Wilson, one of our external directors, would know who to approach. We agreed also that another senior director, Rex Byles, should be brought into the loop but the matter should otherwise be kept confidential until we had a clearer picture.

As I headed home, I recalled that about a year before Christine had met a solicitor from Hamilton at Roy Stevens' wedding, which I had been unable to attend. He had alleged corruption at New Zealand Dairy Company. He provided no information to support his assertion so there was little for me to follow up on. But as I did with such allegations, I tucked it away and kept my eyes and ears open for any evidence. Now there appeared to be some. I phoned him; it was after five but he was still in his office. I asked whether I could come and see him immediately. He was reluctant but eventually agreed. When we met, I recalled his comment to Christine and asked if he would advise me of the basis for his comment. He was very cagey and wanted to know why I was asking, which was fair enough. I told him that we had information which we were investigating and my discussion with him was part of that investigation. He spent some time questioning me about how serious we were and if any action would be taken. In the end, he outlined the reason for his comment, which involved one of his clients. The information was disturbing so I asked him if I could meet with his client together with John Storey. He undertook to consult his client and call me back. When he did so, he again spent some time questioning me about how serious we were, before advising me that his client had agreed to meet us next morning.

When John Storey and I entered his office on Saturday morning and saw the clients, I immediately knew the allegations would have substance. I knew the two individuals; they were fine men and entirely trustworthy. They owned a company which undertook a lot of work for New Zealand Dairy. They told us that they had agreed to meet only because they trusted me completely, but again wanted to ascertain if any action would be taken. I understood their concern because by talking to us they risked losing much of their business if Mac continued as CEO. They finally told us of their experience which was most disturbing and confirmed the information which had initiated the investigation.

It was not too long before the forensic accountants began to uncover a pretty murky pattern of behaviour. While the controls and processes the company had around letting contracts were adequate, they were frequently being ignored, often at significant cost to the company. This was serious enough in itself to warrant dismissal, but even worse an extensive pattern of irregular payments had been discovered. These were unauthorised and had been inadequately and incorrectly documented. Many were at best unethical, some potentially fraudulent or illegal. They included unauthorised payments to the Dairy Workers Union. It was not clear that Mac had benefitted personally from any of this, although his personal expenditure was high and poorly documented, with pretty lax use of his credit card for what seemed to be some personal expenditure. At best it may have been a case of "the end justifies the use of any means". But it displayed poor judgement, a complete lack of integrity and was most serious misbehaviour. It was clear that he had to be dismissed.

What about Graham? He had completely failed in his responsibility to ensure integrity and probity in the management of the company. It was clear that he had been aware of at least some of what was going on and had been complicit in it. Certainly, his own behaviour had encouraged much of it. He had tried to rein in the more serious transgressions while deliberately covering them up. He had managed badly what was a serious conflict of interest, by failing to report serious matters which should have immediately been reported to his fellow directors. He had let the company down, his fellow directors down, the shareholders and himself down. By failing to constrain his brother he had also let him down. The directors were unanimous: Graham had to go also.

There were some tumultuous telephone calls to dismiss Mac as he came through Narita Airport, on his way home from Japan. Then Rex Byles, Storey and I travelled to Graham's home to meet him shortly after he arrived back from overseas, to advise him that the directors required his resignation as chairman. It was one of the most unpleasant things I have ever had to do. He handled it with dignity, but my close friendship with him was a casualty. I do not think he ever forgave me for not at least giving him a "heads up". But by now the Serious Fraud Office was investigating the matter and we did not know where the matter would end up. Ultimately, they did not lay any charges. I am sure that Graham's testimony was crucial to their decision.

John Storey became chairman and acting CEO with Rex Byles as deputy chairman. They had the unpleasant and drama-filled task of finalising Mac's dismissal. It soon became clear that there had been a severe deterioration in the culture of the company with the policies, processes, checks and balances we had so painstakingly built being almost universally ignored. The culture needed to be rebuilt and values restored. So, in the search to find a new CEO, strong disciplines became an important requirement, one which was to dominate the selection process. That led to the appointment of Pryme Footner who at the time was working as a consultant for a small Australian investment bank. I suspect that his CV had been "overcooked". He was a stern disciplinarian but proved to have few other qualities. Truth was certainly not one of them. He said that he had held an executive position in a large Australian company, the CEO of which was a colleague of mine. My colleague could not remember him. He ruled by diktat and fear, was devious and manipulative but not very clever. After his appointment but before he had started, I happened to be on the same plane as him on a flight from Adelaide to Auckland so we arranged to sit together. We spent the flight discussing the New Zealand Dairy Company, the dairy industry and New Zealand Dairy Board. He told me that he had looked at both the New Zealand and the Australian dairy industries. He admired what we had in the New Zealand Dairy Board, was fully supportive of it and assured me that he would never do anything to undermine it. He considered New Zealand to be streets ahead of Australia. After he had taken up the role, a few months later he travelled to

Wellington to see me to repeat the same message. He was to do exactly the opposite. He never understood cooperatives nor was he ever a supporter of them.

The second half of my term was going to become more difficult and less enjoyable.

THIRTY-NINE
AN EMINENT PERSON

I was in the Stafford Hotel in London in May 1994 when I received a phone call from Christine. "You have a letter from Government House," she informed me. "Have you opened it?" I asked, thinking that it was another dinner invitation, which we received regularly. "No," she replied. I asked her to do so. "They are offering you a gong, a knighthood," she said when she had done so. I swore. I was not expecting it, perhaps when I retired, but certainly not now. When the Queen's Birthday Honours List was announced in June 1994, I was staying in Kaikoura where I was to be keynote speaker at the centenary celebration of the Kaikoura Cooperative Dairy Company. I received the first congratulatory telephone call at 6.30 am and they just kept coming. It went on all morning and must have driven the motel owners mad as they had to answer the calls and put them through to me. I did not have a cell phone in those days. About 7 am I checked the messages on my home phone. The message box was completely full and would not take any more calls.

The Dairy Board Staff Association wished to put on a function to honour me. Warren asked me to advise staff how I should now be addressed. I told the staff that in formal situations where they would formerly have addressed me as Mr Spring, they should now call me Sir Dryden, or chairman. But in informal situations they should just continue as they always had, to call me Dryden. The upshot of that was that from then on everyone called me Dryden most of the time. I was comfortable with that, but it upset Cynthia, my PA, a sixty-year-old English woman, who considered it most disrespectful! What pleased me most of all, though, was the reaction of Dairy Board staff, both in New Zealand and right around the world. They were genuinely intensely proud that their chairman had been honoured by the Queen. During my next visit to Asia, in every country a function attended by every staff member was held to acknowledge my honour.

Arise, Sir Dryden. Dame Catherine Tizard.

I was fortunate that my formal investiture at Government House by Governor-General Dame Catherine Tizard was attended by Christine, all of my children and Mum and Dad. We had a great day. Mum had had heart surgery six weeks previously. Before agreeing to the date for her surgery she sought an assurance from her surgeon that she would be able to fly to Wellington to attend my investiture. I was fearful that if he said no, she would have wanted to delay surgery. Fortunately, she made it, which was a real thrill for me. Mum and Dad were so proud. Thereafter Dad, when introducing me to anyone, always said, "This is my son, Sir Dryden Spring."

Mum, Christine, Dad, Kevin, Dryden, Julie-Ann, Annemarie, Mark, Lisa-Jane, Gregory

I was in Washington in early 1994 when I received a telephone call from the deputy secretary of foreign affairs and trade, John Wood. He explained to me that the previous year, sixteen nations in the Asia Pacific region, largely at the behest of Australia, had agreed to establish APEC (Asia Pacific Economic Cooperation), a forum to deepen regional cooperation. They were: Australia, New Zealand, Singapore, Malaysia, Papua New Guinea, Brunei, Thailand, Philippines, Hong Kong, Taiwan, People's Republic of China, Korea, Japan, Canada, USA, and Mexico.

The leaders (presidents and prime ministers) were finding it difficult to decide just what APEC should do, so had agreed to appoint an Eminent Persons Group and ask it to develop a vision for APEC. Each economy (this term was used because China considered Taiwan to be part of China and therefore not a country but were prepared to work with Taiwan in APEC provided it was not recognised as a country) was to appoint one person who was to be a direct appointment by their leader. Prime Minister Bolger was asking me to accept appointment. There were two reasons why I was delighted to accept.

1. It was an opportunity to promote trade liberalisation in the region which more than any other issue had the potential to deliver huge benefits to our farmers. It was therefore a priority use of my time.
2. Asia Pacific comprised around half of the world economy; it had economic growth rates which were much higher that most of the world; it contained the most populous country in the world, China, which was a rapidly emerging economic force; it was the region of the world in which we were located; most Asia Pacific Countries were relatively liberal traders.

The Group was meeting at the weekend in Malaysia; it was important that I be there so I had to immediately change my travel arrangements and depart for San Francisco, where I put Christine on a plane for New Zealand and then caught a flight across the Pacific to Kuala Lumpur. I arrived just in time for the first meeting, over dinner on Friday evening. It was an eclectic group with ex-ministers, academics, senior officials, one or two businessmen and a space scientist. I was the only farmer. I felt a little inadequate as all were individuals of high intellect, most of whom had a PhD or several degrees, while I had no educational qualifications at all. All of them were experienced high achievers. Each was a direct appointee of their country's leader and had a direct line to the leader. The chairman was Fred Bergsten, a former US assistant secretary of the Treasury who was director of the prestigious Peterson Institute of International Economics. He had a very big mind, was ideally suited to the task and did a great job.

APEC Eminent Persons Group

For the next six months we were to meet each month in a different country within the region, usually at an airport hotel. We would arrive in time for dinner on Friday when we would agree our work plan for the next two days. We would work through it on Saturday and Sunday. Then we would depart on Sunday evening, fly home through the night and I would be at work on Monday morning. During the interval between meetings, we would be continuously in contact, exchanging research, views and ideas and drafts. We had to have our report ready for APEC leaders when they met in November. It was full on and exhausting. I can remember flying home from Japan one evening. I had been suffering excruciating back pain so was not a very happy chappy and was unable to sleep. I had to get up to go to the bathroom but was unable to get out of my seat. I had to call the flight attendants to lift me up. Embarrassing!

We were a collegial group and worked well together. I made friends whom I have continued to maintain contact with. Despite my apprehensions about my lack of qualifications, I had rather more business experience than any of them in actual trade. While they understood that there were significant barriers to trade in agriculture, none of them really understood the nature, scale and extent of tariffs and import bans. They were often incredulous when I laid them out. I soon won their respect and was able to make a solid contribution to our deliberations. A significant issue we had to resolve early on was how to handle the difference between the "rules-based", prescriptive approach of western countries, particularly the United States, and the less prescriptive, more collegial approach of Asian countries under which a set of principles was agreed, with each country then deciding for itself how to apply them. Our report, *Achieving the APEC Vision*, recommended that:

- Leaders adopt the long-term goal of free and open trade and investment in the Asia Pacific.
- Begin implementing, by 2000, a programme of trade liberalisation to achieve that goal.
- Achieve complete free and open trade and investment in the region by 2020, with developed countries moving more quickly than developing countries to achieve that objective by 2010.
- Adopt a "Concord" on Investment Principles. (We soon agreed on a set of investment principles but struggled to reach agreement on what to call them. Asian nations rejected "Rules" and "Accord" as too prescriptive. We

settled on my suggestion of "Concord", which of course is a French term).
- Harmonise product standards and testing.
- Cooperate on environmental issues.

Our report was presented to leaders at Bogor, Indonesia. It was adopted by them with only one reservation, a not particularly significant one by Malaysia. Importantly, China was fully aboard. This was a significant achievement. We now had a major trading bloc, comprising over 50% of the world's economy, committing itself to trade and investment liberalisation to a degree which far surpassed anything which the WTO had ever been able to achieve. It was a momentous and exciting achievement and I felt extremely proud to have helped achieve it. In thanking us, the leaders asked us to continue for another year to advise them on implementing the APEC Vision.

The next year we were joined by members from Chile and Peru as we developed our recommendations for implementing the APEC Vision which we had previously authored. Again, it was a year of hard work with meetings every two months. I was happy with our recommendations presented to leaders at Osaka, Japan, in November 1995. Our report, *Implementing the APEC Vision*, included many individual recommendations to speed up trade liberalisation and increase economic cooperation. Some of our major recommendations were:

- Members should make a substantial "downpayment" by accelerating their Uruguay Round commitments.
- Reduce by half the transition period for trade liberalisation.
- Establish a Dispute Mediation Service.
- Broaden and deepen Uruguay Round commitments.
- Adopt the Concord of Investment Principles agreed in 1994.

- Adopt "mutual recognition" of testing standards and procedures.
- Align all new regulatory standards with international standards.
- Strengthen regional monetary and economic cooperation.
- Undertake development and technical cooperation.

Again, our recommendations were largely adopted by leaders who agreed that trade liberalisation should commence in 1997. We were sounded out by leaders enquiring whether we would continue to advise them for a further year. We declined. We believed that leaders themselves needed to take ownership of the task of implementing the APEC Vision and drive it forward. Subcontracting it to an advisory body was a recipe for ensuring that nothing happened. Instead, we suggested that leaders should establish a standing Business Advisory Council, comprising leading business people to advise them on implementation of the APEC Vision.

The decision to disestablish the Eminent Persons Group was a huge relief to me as it had been a most arduous two years, but I had enjoyed working with a group of outstanding and highly respected individuals who all had great minds. I was proud of the work we had done to help establish APEC as one of the largest regional economic groups in the world containing over half of the world's economy, and provide it with a commitment and a plan to liberalise trade and strengthen economic cooperation in what was the most important region in the world for New Zealand.

FORTY
INDIA

In the mid 1970s when I was a young and inexperienced director of New Zealand Dairy Company, Dr Verghese Kurien visited Hamilton and spoke to a board meeting. This was most unusual; we simply did not have guests speaking to us at a board meeting.

An Indian, Dr Kurien had been educated in New Zealand under the far-sighted Colombo Plan of the 1950s and 60s in which the New Zealand Government provided university education to promising young individuals from Asian nations, many of whom went on to become leaders within their own countries. He had been tasked by Prime Minister Nehru with building a "milk grid" right across India to make milk readily available to all of its large population. He was often described as the father of the Indian dairy industry and was highly regarded, both in his home country and right around the world. I found him to be a captivating and most impressive individual.

At the 1985 International Dairy Congress in Auckland, he was not a scheduled speaker but given the regard in which he was universally held there was a clamour for him to be allocated a speaking slot. My high expectations were soon dashed, however, when after stating just how much he owed to New Zealand for providing him with an excellent education he proceeded to castigate New Zealand and the New Zealand Dairy Board. I was to learn that he repeatedly did this at every international dairy gathering. I never knew what his problem was but suspected that he saw New Zealand dairy imports into India as a potential threat if they were ever allowed. Regardless, given the huge regard in which he was held, especially in developing countries which were our major markets, it was cause for great concern. When he became chairman, Jim Graham decided that he had to try to fix the problem. He went to India to meet Dr Kurien. The meeting did not go well and he came back with his tail between his legs. Kurien continued to bag New Zealand, and there seemed to be nothing we could do about it.

I was at the International Dairy Congress in Melbourne in 1995 when I received a call asking if Dr Kurien could call on me. I invited him to visit me in my suite. After exchanging pleasantries, he raised the reason for his call. He needed 10,000 tonnes of ghee (anhydrous milkfat or butter oil) and asked whether we could help. I undertook to see what we could do. I knew that were pretty sold up and fat products were in short supply. I immediately called Warren and asked him to find as much anhydrous milkfat as he could, stressing just how important this was. He came back with 3000 tonnes. I stressed that we needed to do better and he found 6000 tonnes. I went back to Dr Kurien and told him that 6000 tonnes was the best we could do. He was very grateful.

During the remainder of the Congress, we spent some time together. We got on well enough and he invited me to visit Anand. He followed up at a later date repeating his invitation, being very insistent that I accept. Hitherto I had deliberately refrained from visiting India. We did little business there and imports were normally prohibited apart from the occasional shortfall in domestic supply. Most people who visited India seemed to get sick, so there had seemed no good reason for me to visit. However, I now had an opportunity to consolidate a more respectful relationship with Dr Kurien. India was undertaking some major economic reforms and our Indian agents were telling us that there were some signs that restrictions on dairy imports might be eased a little. I decided to visit India.

Anand is located in Gujarat, the Indian province which many of New Zealand's early Indian immigrants came from. It is at the southern end of the Punjab, the great plain which straddles the India–Pakistan border. The giant Amul Dairy Cooperative was located there and Dr Kurien had also established a large agricultural university servicing all of India. They were both impressive institutions. Hanging on the wall of the boardroom at Amul was a photo of every prime minister India has ever had, from Nehru on, visiting the cooperative. I took it as a demonstration of political power.

The milk grid developed by Dr Kurien was an amazing development and an inspiring and incredible achievement. Cows are sacred in India and are roaming everywhere. They are usually underfed and often in very poor condition. Most cattle owners do not own land and have only one or two cows which roam the city, town or countryside. Women cut grass from parks and roadsides with shears not much larger than scissors, bundle it up in a cloth and carry it home to feed to their cows. An India-wide network of small receiving stations had been established. After each milking the women (it is universally women who look after the cows) carry their milk to a receiving station. A chilled, nationwide distribution system delivering milk to dispensing stations all over the country had been built. These dispensing stations are located where poor people live and dispense chilled milk into the consumer's own receptacle. The volume of each purchase is small, usually only a cupful or even less.

I had the opportunity to visit a receiving station. I was taken out into the country to visit a small village of about 6000 people. I was told that it was a village of above-average income, but it was still quite poor. When I alighted from my car there was a huge cheering crowd. A garland was placed around my neck and a "tika" marked on my forehead. There was no road into the village so I had to walk along a footpath for the last kilometre. The footpath was crowded with cheering people, a man cloaked in a tiger skin and waving a First World War Lee Enfield rifle danced along in front of me, from time to time firing the rifle into the air. When we arrived at the village, I was first taken to the milk receiving station. There was a long line of women carrying small cans of milk on their heads waiting to have their milk received. In a country bedevilled by caste, they lined up in the order in which they arrived, with high-caste Brahmin women standing behind the lowest-caste Untouchable women. As each woman presented her milk it was weighed, tested for milk solids by a modern Milko tester, sampled for bacto testing and water adulteration. She then moved to the cashier where she was paid in cash. There was then a small store where she could purchase basic food such as oil, rice or flour, as well as animal feed. I asked several women waiting in line to show me the milk in their can. Volumes were very small: half a litre to two litres. I soon learned that a tiny little frail and obviously poor woman would probably only have half a litre in her can while a large, well-covered more prosperous woman would have a several litres. The receiving station was operated by a cooperative. I was taken into the boardroom where I met the chairman and directors. I was served with refreshments while they showed me the financial and administrative details of the cooperative's operations. In this poor uneducated village, it was pleasing to have them discussing their capital, shareholders' funds, debt and debt to income ratio.

Then it was a further walk to the village square where the entire village had gathered. It was bit like college with the men on one side of the square and women on the other. There were speeches welcoming me and I was presented with gifts, including one from the women of the Mahatma Gandhi Society who presented me with two towels which they had spun and woven from flax. When it came to reply, I was interrupted many times by rapturous applause, none louder than when I told them that New Zealand had just defeated their detested neighbour Pakistan at cricket. Afterwards it seemed that everyone in the village came up to shake my hand. It must have been a thrill for the villagers to have a visitor from afar come and spend five or six hours with them. It was certainly a very memorable experience for me and one which I will always cherish.

That evening it was dinner at Dr Kurien's house, a great honour. He told me that we had to go to the Indian capital, New Delhi, on the other side of India to meet the prime minister. While in Delhi I took the opportunity to meet several Indian ministers and do some media interviews which received widespread coverage. I was also taken to a milk dispensing station located in a poor neighbourhood. The neighbourhood was teeming with people. It was inspiring to see desperately poor people visiting the dispensing station, inserting a token into the dispenser and obtaining half a cup of milk.

When I called on the prime minister I had to alight from my car, a kilometre or so away from his compound. I had to walk 400 metres, go through security into the compound where a car was waiting to take me to the prime minister's office building, and pass through security again before entering his office. Prime Minister Deve Gowda greeted me warmly. He had not met our prime minister or any New Zealand minister so it was a real coup for me to have the chance of meeting him. He was interested in New Zealand's economic reforms of the 1980s and questioned me about them. We also discussed the reforms which he had carried out. I was keen to discover whether there were more to come, particularly if there would be any easing of import restrictions. As Dr Kurien was with me, I had to tread carefully to avoid triggering an adverse response from him. If allowing dairy imports became a political issue, there would be only one winner and it would not be us. The prime minister's response gave me some hope of minor easing, but it was also clear that there would not be any large-scale dairy imports in the foreseeable future.

My visit to India had been a wonderful experience. I had learnt much about that huge and complex country. I had been privileged to see the world-renowned milk grid operating. The highlight was my visit to the village. I had repaired New Zealand's relationship with the influential Dr Kurien and was confident that if dairy import restrictions were eased at all, we could work with him to exploit any opportunities while reducing the risk of an adverse political reaction. But India had a parting gift for me.

During my visit I had been extremely careful about what I ate, restricting myself to dry or steaming hot food. As I sat in the foyer of my hotel waiting for my car to the airport at 8.30 pm, I was congratulating myself on avoiding any problems. It was a little premature as by the time I reached the airport I was going at both ends. The flight home was a nightmare and I had to go straight into chairing a three-day board meeting. It was to be three months before I recovered from the stomach bug I had picked up.

FORTY-ONE
THE GOING GETS TOUGH

The second half of my time as Dairy Board chairman grew increasingly challenging. I continued to enjoy the commercial operations of the board which were performing pretty well. We knew what our farmers wanted as we had surveyed them and received an amazing response of 94% of all farmers, with 94% of all dairy farmers wanting to continue 100% ownership of their cooperative dairy companies and the New Zealand Dairy Board, while 89% agreed that the New Zealand Dairy Board should continue to control the export of all New Zealand dairy products. They were even more strongly supportive of the board continuing to invest in product and market development.

The dairy industry had adopted a vision: "To be the most profitable unsubsidised dairy industry in the world providing farmers with increasing wealth and secure returns superior to other land uses". This required us to have a "farm to the customer" approach. With the success of our industry being built on the efficiency of our on-farm milk production, it was vital that we maintained and improved the efficiency of dairy farming. We broadened the role of the Livestock Improvement Corporation, which was a world leader in the genetic improvement of our dairy herd, to take a more "whole of farm approach". With economic reforms cutting back on government funding of on-farm research, we had created a joint venture with the Crown, to secure the $2 million they were spending, for a ten-year period, with the board matching it dollar for dollar. This increased the amount of dairy research at a time when funding for agricultural research was being reduced.

A vision for the Dairy Board had been developed and adopted by the dairy industry. It was for the "New Zealand Dairy Board to be the world's best dairy marketing organisation achieving superior and sustainable returns from New Zealand milk products by:

- Pursuing an aggressive consumer strategy to position branded products in selected high-return and fast-growing markets
- Focussing on a selective ingredients strategy to achieve high profits
- Continuing to develop our food service business by close alignment with selected international key accounts
- Marketing all products through an efficient global distribution system with high standards of product quality and environmental integrity."

It was aspirational and challenging but clear and easily understood.

We were making serious progress with our branded consumer products strategy, achieving "lead" brand position in some South East Asian and Central American markets. Helmut Maucher, the CEO of Nestlé, told me that they regarded us as professional and challenging competitors. Praise indeed from the CEO of what was undoubtedly the best food company in the world, one which had been largely unchallenged in that position for many years, including in those markets where we had now dislodged them from lead brand position.

For twenty years New Zealand had tried without success to enter the infant formula market. There was a World Health Organisation prohibition on advertising infant formula, due to the risk of contaminated water being used to reconstitute milk in developing countries. This protected incumbents by making it extremely difficult for new entrants like the Dairy Board to break in. In developed markets, "mothers' milk" was favoured by health and nutrition authorities and the use of infant formula discouraged. But the market research undertaken by our marketing team discovered some startling information. During a consumer's life cycle, there was a relatively small spend up to the age of two when infant formula was consumed. The consumer spend through the "follow-on" years of two to six was many times higher. It was much higher again during adolescent years. In the "golden years" (fifty plus), when incomes were higher, consumption was multiple times higher again. This told us that the larger volume areas of the market were not being serviced by existing brand marketers and that we should focus our research into developing specific products for those segments and redirect our marketing to service them. Using that knowledge, a "Nutrition for Life" strategy was developed, aimed at providing products designed to meet the nutritional needs of consumers through the various stages of their life cycle. Anlene had been the first consumer product to bring together science and marketing to meet a specific nutritional need. Anmum 1 was developed for pregnant mothers, Anmum 2 for lactating mothers. As part of the marketing strategy, support was given to the La Leche League and breastfeeding organisations in other countries. Anlene was targeted at adolescents. "Nutrition for Life" became the cornerstone of our branded consumer business. It was a winning strategy.

Our specialised food ingredients business was also growing nicely. With the Dairy Research Institute now closely aligned with the board's objectives and strategy, innovation was burgeoning and the proportion of sales coming from new products had climbed past 20%. A strategy to attack the rapidly growing food-service sector (sales to outlets such as McDonald's and Pizza Hut) was developed and resourced. Progress was being made, albeit more slowly than we would have liked. Overall, our value-adding strategies were delivering strong value growth.

The next statutory Performance and Efficiency Audit again conducted by Boston Consulting Group in 1998 confirmed "significant improvement" over the five years since the previous Audit in 1993. Financial performance had improved on all measurements. The board's performance relative to world best practice had also improved. I was proud of the audit findings; they were a credit to Warren and his talented executive team. There was, however, no cause for complacency; there continued to be room for improvement.

Internationally, milk prices and the New Zealand dollar continued to fluctuate. The Uruguay Round Agreement had removed uncertainty and while the reduction in subsidised export volumes was yet to become reality as the subsidising countries used every trick in the trade to delay its implementation, they were nevertheless slowly bringing their production into line with consumption. The new access created in the Uruguay Round was becoming available, although often under rather unfavourable conditions. We no longer had to lobby on our annual visit to Europe for continuation of our UK butter quota, which had become perpetual and an EU quota, as a result of which our discussions with EU ministers, officials and farmers were now more constructive. While prices ebbed and flowed according to supply and demand overall, the trends were heading in the right direction and the outlook for New Zealand dairy farmers continued to improve.

We had developed a very good relationship with Congressman Bob Smith, the chairman of the US House of Representatives Agriculture Committee. He was a fine and farsighted man. He had observed that over a prolonged period, as subsidies to farmers increased, US farm exports had decreased. This was not rocket science, as subsidies always result in less efficient production. He was a great admirer of New Zealand farming and had taken his Agriculture Committee members on visits to the few agricultural exporting countries which did not subsidise their farmers: Argentina, Brazil, Australia and New Zealand. He wanted to reduce subsidies paid to US farmers and make them more competitive at export. Naturally, we hosted them during their New Zealand visit. I was to sit with Republican John Boehner, subsequently Speaker of the House, during dinner.

While in New Zealand, Bob Smith confided in me that he intended to hold public hearings of his committee as part of his efforts to reduce subsidies and make US farming more efficient. He asked me if I would testify before his committee as he considered New Zealand Dairy to be a wonderful exemplar. In due course I appeared before the US Congressional Agriculture Committee. In presenting me as chairman of the world's most successful dairy exporter, Chairman Smith gave me a wonderful intro:

> "Sir Dryden, New Zealand is a country of five million people, is that correct?"
>
> "Yes, sir."
>
> "We are 350 million."
>
> "New Zealand produces 1.5% of the world's milk. Is that correct?"

"Yes, sir."

"But you have an international market share of 30%. Is that correct?"

"We supply 32% of all milk which enters international trade, Mr Chairman."

"And we supply 5% of international dairy markets, is that correct?"

"A little less than 5%, sir."

"Sir Dryden, if we are a nation of 350 million people and you have 5 million, and you supply 30% of international dairy markets and we supply less than 5%, you have got to be doing something right. Will you tell us how you do it?"

In my presentation I told the committee that we exported 95% of our milk, that New Zealand dairy farmers did not receive any subsidies or government support; they received only what their production earned in the markets of the world. That our industry was totally focussed on markets and customers and was highly sensitive to consumer needs and expectations. That if consumers reduced consumption and prices fell, our farmers just had to adjust and lower their costs. This drove New Zealand farmers to continuously improve efficiency. The base on which the New Zealand dairy industry was built was the efficiency of our on-farm milk production and responsiveness to markets. I observed that in most countries farmers relied on subsidies, government support and government-mandated minimum prices. This meant they became increasingly less efficient and if minimum prices were higher than consumers were prepared to pay, milk production continued unchanged and surpluses arose. This, of course, was the situation in the USA. I did not tell them that, but they knew it. It was exactly what Bob Smith was trying to change and did so in the Freedom to Farm Act in 1996. I told them that New Zealand and US dairy farmers shared a common objective, to liberalise market access for dairy products. We were working closely together on trade reform, and I urged that we continue to do so. American dairy farmers and politicians were all for that, but with their normal selective morality they saw nothing wrong in keeping their own markets closed and subsidy structures in place. As the USA had begun to attack "state trading enterprises", I dealt with the New Zealand Dairy Board structure. Because of our legislative underpinning the board was technically a state trading enterprise so I carefully spelt out that the board was a cooperative owned by our 14,000 farmers and received no government subsidies or support of any kind. No case could possibly be made that our Dairy Board structure was trade distorting.

Commercially, things were looking pretty positive. There were still plenty of challenges, but international market conditions were evolving favourably. We had a Dairy Industry Vision which had been agreed by dairy farmers and dairy companies. Although not complacent, I felt comfortable with our commercial position, and continued to immensely enjoy the commercial and trade aspects of the job; however, the politics were beginning to get pretty heavy.

The New Zealand Business Roundtable had been established in the early nineties to be a forum comprising the CEOs of the top 100 companies in New Zealand. I had been invited by the Chairman Sir Ron Trotter to become a member but had declined as the Roundtable values were not consistent with those of the Dairy Board, although overall it played a pretty useful role in public policy. Following the successful economic deregulation of the 1980s and 90s, the spotlight was being turned on all remaining regulated activities. It was inevitable that they turn their attention to New Zealand's producer boards. The Roundtable commissioned a report by an Australian agricultural consultancy, ACIL. The author, Dennis

Hussey, was an expatriate New Zealander. This formed the basis of their thrust to remove the legislated powers of New Zealand's producer boards and it triggered a major public debate.

The government had also commissioned a study by renowned Harvard professor Michael Porter. He advanced his "cluster concept" in which clusters of new companies formed around successful industries. That was basically correct and many successful businesses have developed around New Zealand agriculture. He also argued that businesses should develop in the domestic market before expanding overseas. Again, that was nothing earth shattering, and this was what happened in New Zealand. But he went on to argue that the existence of producer boards was preventing this from happening in New Zealand, conveniently ignoring the fact that despite having tried at great cost to diversify our exports for over fifty years, the industries covered by producer boards, dairy, meat, wool, apples and kiwifruit, remained the only New Zealand exporters of any scale, sending overseas between 80% and 95% of total production. They were doing so profitably and continuing to grow at a faster rate than the New Zealand economy.

More worrying was that the USA was beginning to question the legislated powers of the New Zealand Dairy Board. They were having difficulty understanding how tiny New Zealand could successfully export dairy products, while they, "the greatest nation in the history of the world" was unable to do so. Ignoring the huge subsidies US dairy farmers received, a small group of Wisconsin dairy farmers convinced some politicians that our Dairy Board structure was somehow unfair. The US administration knew that was rubbish. Their Deputy Trade Representative Peter Scher told me that they did not consider our structure to be trade distorting, but for them, New Zealand dairy farmers were hardly worth a fight with Congress.

So, battle was joined on all fronts. We had known that the Business Roundtable attack was coming and were ready for it. The Dairy Board, and the dairy industry, were generally viewed very favourably by most New Zealanders. While the interest of the USA was most unwelcome, I was not unduly concerned about it in the short term as they had much larger priorities, so it was most unlikely that our structure would be a significant trade objective for the USA for quite some time. But it was unlikely to go away and would probably assume greater importance at some time in the future.

So, I knew that our legislated structure did not have an unlimited life. That there would come a time when the existence of the Dairy Board's legislated powers would be seen as unreasonable in a competitive, deregulated economy. Murray Gough and Jim Graham had put "Plan B" in place in the 1980s. It provided for the Dairy Board to morph into a company to take over the board's assets and liabilities. Cooperative dairy companies would be issued shares in it, in proportion to their milk supply. Any cooperative dairy company could choose to opt out, and they would receive their proportionate share of the net assets of the board and would be free to go their own way. There was room for debate as to whether a "joint stock" or "cooperative" company should be the entity, and whether individual farmers or dairy companies should be the shareholders. But it was a clean and simple plan which could be effected relatively easily, although the Commerce Commission would no doubt provide some hurdles. Importantly, it had complete industry support both from cooperative dairy companies and dairy farmers. I was comfortable that Plan B was in place.

Meantime, continuation of the "single seller" continued to be in farmers' interests. Although the number of "single-buying" agencies around the world had significantly reduced, some continued to operate. Where import quotas were held, such as butter into the EU and the US cheese quota, "quota rents" existed and were mostly able to be captured by the Dairy Board for New Zealand farmers. This would not be the case if the Dairy Board did not exist. In that case the quota rent in each country would go to the importer and the quota rent would be lost to New Zealand completely.

Most importantly, having a single dairy exporter gave New Zealand dairy farmers ownership of a well-resourced entity of significant scale, which could successfully compete with the large food companies of the world. Nestlé, for example, was several times our size, although their dairy business sales were more in line with our own. But that was the nature of the competition at the higher value end of the market. We were up against the best in the world. Our single-exporter structure also brought significant benefits of lower costs in the supply chain. For example, the board was the largest individual customer of Nedlloyd, at the time one of the world's largest shipping companies. I knew that the shipping rates achieved by the board were well below those obtained by any other industry, all of which had a large number of individual shippers. These advantages were significant. Finally, retention of the single seller was what 89% of farmers wanted. They had told us so.

THE KNIGHT AND THE ROUNDTABLE.

Carrying that debate was my responsibility and carry it I did. I never turned down a single request to speak or comment on the matter, anywhere at any time. Unfortunately, I pretty much had to carry it on my own, which was arduous, but I was reasonably successful in neutralising any great public demand for removal of the single-seller powers. The CEO of one of New Zealand's largest companies, a man whom at that time I did not know, congratulated me on how the Dairy Board had demolished the Business Roundtable campaign for dairy industry deregulation, "and I am a board member of the Business Roundtable," he said. Politically, the Dairy Board continued to have very strong support from all political parties. We had the backing of most Members of Parliament and I knew that as long as Jim Bolger was prime minister our legislation remained pretty secure.

But the apple rots from within.

FORTY-TWO
THE END GAME

Despite the assurances he had given me, Pryme Footner soon began trying to undermine the Dairy Board. He would visit the Dairy Board's overseas marketing companies and make it clear to the executive team there that he intended to do his own marketing. He had no authority from the New Zealand Dairy Company board to make such statements, which were most unsettling to our staff. When he returned, he would tell me what a great job our people in the companies he had visited were doing. He did not seem to understand that they always reported on his visits to Warren and me. They told a much different story.

Footner was a physically big man with an ego to match. It irked him that as CEO of one of New Zealand's largest businesses, he did not control the marketing of the products which his factories produced and did not receive the recognition which a CEO of a stand-alone company of similar size would normally receive. He actually resented having to work cooperatively, within a cooperative industry led by the Dairy Board. He never understood farmers or the unique features of cooperatives, nor did he understand that farmers saw their cooperative as an essential extension of their farming operation. At heart he believed a joint stock structure was superior to a cooperative. Nor did he have the slightest understanding of markets and marketing.

The industry continued to evolve. Dairy companies amalgamated with their neighbours to ultimately create a single company within each region, then amalgamated across regional boundaries. Taranaki company Kiwi Dairies took over Tui, the Wairarapa cooperative. The Waikato was an exception. Tatua continued to occupy a small niche and outperform all others. Sunny Park-Hinuera, Cambridge, Morrinsville and Te Aroha-Thames Valley amalgamated to form Waikato Dairy Company located at Hautapu. The South Island companies would eventually become one. This consolidation improved efficiency in milk processing, facilitated the employment of better management and enabled investment in product diversity and innovation. There continued to be fierce competition between New Zealand Dairy and Waikato Dairy Company.

The industry payment system had been designed by a group of experienced Dairy Company executives in which Jeff Jackson and Warren Larsen had played leading roles. It was designed to:

- Maximise the total return from the industry's milk.
- Return to dairy companies the total costs incurred by the industry.

The basic principles on which it was built were that it should:

- Enable the Dairy Board to obtain the product mix required for the market.
- Be cost neutral between different products.
- Encourage quality, innovation and product flexibility.

It comprised a standard price for the fat and protein in milk and a standard cost allowance, designed to be cost neutral between the different products which milk was manufactured into. The Dairy Board then paid extra incentives to reward dairy companies for innovation, quality and to obtain the product mix it required for the market. It had worked well for ten or twelve years, had always enabled the Dairy Board to obtain the products it required for the market at the lowest possible cost and had equitably distributed the industry's total returns. It had also driven huge efficiency and productivity gains. This was absolutely critical, particularly with new products which usually had relatively small volumes. Processing costs could easily consume any market premium the product could earn. The payment system had the support of all companies, but Footner never understood it. He convinced himself that New Zealand Dairy Company was being disadvantaged by the system and being treated unfairly by the Dairy Board.

As a manufacturer he believed that whatever value a product had was created in manufacturing. He did not understand that it was actually marketing which created value. New Zealand Dairy began to press for a change to a payment system which paid companies the actual market returns. Graham Calvert was an advocate. This was simplistically attractive but deeply flawed. For example, average returns for cheese were above average, but driven largely by a few high-priced quota markets which only took modest and fixed volumes. Outside of those markets, cheese usually returned less for the milk than powder or casein. If the Dairy Board paid a higher price for cheese, more milk would be switched into cheese which would then be sold at a much lower price. That would reduce the average return for the milk used in cheese manufacture and lower total returns for milk. There were numerous such examples. A dairy market is a little like a pyramid, with height being the price per tonne and the area being total tonnes. At the top of the pyramid there are very high prices but usually only for a very small number of tonnes. Moving down the pyramid, the price falls but the volume which could be sold at that price increases. Given the huge variation in prices earned from different products and different markets, maximising total industry returns required adroit utilisation of milk at the margin. Fifty dollars a tonne at the bottom end would return many more dollars in total than fifty dollars a tonne at the top end. Of course, we had to try and do both and move all of our production a notch or two up the value pyramid into a higher price.

Footner instructed his staff to take a hard line in negotiations with Dairy Board staff. This aroused the ever-present suspicions of other companies that they could be disadvantaged to benefit New Zealand Dairy Company, and they began to take an equally hard line. This made life unpleasant for Dairy Board executives, particularly David Pilkington who was the Dairy Board executive in charge of procurement. His task was to obtain from the dairy companies the products required to meet the marketing plan. He was a very capable young executive with outstanding potential who had long been viewed as a potential CEO. He had been well trained for senior management roles. He had been in charge of a product division, been managing director of both our Japan and USA companies, each of which had quite different characteristics. He, like all of the board's senior executives, had been sent to the most prestigious business universities in the world, like Harvard, INSEAD, and Stanford. He was skilled at working cooperatively with dairy companies and obtaining the product mix that the marketeers wanted. His integrity was unimpeachable, and he was respected and trusted by most in the industry.

I was still a director of New Zealand Dairy, but meetings of its board were becoming increasingly unpleasant for me. Every month there would be continual whingeing about how the Dairy Board was "treating us unfairly", "not rewarding us properly for what we contribute" and favouring other companies at our expense. Most of my fellow directors recognised the game which was being played, but constant dripping will wear away a stone. They allowed it to continue, doing nothing to modulate it.

Then Footner hired two professors from the University of Chicago to write a report on the Dairy Board at a cost of more than US$250,000. They delivered what they were hired to do by concluding that the Dairy Board was inefficient. They drew attention to the significant increase of $320 million that year in Dairy Board costs. It was a most appalling piece of scholarship. The volume of sales was up 263,000 tonnes (25%). An accounting change now showed tariffs of $400 million as a cost, when previously they had been deducted from sales. Branded consumer sales had increased sharply. These incur higher costs but also increase revenue. For example, whole milk powder cost about $300 per tonne to manufacture and it sold for about US$1800 FOB per tonne. Packing it into 1 kg cans cost around an additional US$1200 per tonne so costs go up to $1500 per tonne. But the product will sell for around $10,000 rather than US$1800 per tonne. On a like for like basis, operating costs had actually declined. They could have discovered most of this had they taken the trouble to properly read the Dairy Board's published accounts! Nor had they taken the trouble to read the statutory Performance and Efficiency Audit undertaken by the internationally recognised Boston Consulting Group. This analysed Dairy Board operations in some detail and compared them against international best practice. It reached an entirely different view. Of course, the professors' report never saw the light of day as it simply could not have withstood scrutiny. As a director of New Zealand Dairy Company, I had to sit through this nonsense at every meeting but my confidentiality obligations as a director prevented me from exposing it.

As an industry, however, we were wasting too much time and resource on the *distribution* of revenue, time which would be better spent on *increasing returns*. If the industry wanted a different system for distributing returns, one which it could live with and which enabled the Dairy Board to obtain the products it needed for the market, the board could live with it. A working party of all dairy company CEOs and key Dairy Board executives was tasked with trying to design an improved system. I wanted every dairy company CEO involved. I did not want any of them sitting outside and firing bullets. I wanted them to have ownership of what emerged. At great cost McKinsey & Company were employed to help. I asked Sue Suckling, a board director who was a skilled facilitator, to chair the group. As the Commercial Pricing Model, as it was termed, began to take shape, I became increasingly sceptical about how effective it would be. It was a very blunt instrument and I doubted that it would deliver the most profitable product mix for the industry. Still, I had confidence that the industry would ultimately give the board the tools it needed.

Sue Suckling did a brilliant job of chairing the group. It was soon obvious that Footner had no understanding of the complex issues being considered, nor the capacity to get his mind around potential outcomes. It seemed to me that New Zealand Dairy would be significantly disadvantaged by the Commercial Pricing Model. I made Graham Calvert aware of this. He clearly did not believe me, dramatically slamming the desk and exclaiming ,"If that is what it does, we will have to fix that." Even worse for New Zealand Dairy was that Kiwi Dairies was likely to be significantly advantaged.

I had retired by the time the Commercial Pricing Model was implemented. My concerns were well founded. Kiwi was advantaged, New Zealand Dairy significantly disadvantaged, and the board's required product mix unable to be delivered. But as I expected, the industry did give the board the tools necessary to obtain the mix of products it required for the market.

Kiwi was the most efficient dairy company in the country. Taranaki had had a lot of small cheese companies. In the early 1970s most amalgamated into Moa Nui in North Taranaki and Kiwi Dairies located at Hawera. These amalgamations created companies of greater scale which could better afford the investment needed to produce milk powder and casein and reduce their reliance on cheese. This was necessary as New Zealand had to sharply reduce the amount of cheese it produced when Britain entered the EEC. Kiwi, which was inaugurated in 1962, displayed great courage and foresight in consolidating all of its milk processing onto a single site at Whareroa, which was opened in 1975. This gave them an initially large debt burden, but with smart design it created enormous operating efficiency. As they worked their debt down, their payout became one of the most competitive in the country. Matching them had been one of my objectives when I was chairman of New Zealand Dairy.

Morris Roberts had become a director of Kiwi when it was formed in 1962. He became deputy chairman six years later and chairman in 1980. He was thus a very experienced director. Following what was then Kiwi policy, he was not appointed to the Dairy Board. As chairman he ran a very tight ship, carefully avoiding any "frills" and keeping overheads down. Kiwi's operating efficiency was thus unmatched by any other company. In 1991 Kiwi swept up Moa Nui, which was unable to match its payout. Taranaki now had one dairy company.

When I became chairman, I persuaded Morris to come onto the Dairy Board, which he joined in 1990. He was a wise and able director who soon grasped the key requirements of running a marketing organisation. His view was uncomplicated. Kiwi should focus on delivering, at the lowest possible cost, the products required by the Dairy Board and leave it to the Dairy Board to obtain the best return for farmers. He was hugely supportive of the board and of me personally. He retired as chairman of Kiwi in 1994 after thirty-two years' service, having been deputy chairman for twelve years and chairman for fourteen. He continued as a director of the Dairy Board until 1996 when he retired. Morris was the driving force behind rationalisation of the dairy industry in Taranaki, doing it in a way which delivered huge benefits to Taranaki farmers. His was a simply outstanding contribution and Taranaki farmers have much to thank him for.

His successor as chairman was John Young, an affable and hospitable man who had been deputy chairman for eight years. He was to prove more difficult to work with. He did not come onto the Dairy Board when he became chairman so I went to Hawera to meet him. I wanted to get to know him better and establish a good working relationship with him. I advised him that I looked forward to working with him; that I greatly respected Kiwi which as one of the board's major shareholders and partners; that Kiwi and its views would always be important to me; that he should feel free to contact me at any time on any issue; that I intended to visit him every three months. I then asked if there were any issues he wanted to discuss with me. To my surprise, I received a diatribe delivered with real feeling on about eight issues where he believed Kiwi had been seriously wronged by the board. Every one of them was news to me, but I took them seriously and undertook to look at the issues and get back to him. On my return to the office, I sent Warren a memo, detailing each of the issues that Young had raised and asked him for a full report on them. The report indicated that each of the issues appeared to be relatively minor, which was why none of them had been escalated to me. The board's officers dealing with them believed each to have been settled reasonably amicably with Kiwi Dairies staff. They were surprised that they had been raised again. After a discussion with Warren, I wrote a long and detailed letter to John Young explaining the board's understanding of them. I took great care to be as diplomatic as I could and invited him to some back to me if he continued to have concerns on any of the matters. I did not hear back from him so assumed that the matters had been laid to rest. I was astounded on my next visit to receive pretty much the same diatribe on the same issues with no reference to my letter to him. He continued to raise them on occasions after that. When I pushed to find out what needed to be done to allay his concerns, he always refused to engage. I was finding that there was another side to the affable John Young I had always known, one which was anything but good natured.

Looking back, it is now clear to me that the retirement of Morris Roberts marked a turning point. For some reason which I have been unable to fathom, John Young seemed to harbour a grudge against the Dairy Board. Rather than come onto the board where he would likely have been able to fix whatever it was that ailed him, he preferred to stay outside of the tent and fire shots into it. That was also how he operated when the negotiations over the future structure of the industry were under way. He preferred to appoint others in his stead and avoid the responsibility of being a member of any negotiating body.

As the debate on the single-seller issue intensified, New Zealand Dairy began to undermine the Dairy Board. They employed a lobbyist in Wellington at a cost of $250,000 annually. Word began to reach us from various ministers' offices that the Dairy Board did not have the support of New Zealand Dairy Company. When Storey and Footner were confronted about this, they always denied trying to undermine the Dairy Board. New Zealand Dairy directors and shareholders had never been consulted and were uneasy about this. They probably should have saved their money, though, as New Zealand Dairy had little credibility while the Dairy Board continued to be trusted and well regarded.

In 1997 John Storey made a public statement urging the industry to work as though it no longer had an export monopoly. He advocated splitting the Dairy Board into two separate organisations: one controlling the granting of export licences, the other a marketing organisation. He advocated the latter should be a corporate model, in other words not a cooperative. This fomented considerable discontent among most dairy companies and farmers including those supplying New Zealand Dairy Company. Most dairy companies were deeply suspicious of the motives of New Zealand Dairy and what its real intentions were, believing that it wanted to control the industry and advantage itself. The other companies and most farmers, including New Zealand Dairy suppliers, had huge confidence in the Dairy Board and expected it to lead the transition to any alternative structure.

As a director of New Zealand Dairy Company, I was in an unenviable position. New Zealand Dairy leadership, although not necessarily its directors, were hell bent on replacing the Dairy Board as the peak industry body and leader. Attending New Zealand Dairy Company board meetings became increasingly unpleasant as its directors were bombarded with misleading information and anti-Dairy Board propaganda. As a director, I had obligations of confidentiality and loyalty to the company. But as Dairy Board chairman I also had responsibilities to the other dairy companies as well as to all New Zealand dairy farmers who were relying on me to steer the industry through any deregulation towards the optimal structure, one which preserved the industry's strengths and farmer control. There was no doubt in my mind that this was one single cooperative marketing company, or even better, one totally integrated manufacturing and marketing cooperative company. Although never actually endorsed by its directors, the leadership of New Zealand Dairy Company wished to take over the assets of the Dairy Board under a corporate structure, desirably with tradeable shares.

Dairy companies which wished to join them would be welcome, but New Zealand Dairy would be running it. Companies which did not wish to join would be free to go their own way and would be paid out their proportionate share of the board's net assets. What a disaster that would have been for New Zealand dairy farmers.

In trying to steer the industry towards an optimal outcome, I was between a rock and a hard place. A single integrated manufacturing and marketing cooperative was by far the best option. Every study undertaken, and there had been many, had reached that conclusion. But I had to tread delicately. New Zealand Dairy Company, which had half of the industry's milk, was opposed to that concept, unless of course they controlled it, and they had half of the industry's milk. I had to respect their position, keep them "in the tent" and try to get them across the line on a single cooperative company. If I strongly advocated a single company, they would switch off. I established a committee of all dairy company chairmen to work through the alternatives and seek a consensus. I was confident that logic and common sense would prevail, although that might take some time. That did not concern me as the "single-seller" status was not under immediate threat. But that was about to change.

In early December 1997 I was in the Koru Lounge at Auckland Airport waiting to catch a flight to Wellington. I noticed Health Minister Tony Ryall on his mobile phone making call after call. Something was obviously going on. I hoped that it was not a move against Jim Bolger as National was polling badly with an election less than two years away. Once the plane was in the air Tony Ryall came back to me and told me a "spill" was on. He was obviously one of the plotters so I asked him if they had the numbers. He assured me they did. As soon as I arrived in my office, I phoned the prime minister's office which confirmed that Jim was being challenged by Jenny Shipley. I asked how I could help and then began working the phones trying to convince MPs to stay loyal to Jim. But it was clear that Jim was gone and Shipley would replace him.

I was devastated. Jim Bolger was a special friend. Our friendship went back almost thirty years. We had stood by one another throughout that time. I knew that I could rely on him. He understood the dairy industry well and had huge common sense, understanding that the dairy industry's cooperative single-seller structure was best for New Zealand's dairy farmers and for New Zealand. He understood that a corporate structure with tradeable shares would soon result in ownership moving out of farmers' hands and probably out of New Zealand. He was strong enough to resist the pressures from the "free marketers" within his own party.

Shipley was different. I had known her for some time and got on well with her. But I knew that she was not a supporter of producer boards and was likely to push for deregulation. I went to see her. "I know that you don't agree with the single-seller structure and that you are looking for us to move away from it," I told her. But I stressed that any move to deregulate had to be carefully managed. We were a large commercial enterprise, employing thousands of staff with tens of thousands of customers. Uncertainty would cause stress to many staff and customers and likely be hugely value destroying. For example, I told her that if she deregulated tomorrow, all of the board's financial borrowings would immediately become repayable. Handled carefully, that could be managed but would take time. She showed how little she really understood when she told me that we should not arrange any more borrowing with that condition. She had no understanding that it would increase the interest bill payable by dairy farmers, or that if we could not borrow under our existing "negative pledge" financial instruments, we would not be able to raise money to pay farmers for their milk as we would be unable to offer potential lenders security.

I outlined for her the existing industry political state. New Zealand Dairy Group wanted a corporate structure with possibly tradeable shares. They did not have any mandate from farmers for that, citing the survey of farmers which showed 94% of them supporting 100% cooperative ownership of their dairy companies and the Dairy Board. Kiwi Dairies Company was strongly committed to a cooperative structure. Other companies were fearful of New Zealand Dairy Company, believing that what was good for it was unlikely to be good for them. They also wanted to retain full cooperative control of their business and industry.

I told her that my task was to get agreement from all companies on what the industry should do if there were no single seller. This was no easy task. I had established a task force comprising all dairy companies' chairmen which was working through the issues. I told her that once we had reached agreement, then I would be in a position to deal with her about removing the single seller. I needed a year to do that. I undertook to come back to her at the end of 1998 with a plan. She responded by saying that she was happy with the leadership I was showing. She wanted the dairy industry to come up with its own plan to operate without the single-seller legislation. She was happy to give me that year. Her agricultural adviser, Owen Symmans, who had been a friend for many years, then asked, "Dryden, is there anything you would like the prime minister to do?" I responded, "Yes, there is. I am trying to lead the industry to an agreed position on how it will operate without the current legislation. There has been a lot of public comment from politicians about what the government does or does not want on the single-seller issue. This is confusing farmers, but even worse is unsettling the board's staff and commercial relationships. It would help if she and her ministers could refrain from commenting on the matter and let us work through it." She agreed to do so. The meeting concluded with me telling her, "I am going to tell farmers that I have agreed with you that the industry has a year to agree an alternative structure. We have issues to work through, but we will hit that deadline." We agreed that if anything changed, we would advise one another. She seemed pretty pleased with what we agreed. I too was satisfied and I was confident that by the end of 1998 I would have industry agreement on the way forward. Events subsequently demonstrated that her word was not her bond!

While legislative and structural reform was becoming a dominating issue, the business had to carry on. It was critical that it did not distract the organisation and impair the board's commercial performance. We were continuing to identify opportunities to improve returns for farmers. Our priority must be to capture them. Warren had implemented a global positioning strategy, "Winning Worldwide", with two major business units. New Zealand Milk would be the consumer marketing arm and New Zealand Milk Products (NZMP) an ingredients business. They would compete where necessary for milk and each would be required to deliver superior and sustainable wealth to shareholders.

- In branded consumer products we had to aspire to be either the market leader or a strong number two in every market we entered. If we were not confident of achieving lead or number two position within a three to five-year period, we should refrain from entering that particular market as there was little prospect of ever making money. Encouragingly, we were getting traction in an increasing number of growth markets in South East Asia and Latin America.
- The ingredients business usually had leading market shares in most of the markets we operated in.
- There was a substantial commodity component where price was the major consideration for customers, so low cost to sell was critical.

- The business had to become even more customer focussed, looking for every opportunity to differentiate our products and increase value.
- There was also a substantial specialised ingredient business which was often high value. This business needed to be built on our superior research and development capability, and our in-market technical support. Close liaison between the Dairy Research Institute and our marketing organisation gave us a distinct marketplace edge over our worldwide competitors.
- Our strength came from robust research, creating points of difference in milk by splitting it into its components and then reassembling them into a wide range of functional products, often tailored to the specific needs of individual customers.

While the demands of the structural reform debate were considerable, Warren and I were in complete agreement that driving commercial performance had to remain paramount. The structural debate became increasingly unsettling to our staff, many of whom were concerned about their future employment. While Warren had to play a role in the structural issue, we agreed that driving the commercial performance of the board would be his priority, while I would shoulder most of the structural debate burden. To his great credit Warren and his staff did just that. They never flinched for one moment and, despite the distractions and uncertainty, continued to make good progress towards our commercial objectives.

In the autumn of 1998, I went round the country talking to farmer meetings, advising them that I had given an undertaking to the prime minister that the industry would have a plan on how it would operate without the existing legislation by the end of the year. I had established a task force of the chairmen of all dairy companies. We would consider the options and come back to them with what was best for farmers, not necessarily what the government wanted. Farmers agreed with how we were dealing with the issue and were highly supportive. It was obvious that they overwhelmingly supported a farmer-owned cooperative structure. Although I did not canvass directly the one company model versus multiple exporter models, it was obvious that they preferred the single-company concept.

But as I worked to guide the dairy company chairmen to agreement on the optimal structure for the future , my job suddenly became much harder. John Young, the chairman of Kiwi Dairies, and John Storey came to advise me that their companies had agreed to establish a joint venture to market dairy products overseas and intended to invite other companies to join them. "Why do you want to do that?" I asked. "You've got the Dairy Board." They were looking past the Dairy Board, they replied. "So, you are telling the farmers of New Zealand that the concept of the single seller has got to go?" No, they were supporting the single seller! I asked them to think about the signal they would be giving to the rest of the industry. "Why would they support something that you guys are running, with 70% control?" I pleaded with them not to go ahead as it would frighten dairy farmers and companies. It would escalate the already high level of distrust and suspicion within the industry and make the differing viewpoints harder to resolve. That then would make a government-imposed solution more likely and that would not be good for farmers. I was a director of New Zealand Dairy Company but the matter had never been discussed by its board. As had often been the case, it was another example of Storey and Footner acting without approval of New Zealand Dairy Company directors.

Predictably, the announcement of this joint venture sent the industry into an uproar. Distrust soared. Even New Zealand Dairy Company suppliers were incensed. The smaller dairy companies felt extremely vulnerable. Although extremely supportive of the Dairy Board and the single seller, no company wanted to be beholden to and dominated by the two biggest players. Every dairy company began to consider how it could do its own marketing if the single seller was removed. Reaching consensus became increasingly difficult as by now the smaller companies refrained from committing themselves.

I was in Ottawa, Canada when I awoke one morning in May 1998 to find a message awaiting me from John Luxton whom Shipley had recently appointed as Minister of Food, Fibre, Biosecurity and Border Control, that mouthful title replacing just one word, Agriculture. It asked that I call him as soon as possible. I did so immediately to be advised by his office that he had just gone into the House to introduce legislation to remove the powers of the nine producer boards, giving them till 15 November to advise the government on how they would operate without their statutory powers. I was furious. There had been no prior consultation, which every government always undertook with parties affected by major legislative developments. But it was much worse than that. It was a most egregious breach of the agreement I had made with the prime minister, that we had until the end of 1998 to come up with a plan and the government would give us that time. I had committed to deliver a plan by the end of the year. I had communicated that to farmers. Shipley had just cut my feet from under me.

I knew John Luxton very well. He was a good bloke. I had been one of the first people to offer him my support and ask him to stand for Parliament. Many years later he advised me that he was unaware of my agreement with Shipley. I believe him. Shipley, though, did not have that defence. I had not heard a word from her. It takes some time to prepare draft legislation and introduce it into Parliament, so they clearly had been working on it for some time, almost certainly months not weeks. She broke her word. Never in my whole career, both before or since, has anyone ever acted so dishonourably. It was a complete and absolute betrayal. It also demonstrated how politically inept she was. I had agreed with her a timetable to do what she wanted. It was pretty dumb politics to breach that undertaking and even dumber to take on the National Party's most loyal supporters, dairy farmers. In doing so she destroyed whatever chance National had of retaining power in the 1999 General Election.

By now Dairy Board meetings had become very unpleasant. When dealing with the commercial business, the directors continued to deal with issues logically and we were all singing from the same hymn sheet. But we were increasingly having to deal with industry structural matters where a wide gulf was opening up between New Zealand Dairy Company and all of the other companies. This was highly divisive with goodwill being largely absent. I tried everything I could think of to improve the atmosphere and reach consensus. The structural issues had always been scheduled for the latter part of the board meeting. As these issues grew more divisive, this resulted in directors leaving the meetings with a sour taste in their mouths. I tried moving them to the top of the agenda. This resulted in the disharmony on structural issues permeating the whole meeting. There was no simple answer. It was made worse by the fact that some companies had not appointed their chairmen as directors of the Dairy Board, and they were trying to control their appointed directors from outside the boardroom, so getting decisions from the board was becoming increasingly difficult as directors refrained from committing themselves until they received approval from their company chairman.

I was determined to steer the industry through deregulation into one single cooperative company into which the assets of the board would be subsumed. I knew that this was by far the best option which would create superior value. I knew that is what the overwhelming majority of farmers wanted. The logical way was to transform the Dairy Board into a single cooperative company. But New Zealand

Dairy Company, with 50% of the industry's milk, wanted to control their own destiny, dominate the industry and take over the assets of the Dairy Board. Storey and Footner clearly favoured a non-cooperative model, although that view was shared by few of their directors. Transforming the Dairy Board into a single cooperative company would thwart their aspirations. Kiwi Dairies, with over 25% of the milk, favoured a single cooperative company. They had become less supportive of the Dairy Board. Most of the other companies favoured transforming the Dairy Board into a single cooperative company. Tatua would likely go their own way. They had a niche position which they continued to cleverly exploit to achieve superior results for their farmers. Westland reserved their position, but both they and Tautua did not trust the two big companies.

Given all of that, consensus was clearly going to be difficult to reach. But the consequences of breaking up the Dairy Board were horrendous, I knew that farmers would view it that way. Farmers particularly did not trust Storey and Footner. Despite the difficulties, I believed that I could guide the industry to a consensus. But I had to consider my position. I had been chairman for nine years. I had always believed that about ten years is as long as any leader should remain. The industry was divided. Was I the solution or was I the problem? If somebody else was more likely to unite the industry behind a single cooperative company, I should retire immediately to facilitate that. After some careful reflection and soul searching, I believed that I was more likely to achieve that than anyone else. I formed the view that if I was not there, the New Zealand Dairy Company model dissolving the Dairy Board and dividing up its assets between two or more companies could prevail. That would be a disaster, one which I could not stand back and allow to happen. I knew that Storey would like me gone, but I needed to have at least majority support from the other companies. The Dairy Board statutory meeting which appointed the chairman for the next year was coming up at the end of June. Kiwi was the key so I sounded them out as to whether they continued to support me or wanted me to retire. It was indicated to me that I should continue. I was reappointed but I indicated that I would retire in 1999. I thought that gave me a year to get the job done, which I was determined to do.

But only two months later in August, on the first day of a board meeting, my deputy, Graham Fraser, slipped me a note indicating that a "spill" was on. I asked him if they had the numbers, and he replied, "They just might have." At lunchtime Storey, John Young (who was not a Dairy Board director) and Harry Bayliss (I cannot recall if any others accompanied them) came into my office. They knew that they could not legally remove me midterm as under the Dairy Board Act the chairmanship was from June to June and there was no provision for a mid-term election. They told me that they intended to appoint Storey as chairman designate to take office in June 1999. During the lunch break I moved among the directors. I still had the support of most of them, but Kiwi had deserted me. With their support New Zealand Dairy Company had the numbers. I continued to run the board meeting as normal for the rest of the day.

At 5 pm I asked the executives to leave as I wanted a directors-only session. I raised the issue of leadership, saying I was aware that some of them thought I should stand down. I said, "Come on guys, you had better put it all on the table, now is your chance." I went around the room ensuring that each director commented. I did not learn anything that I did not know. But every director had to commit themselves. I still had the support of the directors who were not Kiwi or New Zealand Dairy, but there were some who were embarrassed and unable to look me in the eye as they supported change. After about an hour when each director had commented, I thanked them for their comments, indicated that I would consider their views and return to the matter next morning. I then adjourned the meeting.

It was clear to me that my time was up. The artifice of appointing Storey as chairman designate was totally unnecessary and irresponsible, because they were prepared to risk the organisation becoming completely dysfunctional had I faced them down. Not for one moment would I even contemplate taking that risk. If I took the matter public to the farmers where I had very strong support, I would probably have prevailed, but that would have exposed the board's business operations to significant disruption. I would never do that. The business was much more important than me. Throughout my career my guiding principle had always been: what is best for farmers? My bottom line was that I had no desire to be chairman if I did not have the support of my board.

I then went into Warren's office and told him. He asked me, "How long have you known about this?" I said, "Since morning tea." He was incredulous and said, "You have chaired the meeting all day and you haven't given a single sign of this?" I replied, "Yes, I am going to finish. I will finish at the annual meeting in November. It will become very difficult for you and won't be pleasant, but hang in there, continue to run the business as you are now. The job must go on; farmers deserve that. But Storey won't last. He simply does not have the capability."

Next morning, I moved the board into a director-only session. I told them that I had carefully considered their views. I told them that the chairman designate scheme was crazy and, even worse, irresponsible, because it risked serious disruption to the board's business and farmers did not deserve that. But, I told them, it was totally unnecessary as I held office only with their support and had no desire to continue as chairman if I did not have their support. "All you had to do was come and tell me that I no longer had your support." I told them that I would retire at the Dairy Board Annual Meeting in November. I then told them that they needed to put their best directors onto the Dairy Board, stop the "revolving door" of director appointments of recent years and stop trying to run the board from outside the boardroom. I told them that in the Dairy Board, farmers had an extraordinarily valuable asset. "Whatever you do don't impair, break up or destroy that value. It will be gone forever; you will never get it back. Farmers will pay for that forever and will never forgive you," I implored them. We agreed that no announcement would be made for ten days as I wished to advise my family and I was committed to leave next day on a short visit to Taiwan.

As I headed home after the board meeting, I had very mixed emotions. I felt deeply disappointed that I had not got an alternative structure over the line. That I had not finished the job and so had let down farmers, and the Dairy Board staff who were so deeply committed to farmers. But I also felt a huge sense of relief. The last few years had not been pleasant. Increasingly, the larger dairy companies who controlled most of the industry's milk had focussed inwards on obtaining a larger share of the pie, rather than what we needed to be done to best compete internationally and earn a bigger pie. It had been depressing at times. Now that burden had been lifted from me.

But I was also immensely proud of what had been achieved. When I became chairman, the board's branded consumer sales had totalled about $400 million. They had grown to $2.5 billion by the time I retired and were very profitable. The board had been transformed from essentially being a commodity-trading organisation, and a good one, to one which while retaining those core commodity-trading skills had also built a very substantial added-value dairy foods business.

The second statutory Performance and Efficiency Audit, completed two months before my retirement, described the board as having moved from a "product-based organisation to one organised around markets, regions and product categories". It also found that the board had shown "significant improvement since the 1993 audit".

Most importantly, there had also been a "significant improvement relative to world best practice", and the board was now in line with world best practice in most dimensions. I could now confidently assure my farmers that the board's performance was world class. The credit for that goes to Warren and his capable and dedicated staff.

I was also proud of the reform of international trade in agriculture. This was the biggest issue of my career, with a payback of several billion dollars per year for New Zealand farmers. I had put years of unrelenting effort into it, helped by Murray, Warren and the late Nigel Mitchell who was such a capable trade policy expert. I would not want to overstate our role, but our knowledge of the international dairy trade and the strong relationships and credibility we had around the world enabled us, together with New Zealand's outstanding trade officials, to influence the scope and detail of the final agreement.

I had been privileged to have had nearly ten years leading New Zealand's largest and most highly respected business. One which was the leading international dairy business and the only business New Zealand had in any industry which had achieved a world leadership. I was leaving it in good shape and performing at the top of its game. Despite the difficulties of the last few years, it had in the main been an exciting journey. I had enjoyed many wonderful experiences and made many friends, in New Zealand and around the world.

Exactly twenty-five years to the day after I had been elected a director of New Zealand Cooperative Dairy Company, I announced my retirement both as chairman and a director of the New Zealand Dairy Board and as a director of New Zealand Dairy Company at the annual meeting of that company. I told them that the decision to retire was mine, which was true. I did not tell them of the crazy chairman designate scheme because I wanted the industry to concentrate on the challenges ahead, not on me. The farmers were shocked, as for thirty years I had always been there for them in one role or another, and now I would not be at a time which they knew was going to be challenging. Many of them, knowing that I had been having a pretty tough time, began to read between the lines and were suspicious of the role their own company leadership might have played in my decision. But all were most generous in their applause and accolades.

I had one more shot to fire, however. I would make it count.

FORTY-THREE
A FINAL SALVO

Speeches were a significant method of communicating with my farmers and with the general public. Media releases and interviews of course played a role, as did radio which I used extensively. Radio New Zealand's midday farming programme was an excellent way to communicate with farmers, as I could speak directly to them without being edited and had sufficient time to effectively cover issues. But it was my speeches which enabled me to communicate in depth to the mass audience of both farmers and public. I had early in my career mastered the art of using a few colourful phrases to capture headlines. I had always taken great care when writing my speeches. I used direct language as I wanted my message to be clear and easily understood. I usually refrained from extravagant language, preferring to be reasonable and discuss issues in a reasoned manner. I tried to avoid personalising matters and refrained from unnecessarily hurting people's feelings. My maxim was "leave a friend behind if you can, but if you can't, never leave an enemy". I would never be intentionally misleading. But I also was determined to be myself, to be candid and level with my audience.

Throughout my career I always wrote my own speeches. My addresses to the half-yearly and annual dairy industry conferences were the only exceptions. They were comprehensive reviews of Dairy Board operations for the period and as such were written by the CEO, Murray and Warren. But in my final chairman's address to the Dairy Board Annual Meeting in October 1998 there was no longer any need to be diplomatic. I decided to let rip and speak my mind without fear or favour. Warren enlisted the help of Neville Martin who was the Dairy Board communications and public relations manager. Neville was a very experienced journalist and PR person. It was largely due to him that the board had a good public image. Journalists referred to him as "on the level Neville". He had an enviable reputation for integrity, was always straight with the media and was highly respected. He was also a skilled wordsmith. I was both privileged and fortunate to have him as my media advisor.

The Minister of Agriculture always addressed the Dairy Board Annual Meeting. That year it was John Luxton's turn to face the farmers. He was very generous in paying tribute to my contribution to the industry. But he then had to sit and listen while I delivered what was to be perhaps my finest ever speech, one which I had rehearsed repeatedly to ensure that it made maximum impact. It was not to be a pleasant experience for him.

After the usual pleasantries, I went to the issue of deregulation, and I went hard.

"I would now like to turn to the subject of deregulation, although I rather suspect that the minister would prefer that I did not.

"It will come as no surprise to anyone in this room that I am opposed to removal of the single seller. I oppose it because all of the evidence tells me that it is going to cost us, and the country for that matter, a lot of money. And because it is not going to do any New Zealander a blind bit of good.

"I would even go so far as to say that what we are seeing is an attempt to perpetrate a gigantic economic hoax. The seductive myth is advanced that if the magic wand of deregulation is waved in the direction of the producer boards, particularly at the so-called single-desk sellers, such as our board, a much-needed economic miracle will follow and export receipts will skyrocket.

"They won't. In fact, I am very much afraid that the net result will be to cost this country export dollars, rather than the reverse.

"It's easy for some politicians to point to Telecom, the waterfront, or the transport industry (you will note that the health system never gets mentioned in this context) and say, you know, it worked for them so why won't it work with producer boards?

"On the surface that argument is deceptively logical – which makes it attractive if your objective is deception. Competition has brought prices to *consumers* down.

"But should that be our objective – or that of the Apple & Pear Board or Zespri International? No of course not, because our objective is to *maximise* returns for our products, for farmers and for New Zealand. Not *minimise* them.

"The decision as to whether the single seller is best for New Zealand dairy farmers is one for farmers to take. Their view is absolutely clear: they remain overwhelmingly in favour of retaining the board's statutory powers.

"They believe that there is significant commercial value in the single-seller status of the Dairy Board. I have seen that time and time again when I visit overseas markets where our competitors talk about us enviously.

"I also see:

- The market premia which we can extract through the benefit of a coordinated marketing effort
- Our ability to capitalise on, and globally roll out, new product developments, thus maximising the value of our brands
- And our ability to exploit product-mix opportunities as market needs change

"But it is not solely a decision for farmers. If Government is to confer the statutory powers on the industry, it needs to be satisfied that the New Zealand economy is at least no worse off as a consequence.

"The next seven slides tell it all:

- The value of dairy exports continues to rise year on year.
- Growth in dairy exports has outstripped every other significant industry.
- Dairy's share of exports has increased from 14% to 21.7%.
- The dairy industry's contribution to GDP growth is 60% higher than the economy as a whole.
- New Zealand's share of international dairy trade has increased steadily.
- A substantial branded consumer/food service business, sourced from New Zealand, has been created.
- In the last three years, *total New Zealand exports* have grown by $868 million. *Dairy's contribution – $826 million.*

"Could I suggest that something in the economy does need fixing – the bits that are really broken.

"The plain unvarnished truth is that, if the performance of the balance of the export sector over the last three years had matched ours, New Zealand would have had a $6 billion trade surplus - rather than barely breaking even.

"Clearly a case *cannot* be made that the dairy industry under its present arrangements has not performed. If our present arrangements are to be changed, then farmers are entitled to have it demonstrated to them that they will be better off. Thus far the silence is deafening.

"Quantifying the value of a single marketing organisation has always been a difficult question, but nonetheless one which deserves to be answered.

"The board has commissioned two highly regarded organisations to examine the value at risk from fragmentation of the single seller.

"Each adopted a different approach. One was a bottom-up study based on econometric modelling, while the other was a top-down analysis using a standard business model.

"Both studies reached similar conclusions. Rapid and significant value loss occurs as the single seller fragments into multiple marketers. These studies demonstrate what we have known all along – that there is significant commercial value in the single-seller legislation, not only for New Zealand dairy farmers but for New Zealand.

"But it won't be worth it, if by shedding our one advantage against the gross economic evils of protection, subsidisation and dumping, that we face in the market every day, it leads to free trade.

"Nobody could be more passionate about achieving a world in which the playing field is level for the New Zealand farmer than I. And I take no little pride in what has been achieved in that area during my time on the board. But to imagine that if David drops his slingshot, Goliath will disarm is to display a woeful ignorance of the way the real world works. Without David's slingshot the Israelites would have been slaughtered by the Philistines of Goliath.

"When complete free trade depends on removal of the single seller, then, and only then, will the industry answer the call. Until then we are entitled to organise our marketing arrangements in the way which is most beneficial to New Zealand farmers and to New Zealand."

I then addressed the most critical component of a deregulated dairy industry.

"But if, and I sincerely believe when, that day comes, the industry needs to be ready for it. And we will be. We may be principled, but we are also pragmatic. Thus, we have taken the decision to shape our own future, to ensure by that initiative that the strengths which we have worked so hard to give the industry, and in which we have invested so much, are retained.

"Of those strengths, nothing is in my view more important for farmers than the common ownership of all which lies beyond the farm gate and adds value to the raw material we produce. By that means the industry amasses the critical mass necessary to take on the major players in the world dairy business. Without that strength they would bury us. Let there be no mistake, size is critical to success. Our competition are the big hitters in the international dairy market. Meeting and beating them in the remorseless struggle for retail shelf space means having sufficient R&D investment capability to innovate constantly, and the advertising and promotional muscle to keep our brands at the top of their market sectors."

I referred to the increasing concentration of retail strength around the world and showed a slide which made the point that while the Dairy Board was New Zealand's largest company, it did not even make it into the ten largest dairy businesses in the world.

I then went on to urge Kiwi Dairies and New Zealand Dairy Company to get together, which would consolidate three quarters of the industry's critical mass. But even that would result in value leakage of hundreds of millions of dollars, so they needed to give sufficient confidence to the rest of the industry to join them to avoid the leakage.

I then moved to the future:

"Major changes are occurring in the food markets of the world. These are being driven by demographics, globalisation, ethics, cultural beliefs, consumer access to information, technology and rising disposable incomes.

"While specific changes will differ greatly by market, the globalising forces which are remorselessly reshaping our world will be increasingly influential. As living standards rise, food markets of the future will increasingly focus on:

- Nutrition
- Wellness
- Convenience
- Recreation
- Indulgence
- Traditional values

"Increasingly, consumers, particularly among the more affluent nations, are going to look for foods which offer both nutritional and health-enhancing benefits – the so-called wellness foods.

"The exciting thing about milk of course is that it is, and always has been, the perfect food. It is a veritable cornucopia of health and life-enhancing constituents, many of which we have yet to fully understand and utilise.

"I believe that you will see affluent consumers attaching increasing importance to aspects such as food safety, food origin, animal welfare and environmental sustainability.

"The industry is going to have to face up to the thorny subject of biotechnology. Genetic engineering will modify plants and animals and change the attributes of the food components available to them. Similar technologies will modify forage and feed, to change both the products and the profitability of animals. And micro-organisms – such as those used in cheese making for instance – are going to be employed to change the processes to which they are applied.

"These are the technologies which will present both opportunities and threats to our industry:

- We will be able to reduce costs and improve product quality.
- We will have available new product concepts and processing technologies.
- We will be able to reduce environmental hazards.
- On the other hand, threats will arise in the form of consumer resistance to some of these technologies.

"These are the drivers for change that the industry must look at now.

"But whatever the outcome of these particular deliberations, I am prepared to predict that, five years from now, the industry will be earning twice what it does today from its value-added businesses. We know how it is to be done and we are on track to do it.

"Our investment in research and development will be paying even greater dividends, with 25% of the industry's earnings coming from products which don't even exist today.

"Our consumer business will be around 75% larger than it is now and will be very profitable.

"And dairy will still be New Zealand's largest export earner.

"And what of the world market?

"Despite the sacrifice of blood that some appear hell bent on making on the altar of free trade in respect of our statutory powers, my considered judgement is that progress in trade liberalisation will be painfully slow. I have held that view for some time, and I fear that the battering the international economy is taking at present is only likely to weaken the resolve of governments around the world to eschew protectionist policies.

"So accessible consumption growth will be slow and the board or its successor (and note that I use the singular tense) will have around 40% of the international dairy trade against todays 33%.

"And the New Zealand dairy industry? I have said often enough that I believe the number of dairy companies will reduce further. What I have not said before is that I hope the process will eventually lead to a single dairy cooperative, integrated in both manufacturing and marketing.

"While the legislation is there, such a development would not be practical. But it will happen eventually, because it is I believe what will deliver the best result for all of our farmers. A single cooperative, farmer owned, focussed on its customers and competitors, is a superior economic model than other options, and thus will most effectively keep the destiny of farmers in their own hands.

"After all, that is what our overseas competitors are doing. Building the greatest critical mass they can to face an increasingly competitive world."

In my valedictory remarks as I closed the annual meeting. I lambasted the dairy companies for the revolving door of director appointments. In two years, there had been twelve director changes in a board of thirteen. Few companies had appointed their chairman, whom one would usually assume was a company's most competent director. It was simply not good enough. Farmers would pay dearly for this appalling commercial stewardship by Kiwi and New Zealand Dairy.

I expressed my disappointment that the industry was spending too much time on structural issues and arguing over their share of the pie. They needed to be more focussed on creating value to bake a bigger pie and concentrate on markets. On marketing, customers and competitors, I urged them to:

- "Maintain ownership of their industry. In that way you will influence your own future. History has a poor record for those who placed their destiny in the hands of others.
- Continue to work together as an industry. Size, power and commercial performance are inextricably linked.
  Individually each farmer's business is tiny. But collectively our industry, while only of moderate size on a global scale, is big enough to mean we are in with a chance.
- Maintain cooperative principles which link ownership and reward throughput. No proprietary company has a goal of lifting its suppliers' earnings. In fact, the opposite applies: they put their best people onto driving down raw material costs.
- Be resolute with government on deregulation. It can be stopped. At the very least being resolute will improve the industry's prospects of negotiating beneficial conditions with government."

FORTY-FOUR
THE AFTERMATH

As I intended, my parting shot certainly captured the headlines in virtually every media outlet in the country. An independent analysis showed that most articles were favourable to me and unfavourable to Government. John Luxton took a hammering, and he was later to remark to Warren that I had destroyed his political career. I think that was an overstatement and certainly was not my intention, but his credibility was certainly in tatters. Within days Shipley was also in retreat and National Party MPs had no stomach for further fight. A month later media headlines heralded a "back down by Government on producer board reform".

Two years later when I was honoured by Massey University with a Doctor of Science (honoris causa) degree, the Massey University orator, Professor (later Sir Paul) Callaghan, said:

"When the then Minister of Food, Fibre and Biosecurity took on Dryden Spring and demanded an end to the Dairy Board monopoly he was forced to debate the facts, and in doing so he lost that debate and faced political humiliation. For the first time the high ground had been lost by those who espoused market ideology, and the news media so responsible for shaping public opinion discovered that the emperor had no clothes.

"Why did Sir Dryden Spring win that debate? For three reasons.

"First, he was leading New Zealand's most successful industry, an industry which had transformed its fortunes in the face of the most difficult international conditions, which had taken on the world and won.

"Second, he made the compelling argument that while maximising competition lowered prices to the benefit of the consumer, the consumer in this case was the rest of the world whereas we in New Zealand could only benefit by maximising our market premiums. I have wrestled with the writings of the leading economists who tried to defeat that argument. They are obscure to the point of being incomprehensible. For the first time they were thrown onto the back foot on entirely intellectual grounds.

"But the third reason that the debate was won was that the argument was advanced by Dryden Spring, an individual of towering intellectual achievement who not only knew his industry inside out, but who retained the respect and admiration of everyone with whom he had dealt."

My salvo had given the dairy industry more time and a much more sympathetic public opinion. The Dairy Board was able to largely ignore government calls to provide it with a proposal for deregulation and concentrate on the strategy that the Dairy Board and dairy companies wished to pursue. But the road ahead would not be easy. New Zealand Dairy and Kiwi Dairies had nearly 70% of the industry's milk between them, but they had diametrically opposed views. Kiwi was firmly committed to a single cooperative company to succeed the Dairy Board. What New Zealand Dairy Company wanted was less clear, but its leadership appeared to favour two competing companies with New Zealand Dairy becoming a joint stock company with tradeable shares. Their farmers, who had never been asked, almost certainly favoured a single cooperative company.

Within a year, as I had predicted, Storey was gone. He was convincingly defeated in his bid for re-election as a director of New Zealand Dairy by his own Te Awamutu farmers who chose Jim van der Poel, to whom I had given my public support. He paid the price for being out of touch with farmers who were deeply suspicious of his undermining of the Dairy Board, his preference for a corporate structure, and his own poor judgement.

Personnel changes continued apace. Doug Leeder succeeded Storey as chairman of New Zealand Dairy. He was strongly in favour of a single cooperative company which he openly supported. This put him at odds with Footner who a few months later was also gone. He was succeeded by Graeme Milne, a former CEO of Bay Milk and a senior Dairy Board executive. With Doug Leeder and Graeme Milne leading New Zealand Dairy, prospects for a single cooperative company improved. Several different external studies commissioned by the industry clearly demonstrated that it would create by far the most value for farmers. But there was then a setback when Doug Leeder unexpectedly resigned. His successor, Henry van der Heyden, was bright but had never been really committed to cooperatives. Neither he nor the New Zealand Dairy Company directors understood that the new payment system, which they had trumpeted as a major win, was about to deliver them a nasty shock. Doug Leeder and Graeme Milne did, though.

Through all of this the milk kept flowing. It had to be processed and sold. The leadership of dairy companies were absorbed by the structural debate. It was a credit to the operating managers that they kept milk-processing operations going effectively. For the Dairy Board staff, it must have been a most frustrating experience, constrained from undertaking many value-creating activities while worrying whether they would even have a job. But Warren's leadership was amazing. Farmers will never understand how much they owed to him and to his staff through that difficult period. The board directors by now were a woefully inexperienced group. Despite that, Warren and his team kept the organisation operating to a very high standard of performance.

The road to the formation of Fonterra was not an easy one, with many setbacks along the way. A single cooperative company was by far the best option. It was a veritable no brainer. Few people understood what a hugely valuable asset farmers owned in the New Zealand Dairy Board. Any other option would have required breaking it up, which would have been hugely value destroying but would have delighted our competitors around the world. I was thrilled when agreement to form Fonterra was finally reached.

I was now only a spectator from outside so have little inside knowledge of that journey. But farmers paid dearly for several mistakes along the way, ones which were a direct result of having such inexperienced directors. Most experienced directors had been purged through the journey to establish Fonterra. A photograph of the original Fonterra directors is revealing. Fonterra was a large-scale dairy-manufacturing and international-marketing business. Yet out of fourteen directors, including the three appointed directors, only three had any experience in a marketing business, four had experience in international business, six in large-scale business while only five had been a director of a dairy company for more than five years. This was a woefully inadequate experience and skill base for a business which brought together the large-scale international marketing of the Dairy Board and most of the industry's milk-processing activity. But it was even worse than that.

The Dairy Board had outstanding people. Its executive ranks were populated with extremely talented people with international marketing experience. At least two of them were experienced and good enough to fill the CEO role in the new organisation. And there was another generation of equally capable young executives behind them. Over the next fifteen years many Dairy Board executives would go on to hold CEO and other senior roles in many of New Zealand's best businesses. Down in the engine room were several hundred dedicated, capable and hard-working people. The decision to relocate Fonterra to Auckland, while being the correct long-term decision, was poorly executed and resulted in the loss of several hundred proven and highly competent staff and executives, as few of them were prepared to move to Auckland.

There was a huge scrap over who should be CEO. Dairy Board executives Chris Moller and David Pilkington were experienced marketing executives and were eminently qualified, knowing the business and the market from top to bottom. Either would have made an outstanding CEO. They both went on to have stellar commercial careers after leaving the dairy industry. Kiwi CEO Craig Norgate was an outstanding young talent who was clearly a future CEO but was not ready as he did not at that time have the necessary experience or maturity. I was at Sydney Airport boarding a plane for Brisbane when I received a call from Henry van der Heyden. He told me that Kiwi were insisting on the appointment of Craig Norgate whom he could not accept under any circumstances. He was prepared to accept Chris Moller, but only for a short term. They were deadlocked, could I help? I told him that I would call him back when I arrived in Brisbane.

Before calling him back I made a few enquiries. My information was that Kiwi were not insisting that Norgate be appointed. They were insisting that he be considered and given equal opportunity. I called Henry and advised him of this. I suggested that a couple of leading businessmen – I nominated Roderick Deane and Norman Geary – be asked to interview the candidates and make a recommendation to the Fonterra directors. I had ascertained that Kiwi would accept that. Unfortunately, Henry was so concerned that they might recommend Norgate that he would not accept my recommendation. I was sure that they would not, but he would not accept my reassurance on the matter. I do not know the details but in the end Norgate was appointed CEO. Chris Moller was appointed deputy CEO but left after a couple of years. So not only had the Kiwi–New Zealand Dairy cabal eliminated the industry's experienced directors but they had now appointed a CEO who, while he had a good mind and a lot of potential, was neither sufficiently experienced nor qualified for the role. They had also eliminated most of the experienced marketing executives and let go several hundred highly capable and experienced marketing, administration and logistics staff. They then had to try to replace those people, something which not surprisingly they were unable to do even at a much higher remuneration cost. Fonterra quickly earned a reputation among business leaders for paying exorbitantly high salaries as they sought to replace the high-quality team they had destroyed.

Fonterra initially saw the expenditure on brands and marketing as wasteful, and so cut back investment. Sales in this most profitable business which had been growing at over 20% per annum soon stalled. Ten years later total branded consumer sales appeared to be only about the same as they were when I retired. With China emerging as a potentially huge future dairy market, a large investment was made, purchasing 43% of Sanlu, a Chinese dairy company. The Dairy Board had previously looked at buying into Sanlu, but Warren would not touch it. He was very wisely not prepared to accept its unsatisfactory provenance and its inadequate quality and food safety security. In due course Sanlu milk was found to have been adulterated with melamine to lift the protein levels. Several babies died and hundreds of thousands became ill. Several Chinese Sanlu executives were sentenced to death and others to life imprisonment. Fonterra's image was damaged, and it had to write off all of its investment.

In 2007 Fonterra began to invest in dairy farms in China, an ill-considered strategy if ever there was one. At the time Fonterra directors told me that in order to get dairy products into China they needed to invest in milk production in that country. What absolute bunkum! For forty years or more most of our dairy exports had gone to developing countries. They all produced some milk and wanted to increase their domestic milk production. It was not uncommon for governments in many of those countries to seek our help to do this. Of course, they would never give us any commitment to prioritise imports from New Zealand if we did so. They reserved the right, at all times, to buy at the best price available regardless of origin. But helping them increase their own milk production would be shooting ourselves in the foot, as to the extent that they succeeded, they would import less milk from us and others. It could never be in our interest to help them increase their domestic milk production. How Fonterra ever believed it could defies all logic. Fonterra's investment in Chinese milk production exceeded $1 billion, it never made a profit and most of it had to be written off.

By moving to Auckland, Fonterra soon lost the political leverage the Dairy Board used to have. To persuade Government to legislate to bypass the need for Commerce Commission approval, it negotiated legislation which required it to provide milk to other dairy companies on terms which were most unfavourable to it. This surprised me. While this was exactly what Agriculture Minister Jim Sutton, who was no supporter of cooperatives, wanted, I knew that Prime Minister Helen Clark and Deputy Prime Minister Michael Cullen had always been strongly supportive of the Dairy Board and of cooperatives. I thought that negotiations should have been escalated to her. That legislation is still in place twenty years later.

As I had argued several years earlier, replacing "nominal value" shares with "fair value" shares was most unwise. It became a millstone around Fonterra's neck. It was fine while the milk supply was growing, but when milk supply declined the company's capital structure was weakened as capital then flowed out. It penalised those farmers who wanted to join Fonterra and rewarded those farmers who left to supply another processor. They could take a large amount of capital with them which they did not have to reinvest in a milk processor, but they still benefited from the umbrella Fonterra was holding over every farmer as all other dairy processors had to match Fonterra's payout.

After Craig Norgate left, Fonterra appointed Canadian Andrew Ferrier as CEO. A decent enough person, his background with Tate & Lyle, the world's largest sugar company, was quite unsuitable for the task, however. Sugar is the ultimate commodity with few opportunities to add value. A dairy foods business, on the other hand, has a myriad of opportunities to add value through branding, science, innovation and new product development, functional properties, health and wellness characteristics and service.

He was followed by Theo Spierings, a Dutchman. On the face of it, his background with a large Dutch cooperative appeared to be ideal. He will be remembered for two things. He persuaded the Fonterra board to adopt a "30 Million Tonnes of Milk" strategy, of which roughly half would be sourced outside of New Zealand. Investment in the value chain from the "cow to the customer" is roughly 65% or so on farm, 20% in primary milk processing and 15% or so in marketing. Margins earned, and return on capital, however, were the reverse. Marketing providing the highest return and milk production the lowest. So, his strategy was effectively "invest in the lowest margin area of the business". The world's leading dairy businesses, like Nestlé and Kraft, had long since exited milk production and in the 1990s completely exited primary processing. Spiering's was the dumbest strategy I have ever experienced in my whole commercial career. His other notable achievement was to persuade the Fonterra directors to pay him more, much more, than any other CEO in New Zealand.

Fonterra performed very badly for the first sixteen years of its existence. In 2018 John Monaghan became chairman. He inherited a global search which was well advanced to find a CEO to replace Spierings. He had the good judgement to abort the search and appoint Miles Hurrell, an existing Fonterra executive, initially as acting CEO, but shortly thereafter confirming him as CEO. It proved to be an inspired decision which set in motion a complete turnaround in Fonterra performance. Hurrell dumped the "30 Million Tonnes of Milk" strategy, focussed the business on adding value to New Zealand milk, stripped cost out of the business and freed up capital by selling underperforming businesses. Fonterra went from performing very badly prior to 2018 to a very high level of performance within a few years. Miles Hurrell has proved to be an outstanding executive and is now regarded as one of New Zealand's leading CEOs. Today Fonterra is performing well, has a payout which is more than competitive with all other dairy processors except Tatua, and is holding a payout umbrella over every New Zealand dairy farmer. Farmers and New Zealand are fortunate to have a New Zealand farmer-owned cooperative, in such a key industry.

PART SEVEN
A NEW BUSINESS CAREER

FORTY-FIVE
MAJOR CHANGES IN LIFE AND CAREER

After my career in the dairy industry concluded in 1998, my life underwent significant change. Christine and I separated in 1999. She had been marvellously supportive, milking cows and helping on the farm as we built our farming enterprise, then supporting me as I built my commercial career. She was a wonderful mother and it was largely due to her that our children became the fine people they are. But I had met Marg and fallen in love with her. It was a painful time for Christine and for our wonderful children who each coped with it in different ways. But I was pleased that Christine and I handled it in a civilised way and have continued to support one another. In 1999 I moved to Wellington to join Marg.

One day in 1998 I received a call from Evan Rogerson. He was a New Zealander who was chief of staff to Renata Ruggiero, the director general of the World Trade Organisation. Evan was a New Zealander whom I knew quite well. He told me that the position of WTO director general was becoming vacant, that Mike Moore was a credible candidate, that if New Zealand got behind Mike, he would have a very good chance of being appointed. I spoke to Mike who told me that he was seeking the position, believed that he had significant support and was prepared to mortgage his house to fund his campaign, but needed the support of the New Zealand Government if he was to have any chance of success. I phoned Prime Minister Shipley and urged her to support Mike's campaign. I told her that an influential source within the WTO had advised me that Mike was a very credible candidate, who with the support of the New Zealand Government would have a good chance of success. I believed that it would be good for New Zealand were Mike to become director general of the WTO. I then talked to other politicians and prominent New Zealanders, urging them to support Mike's candidacy. The New Zealand Government agreed to support Mike's bid. Negotiations for the role deadlocked and eventually it was agreed that the four-year term would be split, with Mike taking the first two years and former Thai Prime Minister Supachai Panitchpakdi, whom I knew and rated highly, taking the second two years. I felt that the timing was the wrong way around. Supachai was a technocrat, well suited to the huge amount of preparatory work needed before real negotiations could begin. Mike was a wheeler and dealer, good at taking people along with him, just what would be needed in the inevitable scramble of final negotiations to conclude an agreement.

In early 1999 Michael Cullen phoned me and asked if I would address the Labour Party Conference. I immediately said no, as it was election year and I had always supported National. However, under Shipley's leadership the National–New Zealand First coalition had fallen apart and Labour looked certain to win the election later in the year. As I thought about it, I reached the view that if Labour was going to become government, it should hear a business perspective rather than just the views of school teachers, trade unionists and social workers. I called Michael Cullen back and told him that I would accept. I knew that this would be a great coup for Labour. Normally, I would not have even considered doing so because of my loyalty to National, but now I no longer owed them anything given Shipley's betrayal of me and my farmers.

When I arrived at the Takapuna Events Centre on a Saturday morning I was besieged by reporters. Of course, they wanted to know who I would vote for. I told them that was my business. They also asked why I was addressing the Labour Party Conference. I told them that I wanted to ensure that a business perspective was given to potential Labour Members of Parliament. In my speech I told the conference: that it was business which drove the economy; that business had to compete with the best in the world; that if they burdened it with cost and regulation it would impair the ability of business to compete; that would lower the income of every New Zealander. I advocated that New Zealanders needed to work smarter, so we should seek to build a knowledge economy. To do that we needed to rev up our education system to ensure that our young people were better educated and that more of them were learning maths and science. I told them that our international business competitiveness would be improved if all students were required to learn a foreign language when they commenced their secondary schooling. My speech was extremely well received, being frequently interrupted by strong applause even though many of them would have been uncomfortable with some of the comments I made. But the National empire was to strike back.

Preparatory work for the next WTO negotiating round, the "Doha Round" due to commence in 2001, was about to get under way. The trade minister, Tim Groser, wanted to appoint a "Special Agricultural Trade Envoy" to push for further liberalisation of agricultural trade. He had asked me if I would be available and recommended that I be appointed. But after speaking to the Labour Party Conference I was, not unexpectedly, soon out of contention. However, one door closes and another opens. Shipley was sacked by the electorate when Labour won the 1999 election. Helen Clark soon asked me to lead the New Zealand team to the APEC Business Advisory Council (ABAC).

When I retired from the Dairy Board, I was invited to join the International Policy Council on Agriculture, Food and Trade, located in Washington DC. This was a "think tank" of largely "free traders" which advocated globally sound food production and trade policies. It was a most prestigious body led by the influential Lord Plumb, a former president of the European Parliament, whom I had known well for over thirty years. Its members were all people of considerable intellect and were internationally recognised and highly influential. Among its members were a future USA Secretary of Agriculture, the highly respected Ann Veneman, and leading US (Joe O'Mara) and EU (Rolf Moehler) trade negotiators, as well as internationally renowned academics and international business people. We provided an independent and influential input into both agriculture and trade policies which were always closely linked. I resigned, due to the pressure of my workload, shortly after being appointed to ABAC.

Dr Spring

In 1999 I was honoured by the Institute of Directors in New Zealand with the Award of Distinguished Fellow of the Institute of Directors in New Zealand. I believe I was in the first group of individuals to receive that award. That same year I was also appointed the first Distinguished Fellow of the Massey University Academy of Agriculture. That role required me to meet with Massey's science academic staff from time to time to discuss future science trends and other issues affecting science and agriculture. It was a stimulating role. As mentioned earlier, in 2000 I was honoured by Massey University with an Honorary Doctorate of Science.

When I retired from the Dairy Board, I was fortunate to have another career as a director of several leading New Zealand and Australian companies. At the time of my retirement, I was already deputy chairman of Goodman Fielder, and a director of Nufarm and the National Bank of New Zealand. I received many invitations to join company boards but was very selective about which I accepted.

I accepted appointment as chairman of Ericsson New Zealand. Ericsson, a Swedish multinational, was one of the world's leading telecommunications companies. It was a huge worldwide business with several hundred thousand employees. It specialised in networks rather than mobile phones. Mobile telecommunications use was growing rapidly at around 35% annually. It was an exciting but very competitive business to be in. Innovation was the key to success, particularly with handsets. Ericsson was very strong in quality engineering; in fact, the company was run by engineers. Sales staff were all engineers, and even most of the finance staff seemed to also have an engineering degree. But it was less successful in handset innovation and design, eventually exiting the handset business to concentrate on its core strengths of networks and mobile internet where it was a world leader. Innovation was the name of the game. If you could not keep up with the rapid pace of innovation, you would soon be out of business. Ericsson sent me to Stockholm where I experienced the huge R&D function and learned of the direction of telecommunications technology.

Some 70% of Ericsson's global business was the provision of network equipment. In New Zealand, Telecom (now Spark) had been a long-term user of Ericsson network equipment and was Ericsson's largest customer. Shortly before I joined, Ericsson had lost the Telecom contract, when in upgrading from analogue to digital technology Telecom had chosen CDMA technology which it believed would have better voice quality, rather than Ericsson's GSM system. It was not a smart decision by Telecom. GSM was a global system which operated right around the world. CDMA was a US system which operated only in the USA and then in only some states. With CDMA as its operating system, Telecom mobile phones would not work outside of the USA. Telecom had to lend a GSM phone to its subscribers travelling overseas in order for them to have a mobile which worked everywhere. That was most inconvenient. The loss of Telecom as a customer reduced Ericsson's New Zealand business by 40%.

At about the same time there was a major drop-off in new network installations right around the world. Along with all other telco equipment providers, instead of growing by 30 to 40% each year, Ericsson's worldwide sales fell by a similar amount, so there was massive global retrenchment by Ericsson internationally. I retired after five years when the New Zealand operation was merged into Ericsson Australia. It had been quite exciting to be involved in a high-tech industry.

Maersk, one of the world's leading shipping lines, had recently established in New Zealand. At the time of my retirement from the Dairy Board, Christine was invited to be "godmother" to a ship which she was to launch in Taiwan. Maersk took Christine, Julie-Ann and I to Taipei for the launching ceremony, which was a huge event. I was then invited to join the board of Maersk New Zealand. Being new to New Zealand, Maersk had a huge challenge to break into the New Zealand shipping market. But they were a typical Danish company prepared to play a "long game", win business by the quality of their service offering, and avoid price discounting. They provided very good service and steadily built their customer base. But the big prize was New Zealand's largest shipper, the Dairy Board, which they had to win for their New Zealand service to be profitable. They patiently worked to create an opportunity. One finally arrived and the managing director, Jens Madsen, excitedly informed me that they were entering negotiations for a contract. I informed him that the

Dairy Board would be really tough on price so he had better be prepared for a very demanding negotiation. A week or so later he phoned to advise me that they had reached agreement with the Dairy Board for "volumes beyond my wildest dreams, but at rates below my worst nightmare".

Maersk had been founded by Captain Arnold Peter Moller in 1904. He had one ship. During my time on the Maersk New Zealand board, Maersk took over the US Sealand line in 2003 to become the largest shipping line in the world. Two years later they took over P&O Nedlloyd to become twice the size of their next competitor. Maersk was a quality organisation. It was run by Mr Maersk McKinney Moller, the son of the founder. He was a most generous man who donated an opera house costing over US$500 million to the Danish nation. He was a remarkable individual who was 97 years old and still actively running the business. Each year he actually signed our New Zealand annual accounts. Maersk New Zealand was an agency business making good money which we had no need to invest, so a growing pile of cash was sitting in our bank account. I believe that if you cannot profitably invest spare cash, you should give it back to shareholders. I had pushed for this for a few years but to no avail. Eventually, I persuaded my director colleagues to pay a dividend to the parent company, but when I arrived at the meeting, I was given a replacement page in which the dividend had been removed. This was at the direction of Mr Moller, who did not think it right that the profit should be taken out of New Zealand. His view was that the cash should be retained in the company and invested in New Zealand. I resigned as a director of Maersk New Zealand in 2004 when I was invited to join the board of Port of Tauranga.

FORTY-SIX
ASIAN ENGAGEMENT

In 1994 Deputy Prime Minister Don McKinnon asked me to accept appointment as a trustee of the Asia 2000 Foundation as it was then called. It was a joint government and business organisation funded by both government and business. The board of trustees was comprised of prominent, high-achieving New Zealanders. It was tasked with deepening New Zealand's engagement with Asian nations. It was originally intended that it operate only till the year 2000, hence the name Asia 2000. However, it was decided in 2000 that it should continue its work and in 2004 was renamed Asia New Zealand Foundation. It remains in existence at the time of writing.

It was initially largely a grant-making organisation which completed projects inherited from the Ministry of Foreign Affairs and Trade (MFAT). Its priorities were focussed on business, education and media. When he retired from Parliament in 1996, Philip Burdon was appointed chairman and one of our most highly regarded diplomats, Phillip Gibson, was appointed executive director. These appointments indicated how importantly government and MFAT regarded its work. Funding from government and business was increased and the range of activities broadened. Activity was largely focussed on business, education, culture and media. Promoting the use of Asian languages in secondary schools was a priority while Asian cultural festivals were supported. The foundation also began to play a role as a "think tank on Asia", attracting the prestigious international Williamsburg Conference to New Zealand.

In 2000 Philip Burdon retired and I was appointed chairman. My deputy was Sir Anand Satyanand, later to become governor-general. Phillip Gibson had returned to MFAT and been replaced by Tim Groser. Tim has a huge intellect and I enjoyed working with him. As I had just been appointed New Zealand Chair of APEC Business Advisory Council, with Tim's trade background he was a huge help to me. But for Tim it was a case of a "trade negotiator" in waiting as he waited to see if the next WTO round, the Doha Round, would go ahead. When it did in 2001, he was off to lead New Zealand's Doha Round negotiating team.

Chris Butler was New Zealand ambassador to the Netherlands. We were fortunately able to persuade him to return home a year earlier than planned to take the role as executive director. One of his great advantages was that he had been in business before he joined MFAT, so he was more qualified than normal to lead an organisation which was effectively a partnership between business and government. The Labour Government of Helen Clark was keen to increase New Zealand engagement with Asia. We increased our activity on all fronts. Culturally, we sponsored some Festivals of Asia while the Lantern Festival at the time of Chinese New Year became an annual event in Auckland attended by between 40,000 and 50,000 people. We initiated smaller events in other cities around the country. The Indian Diwali Festival had a similar success. Education was a prime focus; we wanted students to learn about Asia and be aware of the opportunities which existed within the region. Teaching of Asian languages was encouraged, Asian cultural programmes provided to schools and Asian SCHOLARSHIPS provided. We worked hard with media programmes, including scholarships and seminars, designed to encourage positive publicity of Asia and its importance to New Zealand. We had to be ready every three years with material to rebut Winston Peters when he went on his usual anti-Asian campaign each election year. Our business programmes were reshaped to be more market driven.

A major breakthrough came in 2002. I was visiting Prime Minister Helen Clark to report to her on ABAC. When we had finished our business, she asked me how we were doing in Asia. I said, "I think that we are going backwards." She said, "Chris Butler was in here the other day and he said exactly the same thing. Why do think that is?" I took her through some of the reasons: there were no ministers visiting Asia on trade missions; there were few state visits to and from Asian nations; I did not think that the government was sufficiently engaged in Asia. If the government continued to accord a low priority to Asia, New Zealand was not going to understand what was happening in Asia and would not be seen as a good partner for Asian countries to whom relationships are important. I reminded her, not that she needed to be, that Asian countries accounted for around 40% of world GDP, which was growing more rapidly than the rest of the world. Asia was our largest export region and would soon become our largest import supplier. Our trade with the region would continue to grow strongly. She asked me, "Well, what can we do about it?" I replied, "I think that it must start with Government leading the way. That means you leading the government and saying we are going to allocate more resources to Asia; we are going to lift our profile in Asia; we are going to become a lot more active in Asia; ministerial state visits and trade missions to Asia will be made." I told her that I would get back to her with specific recommendations in two weeks. Chris Butler and his team worked feverishly to produce a strategy.

The result was "Seriously Asia", undertaken in 2003, which was to become a real game changer. An interactive consultation process was established. Working groups covering subjects such as trade, education, culture, geopolitical, business and media were established. The views of more than 1000 people actively engaged in each area were sought. A group of active participants in each area distilled the submissions into reports with recommendations for action. Over 500 New Zealand leaders were invited to a plenary session in Parliament. It was preceded by a gala dinner at which the keynote speaker was the Prime Minister of Singapore Lee Hsien Loong whom I knew quite well. He very generously flew to Wellington with his wife to be the keynote speaker. That helped to make the point that this was to be a major pivot to Asia of New Zealand's foreign affairs focus.

Helen Clark indicated that she would attend the plenary for the whole day. Not unexpectedly, her office was insisting that she chair it. I intended to chair it because I had other plans for her. I wanted the prime minister to sum up the proceedings at the end of the day. That would give her ownership of the outcomes which would increase the likelihood of action being taken on the recommendations. The submissions, deliberations and recommendations of each of the working groups had been circulated. At the plenary session, each was presented and discussed. We had eminent speakers from Asian countries who were very impressed with the concept, the quality of reports and the discussion. They were amazed that the prime minister was present all day. They received a powerful message that New Zealand was serious about its relationships with Asian nations. The summing up by Helen Cark was insightful and brilliant. I had suggested to her that she might consider establishing a ministerial task force to action the recommendations. She went one further. I was over the moon when she said, "I think that we ought to establish a prime ministerial task force to action the conference recommendations." I will never forget as I walked out of Parliament the highly respected Sir Frank Holmes saying to me, "Congratulations, Dryden, you must be delighted. A prime ministerial task force; it does not come any better than that." It is clear that "Seriously Asia" triggered a reorientation of New Zealand's foreign affairs and trade policies towards Asia.

The next period we worked on implementation of the Seriously Asia Action Plan, assisting Government to deliver it. Asia New Zealand had a very high public profile and was operating an increasing number of programmes. We had to work hard to obtain and hold commercial support and sponsorship to fund them. The fact that we were seeking private-sector funding for some of our activities forced us to focus on practical issues which business believed needed to be undertaken. We increased our research capability to enhance our ability to make a constructive contribution to public discussion, as a think tank on Asia. One of the programmes I was delighted with was the establishment of an Asian Knowledge Working Group with the Ministry of Education. Chris and I visited Korea, Hong Kong, Japan and Taiwan where we had sponsors and supporters.

Chris then resigned, hoping to return to MFAT. I was disappointed as he had been outstanding and had set in motion so many outstanding initiatives. John Austin, who had been a director of the World Bank, was recruited to replace him. But I got his appointment wrong. He was a nice chap but simply not up to the job. I had decided that I had to deal with the issue, but other events intervened.

Winston Peters had become minister of foreign affairs. I had always got on well with him, but he was difficult. He was always reluctant to engage so it was impossible to know what he wanted, which made it difficult to meet his expectations. Trustees of the foundation serve for a three-year term. If at the end of that term they have not been reappointed or replaced, they continue until the minister makes an appointment. It was my job to recommend suitable appointments to the minister. The previous minister, Phil Goff, had always accepted my recommendations, but I was always careful to not put them in writing until he had indicated his approval. This was to avoid placing him in an embarrassing position if he wished to appoint someone whom I had not recommended. Winston, however, never responded to any of my recommendations. This went on for two years or more by which time the terms of two thirds of my trustees, including mine, had expired and they were serving at the minister's pleasure. They were all prominent, highly regarded and busy people who were giving freely of their time and wisdom. Some of them were financial sponsors of the foundation. Peters' failure to act on their appointments left them in limbo. It was unfair, unbusinesslike and discourteous. They deserved to be treated better. But still Winston failed to respond. I was totally fed up and let him know that this was most unsatisfactory, stressing the urgent need to fill the vacancies. This got action. In 2006 he phoned me, told me that he wanted a new board and chairman. This was the only time in my life I have ever been fired. That was the last I heard from him. I immediately resigned in writing to both him and my fellow trustees. He did not even do me the courtesy of a reply, let alone a "thank you" for my service! It was to be several months before a new chairman was appointed. An inglorious end, but I was pleased at what Asia New Zealand had accomplished under my leadership. We regularly tracked public attitudes and activity where our programmes were directed. These tracking surveys showed steady improvements in most areas which we were targeting. They showed that New Zealanders increasingly held a favourable view of Asia and an improving understanding of its importance to our country. In particular, New Zealand's pivot to Asia, initiated by Seriously Asia, was a major achievement.

Of course, that was not the end of my Asian activity. I was in demand to speak on APEC, both in New Zealand and overseas. I accepted every New Zealand request but was much more circumspect if overseas travel was required. But my trade work was far from over. In 2001, a couple of years after I had retired as chairman of the Dairy Board, Prime Minister Helen Clark asked me to lead the New Zealand delegation to the APEC Business Advisory Council (ABAC). Of course, I was delighted to accept, as this allowed me to continue the push to liberalise trade which was where the big dollars for New Zealand farmers still lay. My colleagues were to be Peter Masfen, a well-respected Auckland businessman, and Wendy Pye who was a world leader in the use of digital technology in children's books and education. By now Russia and Vietnam had joined APEC which was making reasonable progress on our recommendations for "Implementing the APEC Vision". Each ABAC member was appointed by their respective leader and was directly responsible to them. This appointment ensured that I was able to have a significant ongoing influence on New Zealand's trade policy and international efforts to liberalise trade.

Like the Eminent Persons Group, ABAC members were all outstanding individuals. The difference was that they were all business people. Many of them were CEOs or vice presidents of some of the world's largest companies, such as Motorola, FedEx, General Motors, Cargill and Sumitomo. Many were high net worth individuals, quite out of my own financial league. While most of my experience and interest had been in liberalising trade in goods, the majority of my APEC colleagues were much more interested in the new and rapidly growing services trade, which was where most of their effort was focussed. Political resistance to liberalisation of services trade was not nearly as pronounced as trade in goods, which meant gains in services liberalisation were easier to achieve.

ABAC met four times a year in a different country on each occasion. Our meetings occupied three days. Our mandate was to advise leaders on business issues arising from implementing the APEC vision. Some issues were referred to us by the leaders, others from our own leader or officials, or from business in our own countries. I regularly liaised directly with Helen Clark and her officials to ensure that she was aware of what we were trying to achieve and to make sure that she was on board with it. She was always across the issues and just as enthusiastic about trade reform as I was. Most of my ABAC colleagues did the same with their own leader. My ABAC membership fitted well with my Asia New Zealand work. The regular travel to Asian capitals made it convenient for me to further build my already extensive Asian network.

The chairmanship of ABAC rotated annually, being held by the host country each year. At our first meeting of the year, we agreed a work plan for the year and then at each meeting we worked our way through it. We usually established between four to six working parties to undertake the detailed work in our more important areas of work. I was usually appointed chairman of a working party, mostly either "trade liberalisation" or "trade facilitation". Other working parties usually covered IT, standards and finance. Holding a chairmanship role gave me real influence over what we worked on, the working party's recommendations, and the drafting of reports and communiques. The words of one of my early mentors, the wily Sir William Dunlop, were always front of my mind. He used to say, "If I have control of the person who writes the minutes, I will always get 90% of what I want."

We were tasked with reporting to leaders when they met in November of each year. At our first meeting of the year, we decided what we were going to work on and prepared a work plan. We then pulled together our views through the year, finalising our report and recommendations at our November meeting, immediately prior to presenting them to leaders. ABAC then met with leaders to present our report and recommendations, and then discussing them with leaders. The format of this critical meeting evolved over time. It had been the practice to have a very formal meeting between all of the leaders and all ABAC members. Our report would be formally tabled, the ABAC chairman would make a statement summarising it followed by discussion, in which individual leaders and ABAC members would have been pre-delegated to ask and answer questions. The discussions were always constructive and leaders' comments perceptive. It was clear that they had read our report. I was most impressed in Shanghai when Chinese President Jiang Zemin conducted the whole three-hour meeting in English. When we met in Brunei, however, it became a great farce. The leaders' chairman, the King of Brunei, who held absolute power and was not a politician, was not accustomed to answering to anyone on anything, and was totally out of his depth. We were required to submit written questions in advance, to which we received written replies in advance. But we had to also submit our supplementary questions in advance to which we also received written replies. All of this before the meeting had even convened. Then when we met, we would go through the charade of reading out our question, a leader would then read their reply, we would then read the supplementary and so on. It was an absolute farce and a complete waste of time. We could not even skip the meeting and go to the bar to console ourselves, as Brunei being a strictly Muslim country did not allow alcohol.

We then changed the format to one in which we broke up into about six or seven small groups, two or three leaders and about ten ABAC members in each group. This allowed for a good interactive discussion for a couple of hours between ABAC members and leaders, with plenty of what was sometimes robust discussion. This enabled issues to be put on the table and discussed in depth. It also enabled us to meet individual leaders and observe them at close quarters. During my term I met most of the leaders in this way, including some of the most powerful people in the world, such as President Putin of Russia, a cold calculating man, and President Hu Jintao of China. We balloted for which group we were to be in. Everyone, of course, wanted to meet the president of the USA. I was upset over the invasion of Iraq; in fact, I was pretty wound up about the needless loss of life and suffering caused by an illegal and unjustified war. I had no time for the perpetrator of the war, George Bush, so I asked the staff to ensure that I was not in his group. I was the odd man out as most ABC members wanted to be in the same group as the United States president. But I knew that if I was, there was a fair chance that I would be rather less than diplomatic. I knew I had drawn his group on a few occasions, when the APEC officer conducting the draw had to redraw my name. In my last year a good American friend, Mike Ducker, who was vice president of FedEx, came over to me and said, "I know that you don't like him, Dryden, but you had better come and meet him." He then took me across the room, straight through the crowd and security surrounding the US president and introduced "my dear friend from New Zealand, Sir Dryden Spring". President George Bush had a firm handshake, looked me in the eye and said, "How ya doin, Dryden?" We then chatted for about five minutes before his security ushered him away. He was personable, continued to look me in the eye and kept calling me by my name. Against my prejudice, and much to my surprise, I found myself actually liking him.

Overall, APEC was making good progress towards the vision drafted by the Eminent Persons Group. However, progress was variable between segments. Foreign direct investment within the region was increasing steadily as was intra-regional trade. Progress on standards was slow, yet there were many examples of successful cooperation. For example, some useful help was provided to developing countries to improve food storage as inadequate storage facilities and processes resulted in large wastage. Another was the development of a "Model Port" project for China. Trade liberalisation was slow to start and progressing more slowly than we hoped, but it was nevertheless under way. But trade between APEC members was growing strongly, which was encouraging.

The dialogue between ABAC and leaders was very good. Leaders appeared to value our recommendations, adopting most of them. The host country of the Leaders' Summit each year chaired both APEC and ABAC. During my time, Brunei, China, Thailand, Mexico, Korea, Chile and Vietnam each held the chairmanship. Some countries were just much better at getting things done so progress varied from year to year. Chile and China were the standouts. Most countries usually hosted a Leaders Gala Dinner to which we were invited. Again, the quality of the entertainment in Shanghai was outstanding, while the fireworks display on and along the Huangpu River was unbelievable, costing over US$100 million.

President of China Hu Jintao and the New Zealand business delegation

The weakness in the APEC model was that in allowing countries to set their own pace towards the APEC objective of "Free and Open Trade in the Asia Pacific", the rate of progress became effectively determined by countries least committed to liberalise trade. While a lot of good things were happening in foreign direct investment and in "cooperation" activities among APEC countries, progress in trade liberalisation was minuscule, being geared as it was to the *slowest* common denominator. One of our Canadian colleagues, Pierre Lortie of the Canadian aircraft manufacturer Bombardier, and I began to push the concept of a "Free Trade Agreement of the Asia Pacific". The concept was relatively simple. On a voluntary basis, countries which wanted to liberalise trade more quickly should jointly negotiate and agree firm commitments to achieve free and open trade in goods and services significantly in advance of their APEC commitments. While it was desirable to have as many countries as possible involved, no minimum number of participants was required. We knew that if such a deal could be pulled off, even with a small number of participants, others would soon join for fear of being left behind. Negotiating such an agreement would not be constrained by those who were not enthusiastic about liberalising. Thus, it had the potential to be a circuit breaker and pick up the pace of trade reform. It was at our meeting in Auckland in 2004 that we managed to convince our colleagues to support it and ABAC publicly called on APEC Members to negotiate a Free Trade Agreement of the Asia Pacific.

The New Zealand Government then played a leading role in negotiating what became known as the "Trans Pacific Strategic Economic Partnership" (P4 Agreement) between New Zealand, Brunei, Singapore and Chile which came into force in 2006. While this was a relatively minor grouping, the four countries had a population of 36 million people and a combined GDP of US$736 billion. For New Zealand it was a big number.

Importantly, the framework of the P4 provided for other countries to join. In 2016 Australia, Canada, Japan, Malaysia, Mexico, Peru, Vietnam and the USA joined the original four members in what became known as the "Trans Pacific Partnership", or TPP. USA under Trump, and New Zealand's Ardern Government, refused to ratify the agreement, causing it to collapse. But within two years the same participants, though without USA, had concluded the Comprehensive and Progressive Agreement for Trans-Pacific Partnership (CPTPP). With the TPP being called another name (CPTPP), New Zealand joined. This was a very significant economic grouping which had a combined GDP of US$10.6 trillion.

Although the expansion of the P4 occurred long after I retired from ABAC in 2006, I was delighted with the outcome of all of the work the Eminent Persons Group had put into crafting the APEC Vision in the mid-nineties, and our efforts in ABAC to achieve the vision. I remain particularly proud that the seed of a Free Trade Agreement of the Asia Pacific, which Pierre Lortie and I had sown two decades ago, has grown into a major Asia Pacific Trade Agreement, the CPTPP. It is an agreement which brings huge benefit to New Zealand and to our farmers.

I had one rather surreal experience when the APEC Summit was held in Bangkok, Thailand, in November 2003. Marg and I usually stayed somewhere in the host country for a few days after the summit concluded. We had decided to visit Chiang Mai, which is a provincial capital in the northern highlands area of Thailand. The Lan area of Thailand is located in the north where Thailand bulges into Myanmar. The border with Myanmar is not far away. The Lan region is quite different from the populous regions adjacent to Bangkok on the Mekong River delta. The topography, people, culture and food all differ markedly. It is a great place to visit. When one of my APEC Philippine colleagues, Benny Ricafort, became aware that Marg and I were going to visit Chiang Mai he told me that he had a friend there and he would let him know that we were coming. I thought nothing more of it. Marg and I arrived in Chiang Mai late morning and caught a taxi to our hotel. We hired the taxi for the afternoon to do some sightseeing. We had a wonderful afternoon, arriving back at our hotel at 5.30. I had just finished having a shower at about 6 pm when the phone rang. It was Puvakul Supavai, Benny Ricafort's friend. He had come to take us to dinner! I told him that we had just got in but would be down in fifteen minutes. Marg exploded when I told her that she had fifteen minutes to shower and dress, but she made it, creating a world record in the process. Puvakul and his wife took us to a Chinese restaurant, one of those loud family places with pretty ordinary food which was served extremely rapidly. Your plate was removed and replaced with another dish before you had put your chopsticks down. I wondered what all the rush was about. He then explained that we were in a hurry because he and his wife were going to the funeral of his brother-in-law. I apologised and suggested that they leave us and go. They would have none of it. We were going to the funeral with them.

Off we went to the Buddhist temple. We were guests of honour so were taken up onto the dais and introduced to the family. They were all impressed when told that we had been at APEC. There was a special APEC TV channel and everyone seemed to have been watching it. I was sitting next to a brother-in-law who was an air marshal in the Thai Air Force. He spoke excellent English so we had an interesting discussion. Two grandchildren who spoke fluent English were seated behind each of Marg and me to interpret for us and describe what was happening. I could not see a casket but there was a huge mound of flowers with the deceased's photo in front. From time to time there would be the sound of ice being shovelled behind the flowers so I assume that the body was there. Then the monks began to speak. There were five of them and they each went on for about 30 minutes. About halfway through there was a short break and we were served food and drink. When the proceedings came to an end, we made our farewells to all of the family and were taken back to our hotel. Our host then very generously put his car and driver at our disposal for all of the next day. What an unbelievable experience.

FORTY-SEVEN
GOODMAN FIELDER

Goodmans Bakery was a small family-owned bakery in Motueka. In those days the baking industry was comprised entirely of similar small, family-owned bakeries and was highly regulated. However, by 1965 deregulation was looking inevitable and it was clear that many of the smaller players would not survive. In 1968 Pat Goodman brought together eight New Zealand bakeries into a cooperative, Quality Bakers Ltd, which then began to purchase other bakeries and sign up new members. Quality Bakers then merged with AS Paterson, a flour milling company. When foreign bakers and flour millers Westons and Allied entered New Zealand, Quality Bakers merged with Australian company Fielder Gillespie Davis, which gave it a trans-Tasman presence and a much broader product range.

When I was chairman of New Zealand Dairy Company, as part of our strategy to improve the company's access to capital we had established a commercial paper (short-term borrowing) facility for $150 million. During the holiday period at the end of 1985, I received a call from Jim Graham who advised me confidentially that Goodman Fielder was intending to launch a takeover of New Zealand's leading food company, Wattie Industries Ltd. They then intended to take a stake in European food giant Rank Hovis McDougall, intending to mount a full takeover at a later date. Goodman intended to become a leading food company, not only in Australia and New Zealand, but in Europe as well. Bernie Knowles had worked with Pat Goodman and regarded him highly. Jim and Bernie believed that the Dairy Board should take a stake in Goodman Fielder as it would materially assist the Dairy Board's effort to move further up the value-creation chain. However, the consent of the Minister of Agriculture would be required and that was likely to take some time to obtain. Jim was aware New Zealand Dairy had just established the commercial paper funding line and suggested that we use it to fund the stake in Goodman Fielder until the board could obtain ministerial approval. He asked would I meet with Goodman Fielder, him and Bernie, at the Dairy Company office in Hamilton. For a range of reasons, I was not at all enthusiastic about the Dairy Board, of which I was a director, investing in Goodman Fielder and even less so about the Dairy Company funding the investment even short term. However, I agreed to meet.

On New Year's Day 1986 I drove to Hamilton and opened up our office, which was closed for the holiday. Jim and Bernie arrived as did the Goodman team who had flown from Motueka and Wellington on the Goodman plane. There were four of them: Pat Goodman, the chairman, elder statesman and visionary; Bob Gunn, the finance guy with a mind like a calculator for numbers; Peter Goodman, Pat's younger brother, who ran the baking and milling business; Peter Shirtcliffe who was the operations guy. They were an impressive team who worked together like a well-oiled machine. I was pretty much an observer as options for a strategic alignment between Goodman Fielder and the Dairy Board were discussed. My main concern at that time was to avoid any commitment to New Zealand Dairy Company being used to warehouse Goodman Fielder shares until the Dairy Board could obtain ministerial approval.

The Minister of Agriculture subsequently approved the New Zealand Dairy Board purchase of a stake. Then in 1987 Goodman Fielder took control of Wattie's to form Goodman Fielder Wattie, the largest food company in Australia and New Zealand. Pat Goodman had visions of building Goodman Fielder Wattie into the No. 1 food company in the world. As a director of the Dairy Board, I did not consider a large investment in Goodman Fielder Wattie to be sensible. It had an extremely broad product range, baking, milling, cereals, starch, speciality food ingredients, oils and fats, stockfeed, vinegar, meat, poultry, textiles, restaurants and cafés, as well as the extensive Wattie's range of canned, chilled, frozen, dry, snack and convenience foods. They used only a tiny quantity of dairy products so there would be few synergies. Synergies were largely limited to margarine, which was important to the board as it was pretty effectively managing the margarine market to avoid margarine taking market share from butter, and ice cream as Wattie's owned Tip Top Ice Cream Company. Bernie Knowles was smart but he had a blind spot with ice cream which affected his judgement. He saw it as a great opportunity to add value to our dairy products, one which could be built into a world-leading position. I knew that was far from reality. New Zealand Dairy Company sold dairy ingredients to Tip Top and most of the smaller ice-cream companies. It was a terrible market where ice-cream makers were constantly chopping and changing their dairy suppliers as they attempted to lower their ingredient costs, often by purchasing lower quality products, to enable them to compete in an extremely price-competitive market. Our returns from sales to ice-cream companies were below average. However, the board approved the purchase of a 4.5% stake and Jim Graham was appointed to the Goodman Fielder Wattie board.

When I was appointed chairman of the Dairy Board in 1989, Jim was adamant that I take his place as a director of Goodman Fielder Wattie. The other major shareholders supported my appointment as did the Goodman Fielder Wattie Board. I found that Goodman Fielder Wattie had not lived up to its early promise. Although it had been formed, and was initially controlled, by New Zealanders, it had been headquartered in Sydney. Peter Shirtcliffe, who would have been a brilliant CEO, was not prepared to relocate to Sydney, neither was Cliff Lyon, the CEO of Wattie's, who would also have been a great choice. The directors defaulted to Australian Duncan McDonald who was not the correct fit for the job. He did not last long so when I joined the board in mid-1989 Pat Goodman was acting CEO as well as chairman. Pat had been acting CEO for some time, was a good chairman but was not well suited to be CEO. Little effort was being made to find a suitable CEO.

When Goodman Fielder Wattie was established in 1987, it gave Australia and New Zealand a food company of international scale which was predicted to have a bright future. But later that year came the 1987 stock market crash, the company was not preforming well and the share price had fallen to half of the 1987 value. The 1980s were heady days during which world share markets had soared, the "cowboys were off to the races", and many of them became very rich for a short period. The normal constraints on corporate behaviour had been put aside and a culture of excess permeated many companies. Goodman Fielder Wattie was no exception. It owned a very expensive Sydney house for its chairman, and two jet planes which each cost $20 million annually to run. Large and unwise investments had been made in all sorts of irrelevant activities; for example, $100 million had been invested in Harlin, a company established by John Elliott to try to take over Foster's Brewery. That $100 million ultimately had to be completely written off.

Over $1 billion had been spent buying several bakery businesses in Europe. While these were good businesses, little thought appeared to have been given to any serious consideration of what the investment might earn. The Asian expansion consisted of several chains of ethnic restaurants and cafés in Singapore, Malaysia and Thailand which were delivering very poor returns. When we visited the region, we lunched and dined at some of our Asian restaurants. Most of the original Australian and New Zealand businesses were good ones, although some of the Australian companies were not delivering the performance they should have been.

A large chunk of company shares was held in trusts, the control and ownership of which were opaque. This created the possibility that the company owned a large volume of its own shares, which was illegal, so the directors urgently needed to find out who owned and controlled those shareholdings. At my third meeting we received a report from a leading Sydney legal firm, Blake Dawson Waldron, which cost $250,000. It traced the details of several trusts; who the beneficiaries of each were; the number of Goodman Fielder Wattie shares each trust owned; and what we should do about them. All of the directors were horrified to learn that they were each beneficiaries of these trusts. I was the only director who was not a beneficiary of any of them.

We decided they should be wound up pronto. At the next board meeting, under the guidance of our lawyers, we had to go through a formal process for each trust, in which each director waived his rights in respect of each trust and the trusts were formally wound up. As each director had to absent themselves from the room while their own interest in each trust was being resolved, the boardroom was like Sydney's Central Railway Station with directors constantly leaving and re-entering the room. All of this took about three hours, and I was the only director to remain in the boardroom for the whole proceedings.

Not surprisingly, the company was being very harshly criticised by shareholders. Australian annual shareholders meetings of companies which are not performing well are brutal. They can go on for several hours with the directors being hammered unmercifully. It is not a pleasant experience. Some of the larger shareholders were pressing strongly for change. Most of the criticism was being directed at Chairman Pat Goodman, which was a new experience for him. After a stellar commercial career, Pat was finding that it is one thing to build a large business through takeovers, and that is the easy part. Making it pay is much more difficult, which is why research shows that in about 70% of corporate takeovers the winners are those who sell. Shareholders now believed that he needed to move on, but he was not showing any inclination to do so and appeared to be doing little to find a permanent CEO. They also wanted some board changes. We agreed to immediately commence a search for a new CEO. We finally chose a South African who was running a smaller company in the milling, baking, cereals sector whom we thought could do the job. He had accepted, a remuneration package had been agreed, even to the extent of repainting a Mercedes to the colour he wanted. Then a bombshell, he pulled out. I never did understand why.

One of our directors was Michael Nugent, general manager of Elders Ltd. As we sat around the table, shellshocked and trying to work out the way forward, someone turned and said, "Michael, what about you, would you be interested?" In due course negotiations were concluded and Michael Nugent was appointed. Michael was a thoroughly decent man, but his appointment was a lesson that simply being available is not itself a qualification for any job. He started well and made some useful changes. He then recommended that we purchase Uncle Tobys, a very good snack food and cereals company with a very strong "healthy food" brand image. He also recommended that we sell Wattie Frozen Foods. There was some logic in that as frozen foods was a low-margin, high-working capital business, as the products were harvested in the autumn but sold all year round. I was reluctant to sell as I saw frozen foods as a useful adjunct to Wattie's fresh and canned products. Then the discussion turned to whether we should sell the entire Wattie business. This was not a very good idea as Wattie's was the best performing business in the group. But I did not believe that it would ever deliver its potential controlled from Australia. I believed that it would be better for Wattie's to return to being a stand-alone New Zealand company. We agreed to consider an IPO to float the entire Wattie business. That progressed, a New Zealand board had been established, they had completed due diligence, and the IPO had been announced. Then Pat received a call from Tony O'Reilly, the former Irish and British Lions rugby star who was CEO of the American company HJ Heinz. Within a week the O'Reilly roadshow arrived in New Zealand, charming everyone from Prime Minister Jim Bolger to the Wattie workers, and the fruit and vegetable growers who supplied Wattie's. He quickly offered about $45 million more than the highest price we could expect from an IPO. A sale to HJ Heinz was soon a done deal. I got on well with Tony O'Reilly and when he visited New Zealand each year we always got together. We shared a common interest in dairy. His very first CEO role had been with Bord Bainne (Irish Dairy Board) where he had done an outstanding job in upgrading their marketing capability. He was always grateful to the Irish farmers who had taken a chance on him as CEO and given him an opportunity.

Pat Goodman stood down as chairman in 1992 and was succeeded by John Studdy. The board was strengthened with some very capable directors being appointed, including the first woman director, Janet Holmes à Court. Her husband, who was a successful and wealthy investor, had died suddenly. With six children she had taken on the responsibility of running the family's businesses. She was highly regarded and a charming and very smart lady with a highly developed social conscience. She added much to our deliberations.

Uncle Tobys' performance was disappointing, and so I suggested that we visit the factory at Wadonga, close to the New South Wales and Victoria border. At the airport I was introduced to "Phil", the Uncle Tobys plant manager. Sitting next to him on the flight, I elicited that he lived in Sydney and visited the plant once or twice a month. Alarm bells immediately rang. When we entered the plant, it soon became obvious what the problem was. It was a very complex plant making a large volume of high-quality, premium-priced products. It was very inefficient with a huge amount of wastage, product on the floor, machines down and finished product not meeting specification. Costs were obviously out of control. Like all complex manufacturing sites, it needed continuous hands-on management. Within weeks Phil was relocated to Wadonga.

As Michael Nugent exhausted the very obvious fixes, the overall performance improvement stalled and the job got much harder for him. As he came under pressure for results which he was not delivering, he began to withdraw into himself and spend less and less time in the business units. He sacked John Baird, who ran the New Zealand operations which were performing well; John was a possible successor to him. That prompted the resignation of Dr John Keniry, the other executive who was another possible successor and who was doing a great job building a highly profitable ingredients business. It became clear that Michael had to go. But we repeated an earlier mistake when John Studdy persuaded the board to appoint Barry Weir who was running the European Bakery Group. Barry was an experienced bakery manager who went back a long way with John Studdy. Located in Europe, he had been largely out of sight of the board, apart from his annual visits to report to us. The European business was a good one which, while not performing badly, was making only a very modest return on the large investment we had made on Barry's recommendations. He was a Machiavellian character whose communications were always obscure. His greatest qualification for the position seemed to be that he was available. That is never much of a qualification.

Chairman John Studdy was now coming under heavy criticism from shareholders. He felt that he should resign. The directors decided that the new chairman needed to be a widely respected leader who should come from outside of the existing board members. David Clarke was identified as a suitable candidate. He was highly regarded, being the founder and executive chairman of the hugely successful Macquarie Bank. To be persuaded to accept the position, he required a grant of share options which would be vested if Goodman Fielder met certain share price performance targets. Although common for executives, incentive schemes like this were unusual for directors. However, consultation with shareholders indicated strong support for his appointment and they were prepared to accept his remuneration arrangements. We considered ourselves lucky to have attracted such an outstanding individual and the market reacted very favourably.

David soon reached the view that Barry Weir had to go. An international search was carried out which turned up a few interesting candidates. We settled on David Hearn, who although he had not been a CEO, was a high-performing UK divisional managing director. He was clever, a great salesman and an extremely good communicator. He made an immediate impact, company performance improved, the market reacted favourably and the share price lifted. For a while he was a market darling. But, again, the improvement in performance stalled.

Goodman Fielder was a "conglomerate", a collection of many businesses which had little in common with one another other than that they were all in food. Each of them had quite strong market positions. As was the case in most businesses I have been involved in which operated in both Australia and New Zealand, the New Zealand businesses were outperforming the Australian ones on most measures. Market share which for some products was 80% or more, return on sales, and return on capital were invariably significantly better in the New Zealand businesses. The basic reason for this was that most of the New Zealand businesses had strong market shares for each product group and competition was less than in Australia. While the Australian market was five times larger, competition was much more vigorous. Australia seemed to have many large family businesses, which were still being run by their founders. They had low overheads and competed on price and service which kept selling prices under pressure. Overall, their costs were lower than ours. In some cases, while Goodman Fielder was the largest player in the industry, it had failed to invest in upgrading the actual production sites, which as a consequence were often small and below the scale of our competitors. Thus, our plants were often less efficient, and it was difficult to obtain adequate margins. Goodman Fielder Wattie had been built by acquiring many businesses, some of them large but many small. Starting with the company's founder Pat Goodman, no one had ever applied themselves to the hard work involved in taking a disparate group of businesses and welding them into a cohesive business which had true scale, and then using that to create market leadership. This was how Pat had built Quality Bakers. He failed to do it when he founded Goodman Fielder Wattie.

Successive CEOs had continued the helicopter approach of sitting above the playing field, moving businesses around and buying and selling them. They had failed to do a deep dive into each business, ascertain what its issues were and invest in achieving the lowest cost position our scale should be delivering. Uncle Tobys was a good example of buying a good business but allowing it to underperform through gross inefficiency in the production factory which the CEO had never visited. There were other striking examples. The large poultry business Steggles continued to badly underperform. After much probing from the directors and some external advice, poor livestock performance was identified as the problem. Two factors contributed to that. With the short breeding cycle of poultry, best-practice breeding programmes were delivering genetic gain of about 5% annually. This was much higher than the 1.5% to 2% achieved with sheep and cattle which I was familiar with. But Steggles was delivering only 3%. Thus, our birds produced less saleable meat per tonne of feed than our competitors and the gap was increasing each year. The other reason was even more basic. With thousands of birds in close proximity, an outbreak of disease can kill thousands of birds. Most chicken farmers adopted very strict regimes to keep disease out. An alternative regime was what was called "dirty" farming. In this model a much less stringent regime to prevent the entry of disease was practised, on the basis that while disease may enter, natural immunity would soon build up among the flock and keep losses to acceptable levels. I was incredulous: this was the regime that we practised. Not surprisingly, our mortality rate was higher than our competition's. Just to round off the picture the company also owned the chicken farms so was taking all of the farming risk. Our very profitable Tegel business in New Zealand contracted chicken raising to individual farmers. This not only lowered our risk and the amount of capital employed, but the individual farmers achieved better production than corporates did so we benefited from that also.

There were many more examples. To create world-class businesses requires analysing every activity and every step in the value chain: identifying every issue both large and small and rectifying them. It is hard, painstaking work with a meticulous focus on line-by-line detail required. Although he had a quick mind, David Hearn seemed to be easily distracted and find difficulty in following through on issues. Unfortunately, he did not get the support from Chairman David

Clarke that he both wanted and needed. It was Hearn's first CEO job; he needed greater guidance and support from his chairman than he received. David Clarke was a good chairman who had much to offer. But in Macquarie he was used to direct reports who were highly competent people, whom he could rely on to work out what to do and get it done. Hearn needed more than that and frequently sought mentoring from individual directors.

One area where David Clarke can take much credit was in health and safety. He asked for an analysis of the company's health and safety record. It was appalling. He established a Board Health & Safety Committee, set a target of a 30% reduction in accidents for the year and made every performance bonus conditional on meeting the health and safety target. In other words, regardless of how well any executive performed on all other measures, if the health and safety target was not reached that person would not receive any bonus at all. That, together with establishing a highly visible directors' committee, provided a strong signal to all staff that we were taking health and safety very seriously indeed. Hearn also applied his not inconsiderable ability to driving the improvement programme forward. Pleasingly, the 30% reduction target was hit out of the park, with most business units achieving a reduction of over 50%. Hearn kept the pressure on to further reduce accidents. Within a couple of years Goodman Fielder was achieving best practice in harm reduction and was being cited as an example for others to follow.

When, after five years, David Clarke's share grants were about to lapse because the share price was well below the performance target, he requested that we enter into a new grant for a further five years. The directors refused to do so. Share grants for directors were highly unusual and the circumstances which had justified it five years earlier no longer applied. We knew in declining a new share grant that Clarke would probably resign. We would prefer him to continue but on principle were not prepared to have director remuneration significantly out of line with common practice. Unfortunately, he chose to resign. Deputy Chairman Jon Peterson replaced Clarke as chairman in 1999. Jon was a former vice president of the giant international food company Unilever, who had retired back to his native Australia. He was a highly competent and very experienced executive. I became his deputy chairman.

David Hearn was by now under pressure. The share grants which he had received when he was appointed five years ago, and which would have made him rich if they vested, were about to lapse because the performance targets had not been met. Although we extended the qualifying period by a year, they were still likely to lapse as there seemed little prospect of the performance targets being met. His focus was no longer on the hard grind necessary to lift performance but on any short-term action, including a takeover, which would cause his share grants to vest.

Goodman Fielder's poor financial results made it vulnerable to a takeover, although its conglomerate nature made that less attractive, which was probably why a takeover offer had not been made. Funded by Bain Capital, Pacific Equity Partners approached us with an indicative takeover offer of $1.60 per share which was sufficiently attractive to interest us, being close to 25% above where our stock was trading. Unfortunately, it was not a firm offer. They required that we allow them to undertake due diligence for an exclusive period of seventeen weeks. We negotiated them up to $1.68 and agreed to allow them into the business to undertake due diligence. They descended on Sydney with a team of about seventy investment bankers, accountants and lawyers and went through the business with a fine-toothed comb. During that period, all of our senior staff were tied up almost exclusively providing them with information. Virtually all action on the performance improvement initiatives we had under way were suspended during that period.

When the seventeen-week due diligence period ended, Pacific Equity Partners came back with an offer which was 10 cents lower than the indicative offer. Had that been the original offer we would never have allowed them to do due diligence. We quickly sent them packing. I was annoyed that the company had its normal business operations virtually suspended for four months. There was a significant cost to our shareholders from that. I learned from that experience to not allow any bidder an extended due diligence period. Any potential offeror should put a firm bid on the table which we would deal with according to the corporations law. Another issue that as directors we had to wrestle with was our obligation of disclosure to ensure a fully informed market. There was no certainty that there would be a firm and acceptable bid. To disclose the indicative bid and then not receive an acceptable offer could mislead the market. On the other hand, if we did not disclose and an acceptable bid was forthcoming, the market would have been not properly informed during that seventeen-week period and shareholders who had sold during that period would feel aggrieved. Fortunately, we had an excellent commercial lawyer who guided us through the maze of our obligations as directors. His advice was not to disclose, but to do so immediately if the indicative offer became public. Remarkably, given the number of people involved in the due diligence process, it did not become public. Given similar circumstances again, I would opt in favour of a fully informed market and fully disclose.

Several years previously, David Hearn had hired Doug McKay, a top-quality New Zealander whose career with Lion had been stellar. He was a very rounded executive who had deliberately set out to gain experience in every discipline from marketing to manufacturing. He was hired to give us a future potential CEO option. Unbeknown to us, Hearn had done a crazy deal which provided for a large payout to Doug in five years if he was not CEO. Doug brought much to Goodman Fielder, quickly earning unofficial recognition as second in command to Hearn. We were comfortable that he was likely to become a credible successor to Hearn. But Hearn had a habit of undermining anyone who might become a competitor for his job. Jon and I were conscious of this and resolved to guard against it, but it happened insidiously anyhow. The directors reached a view that we needed different qualities than Hearn was providing us with. Jon did a good job of convincing him to move on.

We conducted a comprehensive search for a new CEO. After the search had commenced came another significant event. Jon Peterson suffered from depression, a terrible disease which can often affect high achievers. One Saturday morning he phoned to tell me that he was suffering another severe episode of depression and had been advised to step down immediately. He handed the chair over to me and I became acting chairman at that moment. The responsibility for completing the search and finding a new CEO was now mine. Eventually, Tom Park emerged as our preferred candidate. I had known Tom for over ten years, first meeting him when he was Asia Pacific director of Kraft, the leading global cheese brand. He was an American who had married an Australian girl but chose to remain in Australia when Kraft wished to promote him and move him out of Australia. I had always rated him and felt that for the first time since Goodman Fielder was formed, we had a CEO who had the attributes which the job required.

I had the unpleasant job of telling Doug McKay that he had missed out on the CEO job. He was devastated. To my consternation, when I boarded my flight at Sydney Airport that evening, he was also boarding the same flight. I breathed a sigh of relief when he took a seat several rows away from mine. But when the seatbelt sign was turned off, he came and asked if he could sit with me. I could hardly refuse. Of course, he wanted to know why he had missed out. I had no obligation to justify our decision to him and had no intention of doing so. But he was feeling pretty low and I wanted be empathetic.

We finally turned to his future career. I informed him that I considered him to have CEO capability but that he was not yet quite ready for a company with the size and complexity of Goodman Fielder, that he should seek such a role in a smaller business for a few years to prepare himself for a larger role. He thanked me for my advice and appeared to follow it as I subsequently received a call from Murray Gough who was chairman of Sealord. He wanted to discuss Doug's capability with me and of course asked me why he had not been appointed CEO of Goodman. He was appointed CEO of Sealord where he did a good job, became CEO of Auckland City Council and subsequently had an outstanding governance career.

There was another issue which had to be dealt with: the appointment of a permanent chairman. Had I lived in Sydney I would have relished the opportunity of taking on the chairmanship, but I felt that the chairman needed to reside in Sydney. The CEO appointment process had demonstrated just how difficult it was to do the job from Matamata. The process of interviewing the CEO candidates selected for the "long list", to prepare a "short list" for the directors to consider, had been arduous. With candidates coming from overseas as well as other Australian states, it was impossible to orchestrate interviews into a concentrated period. On occasions I had two or three visits to Sydney in a week just to conduct interviews that took at most half a day. Also, given that I had been on the board for ten years and the low regard in which Goodman Fielder was held by the market, I felt that a highly regarded Australian chairman would have a much better chance of maintaining shareholder support as Tom Park set about the task of rebuilding the company. The directors agreed with me so we initiated another search to find a suitable chairman. Despite its poor performance and image, Goodman Fielder had never had any difficulty in attracting high-quality directors and the chairman search was no exception. We had some first-class candidates. The directors in the end appointed as chairman the highly regarded former CEO of James Hardie Industries, Dr Keith Barton.

One potential acquisition that Goodman Fielder had been watching closely for several years was the venerable Australian company Burns Philp. Originally a shipping and trading company, it had moved into food products as trading opportunities declined. In the 1980s it had purchased the world's second-largest spices business. But it had not been able to handle the competition from the market leader McCormick, a Fortune 500 company, and had got itself into a weak financial position with its share price steadily declining. It appeared to be a good fit with Goodman Fielder, but for a range of reasons we decided to wait while we gained further knowledge about it, and as we expected, its share price declined further. Then out of the blue, New Zealander Graeme Hart swooped in and purchased a controlling stake. It was an audacious move which appeared to be foolhardy when the true parlous state of Burns Philp was revealed. It was sufficiently bad to take Graeme Hart down, but unbeknown to anyone he had a "buy back" agreement with the investment bank which had funded his purchase, under which he could "put" the shares back to the investment bank, if Burns Philps' financial position was not what it was believed to be. He exercised that right and negotiated with the bank to retain his shareholding at a price he believed he could make it work. Applying his usual practice of meticulously reviewing every single activity and an invoice-by-invoice examination of expenditure, he stemmed Burns Philp losses and stabilised the company.

Tom Park was doing exactly what we expected him to do. Doing the hard yards in understanding the detail of every business, its markets and customers, costs and performance at every step of the value chain, then taking action to permanently fix the problems. Steps were being taken to simplify the business and the ingredients business was sold for a very good price. It was a good business with a leading international position, but we needed to narrow the scope of

Goodman Fielder and concentrate on excelling in a smaller range of businesses, in particular on our very strong retail brands. For the first time in twelve years, we had a CEO with the ability to run the business properly. This was showing up in the financial results. In the 2002 financial year we delivered the company's highest-ever profit of A$168 million. For the first time the market was viewing Goodman Fielder favourably. But time had run out on us.

In 2003 we became aware that someone was building a stake in Goodman. It was obvious that a takeover offer was coming. When it did come, it was from an unexpected party. Ironically, it was a company we had been looking to purchase, Burns Philp. Graeme Hart had stabilised it and was now looking to expand. The offer price of $1.85 per share was above the $1.50 where it had been trading only a few months earlier, but it was below what we believed to be the intrinsic value of the company. We decided to fight the offer. We set out to test the market for some of the individual businesses, but in the time available were unable to conclude the one big deal which would demonstrate the company was worth more than was being offered for it. Meantime, our long-suffering shareholders were voting with their feet and selling their shares to Burns Philp. We had little choice but to accept the inevitable. We negotiated the price up a couple of cents to $1.87 and recommended that shareholders accept the offer. By early 2004 it was all over; Goodman Fielder became owned by Burns Philp.

The night before we were to meet to formally accept the offer, I was dining in the restaurant at the Four Seasons Hotel, where I always stayed when in Sydney. I saw Graeme Hart come in with a group. I had never met him, but he obviously recognised me. After a while he came over with a bottle of wine and introduced himself. I invited him to sit down and poured him a drink. While we did not discuss the takeover or Goodman Fielder, we both knew that the next day his offer would be formally accepted. We had a great discussion for about one and a half hours. He seemed to be a very decent bloke, who is extremely clever. After taking control, he broke the company up and sold off the various divisions at significant profit. That became the foundation of the several-billion-dollar commercial empire he has built, making him New Zealand's richest man – an amazing achievement by a guy who started out as a truck driver.

I was sorry to see Goodman Fielder broken up. It was the end of Pat Goodman's vision to build a world-class food company. But as directors we had made a series of poor CEO appointments so could take little credit for our stewardship. The tragedy was that in Tom Park the company now had a CEO who was good enough to deliver on its potential. But it was too little too late. Our long-suffering shareholders deserved better.

FORTY-EIGHT
ANZ

In 1994 I was invited to join the board of the National Bank of New Zealand, which was owned by Lloyds Bank of London. The National Bank was New Zealand's third largest bank, and was strong in both personal and business banking. It had been our bank when I was chairman of New Zealand Dairy Company as well as banking many other companies I had been involved with, including the Dairy Board. I knew all of its senior people well including its chairman, Sir Spencer Russell, one of New Zealand's great bankers. It was very British and always seemed to have about five knights on its board; perhaps that was why I was invited.

I also knew the CEO, John Anderson, and rated him highly. He had been CEO of New Zealand's leading investment bank, Southpac, which had been absorbed into the National Bank. When doing my due diligence after receiving the invitation to join the board, I was to find that he was highly regarded by management and staff and his philosophy and values had permeated the whole bank. I was pretty impressed by what I saw so was delighted to accept the invitation to become a director of the National Bank.

With my Rural Bank experience, I was not a complete novice about banking, but a retail bank is quite different, so I was on a steep learning curve. I soon learned that banking is all numbers. In a bank most things are capable of being quantified and banks are skilled at doing just that. Then there is risk. Banks deliberately take risks; after all, every loan is a risk, but measuring and managing risk is a core skill which banks are good at. They do not survive if they are not. In hard times banks often lose money, sometimes large amounts of it, so evaluating, measuring and managing risk is critical to success. Margins are fine. Most businesses I had been involved in had a capital to total assets ratio of 45% to 50%. In banking it was much lower, about 14%. In other words, every dollar a bank lends is comprised of 14 cents of the bank's own money and 86% is money which the bank has borrowed. Profit after all expenses is only about 1 cent in every dollar lent. I also found that banks employ lots of very clever people and therefore pay remuneration which is well above average.

The National Bank was a quality organisation which reflected the values of its owner, Lloyds Bank. It was consistently rated No. 1 or No. 2 among banks for customer service. It was also steadily gaining market share. Its bad-loan management was excellent, with low loan losses by industry standards. Its profitability was reliable and at the high end of the banking industry. It was a comfort to me as a director to have one of the best banks in the world, Lloyds Bank, as owner. Lloyds kept a close eye on National, and CEO Sir John Anderson had a joint reporting responsibility to both the Lloyds parent and the National Bank boards. Every six months either the CEO of Lloyds or the chairman or deputy chairman visited. The opportunity was taken on each visit to have a formal black-tie dinner with partners attending, which was all very pleasant.

Lloyds were very proud of the National Bank. It was one of their best-performing units and often described as the "jewel in our crown". While the National Bank was making satisfactory and increasing profit, it was relatively small for Lloyds which at that time became the most valuable bank in the world by market capitalisation. Lloyds' CEO Sir Brian Pitman was an outstanding operator. During one of his visits, I asked him what we could do better. He replied, "Get your costs down and improve your cost to income ratio. Lloyds is at 48% and we will get it below 40%." At that time the National Bank was about 68%. We clearly had a lot of scope for improvement, but we needed greater scale to get anywhere near 40%.

John Anderson, with whom I had served on the Prime Minister's Enterprise Council, had a rather unusual background for the CEO of a retail bank. He was a merchant banker, unquestionably the most highly regarded in New Zealand. But he was a visionary who believed that the National Bank needed to become much more customer focussed. He brought new ideas to the role, had great judgement and was extraordinarily effective at developing quality people and building teams. Lloyds always had a senior executive from London as his second in command. Profitability grew steadily year on year, reaching an outstanding post-tax return on shareholder funds in 1993 of 22%.

In 1994 Jim Bolger asked Sir John to chair a multi-party Employment Task Force. This occupied a huge amount of his time through most of 1995. There were some funding and hedging misjudgements by the bank's treasury which were related to a proposed takeover of Trust Bank, which caused a sharp, 39% drop in profit in 1996. Lloyds were most unhappy and insisted on change. Chairman Malcolm McCaw resigned and was replaced by former All Blacks Captain Sir Wilson Whineray who was an astute businessman. The management team was modified and their responsibilities realigned. Costs were aggressively driven down. Post-tax profit reached a record $200 million by 1998.

The National Bank was increasing its market share each year but would benefit from greater scale. Most of the regionally based Trustee savings banks had merged to create New Zealand Trust Bank and had obtained a full banking licence. Auckland Savings Bank had become a subsidiary of the huge Australian bank CBA, while Taranaki Savings Bank had remained independent. Banking is extremely competitive and also inherently risky. Banks need ready access to capital. Small banks find life very difficult and rarely survive. Southpac, the National Bank's investment banking arm, had persuaded the directors and management of Trust Bank to sell to the National Bank. In 1996 a deal had been agreed for the National Bank to take over Trust Bank. However, having previously supported the purchase, Lloyds backed out at the very last moment. At the time they themselves were preoccupied with a major takeover of the Scottish bank TSB and did not feel that they could handle both. This was a major blow as a takeover of Trust Bank would have been a game changer for the National Bank which would have resulted in it becoming the largest bank in New Zealand. Trust Bank was soon sold to Westpac.

Countrywide Bank had been formed by an amalgamation of most of New Zealand's building societies, obtained a banking licence and established as a retail bank. It had been purchased by the Bank of Scotland. Countrywide was struggling and in 1998 Bank of Scotland offered Countrywide to Lloyds. Negotiations for National Bank to acquire Countrywide were quickly concluded. Countrywide was the "last on the block" bank available for purchase. It gave National Bank sufficient scale to be fully competitive. John Anderson set the ambitious target of implementing the merger plan within one year. Countrywide's branch network largely duplicated that of National, so effectively Countrywide's expensive branch network could be completely shut down and the business absorbed into the existing National branch network. The most challenging task was to get the

Countrywide customer base onto the National Bank Systematics system, at a time when a great deal of systems work was being carried out to get ready for year 2000. The merger was completed on time and gave a huge boost to National Bank's efficiency. Within two years the cost to income ratio had decreased to 48%, while profit had almost doubled and then increased by a further 30% over the next two years. This was outstanding and the National Bank was the best-performing bank in New Zealand by a long shot.

But for Lloyds Bank, the National Bank was an orphan which was a long way from home. It had no other business in Australia or New Zealand. It decided to concentrate on its home ground in the UK where it had made several large acquisitions. In 2003 it decided to put the National Bank on the market. Most of the top Australian banks had a look but it was Melbourne-based ANZ Banking Group which came out on top. This was ironic because National Bank was the highest-rated New Zealand bank on service and customer satisfaction, while ANZ was the lowest. In a takeover it is invariably the offeror executives who take the top jobs in the merged entity. That had serious implications for National Bank's customers who were accustomed to superior service. But ANZ Chief Executive John McFarlane displayed great judgement in stipulating that he would not buy National unless the National Bank management were available to run the combined bank.

Norman Geary and I were invited to become directors of the ANZ National Bank as it was named. We joined Roderick Deane who was chairman of ANZ New Zealand. Three ANZ Banking Group executives from Melbourne also joined the board. ANZ had negotiated a right to use the National Bank brand including the Lloyds Bank black horse logo, for seven years. It was not too difficult to merge some of the functions, such as treasury and risk, of both ANZ and National and this brought significant cost savings, but it was decided to retain the two retail banks and run them separately. The reasons for this were, first, to avoid destabilising the customer base of each bank. But more importantly, each bank had different systems which would first need consolidating onto one system which would be a huge undertaking. Finally, and perhaps most importantly, each bank had separate cultures. National was built around customers and their needs, while ANZ was product centred. The downside was that the full efficiency benefits could not be gained while we ran two banks. In that first year, 2004, ANZ National made a post-tax profit of $584 million.

I was appointed chairman of the Risk Committee. Risk identification, evaluation and management was a critical component of running a bank. ANZ requirements and processes were rather more comprehensive than Lloyds had required of the National Bank. Stress testing plays an important role in enabling an understanding of the consequences of shocks and the response which may be required. At an early date I wanted to know what the impact would be of a major global economic recession. I suggested we model based on the 1987 crash. When completed that work showed that while the Bank would suffer huge losses, it would remain in a sound position and profit would be restored to normal levels by year three. That gave the board considerable comfort that the bank would be able to withstand a serious economic downturn. ANZ was going to need all of its financial strength during the 2008/2009 Global Financial Crisis.

The National Bank management team led by Sir John Anderson was doing a grand job leading the merged ANZ National Bank. The customer base of both banks remained stable with no customer attrition despite a vigorous attack by our competitors. By 2006, post-tax profit had almost doubled to $1067 million. But relations between Melbourne and Wellington were not easy. The National Bank management did not find it easy to accept the more hands-on approach of the new owner ANZ, compared to the more light-handed style of the previous owner, Lloyds. The ANZ Chief Executive John McFarlane genuinely wanted the National team to manage the combined bank, but he was probably the only executive in Melbourne holding that view, so his Melbourne team did not always reflect that intention in their own areas of responsibility. This caused friction with the Wellington team. I had an occasion as chairman of the Risk Committee when I had to speak quite sternly to the group head of risk about his treatment of ANZ National head of risk. Normally, this would be sorted out at chief executive level, but the relationship between Sir John and John McFarlane was anything but warm and, unfortunately, they rarely spoke. I did my best to try to get them together more frequently but with little success.

At the end of 2005 Sir John retired as chief executive after an absolutely stellar career. He was clearly one of the very best CEOs in New Zealand and was a giant among bankers. He had an amazing ability to develop young executive talent. At one time the CEOs of each of the other four major banks in New Zealand had been trained by John Anderson, and there were another five individuals who were CEOs within the financial services industry in Australia and New Zealand. What a record! He had done a great job for ANZ. He had brought together the two banks and integrated those functions which were able to be integrated. He had retained the customer base of both banks during what was a difficult and uncertain time for staff through the change of ownership period, despite vigorous efforts by the bank's competitors to convince customers to change. Importantly, the post-tax profit doubled in two years. He left ANZ a great legacy, the most profitable bank in New Zealand with more to come. Melbourne appointed ANZ Chief Economist Graham Hodges to succeed him. The New Zealand directors had been given the opportunity to participate in the process to select him. I believed that it was time for ANZ National to have a CEO who came out of Melbourne. It needed to become ANZ New Zealand, an integral part of the parent ANZ

Banking Group. That would occur more readily with a career ANZ Melbourne leader.

In 2006 Roderick Deane retired and ANZ Banking Group invited me to become chairman of ANZ National Bank. I immediately began searching for a New Zealand director to replace Roderick. It was most prestigious appointment so I had no shortage of high-quality directors to select from. In making an appointment I was looking to the future for a younger person who had the potential to succeed me in five years or so. I identified two highly qualified individuals who met those criteria for the Melbourne leadership to choose from. John Judge was appointed. As a former CEO of Ernst & Young I asked him to chair the Audit Committee and my good friend Norman Geary to chair the Risk Committee.

Graham Hodges was a good CEO; we got along fine and worked well together. But we had a major issue. We had to continue to run two retail banks because each bank had a different operating system. That is not unusual in a merger. As long as that continued, the full benefits of the merger could not be obtained. Invariably, the solution is to consolidate onto the system of the acquiror at the earliest possible date. That was the intention of ANZ when it acquired National, to consolidate both banks onto the ANZ "Hogan"

The author and Marg with tennis great Rod Laver

system. It would probably have happened if Sir John Anderson had not dug in and refused to do so. He had very good reason. National Bank was a "customer-centric" bank and its system, Systematics, was designed to serve a customer-focussed bank. ANZ, though, was "product centric" and Hogan was designed to serve a product-focussed bank. Had ANZ National migrated onto Hogan, much of the value ANZ purchased with National would have been destroyed. So here was a conundrum. ANZ National needed to move to a single system to realise the full benefits of the merger. That needed to be Systematics to protect the value which ANZ had purchased. But Systematics was not ANZ's system. Naturally, it would prefer to have one system, its own, across the whole ANZ family.

Profit increased each year to reach $1163 million in 2008, but through 2007 storm clouds were gathering on the world economy horizon. A combination of low interest rates and easy credit worldwide had pushed asset prices up to excessive levels. Inadequate regulation, particularly in the United States, allowed increasing risks to be taken by lenders. Then good and bad loans were parcelled into packages which were then sold off to investors. These were called subprime mortgages, which further increased risk. As a result, assets, including mortgage assets had become grossly overvalued. In New Zealand, banking regulations are much stronger than in many countries and were stringently applied by the Reserve Bank of New Zealand. Banks in New Zealand and Australia also had much stronger capital adequacy, around 14% of total assets, compared to 3%–4% held by the failed giant US investment bank Lehman Brothers. What that actually meant for a bank with 4% capital was that if the assets it had lent on fell by more than about 10%, it was effectively insolvent. Ten per cent is not much given that when property prices fall it is often by 20% to 30%.

As the financial contagion spread around the world, we could see what was coming to New Zealand and Australia and had begun to prepare to face it. The Reserve Bank officials were in daily contact with the management of New Zealand's banks. The Governor of the Reserve Bank Dr Alan Bollard, whom I regarded highly, called me in to seek my assessment on how well prepared we were. We had pulled back on lending, particularly higher margin more risky lending, through 2007, and were now restricting lending even more tightly. We had arranged more committed "stand-by" credit lines. Our shareholder ANZ Banking Group had committed more funding if required and we had more than doubled the amount of our liquidity buffer (actual cash on hand). I felt comfortable that we were well prepared, but of course it would depend on how ugly things became.

And they became very ugly indeed. World finance markets reeled when the venerable US investment bank, Lehman Brothers, closed its doors in September 2008. Others soon followed. Altogether twenty-five banks, most of them US, failed. Many more, including many of the largest banks in the world, were either bailed out by governments around the world or forced to merge with sounder banks on "give away" terms. The contagion spread to the insurance industry, which is a large investor. Most insurance company profit comes from investing the cash premiums while awaiting claims. Many insurance companies were in difficulties. This compounded the problems for many banks which had insured some of their riskier loans, only to find that the insurer defaulted on claims.

The author and Marg with former UK Prime Minister Tony Blair

Marg and I were on holiday in Crete when Lehman Brothers failed. Day after day, other banks either failed or were forced to merge. I was on the phone every day with Graham Hodges to keep abreast of how ANZ National was handling what was a most difficult and dangerous situation. The most serious issue was that term funding markets had dried up. It had become impossible to arrange any term funding at all, even at high interest rates. We went for nearly eighteen months into the second quarter of 2009 without being able to arrange any term funding. Although no term funding was available, there was plenty of overnight funding available. But relying on that would normally be poor practice and very dangerous, as matching borrowing and lending is the foundation of risk management. The New Zealand Government introduced a "Wholesale Guarantee Facility" which guaranteed the borrowing of financial institutions. The Labour Government charged the major banks a fee but did not charge smaller financial institutions. This was not only unfair but also unwise. While the five large banks did not have to call on the guarantee at all, others did. Finance companies, in particular, became able to borrow easily and their lending soared. With few exceptions, the government later had to pay very large sums under the guarantee as most finance companies were unable to meet their obligations. The government had to pay over $2 billion under the guarantee to the creditors of South Canterbury Finance, for example. Our increased liquidity buffer, the "stand-by" credit facility we had arranged, support from ANZ Melbourne, support from the Wholesale Deposit Guarantee Scheme and the Reserve Bank of New Zealand kept us in business, but it was a worrying time to be chairman of a bank. As expected, our loan losses soared. As a result, profit fell by a whopping 75% from $1163 million in 2008 to $298 million in 2009 before recovering sharply to $827 million in 2010. This was pretty much in line with the modelling I had commissioned as chairman of the Risk Committee in 2005, even though the Global

Financial Crisis was rather more serious than the scenario used in the model.

Graham Hodges reached the view that we should consolidate onto the National Bank's Systematics. This would be costly and was not warmly welcomed by Melbourne. However, in early 2009 he was promoted to deputy CEO of the parent company so the major issue of systems slipped off the radar. He was succeeded by Dr Jenny Fagg, a young but long-term ANZ executive who was a high achiever with a stellar career to date. She had a great mind and was a lovely person, who was both highly regarded and very popular with colleagues. Unfortunately, about eighteen months later she was forced to retire through ill health. Luckily, she was to make a complete recovery.

A very experienced and tested banker, David Hisco, was appointed CEO New Zealand. He had been head of Australian Commercial Banking for some time. He had previously been stationed in New Zealand as CEO of ANZ's UDC New Zealand business. He was a seasoned commercial and retail banker, exactly the qualities and experience that I believed were required. He retained overall responsibility for commercial banking across the whole ANZ Banking Group. He also brought new energy to the job and like all good CEOs spent a good deal of his time out visiting branches, workplaces and customers. He quickly understood what the important issues were, set clear objectives for his people and was a very good leader able to motivate staff. I rated him highly and he was to prove to be one of the very best CEOs I have ever worked with.

Only months after he took up the CEO role, Christchurch was hit with a major earthquake. As it occurred at 4.35 am casualties were minimal. However, the city was not so lucky six months later when on 22 February 2011, another severe quake occurred at 12.51 pm. In the earthquake 185 people were killed, several thousand injured and damage was widespread with several multi-storey buildings in the city centre collapsing. Our Christchurch Central branch was badly damaged. Three of our staff lost family members while many staff members' homes suffered major damage. I was proud of our response. We immediately resolved that our priority would be our staff and their families, followed by our customers. Our head of HR flew to Christchurch as soon as the airport opened to assess the need of our people. We rented a motel to provide accommodation for our staff and their families, and to provide a refuge where they could shower, rest and receive support. Grants were made to those in need. I visited Christchurch as soon as I was advised that it was appropriate for me to do so. We also resolved to support those of our customers who needed help.

The clock was also ticking on another issue. When ANZ purchased National Bank it was allowed to continue to use the National Bank livery and black horse logo for seven years. The expiry of that term was approaching. The expectation was that the right to use the brand would be renewed. But the livery and black horse was Lloyds' and were used by them. There was nothing in it for them to extend the right to use the brand to a bank on the other side of the world, so while they were prepared to agree to a short extension, they wanted a final end point a year or two away. This was actually a good development as it forced ANZ to confront a major issue.

Although ANZ National Bank was the largest bank in New Zealand with close to a 40% market share, and was about 50% larger than the next largest Westpac, because we were running two retail banks, National and ANZ, in reality we were only the fourth and fifth-sized retail banks in the country. We thus had smaller scale than each of our competitors so were actually at a disadvantage in costs as well as in marketing heft. But it was within the power of ANZ to turn that equation on its head and have a major competitive scale advantage, as well as much more marketing hitting power than any of our competitors. But to do that we had to merge the two banks into one, on a single operating system. Hogan was the parent bank's system and obviously the one which they would prefer. But the ANZ Hogan system was product-centric, while National's Systematics was customer-centric. If ANZ New Zealand was to become a product-centric bank it would lose a great number of its customers who were accustomed to the service National was renowned for.

Like Graham Hodges before him, David quickly concluded that the two banks should be merged into one, ANZ New Zealand. A customer-centric bank consolidated onto a single system, Systematics. He knew that it would not be easy to convince Melbourne to do that. There were some serious issues. Changing an operating system in a bank is a challenging undertaking. Bank systems operate 24/7 and require 100% accuracy. The risks are high that there could be serious commissioning problems. Changing a bank's operating system is a little like trying to change the control systems on an airliner while it is flying, with similar consequences if it goes wrong. It is not something to be attempted unless it is absolutely necessary. Then there was the cost: initially around $118 million but likely to end up around $150 million. The business case was in my view overwhelming, that consolidation onto Systematics was by far the preferred option. David went to battle with ANZ Melbourne and succeeded in persuading them to agree. The fact that the National Bank brand would soon not be available and have to be replaced by something else prevented the issue being kicked for touch again. It had to be dealt with now.

One day I received a phone call from a lady who believed they were being very badly treated by ANZ and were likely to lose their farm. The issue involved foreign currency loans. These had a much lower interest rate but carried the risk that if the New Zealand dollar fell, the amount of the loan increased. I was familiar with the issue. In the 1980s when mortgage interest rates had reached just under 20%, some farmers converted their loans into Swiss francs at interest rates of around 4%. The NZ dollar fell sharply against the Swiss franc, so the loan amount shot up, causing some farmers to become insolvent. A number lost their properties. I asked the lady to write to me, setting out the details of the case. When I read her letter, I was troubled. I asked David to have the matter investigated. I wanted an independent person to undertake the investigation and expressly stipulated that no person who had been involved with the client should have anything to do with the investigation. When the person who undertook the investigation concluded his work, he called me. His first words were "I do not want to write this but..."! He was disappointed in how the client had been dealt with and believed that we needed to make amends. In discussing the matter with him and David, I advised them to be generous in any settlement offer. "Do not be parsimonious and leave behind a disgruntled client. Be generous and leave a satisfied customer," were my words. In due course I received advice that the matter had been satisfactorily settled with the customer. A week or two later a large liquor basket was delivered to my home. It was from the couple concerned and was accompanied by a letter which thanked me for my help and for saving their farm. To my embarrassment I continued to receive a similar gift from them for many years until we shifted to Tauranga.

The business had weathered the storm of the GFC and quickly recovered. In 2012 profit hit a record of $1325 million. The systems conversion project was proceeding satisfactorily but slipping behind schedule. That of course was increasing the cost, and David was under considerable pressure from Melbourne about the delay in completion date and the increasing cost. But I was counselling him to resist that pressure, advising that getting it right was the most important issue. In particular, I advised against the project going "live" until it was 100% right. I advocated this point of view when I had my regular meetings with the ANZ Banking Group directors. David followed that advice, and the project did not commission until

September 2012, a year later than scheduled and three months after I retired as chairman and as a director. However, by that date some thirty full dress rehearsals had been conducted. The integration was seamless with almost no problems. Our competitors were waiting to attack our client base when we ran into the expected commissioning problems. They were hugely disappointed as customer losses were almost nil.

From my early days in business, I had believed that one should not stay too long in any one position. I had frequently observed how so many people stay too long and past the peak of their contribution. I had also seen too many long-serving directors who made little contribution and were merely keeping a seat warm. "Get in, make a difference and get out" had been my mantra. As a chairman I had supported term limits and introduced retirement policies as part of the governance policies of the companies of which I was a director. Ten years was a reasonable and normal term for a director. Being required to retire was often a shock to long-serving directors so, when some long-serving directors were reaching the end of their ten-year term, I usually set an example by being first up for retirement. In 2012 I advised my board and the parent company that I would retire at the end of the 2012 financial year on 30 June.

New Zealand is extraordinarily fortunate to have strong banks with each of the four major banks backed by a much larger Australian parent. The robust regulation of the Australian Prudential Regulation Authority (APRA) in Australia and the Reserve Bank in New Zealand ensures that our banking system is one of the soundest in the world. That is important for bank customers who can have confidence that their deposits are secure, particularly as there is no government guarantee of savings as there is in Australia and some other countries. The revolution in information technology has dramatically reduced the operating costs of banks but vigorous competition has also reduced pricing. When I joined the National Bank in 1993 it earned a net interest margin of over 5%. It is now around 2.4%. The difference has been passed onto borrowers in lower interest rates. Banks do make good profits but are also required to continually invest more capital to keep operating. New Zealanders often comment on the amount of dividends paid to their Australian parents by New Zealand banks. They have no understanding that those parent banks are continually providing more and more capital to their New Zealand subsidiaries. For example, during my time as chairman, the parent ANZ pumped about four times more capital into New Zealand than ANZ New Zealand paid to them in dividends. Likewise, since establishing Kiwibank in 2001, the government has pumped many times the amount of capital into Kiwibank as it has received from it in dividends.

I had been privileged to be a director of the premier bank in New Zealand, the National Bank, for ten years and ANZ National Bank for nine years, chairman for six. I had enjoyed it immensely. Without doubt the ANZ Board which I chaired, where every director was highly experienced and extraordinarily competent, was the best board of which I had been a member. We had been able to make a real difference in merging the two banks and creating a highly profitable bank for our shareholders. The full benefits of integration were delivered after my retirement, but they were in line with expectations. A few years later profit reached $2 billion. I was also pleased to have recruited John Judge to follow me as chairman, knowing that the bank would continue to have a very able leader.

FORTY-NINE
BACK TO THE WAIKATO

From 1999 to 2001 I lived with Marg at her home in Island Bay, Wellington. She was a high achiever who had worked in National Party headquarters for some time, being director of administration and had then been appointed to the top job, the influential position of executive director. She resigned from that role in 1997. She was then appointed to the position of administration manager at the prestigious Wellington boys' school, Wellington College.

Wellington had been a good city to work in when I was chairman of the Dairy Board. It was compact, and being small everything was nearby so it was easy to get around. It is, however, not the most beautiful city. The hills covered in that worst of all weeds, gorse, offended the farmer in me. I had always tried to keep my farm tidy and clean of weeds. The climate also was not the greatest to live in. When I returned from visiting Matamata each month, Marg asked me why I liked Matamata. I always replied, "The beauty of it; it is so green, colourful and tidy." She did not understand what I meant until she made her first visit when she said, "I see what you mean; it is beautiful." For Christmas 2000 I took Marg to Rotorua to meet Mum and

Dad. My siblings, Michael, Paul and Denise, were there. Normally when I arrived, Mum stood at the top of the back steps to greet me, as it was not easy for her to climb down the steps and then back up again. But when we arrived, Mum, with some difficulty, walked down the steps to greet Marg and to put her at ease. "I wanted to make you welcome but I was not going to do it looking down from the top of the steps. I wanted you to feel part of our family," Mum said.

Dryden with Paul, Denise and Michael

Two of my boards, National Bank and Ericsson, were located in Wellington but the rest were in Auckland, Hamilton, Sydney and Melbourne so, together with my role with the APEC Business Advisory Council, I was travelling a lot. Still, Wellington Airport was close by and we enjoyed frequent use of the National Bank suite at Wellington Stadium. But my heart was in the Waikato and in 2001 Marg made a huge sacrifice for me, giving up her job and leaving her family behind to move with me to Matamata. Marg's mum was suffering from Alzheimer's and was in a home in Berhampore. We moved her to Country Lodge Matamata. Being back in Matamata meant that I was closer to my parents, both of whom were in their late eighties and living in Rotorua. They warmly welcomed Marg into their family and soon loved her dearly, as she loved them.

Marg had lived in Wellington all of her life. Her friends and family were all there, so moving to a country town was a major change for her. The only people she knew in Matamata was our local MP Lindsay Tisch who had been acting president of the National Party when Marg was executive director, and his wife Leonie. She found Matamata quite different, noting that people had more time for one another. Although she did not know anyone, she was amazed that so many people seemed to know who she was. For example, a lady behind her in the checkout queue at the supermarket, whom she had never seen before, commented on the wonderful job she was doing with our garden. One day I was in Sydney and I received a call from Marg. We had previously decided that when our granddaughters turned sixteen years of age, we would give them a nice ring. She had seen a suitable ring for her grandaughter Nicole in Arawa Jewellers in Arawa Street. She had asked the owner, Barry Simonsen, if he would put it away for her until the end of the week until her partner returned home. To her amazement, he said, "Take it home now and show it to Dryden when he returns." She asked if he would like her to put down a deposit. "No, that will not be necessary; I know where to find you!" That would never happen in a city.

A community group wanted to turn the disused railway station into a Community Resource Centre. Marg was asked to become a founding trustee and help establish it. Today it is a much-used facility for the Matamata community. Marg was then approached by Health Waikato District Health Board, to join a Community Health Forum covering the Matamata, Morrinsville, Te Aroha, Cambridge and Te Awamutu districts. Its role was to advise Health Waikato on community health matters in those districts and have an input into the Strategic Plan of Health Waikato. She was appointed chair of that forum.

Then Dr Neil Algar, a former mayor and a wonderful and long-serving contributor to the Matamata community, came to see Marg. He had been chairman of the Pohlen Hospital Trust for many years. He asked Marg to become a trustee of the hospital. She initially declined but over the weekend I persuaded her to reconsider. She reached the view that to be accepted into the community she needed to put something into it. She advised Neil that she would accept but told him that in doing so she would be looking to become chair. That suited Neil who realised that he should stand down but could not quite bring himself to do so. After a year Neil stood down and Marg became chair. The leadership change was timely. The existing trustees had been in office for ever. The organisation had lost momentum and it needed fresh ideas and a good rev up. Marg hired a new CEO who had considerable experience in health and renewed the membership of the board to bring in fresh thinking. It was an ongoing battle for a while as, although she received good support from the trustees, every suggestion faced a degree of resistance. The "we don't do it like that", or "we have never done that" syndrome was alive and well. But she pushed on, won acceptance and made progress.

Finance was an issue. It is always an issue in health and more so for community hospitals. Most of the revenue came from district health boards, in this case Health Waikato. They didn't give money away easily. Health funding rules are fiendishly complex, so a good knowledge of what is available, for what purposes and from whom, is essential as is building strong relationships with Health Waikato staff. A hospital is also like a hotel. Occupancy is everything. If occupancy is below 85%, the hospital will be losing money. Marg had much to do to turn around the financial performance of Pohlen Hospital and make it profitable. At the same time new certification standards had been introduced and Pohlen was well short of the standard required to meet certification, so a major effort went into upgrading the hospital's facilities and operating processes.

Another issue was capital. Even a profitable hospital could not generate sufficient funds to replace major items, or refurbish and upgrade facilities, let alone fund any expansion. Marg decided to establish the Pohlen Hospital Foundation to raise funds for Pohlen. After five years as chair and having got Pohlen Hospital into a healthy financial and operating position, Marg retired as chair of Pohlen Hospital Trust to take the chair of Pohlen Hospital Foundation Trust, a role she continued for eleven years until we left Matamata in 2016.

Governor-General Dame Patsy Reddy and Marg QSM

Marg had a very high profile in Matamata. In fact, she soon became even better known than me. She was seen as the face of the hospital, which continued even long after she had ceased to be a trustee. She had established Pohlen as top of mind for Matamata residents who understood what an important community asset it was and made them realise that it had to be nurtured. Her work for Matamata was recognised by Rotary in 2014, with the award of a prestigious Paul Harris Fellowship. In 2016, Matamata-Piako District Council recognised her contribution by awarding her the Key to The City of Matamata. In 1993 she had been awarded a New Zealand Suffragette Medal, one of only 500 awarded throughout New Zealand. She was recognised in the 2016 Honours List, when she was awarded a Queen's Service Medal (QSM) for services to health and the Matamata community. I am intensely proud of her.

Rotary Paul Harris Fellows both

One day in 2002, Marg and I were in Sydney when I noticed a nice diamond ring in a jeweller's shop. She liked it so I bought it for her. On the flight home I asked her to marry me. She asserted herself right from the start, insisting that I get down on my knee to ask her, but she accepted. She then told the whole business-class cabin that I had just proposed and she had agreed to marry me. The cabin crew then broke out the champagne for us. We did not tell people that we were engaged but one day Dad said, "I notice that Margaret has a lovely new ring. Did you give that to her?" "Yes," I replied. "Are you engaged, Dryden?" "Well, yes we are." Dad then said, "I want you to know that Mum and I thoroughly approve. We would like to see you marry while we are still alive". Mum and Dad really loved Marg and she loved them. Mum actually thanked Marg "for giving me my boy back" and "for making him happy".

We were married on 15 February 2003 on the deck of our lovely home in Burwood Road. The reception was held in a marquee on the lawn. All of Marg's family were there and most of my mine. A particular pleasure to us was that we had three of our parents present. Marg's mum (eighty-seven); her father had passed away many years before at the age of sixty-four. My dad (ninety) and mum (eighty-eight) were thrilled. It hurt me that I could not get married in the church but Father Frank O'Regan attended our reception and gave us a blessing.

Marg and Dryden on their wedding day

In 2005 Christine and I decided that it was time to sell the farm to Jul and Graham. They had earned the right to own it and it was the right thing to do for all of our family. But it was still a wrench for me, as for the first time since we had arrived at Paratu in 1949 I was no longer a farmer.

Mum and Dad continued to live in their home in Rotorua, but it began to get more difficult for them. However, we were able to see them frequently. In 2003, Dad moved into Cantabria rest home in Rotorua. He had suffered severely from arthritis for close to fifty years and had received six hip replacements. He passed away on 6 May 2004 at the age of ninety-three. Mum wanted to move into a retirement village as soon as possible after Dad died. She moved into Cedar Manor, Tauranga where she had her own apartment. She loved it and before she died told me that her almost three years there had been three of the happiest years of her life. In 1993 she had three heart valves replaced. They do not last forever and began to fail in 2006. She died peacefully on 6 November 2006, like Dad at the age of ninety-three. Her passing left a huge gap in my life as she had always been there for me. One of the advantages of living in Tauranga has been that I have been able to visit her grave frequently.

FIFTY
WEL NETWORKS

FOR SOME TIME, GOVERNMENT HAD BEEN UNDERTAKING reforms designed to improve the efficiency of the electricity sector. In 1990 power boards and municipalities supplying electricity were required to form commercial companies to sell and distribute electricity. The shares of those companies were to be held by a trust or distributed to electricity consumers. In 1998, Government went much further and announced a major package of reforms designed to create competition in the sector. The state generator, Electricity Corporation of New Zealand, was split into three generating companies, Mercury, Genesis, and Mighty River. Roughly 48% of the shares in each were sold to the New Zealand public. Contact Energy had previously been privatised and all of its shares sold to investors. These four major generators were to compete for the sale of electricity. A national distribution company, Transpower, was established to distribute electricity from the generators through the national high-voltage grid. Power was then to be purchased by retailers, mostly owned by power boards or municipalities, distributed through their power lines networks and sold to consumers. As each electricity user had only one powerline connected to their home or business, it was difficult to avoid a monopoly at the retail point of the electricity supply chain. To prevent that monopoly from being created, the reforms required retailers to dispose of either electricity retailing or distribution by 2003. They could do one or the other but were not allowed to do both. Virtually all retailers chose to keep their low-risk distribution business and became "lines companies". They disposed of their electricity sales business. These retail electricity sales businesses were quickly snapped up by generators who needed customers for the electricity they were each generating.

In 2000 I was approached by Margaret Evans, who was a trustee of Waikato Energy Trust. She explained that the trust owned 60% of the shares in Waikato Energy Ltd. It wished to buy the remaining 40% of the shares from the private and corporate shareholders. Waikato Energy was the fifth-largest power company in the country after the four main city power businesses. She advised that the company would need a new board and asked if I would be prepared to consider becoming chairman. I indicated that I would be prepared to have a look at the business. A week or two later I received a call from Don Jaine, an executive search partner who had been tasked with putting together a new board. I was aware that the Waikato Energy Trust had a reputation as a largely dysfunctional entity, prone to irrational and disruptive behaviour. Before accepting, I needed to have a clear understanding from the trust that the directors would have a free hand to run the company subject to complying with the provisions in the constitution requiring shareholder approval on "major matters". I set up a meeting with the trust and included Roger Fisher, who was to be deputy chairman, in this discussion. I undertook to operate a "no-surprises" policy and keep the trust as shareholder informed on any significant issues. Roger and I were satisfied with the undertaking we received.

At the meeting with the trust, they had invited the CEO of WEL Energy, Graham Coxhead, to meet me so we took the opportunity to meet with him in his office after our meeting with the trust. Roger and I wanted to gain an understanding of the company. Graham played it absolutely straight, told us that he would be happy to answer questions on anything which was publicly available, but beyond that I should contact the chairman, Michael Stiassny, and get his approval. That was perfectly proper and I undertook to do that. I did not know Stiassny but phoned him that evening, advised him that I had been invited to become chairman and sought his approval for the CEO to facilitate my due diligence process. I was astounded to receive a very frosty reception in which he suggested that I was out of line in even talking to the CEO without his approval. He curtly told me to put my request in writing and the board would consider it. I had never experienced anything like that before.

With Don Jaine's help Roger and I pulled together a good board. Graham Coxhead was a very competent CEO whom we were pleased to have. He lived in Auckland and commuted to Hamilton. He indicated that he would probably retire in a year or so. I was anxious to retain him so set out to ensure that he enjoyed working with me. The two previous chairmen had received fees of over $250,000 per annum. This was grossly excessive. The reason for this I did not know but it probably was due to the difficulties of working with the trust as a shareholder. The total fees we fixed for a board of six directors were in line with market and totalled less than the previous chairman's fee.

Shortly before I became chairman, Graham Coxhead had sold the retail energy business to one of the generators for $2700 per customer, an amazing deal and the highest price received for the sale of any retail energy business. This left the new WEL Energy line business, or WEL Networks as it became, in a very strong financial position. WEL Energy Trust employed an energy advisor, one Dave Cook, a former senior executive in the Electricity Corporation. He had a lucrative consulting business as he also consulted to several other energy trusts and seemed to pick up about $250,000 every year from each of them. Any tension between the company and the trust increased his value to the trust. At the time of my becoming chairman, he had convinced the trust that the high price received for the sale of the retail business could only have been obtained if some other assets had been included in the sale. What were they? I undertook to investigate the sale and report to the trust. My investigation showed that the deal was all above board. That the deal was exactly what had been disclosed, the customers which WEL was obliged by law to divest had been sold. The price was the highest price realised by any power company from the sale of its customers. Management and the previous directors were to be congratulated on what was the deal of the year. Of course, that did not satisfy him and with the support of the trust he kept coming back asking to see all of the documents, which I declined to provide. There could be no other reason than to keep his charge-out meter ticking over. Over the next few years, he continued to be a problem as he sought detailed information and tried to second guess everything the company did.

I was looking for opportunities the grow the business. The Taranaki power company Powerco had been successful in building a business into other regions. They had acquired Whanganui and Manawatu. They looked to be the best opportunity to over time build a nationwide lines company. They then acquired Hutt Valley. Graham and I worked hard to establish a relationship with them and create an opportunity for future growth. It soon became evident that we shared similar aspirations. We finally reached agreement to take a 13% stake in Powerco which we believed would provide a springboard to future growth. Unfortunately, our trust refused to support the proposal so a wonderful opportunity was lost. That had future implications for WEL.

After a year or so Graham Coxhead resigned. He was a good CEO so I was sorry to lose him, even though I knew when I became chairman that his time with us would be limited. We were fortunate to attract Mike Underhill who had exactly the background and experience we were looking for. Mike was an electrical engineer who had been chief operating officer for the Wellington-based TransAlta. He had master's degree in economics and had completed the Advanced Management Programme at Harvard University. He was uniquely qualified for the role. He was to prove to be a very good CEO whom I enjoyed working with.

The trust continued to be difficult to work with. They were a largely dysfunctional group who fought like Kilkenny cats. At one stage they enlisted the services of the respected former judge, Dame Augusta Wallace, to mediate. Success was beyond her formidable skills. Russ Rimmington became chairman. While he had his own problems with his trustees, he improved the working relationship between the trust and the board and soon terminated Dave Cook from his golden sinecure as energy advisor to the trustees. When trustee elections were held, a ticket to introduce customer rebates was led by Garry Mallett. They swept the floor, defeating almost all of the sitting trustees. The new trustees were much more reasonable and the relationship between the board and the trust improved. The trust had been distributing its dividends as grants to worthwhile causes in Hamilton. This provided a useful source of funds for Hamilton organisations. The Centre for Performing Arts at Waikato University was an example of a facility which was made possible by grants from the trust, funded by WEL dividends and from which the community benefited. That facility would not have been built without the WEL dividend. The new trustees wanted to pay the bulk of the dividend they received from WEL, as a rebate to WEL customers. I would have preferred to pay a rebate (paid from profit) as I wanted WEL to stay resolutely focussed on efficient performance and maximising profit. However, tax would have to be paid on the rebate and that would be inefficient, so we gained approval from the IRD which allowed us to pay a discount from pre-tax profit twice a year.

WEL was a very good business. Power consumption was pretty steady so the sales line was very reliable, growing by about 3% per annum. Costs were largely fixed so provided costs were kept under control, profit increased each year. WEL posted a tax-paid profit of about $13 million in the first year I was chairman. Health and safety was a major focus. Electricity is very dangerous, mistakes can be fatal, so we had zero tolerance for accidents. The other important area was reliability. We were in the business of delivering electricity to our customers. Their demand was continuous, so our objective was to deliver power continuously. Reliability is measured by a term called SAIDI, which is essentially the total number of minutes that power is off across the whole network. We set a searching target of 90 minutes downtime per year across the network. That meant that power was available to consumers 99.9% of the time. Our objective was to get that number down even lower. We did get it below 60 minutes.

The other key metric was cost per customer. WEL was the fifth-largest lines company in the country. Our objective was to achieve the third lowest cost per customer of any lines company. As costs were largely fixed, there was a strong relationship between size and cost per customer. To achieve the third lowest cost per customer we would need to sharply reduce costs without compromising reliability. We decided to contract out network servicing instead of doing it ourselves. To guard against the contractor reducing service to save cost, there would be heavy penalties if network reliability targets were not met. We were fortunate to conclude a very favourable contract with a Queensland lines maintenance company which wanted to break into the New Zealand market. We achieved an excellent 45% reduction in our servicing cost which enabled us to meet our cost per customer target of having the third lowest in the country.

WEL was performing well. Customer service metrics were impressive and profit was increasing each year. We were searching for growth opportunities, but I was committed to staying within our core competency which was operating networks. But with most lines companies owned by trusts there was almost no opportunity to purchase other lines businesses. With the internet in its early days, we extensively researched establishing a fibre network in Hamilton. But finding sufficient content was a problem so the economics looked bad. We decided to defer but keep a close watch on trends and put the company into a position where it could move quickly when we felt the time was propitious. We investigated wind power and put in process a project to establish a wind farm at Te Akau. After I retired that was sold to Meridian Energy. Then Utilico, which owned lines companies in Thames Valley, Coromandel, Tauranga, Rotorua and Taupo, came onto the market. It was too big for us, but we endeavoured to set up an arrangement with Vector under which we would jointly bid for Utilico. WEL would take Thames Valley for $308 million and Vector the rest. WEL would then sell Coromandel and a small area in the north of our territory to Counties Power for $100 million. This would result in WEL purchasing the old Thames Valley Power Board business for a net cost of $208 million, which we could comfortably fund and which would increase profit by almost 50%. Unfortunately, we were trumped by our old friends Powerco, who became the second largest lines company in New Zealand. Had the opportunity available to take a stake in Powerco a few years earlier been taken, WEL would have been in a very strong position.

I retired as a director in 2006, having completed my contracted two terms. I was delighted that the trust appointed my deputy Roger Fisher to succeed me. He was highly competent so I was confident that WEL would be in good hands. I left knowing that WEL was operating efficiently with low costs, a very good health and safety record and excellent system reliability. Profit had increase from $13 million when I joined to just on $20 million when I retired. I had enjoyed my time as chairman and was proud of what we had achieved.

FIFTY-ONE
FLETCHER CHALLENGE

Fletcher Challenge had for many years been New Zealand's largest listed company. It had been created in 1981 when the long-standing and highly respected companies Fletcher Holdings and Challenge Corporation merged with Tasman Pulp & Paper under the leadership of Sir Ron Trotter as chairman and Hugh Fletcher as CEO. It had some good years, turning a profit of $602 million in 1990 when paper prices were high, but that was never repeated and the value of the company began to decline. Total shareholder return through the 1990s had averaged a miserable 1.7%, so billions of dollars of value had been destroyed. Fletcher Challenge was a conglomerate engaged in four main industries, pulp and paper, forestry, building products and energy (oil and gas). In 1993 Hugh Fletcher persuaded the board, despite opposition from the greatly respected chairman, Sir Ron Trotter, to split Fletcher Challenge into four "letter stocks", essentially four separate companies, each of which was listed on the stock exchange. The rationale was that it would be easier for investors to understand the individual business, and they could choose for themselves which industries they wished to invest in.

Had the four letter stocks been structured as separate stand-alone companies it would have been a sensible move. But they were effectively subsidiaries of, and were controlled by, Fletcher Challenge. So it proved to be anything but. The expensive Fletcher Challenge corporate structure imposed a heavy cost burden on the four operating companies, each of which also had their own management and corporate costs. The structure was even more complicated and difficult for investors to understand. The normal ability of a company to use the cash flow from strong businesses to fund any weaker business was not available, causing sub-optimal use of cash. There was no accountability as Fletcher Challenge controlled each letter stock. In addition, the weak letter stocks caused the stock market to mark down the value of the stronger letter stock businesses, in accordance with the value of the weakest, thus undervaluing the combined Fletcher Challenge. The combined Fletcher Challenge was clearly worth less than the sum of its parts. The letter stock structure had nothing to commend it. I could find no advantages, but disadvantages were numerous.

Hugh Fletcher operated an executive board comprising about seven executive directors. They sat between the board of directors and the operating businesses to which they seemed to add very little. Several of them were appointed directors of Fletcher Challenge. It was a very expensive structure of doubtful value, while having five executive directors on a board of eleven ensured that CEO Hugh Fletcher effectively controlled the board. There was a fundamental disagreement between Hugh and Ron Trotter who believed that the company needed major reorganisation. In 1995 this culminated in Sir Ron being rolled as chairman, leaving Hugh in undisputed control to continue the underperforming strategy.

In 1993 Sir Ron Trotter had invited me to lunch at the Wellington Club. He explained that he was planning director succession for Fletcher Challenge. He was searching for someone with leadership ability as a potential chairman when he stepped down in due course. He believed that I had those qualities and invited me to join the Fletcher Challenge Board. I was flattered, but declined as it was early in my term as Dairy Board chairman which I wished to concentrate on. In 1998, shortly after my retirement from the Dairy Board, Kerry Hoggard approached me. He was to become chairman of Fletcher Challenge and intended to give it a massive shake-up, eliminating the letter stocks by converting each of them into fully stand-alone companies. He wanted some new directors who understood the need for fundamental change in the structure of Fletcher Challenge and how it operated. Would I help and accept appointment as a director? I was delighted to do so. Kerry was a friend for whom I had huge respect. But before taking up the role I undertook due diligence, as I always did before accepting appointment to the board of any company. I needed to go into the role with my eyes wide open, having familiarised myself with the company and being satisfied that it was in a sound financial position. I needed to be aware of any issues which could materially weaken or threaten the business. Given the woeful financial performance of Fletcher Challenge, I was surprised to find that most of the operating business units were well managed and performing acceptably, some of them very well. It was clear that the poor performance of the company was a result of poor strategic decisions, as well as several very unwise major acquisitions, particularly in pulp and paper and forestry.

A couple of years earlier Michael Andrews had replaced Hugh Fletcher as CEO. While he was a good solid chief executive, the business continued to perform badly and destroy value. However, he had cleaned out the executive ranks, bringing in outsiders to several key operating roles. These people could see little merit in the unusual letter stock structure and favoured separation. Work on a strategic review of the business was under way and was considered by the directors shortly after I joined the board. Kerry had driven the conclusions that the four letter stocks should be separated into individual entities and those which were underperforming sold. There was no doubt in my mind that this needed to happen. Despite the reluctance of Hugh Fletcher, the directors agreed.

The decision was welcomed by the market which responded favourably. But, sadly, there was one major casualty. The chairman Kerry Hoggard had decided to make a personal statement of his confidence in the new direction of Fletcher Challenge, by purchasing a lot of shares. Unfortunately, he jumped the gun and executed the purchase prior to it being announced to the market. This was a breach of "insider trading" rules, both of the company and of the New Zealand Stock Exchange Listing Rules. The directors had no option but to require his resignation. Subsequently, two shareholders successfully brought a private prosecution against him. It was very sad for me to see the career of a friend whom I greatly respected and who was an outstanding business talent end in this way. But integrity is the most important requirement of business and directors must meet the most exacting standards of probity.

Roderick Deane was the obvious choice to take the chairmanship. He was experienced, wise, had a huge intellect and outstanding business acumen. His track record of creating value as CEO and chairman of Telecom was unmatched. However, he was reticent to accept appointment as in the process of appointing Kerry Hoggard as chairman, he had been told that he did not have the support of the directors, a number of whom remained on the board. We had a long informal meeting in Wellington during which every director expressed support for Roderick. He also wanted to be assured that every director was committed to the strategy agreed prior to Kerry's resignation. Having received those assurances from every director, Roderick accepted the chair.

In 2000 we set about the task of breaking up Fletcher Challenge. It was a monumental and complex task. Every step needed to be carefully considered, not least to ensure that $3 billion of existing tax losses were not lost and other hidden liabilities triggered. This was no easy task. "Financial engineering" had been regarded as a core skill so Fletcher Challenge was a complicated beast littered with hidden "bear traps" and a host of potential liabilities. We agreed that every business should be analysed. Any unit which could not earn the cost of its capital would be sold. The priority was to sell the pulp and paper assets which accounted for 60% of the company's debt and showed no prospect of ever covering its cost of capital. We were fortunate to receive a very good offer of $5 billion from Norske Skog, a premium on the market price at the time of 82%. Norske Skog also took over the $2.1 billion debt owed by the paper business.

By October an offer of $4.6 billion had been received from Shell and Apache Corporation for Fletcher Challenge Energy, a premium of 43% on the then energy letter stock share price. This enabled us to put the full break-up proposal to shareholders. Fletcher Challenge was to be dissolved, Fletcher Energy sold to Shell and Apache, and three new stand-alone companies created: Fletcher Building, Fletcher Forests, and Rubicon, a small company which had been created to mop up some non-core energy assets, as well as Forests' biotechnology assets and to underwrite a Forests "rights issue".

There was a last-minute hiccup as the Extraordinary General Meeting approached. Greymouth Petroleum launched a counter offer for Fletcher Energy. The price was similar to that offered by Shell and Apache but was highly conditional. Shell and Apache sweetened its offer by 21 cents per share and shareholders approved the break-up. Fletcher Challenge had destroyed around $5 billion of shareholder value through the 1990s. However, we had restored most of that and total shareholder returns from the break-up in 2001 were over 60%.

The separation had been a most difficult exercise. Over twelve months the board met fifty-three times as we laboured to complete it. Michael Andrews had done an outstanding job in executing the break-up and establishing Fletcher Building, Fletcher Forests and Rubicon as stand-alone companies. Together with his team, he deserves considerable credit for getting the job done. He retired as CEO when the reorganisation was completed.

Fletcher Forests was in bad shape. In 1996, at the peak of the cycle, Fletcher had, together with CITIC, a Chinese investment company, purchased the Central North Island Forests from the government for $2 billion. Two years later timber prices had collapsed, and the forests were only worth around half of that. In February the Central North Island Forest Partnership was placed in receivership by the partnership's banks. Fletcher Forests had to write off $529 million of its investment. The Forests letter stock was thus laden with debt and needed a cash injection to be able to stand alone. A "rights" issue was the obvious answer but needed to be underwritten to guarantee that the funds would be raised. But no one was prepared to underwrite the issue. As we wracked our brains to find a way forward, Hugh Fletcher suggested that Rubicon underwrite the issue. This enabled Forests to receive the cash injection it needed to stand alone. A consequence was that Rubicon became the largest shareholder in the new Fletcher Forests. This was to have future implications.

The jewel in the crown was Fletcher Building which was a very good business earning better that its cost of capital. It too had been offered for sale, but offers fell short of what we believed it was worth. The top offer was around $1.65 per share, which was in line with a second valuation commissioned by the directors. However, we decided that we could do better than that by forming Building into a separate stand-alone listed company. Events were to massively vindicate that decision. From a starting value in 2001 of $298 million, the value of

Fletcher Building had reached $4.8 billion by 2009, making it the most valuable company in New Zealand.

The board which had steered Fletcher Challenge through the fiendishly complex break-up process in 2000/2001 was largely comprised of directors who were not involved in Fletcher Challenge's huge value destruction through the 1990s. Most of the directors who worked on the reorganisation, including me, became directors of the new Fletcher Building. It was a very good business and there was no lack of candidates to join the board. I offered to take the chair of Fletcher Forests. I knew that it would not be an easy ride, but I believed that with my international experience, and experience in adding value to a New Zealand natural resource, I could guide it to success.

FIFTY-TWO
FLETCHER FORESTS

In accepting the chair of Fletcher Forests, my vision was to "build a significant international business adding value to New Zealand's outstanding forestry resource". So often New Zealand has excelled in growing things but has had limited success in adding value to our natural resources. Forestry was in that category. I knew what needed to be done, but I also was well aware that it would be no easy challenge. Timber prices were depressed and showing no sign of improvement. Fletcher Forests was laden with debt, much of it being denominated in US dollars. The debt was escalating as the New Zealand dollar weakened against the US dollar and we were heading for a breach of the company's borrowing covenants. The break-up of the partnership with CITIC had lost us ownership of the prime forestry resource of the Central North Island Forests, although we continued to manage it for the receivers. The high-cost structure which we had inherited from Fletcher Challenge was unsustainable. We needed to act quickly or the company would slide into receivership.

Terry McFadgen had been appointed CEO. He was a seasoned executive who was experienced in dealing with difficult circumstances. He had Ian Boyd, a very experienced forestry executive, looking after forests and milling. John Dell, a talented young executive and former Air New Zealand CFO, was recruited as CFO, with lawyer Paul Gillard rounding off a small but strong executive team, to lead what I intended to be a lean organisation. I recruited a board comprising my former Dairy Board CEO colleague Warren Larsen; Michael Andrews, the CEO who had driven the break-up of Fletcher Challenge and who was probably the most experienced forestry executive in New Zealand; Rodger Fisher, former CEO of Owens Group and a very respected company director; Michael Walls, senior partner of Chapman Tripp who was one of New Zealand's most highly regarded corporate finance specialists; Stephen Hurley, managing director of Xylem Investments, a leading international forestry investment fund manager; and Luke Moriarty, one of Fletcher Challenge's most capable finance executives who was managing director of Forests' major shareholder Rubicon. I was confident that I had a team capable of dealing with the significant challenges Forests faced.

Fortunately, the "rights issue" shortly before separation gave us some financial breathing space, but the most urgent need was to get the company into at least a break-even position. Costs were slashed and tree-harvesting volumes increased to improve cash flow. Capital investment was paused, and assets not absolutely essential, or not earning their cost of capital, sold to reduce debt. These measures got us to break-even and as we got the debt down, debt-servicing costs reduced. But this was only a holding situation; the challenge to build profitability sufficiently to enable the company to earn the cost of its capital would be much more difficult. We commissioned the Boston Consulting Group to undertake a strategic review. Their work gave us much valuable information. We set out to run a very efficient, low-cost forestry operation and focus investment on adding value to New

Zealand timber. This was mainly centred on the high-quality timber from our pruned forests and included offshore investment in marketing and distribution. A couple of small businesses in the United States were purchased which returned good profits. But we needed to do much more.

The receiver of the Central North Island Forests had been unable to find a buyer. It was clear that Fletcher Forests would benefit if it could regain control of that resource, but we could not afford to buy it back from the receiver. The decision by Fletcher Challenge to let the partnership with CITIC fail had been most short sighted. As we wrestled with how we could fund its purchase, CITIC appeared to be the only possibility. We reached the view that establishing a new arrangement with CITIC should be explored. I was scheduled to attend the APEC Leaders Summit in Shanghai in November 2001 so sought a meeting with the chairman of CITIC, Wang Jun. CITIC felt very badly aggrieved by how it had been treated by Fletcher Challenge, sufficiently so that the matter had been raised by the Chinese premier in a meeting with Prime Minister Helen Clark. Given the history between Fletcher Challenge and CITIC, Wang Jun was very generous in agreeing to meet me. But he would have done his homework on me and believed that I could be trusted. I flew from Shanghai to Beijing and met him over lunch.

Wang Jun was a very senior and influential Chinese official who was on the fringe of the Communist Party Central Committee. He was a chain smoker who spoke no English but was clearly a leader and a very smart individual. I expressed my regret about the circumstances which had caused the partnership with Fletcher Challenge to collapse, acknowledging that in my view CITIC had a right to feel aggrieved. I apologised to him and explained that Fletcher Forests was a new, and now completely separate, organisation from Fletcher Challenge, with a new board and management. I advised him that we had considered the reasons for the original decision to partner with

CITIC and believed that they were still valid despite the breakdown in the relationship. I could tell that my remarks were resonating with Wang Jun, so pressed on to suggest that we would be willing to discuss a new relationship if CITIC felt so inclined. Wang Jun responded by commenting that they saw their future being with Fletcher. Given that was the view of CITIC, our discussion turned to what that future might be. I advised Wang Jun that we would be willing to consider all options including CITIC taking a significant shareholding in Fletcher Forests. Wang Jun welcomed that comment and agreed that we should commence negotiations. He undertook to send a senior person to New Zealand to negotiate with us. This had all taken place within a period of ninety minutes before I had to depart to fly home to New Zealand, but I was delighted with the agreement we had reached to endeavour to negotiate a new arrangement.

CITIC sent a very smart and affable Hong Kong man, Peter Kwok, to initiate discussions. We negotiated an arrangement for CITIC to purchase a cornerstone shareholding in Fletcher Forests. Another visit to Beijing to meet with Wang Jun and then CITIC Vice President Zengxin Mi arrived in Auckland where we finalised a deal. CITIC would purchase a 35% shareholding in Forests for $439 million. The price of 37 cents per share was an 85% premium to the then market price. There would be a two-year stand-still provision under which CITIC agreed not to increase its shareholding. We negotiated a new loan of $550 million from the banking consortium which would enable us to purchase the Central North Island Forests from the receiver and restructure our debt, including bringing it onshore. As we concluded the deal, Mr Mi advised that he had one "condition precedent". CITIC would only go ahead if I agreed to remain as chairman. While this was most flattering and confirmed that I had gained the respect of CITIC, I advised him that while I felt warmly about CITIC, and greatly respected he and Chairman Wang

Jun, and was satisfied that our deal was in the best interest of my shareholders, I could not even consider accepting his proposal. My duty was to the existing shareholders, and it was my responsibility to get the best deal for them. When the deal was concluded, then we could discuss membership of the new board.

This was an excellent deal which would enable us to buy the valuable Central North Island Forests, increase the scale of the business, place our finances on a very sound footing and have the assistance and influence of CITIC in penetrating the potentially valuable Chinese market. But it would need the approval of our shareholders and there was a last-minute snag. Rubicon, which owned 17.6% of our shares, would not support the proposal unless they were bought out and their support would be required to gain approval. After some torrid negotiations, agreement was reached for them to accept one of our forest blocks in return for their shares. This stuck in my craw as it meant that Rubicon was receiving something which was not available to the rest of our shareholders. Unfortunately, one of my directors, Stephen Hurley, president of forestry investor Xylem which held 7.6% of Forests' shares, was opposed. He objected very strongly, principally to the favourable treatment of Rubicon. Understandably, he would have liked the same opportunity to sell his shares at the price Rubicon was to receive. I would have much preferred a unanimous board and no special treatment for Rubicon. But the overall benefit to our shareholders was so great that I believed that the proposal should be put to them and they should have the opportunity to accept or reject it. I believed that the outlook for Forests was bleak if the proposal did not proceed.

Gaining shareholder approval under those circumstances was always going to be a tough ask. The company had a poor history of performance under Fletcher Challenge ownership. Preferential treatment for Rubicon; sale of a cornerstone shareholding in an iconic New Zealand forestry resource to a Chinese company; the debt which would be incurred to buy back the Central North Island Forests – these were all matters which some shareholders objected to. I received advice that I should not chair the Special Shareholders Meeting as the National Bank of which I was a director was a member of the banking syndicate for the Central North Island Forests which we were purchasing. Michael Walls, chairman of the Audit Committee, chaired the meeting, but I was able to lead the discussion as I would normally have done had I been chairing the meeting. A 75% vote in favour was required for the proposal to go ahead; we came up short at 71%. The opportunity to significantly improve the company's performance was lost. The dream of Fletcher Forests being a national icon utilising the New Zealand's outstanding forest resource had been strangled.

Chairman in full flight

But life goes on, so it was back to square one to develop an alternative strategy from pretty limited options. Log prices were at near record lows and seemed likely to remain depressed for the foreseeable future. Capital was limited and the contract for the management rights for the Central North Island Forests, which contributed close to 15% of our revenue, was expiring and therefore at risk. But forest ownership was the real issue. Forests have a very long-term horizon. The "plant to harvest" cycle for trees was twenty-six to thirty-five years depending on the land and growing conditions. Most of the costs are incurred in the first few years, while revenue is highly volatile and mostly earned in the final year. Public listed companies are not natural owners of forests. Their half-yearly reporting cycle inevitably causes them to think relatively short term, and to adopt strategies which are less than optimal for a long-term investment cycle. Around the world many forests are owned by pension funds which are able to take a long-term investment perspective. We decided to run a lean business and ruthlessly reduce operating costs; focus investment on higher margin front-end processing, marketing and distribution; reduce investment in trees, and use freed-up funds to reduce debt. Capital which we could not profitably invest for above cost of capital returns would be returned to shareholders. Fletcher Forest would be a much smaller company but one which we believed could be profitable, earning good returns for shareholders.

Terry McFadgen decided to retire. Ian Boyd and John Dell were both very good executives. Ian was very experienced in forestry operations, while John was a young and talented CFO but was not quite ready to be CEO. We conducted an external search without turning up any better candidates. Between them Ian and John had every quality we needed, and it was Warren Larsen who eventually suggested that we consider appointing joint chief executives. After much discussion and thought, my board decided to appoint Ian and John as joint CEOs. This is something which normally would never be contemplated; there are just too many inherent disadvantages. But in John we had a unique talent who needed a little more time, and broader experience, which Ian was able to provide, so their skills and experience complemented one another. Importantly, we were confident that they would work well together. The directors asked me to be a little more hands-on than I would normally be. It was an arrangement which we intended would not be long term, one to two years maximum. It says a lot about the character of Ian and John that it worked extremely well and John Dell grew enormously. After a year or so Ian Boyd generously suggested to me that the time was right for John to become CEO and that he would be prepared to accept the role of chief operating officer. The directors agreed and appointed John CEO.

We made reasonable process with our strategies, but log prices continued to fall. We were making progress with our added-value processing and marketing activities and increased our investment in those activities. But despite the fact that we were earning operating profits, decreasing forestry values resulted in our annual results being affected by large forest asset write downs. We decided to sell the forests. With depressed log prices, the timing was not ideal, but we needed to invest in and focus on our profitable value-adding activities. Any capital which we believed could not earn above its cost would be returned to shareholders.

In September 2003, a conditional agreement for the sale of the forests at a price of $685 million was entered into with Campbell Group, a US investor backed by pension funds in North America. This was trumped by a bid of $725 million from Kiwi Forest Group, a New Zealand consortium. Like everything connected with the former Fletcher Challenge, the sale of the forests was a devilishly complicated process. But it was consummated by the middle of 2004. To better reflect the changed nature of the company's operations the company name was changed to Tenon Ltd. Tenon was now a processor and marketer of high-value specialised wood products and mouldings with processing and marketing operations in both New

Zealand and the USA. When it was completed, Tenon was able to return $495 million to shareholders.

With the sale of the forest completed, and cash from the capital return in Tenon's pocket, its largest shareholder Rubicon swooped. In June 2004 I was driving home from a Tenon board meeting, when John Dell called me to advise that a takeover offer had just been received from Rubicon which was offering $1.85 a share for 50.1% of the company. Our Takeover Response Plan was immediately activated. After receiving professional advice, the directors concluded that the offer was inadequate. The price was too low while conditions were less than satisfactory. As it was only a "partial offer" for 50.1%, shareholders would be locked into a minority holding in Tenon for 49.9% of their shares. Accordingly, we decided to oppose acceptance. We managed to get the price up to $1.95 per share but when it became obvious that the "partial offer" would be accepted by 50.1% of shares, agreed to recommend acceptance.

With the takeover completed, my time at Tenon was at an end. I could hardly regard my stewardship as a success; however, it was not a failure either. When it was spun out of Fletcher Challenge, Fletcher Forests was in a desperate situation. In fact, its weakness threatened the whole break-up process of Fletcher Challenge. Forestry product prices were depressed; it was burdened with excessive debt; the forest assets were overvalued; and it was burning cash. Our new team of management and directors had stabilised the business, reduced costs and stopped the cash burn. We had faced up to valuing the forests at their true market value rather than their historical cost and had established a profitable value-adding processing and marketing business. After allowing for the share consolidation in 2003, the share price which was $1.25 at separation was equivalent to $1.45 for those shareholders who accepted the Rubicon takeover offer. We had pulled together a very favourable deal with CITIC, which if it had been approved by shareholders would have given the business a long-term future with a good chance of delivering on my vision of "building a significant international business adding value to New Zealand's forest resource". It also would have kept the forests in New Zealand ownership. Sadly, after taking over Tenon, Rubicon steadily destroyed shareholder value, both of Rubicon and Tenon.

There was a sequel. I have always believed that directors should align their interests with those of shareholders, by holding shares in any company of which they are a director. I always pushed for that obligation to be included in directors' governance obligations of every company of which I was a director. My normal guideline was that I should have a shareholding equivalent in value to one year's directors' fees for that company. Fletcher Challenge rules required shareholding by directors to be held in each letter stock proportionate to the market capitalisation of each letter stock. With Forests being the weakest of the four letter stocks, this meant that when Fletcher Challenge was broken up my Forests shareholding was well below the guideline of one year's fees. So, when Forests launched as a stand-alone company, I needed to top up my shareholding to meet my guideline. But that was not so simple. There are very strict rules around when directors can buy and sell stock and windows to trade shares are limited. Some were NZX requirements and some were company rules. The basic principle was that if a director has any knowledge of a company which is not available to the market, then trading company stock is prohibited. We had a robust process in place which required directors to seek approval before buying and selling stock. But when it was formed, Forests had a continuous stream of activities under way which precluded its directors from trading stock. Some were positive, most were negative. Regardless, for several years I could not top up my shareholding. We were very careful in granting approval. On a couple of occasions, I considered that the market was fully informed and therefore I could buy, but approval was declined. In 2004 we had sold the forests and released a market update. I considered that the market was fully informed, so I sought and received approval to buy, which I did on a Friday. At a board meeting on Monday, as I was obliged to do, I declared my purchase to the board, which in turn was obliged to declare it to the NZX. Some of the executives who were in a similar position had also sought and received permission to buy. When I declared my purchase I noticed Luke Moriarty, who was also CEO of Rubicon, suck in his breath. I was soon to learn that he knew something that the rest of us did not. That afternoon, in June 2004 as I was driving home from the meeting, out of the blue I received advice that a partial takeover offer from Rubicon had been received. I immediately knew that I was in trouble. I had just purchased shares immediately before receiving an offer to buy Forests shares, at a higher price than I had paid for them. It looked bad and there was at least a prima facie case that I had been trading with inside information even though that was not true, but it was a very serious matter. As I expected, the media quickly made the link and my integrity was on the line.

In due course I was summonsed before a Securities Commission hearing and interrogated under oath on what I did, and did not know, at the time of my purchasing the shares. Having my integrity challenged was not a pleasant experience, but the evidence that I had no knowledge of the offer at the time of my purchase was clear, and the Commission concluded that there was no case to answer. I had always taken great care when buying shares in a company of which I was a director, and I had never ever sold stock. I had also always ensured that a robust approval process was in place. But the whole episode was a clear demonstration of how careful company directors must be when trading in company securities.

FIFTY-THREE
FLETCHER BUILDING: THE PHOENIX

THE JEWEL OF THE FLETCHER CHALLENGE CROWN WAS Fletcher Building, which had been the rump of the original Fletcher Industries. It was involved in construction, steel, cement, Placemakers retail, aggregates and a range of building products. It was a decentralised business comprised of several operating companies, most of which had very high market shares, a few being market dominant. As I had found when doing my due diligence prior to accepting appointment to Fletcher Challenge, most of the operating companies were very well managed. It was a profitable business which earned a reasonable return on its capital. We had no doubt that it could do much better.

Terry McFadgen was an experienced manager who had been CEO for some time, but the directors were determined to drive a major uplift in profitability so felt that an appointment from outside would be beneficial. Alexander Toldte, who had recently joined Fletcher Challenge, was our original choice. He was experienced and very highly rated. Unfortunately, he had little respect for the directors who would form the new board of Fletcher Building and began to dictate to Chairman Roderick Deane and the directors those who he would accept as directors. His lack of respect for the directors of Fletcher Challenge, who had presided over huge value destruction through the 1990s, was understandable, but he failed to understand that it was a different board which had guided Fletcher Challenge through the break-up, in the process lifting the value of the Group by 60% in a little over a year. The members of that board deserved considerable credit. His attitude also demonstrated poor judgement; a manager telling the board what to do is not acceptable so it was obvious that he was not suitable. We resolved to conduct a search for a CEO but in the meantime were fortunate to have Michael Andrews willing to act as interim CEO. Although a long-term Fletcher Challenge executive, he was highly competent, had done an excellent job executing the break-up of Fletcher Challenge, understood the need for significant change and was prepared to get on and implement it.

The first thing we decided was that the company should be decentralised, with responsibility and profit accountability moved down to the operating companies. The costly Fletcher Challenge head office multi-layered superstructure was removed in favour of a very small but highly capable executive team. When we initiated the search for a CEO, we wanted somebody with a manufacturing background; who understood how manufacturing businesses operated; who could be hands-on when necessary; who knew where to look; who knew what levers to pull. The last thing we wanted was a CEO who was a grand strategist sitting above the business in a helicopter, or one who had been a management consultant. Fletchers had enough of those over the years. We wanted a person with a proven record of hands-on management and successful execution. We turned up some interesting applicants, several of whom we believed could do the job. But one person stood out. Ralph Waters seemed to ideally meet our requirements. A mechanical engineer with significant experience as CEO of the successful manufacturing business Email Ltd, a good track record and with good judgement, his background was ideal. For me he was an obvious choice, one which we considered ourselves lucky to have available.

In 2001 Fletcher Building earned an operating profit of $18 million from sales of $2.3 billion and an overall loss of $272 million, although that number was distorted by the break-up process and the costs of establishing Building as a stand-alone company. At the end of that year the share price was around $1.80, only a little above where we had started. We clearly needed to do much better. Ralph set out to demonstrate a clean break from Fletcher Challenge practices. He restructured the company into four operating groups: building products; construction; concrete; and distribution. Of the seven-person executive team, only two came from the previous management team. Implementing a decentralised management structure, Ralph stressed accountability and insisted on a much greater level of ownership and accountability for results from the operating business managers.

Roderick asked me to chair the Remuneration Committee. I shifted remuneration emphasis from complicated structures designed to justify maximum remuneration, to simple principles designed to reward actual results. Performance remuneration changed from comparison with the previous year to achieving an overall satisfactory return on capital. A business might achieve increased profit each year, but unless a satisfactory overall return on capital was achieved, performance pay was withheld. This was a massive change from the Fletcher Challenge practice but really drove performance. To better align the interests of executives with the interests of shareholders, Ralph required executives to invest half of their performance pay in company stock. These measures helped establish a real "performance" ethos across the business.

Fletcher Challenge had been a rich feeding ground for consultants. Ralph wanted executives to take ownership of issues right from inception of a proposal to its implementation. Use of consultants was virtually eliminated, which must have had a significant impact on McKinsey's New Zealand operations. Challenging return-on-capital hurdles needed to be met to gain approval for capital expenditure, while a searching post-review process for all capital projects over $1 million was introduced. This resulted in poor planning, control and execution of projects being identified, sanctioned where necessary, and helped avoid similar errors occurring again. As part of Fletcher Challenge, Fletcher Building's earnings had a history of being inconsistent and unreliable, and consequently some major investment funds would not buy Building stock. Earnings reliability became a key priority and a dividend policy of "increasing dividends each year" was introduced. Funds which had not been prepared to invest in Fletcher Building welcomed this and began to appear on the Share Register.

The 2002 financial year saw a tax-paid profit of $98 million compared to a loss of $288 million the previous year. Importantly, earnings before interest and tax (EBIT) of $210 million delivered a cash return on assets of 23.1%. With the business now performing well, the directors turned their attention to the future. One of the issues was that most of the businesses had very strong market shares in New Zealand; for example, 95% for plasterboard and cement 50%. While this was great, it meant that the company was at the mercy of the New Zealand building cycle and opportunities for sustained growth were limited. Roderick Deane and I suggested to Ralph that he turn his attention to developing a growth strategy and seek growth opportunities, including geographical diversification. He was initially reluctant, as by nature he was an inherently cautious individual. Also, Fletcher Challenge had a long history of making unwise acquisitions. Ralph was determined to avoid repeating that at all costs.

The board agreed a goal of becoming a major Australasian building materials company. Tight criteria were set for acquisitions:

1. Any acquisition must be No. 1 or No. 2 in its market.
2. It must have a good and sustainable industry structure. There is a saying that, "If a good company and a bad industry meet, the bad industry will win every time". So being No. 1 in a poor industry was not acceptable.
3. It must have good management who would be prepared to stay and work for the company. Too many good companies are destroyed after being acquired because the acquiror replaces the management with its own people who know nothing about the business. This is particularly the case when the acquisition is in a different country.
4. The purchase price should allow the company to earn its cost of capital within three years.

Laminex was an obvious target. It was Australia's No. 1 in decorative laminate wood panels. In 2002 its private equity owners wished to sell but wanted more than we were prepared to pay. Ralph played it brilliantly. He withdrew from the process and waited. The owners could not find a buyer at the prices they wanted so moved to an initial public offering (IPO). A board of directors was appointed which completed extensive due diligence and negotiated the float price. Then Ralph swooped with an unconditional offer of $759 million, some $15 million below the IPO price. The sellers avoided significant cost and received an unconditional offer. It was one which they could not refuse.

Over the next five years until 2006, we invested more than $1.6 billion in Australian acquisitions. Laminex was followed in 2003 by Tasman, which was the leading glass wool insulation business in Australia and New Zealand and the New Zealand leader in metal roof tiles. Amatek, which owned several building product businesses ranging from steel reinforced concrete pipes to roll-formed steel roofing and foil insulation, was purchased in 2005.

The original Fletcher business, decades previously, was construction. When I joined the Fletcher Challenge Board in 1998, it was still dealing with the consequences of a series of construction job disasters, many of them in Australia, which had occurred in the mid 1990s. For example, there was a job in Melbourne which had not gone well and we were being sued by the client, originally for about A$12 million. Six years later we had spent almost $20 million on legal and other costs and settlement was still years away. We were advised that costs could reach a total of $30–40 million. The directors could see no sense in that and instructed our lawyers to settle, which we eventually did for almost $40 million. Fighting a claim of $12 million had cost us almost $60 million. This was really dumb. We resolved that all claims should be settled and that in future no litigation should be initiated without board approval.

Mark Binns, by profession a lawyer, had been brought in as CEO of Fletcher Construction, to clean up these problems. He was a capable manager who ran construction very competently. He also believed that it was better to settle disputes in good faith rather than litigate. Under Mark's stewardship, Construction became a reliable earner of around $100 million of profit each year, also utilising huge quantities of Fletcher products – plasterboard, steel, panelling, cement, aggregates, concrete, timber, roofing iron etc. – all at good prices, thus making a major profit contribution to the company. Mark was by nature risk adverse which is just what is wanted in the CEO of a construction business. Construction is an inherently risky business. It is not an accident that a higher proportion of building companies go broke than any other industry. We adopted a policy that Construction could not undertake a "fixed-price" contract without specific authorisation by the board. When we had made clear that the board would rarely, if ever, authorise a fixed-price contract, management stopped recommending them to us. This no-risk policy confined us to low margins of around 1.5%–2.5%, but that was all we had at risk on any job. In the event that the job went badly, that margin was all we had at risk and a bad job disaster was survivable. This policy de-risked the riskiest part of Fletcher Building's business. Building began to earn a steady $100 million or so profit each year. Construction earned a great reputation with satisfied customers and became adept at extracting higher margins from client-requested variations.

Ralph retired as CEO in August 2006. For the 2007 financial year tax-paid profit reached $484 million on $5.9 billion of sales. Return on funds was an excellent 24.8%. Since inception the dividend had been increased every year. Boston Consulting Group advised that total shareholder return for the five years to the end of 2006 was a staggering 38% per annum, the highest among large listed companies in New Zealand. Fletcher Building was New Zealand's most valuable company by market capitalisation. The share price, which in 2001 was less than $2, had reached $13. Ralph was retiring on a very high note and a much wealthier individual than when he had become CEO. He deserved every penny of it.

Ralph had given the directors several years' notice of his intention to retire after five years' service in 2006. Developing potential successors was a significant personal objective which the board set for him over that period. Every six months he provided the directors with an in-depth evaluation of the four executives he considered to be potential successors, all of whom he considered could do the job. It was clear that we had plenty of talent in house. When the time came to appoint a successor to Ralph, Jonathan Ling was an obvious choice. Ralph had hired him three years earlier to run laminates and panels. An Australian, he was an experienced manger with a good track record. Ralph stayed on the board as a director, something which is not normally recommended, but which we felt was appropriate under the circumstances.

Fletcher Building held dominant market positions in New Zealand right across the building products spectrum. While not dominant in Australia, it held leading positions there in the products it was involved in. But opportunities for growth in both countries were limited so we would have to look further afield if we wanted to continue to grow earnings. Entering new geographical jurisdictions would not be without risk so we were cautious as we searched for opportunities. Ralph had identified Formica, a global company and the pioneer of laminated boards, as a possible opportunity. Put together with our Laminex business it would give us the world-leading position in laminates. It was located in the USA and was owned by a private equity company which was in the process of centralising manufacturing onto a single site. Naturally cautious, Ralph had pulled back, deciding to wait until the centralisation project was completed and the new plant successfully commissioned. This had largely been completed by the end of 2006. By that time Ralph had retired and been succeeded by Jonathan Ling. Jonathan decided to make a move and by the middle of 2007 had negotiated an agreement to purchase Formica. I was a little surprised at the price he had agreed, $960 million, which was a multiple of 7.2 times Formica's expected profit for the 2008 year. The businesses which Ralph had bought were all at lower multiples of around six times. However, the directors approved the purchase. But our timing was wrong and the price too high. The manufacturing centralisation project still had some way to go to completion, while the Global Financial Crisis in 2008 caused a sharp contraction in building activity right around the world. Formica returned a meagre profit of $2.9 million for the second half of 2008, abysmal on an investment of nearly $1 billion.

The severe global recession caused by the GFC savagely hit New Zealand businesses. Operating profit for 2009 was down to $314 million, but "Unusual Items" of $360 million resulted in a net loss for the year of $14 million. The "Unusual Items" arose from redundancy payments, as the business had responded to the sharp decline in sales by reducing staff numbers by 15% and closing manufacturing capacity which had become surplus. Also, with lower sales reducing profitability, the value of some assets became impaired and had to be written down. Share markets around the world fell sharply. Fletcher Building was not immune from that trend and the share price fell from around $10 at the start of the year to a little above $5 by year end. Fletcher Building's sterling run had come to an end. The effects of the GFC persisted until 2012 so it would be a tough haul back.

Roderick Deane retired in March 2010. He had been an outstanding chairman, quite the finest I have ever worked with. He was the driving force behind the startling turnaround of Fletcher Building. Ralph's outstanding decision making was often due to Roderick's wise guidance. Subsequent events would show what a loss Roderick was to the business. He was succeeded as chairman by Ralph who appeared to be a pretty obvious choice. Subsequent events suggested that was not necessarily so. By 2010 profit had recovered to $270 million. Formica had improved a little to operating earnings of $34 million, but it was still a pathetic result.

I retired at the end of the 2010 financial year. It had been an exhilarating journey and a pretty successful one for our shareholders. Since being appointed a director of Fletcher Challenge in 1999 I had the good fortune to be part of a team which had increased shareholder value by 60% through the break-up of that company and then took the share price of Fletcher Building from under $2 to $10 when the Global Financial Crisis hit in 2008. Despite the effects of the GFC, that $2 share was still worth $5 when I retired in 2010. It was an achievement to be proud of.

The vision of Fletcher Building to be "the leading Australasian building products company" did not survive for long. It clearly had changed its policy and had entered into fixed-price construction contracts. Why I do not know, but the inevitable happened and in 2017 the company got caught with huge losses on several fixed-price building jobs which brought it to its knees. That was precisely the reason why we had refused to enter such contracts. It had to retrench and shrink its operations to survive. Its share price halved. It had been a great ride, but the dream was over!

FIFTY-FOUR
SKY CITY

I HAD NEVER BEEN A GAMBLER. I WAS NEVER INTERESTED in horse racing, so a ticket in the Melbourne Cup sweepstake was about the extent of my betting. I had been to Las Vegas and found it spectacular and thrilling but regarded gambling as mindless. When the law was changed to allow casinos to be established in New Zealand, albeit under very tight regulation, I would have preferred that not to happen. But as an investor, it was hard not to notice that Sky City Entertainment Group began to create a record of steadily increasing profit with a rising share price. My good friend Sir Peter Elworthy was a director of Sky City Entertainment Group. One day in 2003 he informed me that he was retiring from Sky City and had recommended that I be appointed. He hoped that I would accept. An invitation from the chairman, Jon Hartley, followed, accompanied by calls from other Sky City directors whom I knew. They all stressed that it was a strong and fun company. I agreed to undertake due diligence before deciding. When I did so, I was impressed by the high probity standards which the company followed. When I walked into the casino for the first time at 9 pm one evening, I was even more surprised. There were several thousand people who all seemed to be enjoying themselves. Although alcohol was readily available, the standard of behaviour was much better than would normally be found in a bar at that time of night. While there would obviously be people who had a gambling problem, the majority of visitors appeared to be having a pretty good time. I was to learn that the average visitor to the Auckland Casino spent $71 per visit. For that they had a few drinks, some food, enjoyed a range of entertainment and spent some time at the gaming tables or machines. I decided to accept appointment as a director of Sky City Entertainment Group.

Sky City had been established in 1996. Brierley Investments Ltd had been a leading founding investor. The Las Vegas casino operator Harrah's operated the casino under a management contract. Evan Davies had led both the licencing and building projects when Sky City was founded, becoming its CEO. In 1998 he convinced the board to buy out Harrah's management contract and manage the business itself. It was a smart decision. Evan was a very good CEO, profitability rapidly increased, reaching $107 million in 2003 when I joined the board. Jon Hartley was chairman but resigned shortly after I joined the board. He was succeeded by Australian Rod McGeoch, a larger-than-life individual with whom I was to develop a special friendship.

Each director and all senior executives had to be approved by the New Zealand Gambling Commission. Probity standards were very high. The application I was required to complete was over 100 pages. A huge amount of detail was required, including every exit and entry to and from New Zealand for the past ten years. As can be imagined, this was a major exercise for me given the amount of international travelling I had done. Police checks, including being fingerprinted, were required, as well as credit checks. My fingerprints were taken at Matamata Police Station where the fingerprinting facilities were in the cell block. It was a pretty forbidding environment. Consideration of each application took between four and six months while the information was checked. As Sky City owned a casino in Adelaide, a similar, process was also required for Australia. Eventually, I was approved in both jurisdictions.

When I joined, Sky City owned casinos in Auckland, Adelaide, Queenstown and Hamilton. The Auckland complex also included a hotel, the largest conference centre in New Zealand and a theatre. Auckland's iconic Sky Tower was owned by Sky City and was a major tourist attraction for the city, being visited by one out of every three visitors to the city. In 2004 we purchased the Darwin Casino from MGM Mirage, as well as a 41% stake in Christchurch Casino from the London-based Aspinall. Hotels are an integral part of casino operations. Darwin also had a hotel. A second Auckland hotel, Sky City Grand, was opened in Auckland in 2005 as part of a deal which allowed an increase in the number of gaming machines and tables in the casino. The Auckland, Hamilton and Darwin sites were pretty successful, but Queenstown and Adelaide always struggled. Sky City also owned a half share in the largest cinema chain in New Zealand which was a perennial underperformer. There were many restaurants and bars at all sites, as, again, the provision of food and beverage is an integral part of casino operations worldwide. The company saw its business as entertainment rather than gambling. It was an easier story to sell, but the reality was that it was gambling which earned almost all of the profit. Sky City was a fun company. Being in the entertainment business meant that there was a never-ending stream of events and functions, which Marg and I enjoyed immensely.

As a board we seemed to spend a lot of time discussing new bars, restaurants and hotels, and we were certainly investing a great deal of capital in them. The problem was that they did not make much money. Profit was essentially flat. But the amount of capital invested in the business continued to increase and over five years almost doubled. We had fallen into the trap of investing more and more capital to earn the same profit. Quite frankly our use of capital was poor and becoming worse. The cinema business was an example. We owned a 50% stake in Sky City Cinemas. It made a very poor return on capital. Returns were not improving, and we were facing an impairment charge because the profitability did not support the book value of the assets. For some time, I had been a lone voice advocating selling the cinemas business. The board finally agreed that we should sell and a buyer was located. Then at the last-minute Evan proposed that we buy the 50% we did not own and to my amazement the directors agreed. Profit never got near the profit forecast in the business case submitted to the board. Two years later we had to write off $61 million when we sold the business as we could only attract bids for less than half of its book value.

I was appointed chairman of the Audit Committee. It was not a role which I particularly enjoyed but an important one, nevertheless. While the business had a monopoly over most of the country, it was licenced and closely regulated. It was required to meet exacting probity standards and depended on a social licence to operate. Problem gambling was an ongoing issue as was responsible use of liquor. The business was required to meet high standards of host responsibility and have effective harm-minimisation processes in place. If use of liquor or problem gambling issues occurred, our licence to operate would be in jeopardy. In addition, being a largely cash business, the risks of defalcation and money laundering were ever present. Following the terrorist attacks on the World Trade Centre, New York, on 11 September 2001, the United States demanded the introduction of strict anti-money laundering legislation right around the world. While aimed principally at financial institutions, it applied virtually everywhere cash was handled, including casinos. The regulations and their enforcement grew increasingly onerous each year, with huge financial penalties for non-compliance, and personal liability for directors and executives. Sky City values prescribed that the business should meet the highest standards of probity and that the business should have a policy of "compliance plus". In other words, don't just comply with the standard, exceed it. We beefed up our internal audit capability and each year I would meet with the gaming regulators at the Ministry of Internal Affairs to make sure that I was aware of what their concern were and to discuss what we were doing to manage or rectify them. We worked diligently to maintain high standards and continued to receive a clean bill of health.

When I undertook my due diligence prior to accepting appointment, Evan Davies had advised me that his wife, Heather Shotter, was a marketing executive. This had been disclosed to the directors who had accepted it. I was surprised, as it was a far from ideal situation, one which would not normally be accepted. It was to have fateful consequences. Evan began to promote her and in a couple of years she was in charge of New Zealand operations which comprised more than 85% of the total Sky City Group. Executive turnover began to increase, which is always a worrying sign of personnel problems. The management structure became complicated with dual reporting and dotted lines, and accountability became blurred. Annual profit was flat, yet over five years we had injected $700 million of additional capital into the business, an increase of 75% for no increase in profit. A totally unsatisfactory performance. Evan had been a very good CEO; in 2000 he had been named CEO of the Year and deservedly so. But Heather was now running much of the business. Then Evan and Heather split up. Against Evan's opposition the board insisted that she exit the business. By this time, some of the key New Zealand executives were largely her appointments and were mostly not up to it. Management had become largely dysfunctional, but the board was unwilling to take action.

Then in 2007 Warwick Hunt, the managing partner of our auditor PwC, asked to see me as chairman of the Audit Committee. He was accompanied by Senior Partners David Randell and John Harvey.

They conveyed to me their concerns about the management of the company, stating that it had become dysfunctional and excessively costly. When I asked them to quantify the extent of this, they advised me that operational costs were $50 million higher than they should be. None of this was news to me. For some time, I had been suggesting to my director colleagues that we had a serious problem, but they had been unwilling to act. I immediately advised Chairman Rod McGeoch. We both met with PwC and questioned them closely. Rod then moved quickly to tell Evan that he had lost the confidence of the board and sought his resignation. The board was reluctant but finally agreed to accept Evan's resignation. The severance negotiations were difficult and unpleasant, particularly for some of the directors who had been with Evan from the founding of the company. It was a sad ending for a man who had built the company from nothing but who was no longer delivering satisfactory results. But it was also an apposite warning about the risks arising from personal relationships at the top of a company. A warning which we were to remember later.

A search for a new CEO will usually take at least six months, often more. As we initiated a search, we were fortunate that one of our directors, Elmar Toime, had been an experienced and successful CEO. Although he was now living in England, he offered to fill the CEO role until we made a permanent appointment. This was most fortunate because he quickly began to discover just how dysfunctional the management of the business had become. He discovered that things were much worse than we thought and discerned that we were facing serious consequences if action was not taken quickly. However, Elmar was sufficiently experienced to immediately understand what had to be done and start rectifying the more serious issues.

The executive search turned up some interesting candidates. We settled on Nigel Morrison who was CFO of Galaxy Entertainment in

Macau. Nigel had been chief financial officer of Crown Melbourne and CEO of Federal Casino, Hobart in Tasmania. Clearly, he was a very experienced casino executive. Nigel was a capable CEO. He pulled together a competent executive team and soon had them working cohesively. Casino people are very mobile, so churn of executives is always greater than desirable. He had a flair for knowing what appealed to customers. Casino operations were soon delivering a more enjoyable customer experience. Restaurants are an essential part of casino and hotel operations. But they are capital intensive, struggle to make money and overall have a very poor return on capital. Nigel established some good restaurants on the Grand Hotel side of Federal Street and brought in well-known chefs to run them. Al Brown at Depot and Sean Connolly at The Grill were very successful as was El Gusto which replaced Dine. The restaurants in the casino were also improved.

Profit began to improve modestly but was mostly due to increased investment in the business. Return on capital was inadequate, with little sign of improvement. Significant investment was made in luxurious facilities for high rollers, wealthy foreign individuals, mostly from Thailand, China and Taiwan. "Junket operators" organise groups of these individuals who fly in for a few days' gambling. They receive complimentary lodging, food and beverages. They gamble heavily, mostly on table games where $250,000 per hand is a typical bet. Casinos around the world compete for these very mobile individuals and trim their margins to attract them. While the house usually wins, because of the fine margins this business is conducted on, it is not unusual for the punter to win and go home up a million or two dollars. Soon the directors were receiving a request to buy an executive jet plane to fly more of these groups to Auckland. Fortunately, that did not proceed.

In late 2007 we received an expression of interest from TPG, a private equity financier, to take over the company. The indicative price was at a 25% premium to the then-market price. It was a price which we needed to seriously consider. The problem, though, was that it was only a non-binding expression of interest and was conditional on an exclusive right to do due diligence for a period of four months. If we agreed, we would tie the company up for that period, during which we would be unable to take any major decisions. Our executives would be focussed on the provision of information to TPG and distracted from the task of improving performance. This would be hugely disruptive with no guarantee that an offer would be made at the indicative price or any other price. I had been through this process previously and found it to be most unsatisfactory. The pattern usually followed was for the indicative price offered in the initial approach to be negotiated up to a level sufficient to persuade the directors to let the process go ahead. Then when the company had suffered four months of disruption, and due diligence was completed, the offeror would use the information gained during due diligence to justify a lower offer. This was not a situation I wanted Sky City to get itself into. My view was that TPG should put a takeover offer on the table in accordance with the Companies Act and Takeovers Code and the matter should take its course. The board, however, had a different view and agreed to allow due diligence. A firm offer at the indicative price would likely have succeeded as I was not confident that we would get profitability up to the level needed to sustain a share price above the initial offer. In the event, the onset of the Global Financial Crisis in 2008 prevented the process from actually getting under way, and no offer was forthcoming so we were spared the disruption.

A move got under way in Auckland for a large-scale convention centre to be established to enable large international conferences to be attracted to the city. Conference centres are not profitable. Around the world conference centres are often built by casinos as a condition of their licence and rely on the extra gaming business they bring to cover the losses they incur. Where not associated with a casino they are invariably funded by local or central government. They are vanity projects. Those who promote a conference centre for their city invariably want someone else to pay for it and have inflated ideas about how much business will actually be attracted. "If we build it, they will come" is the mantra, regardless of the facts. But that is rarely the case. For example, our existing conference centre could seat 4500 people and cater for 2000 at dinner. The number of events with gross revenue over $100,000 was only six per year, hardly over-used, yet pressure was building for a facility which could accommodate 6500 participants. New Zealand is a long way from the major cities of the world where most of the large corporate headquarters are located. That means New Zealand is a very expensive place to hold a large-scale international conference. Still, for Sky City it was an opportunity to perhaps get regulatory approval to increase the footprint of the casino and install more gaming tables and machines as part of a deal to build a conference centre.

Running a conference centre was a core skill in our business. We did our homework, saw it as an opportunity, and had a clear idea of the expansion of our gaming facilities which would be required for us to build and profitably operate a facility of the scale sought. It was clear that no other organisation, except perhaps the government, who did not wish to do so, could afford to build and operate such a facility. Prime Minister John Key was a strong advocate of a large conference centre so we set up a dinner meeting between him and the directors. We naively hoped to obtain his support. He acknowledged the advantages of our proposition but played it dead straight and said the Ministry of Business and Innovation would be running a competitive process which we would need to enter. Despite trying very hard, we could not move him from that position. He proved to be very wise. We were the only contender in the ministry's process who could possibly meet the conditions the government had set. We negotiated a deal in which we undertook to build and operate the facility, as part of a deal which allowed the expansion of our gaming footprint which was required to make the overall proposition stack up. A couple of years later there was media controversy when it was alleged the prime minister had done a deal which was in some way improper at a "secret meeting" with Sky City directors. Fortunately, the evidence was clear that that was just not true.

I retired as a director in 2012 having reached the nine-year term limit which I had largely been instrumental in introducing. Profit had lifted to around $125 million as a result of the improvements Nigel had effected. But I was worried by the huge capital expenditure being planned: the international conference centre which I believed was justified by an expansion of gaming facilities, which would bring increased gaming profit; a hotel at Hamilton; a jet plane to transport in high rollers; and several hundred million dollars to massively transform Adelaide and build a new hotel there. I could not see those investments paying off. That would prove to be the case.

As I retired, I reflected on my time as a director. It had been a fun experience which I had enjoyed greatly. The casinos and other facilities had been improved and now gave our customers a more pleasurable experience. I was proud that we had maintained high standards of probity with an outstanding record of regulatory compliance. However, on the most important measure of all, creating shareholder value, we had failed. There had been too much low-quality expenditure which, while improving the facilities and customer experience, simply did not deliver its cost of capital. The shares which I had purchased at a price of $4.40 nine years earlier when I became a director were worth only $3.26. I was pretty disappointed in my stewardship.

FIFTY-FIVE
PORT OF TAURANGA

When I was deputy chairman of Ports of Auckland Ltd, we had outperformed Port of Tauranga on almost every metric. But a lot changed over the next ten years. Port of Tauranga had established MetroPort, an "inland port" at Wiri, where cargo was received and railed to and from Tauranga. Ports of Auckland suffered from its owners changing frequently from one publicly elected trust to another, before being taken over by Auckland Regional Council, now Auckland City Council, in 2005. None of those organisations were suitable owners of an asset-intensive, long-term business, like Ports of Auckland. Therefore, its profitability and its service performance deteriorated, and Port of Tauranga with superior service performance began to win market share from Auckland. When Port of Tauranga had been established, local government politicians in the Bay demonstrated great wisdom in taking great care to structure ownership of the port to prevent local body politicians from being able to interfere in, or control, the port company. Port of Tauranga was 54% owned by Quayside Holdings, the commercial arm of Bay of Plenty Regional Council. Quayside expected the port company to operate a successful business and was a supportive and stable owner.

Port of Tauranga was thus able to focus exclusively on operating a profitable and efficient port business.

I was approached in 2004 by Fraser McKenzie, chairman of Port of Tauranga, to join the board. I was a director of Maersk, which would create a conflict of interest, so I needed to resign from Maersk if I wished to accept the Port of Tauranga offer. A few years earlier I would not have even considered doing so, but the Maersk CEO Jens Madsen, with whom I had a great relationship, had been promoted to head up refrigerated container services for Maersk worldwide. Although I got on well enough with his successor Flemming Gamst, he ran the business in a different way, and I did not feel that I was making the contribution which I had previously. So, I resigned as a director of Maersk and accepted appointment to the Port of Tauranga Board.

A few months after joining the board the chairman, Fraser McKenzie, retired. He had been an excellent chairman who like me was a strong advocate for the use of economic value added (EVA) to measure performance and the use of capital. I have always found it to be a very powerful tool. The basic premise of EVA was simple: a company does not earn an economic profit until it has earned at least the cost of the capital employed in the business. So, the cost of capital is deducted from net profit to show the actual economic value added. EVA also had the advantage of being an external measure, so was transparent and impossible to fudge. Most companies do not actually earn an EVA profit so it was a tough measure which I found managers often strongly resisted. Those which employed it were invariably the better performers. In the companies of which I was a director, Fletcher Building, Fernz/Nufarm and Port of Tauranga all used EVA and were outstanding value creators for their shareholders. Fraser was succeeded as chairman by my former Dairy Board colleague John Parker, whom I greatly admired. John thought a little differently from most people on many issues, but he had a fertile and innovative mind and outstanding business judgement. He was to prove to be a very good chairman.

In my first year the profit was I think about $22 million. Market share was being won from Auckland but clearly pricing was too aggressive, as profit reduced as volumes went up. Long-serving Jon Mayson, who had been a very successful CEO, retired. Mark Cairns, a civil engineer who was CEO of Owens Group Ltd, a subsidiary of Port of Tauranga, was appointed to succeed him. It proved to be an inspired decision. Port of Tauranga became a very good business. It was New Zealand's largest port, being mainly an export port with huge forestry volumes and large dairy and kiwifruit trades. It was number two to Auckland for both imports and containers but was competing ferociously for customers to increase its throughput. It had an exceptional customer service ethos and great relationships with its customers. Its performance statistics for containers, such as containers moved per hour, ship turnround time and truck waiting times, were the best in the country. It was also an extremely efficient user of capital and was adept at optimising the timing of capital expenditure.

Import freight was valuable. Tauranga was mainly an export port, but it needed to attract more imports as ships preferred to unload imports and load exports during the same port stop. Obviously, it was much more cost efficient if the trains which brought exports into Tauranga backloaded imports to Auckland for their return journey. Most imports went to Auckland so MetroPort, the inland port at Wiri connected by rail to Tauranga, was established to service Auckland. Obviously, the rail service between Auckland and Tauranga was critical. Mark decided to compete to win business through providing superior service rather than on price. Ships only earn revenue when sailing. They earn nothing for their owners when tied up at a wharf. Ships which unloaded and loaded more quickly made more money for their owners, while service which moved goods more quickly and reliably lowered costs and made more money for export and import shippers. Port of Tauranga was skilled at investing capital wisely to improve efficiency, reliability and the quality of service. For example, from having only two container cranes when I joined, we seemed to receive a request for a new container crane almost every year. Volumes increased steadily both in bulk and containers. From 2004 to 2014 total tonnage increased by 37% to 19.7 million tonnes while the high-value container business grew from 450,000 containers to 759,000 over the same period.

When I became a director of Port of Tauranga, the Dutch shipping line Nedlloyd, which was a very good operator, was the largest customer. They soon acquired the British line P&O to become P&O Nedlloyd. I suggested to my colleagues that the company ought to have a strategy to persuade Maersk to use Tauranga. With the takeover of the US line Sealand, Maersk was now the largest shipping line in the world. I knew from my previous association with Maersk that it was a top-class operator, with a strong customer service ethic and similar values to Port of Tauranga. I opined that without Maersk, Tauranga was at risk of becoming New Zealand's No. 2 port. This was heresy to my colleagues. But my words were prophetic as Maersk then took over P&O Nedlloyd and soon decided that Auckland would be their New Zealand hub port. This, while not surprising, was a huge disappointment to Tauranga. However, the management team responded positively and developed a strategy to win Maersk as a major customer.

While not neglecting its core business, Port of Tauranga also looked for opportunities to expand in ancillary businesses. Owens Group, which operated a nationwide stevedoring business, had been purchased several years earlier. Anything we could do to make Tauranga and other New Zealand ports more efficient would benefit New Zealand shippers and Port of Tauranga. A 50% stake in Northport was purchased. Then an Auckland transport company, Tapper

Transport, was acquired. It was a relatively small company, but it was the largest transporter of containers to and from Ports of Auckland and Port of Tauranga's MetroPort at Wiri. Auckland carriers were charging a higher rate to service Port of Tauranga's MetroPort than they were Ports of Auckland. Controlling Tapper would provide the opportunity to level the playing field and thus attract increased cargo to Tauranga.

The large Australasian logistics company Toll intended to enter cargo marshalling and stevedoring in New Zealand, which would pose a strategic threat to Owens Group. Port of Tauranga decided to sell 50% of Owens Group to Toll. Owens would become more profitable with the Toll business included. We believed that it was better to have 50% of a more profitable business rather than 100% of the existing business which would have its profitability reduced by competition with Toll. Toll was also a significant freight and logistics business which Tauranga wanted as a partner rather than a competitor. Owens was renamed C3. The relationship with Toll worked well enough, although Toll did not bring the anticipated throughput to the business. Then Toll Holdings restructured their activities and demerged their share of C3 to Australian company Asciano. They were reasonable enough partners but brought little to the business as C3 was really a New Zealand orphan for them. Port of Tauranga was keen to get back control of C3, believing that we could more effectively improve the efficiency of port operations if we completely owned it. But it was making good money for Asciano with little effort, so they were not keen sellers. They declined to engage on selling to us. Eventually, we decided to submit a bid under the "shoot-out" clause in the shareholders agreement. This is a very common provision in joint venture-type companies where there is a stalemate in which one party is keen to buy, but the other is unwilling to sell. Either party may lodge a formal offer to buy. The other party then has the option to either sell at that price or to buy the offeror's shares at the same price. This forces the original offeror to submit a good price or risk having to sell if it submits a low price. Unfortunately, we were too parsimonious in the price at which we offered to buy. Asciano considered that C3 was worth more to them at the price we offered so opted to buy our shares. So C3 was lost. Tauranga then purchased Quality Marshalling, a Tauranga log-marshalling business. It made a bucket of money in the first year but then lost several large customers. It had to be wound back in scale to deliver a more modest contribution.

The company continued to drive efficiency improvements. It was very good at planning ahead and displayed extremely good judgement in timing the investments necessary to handle increasing volumes of trade, particularly the high-value container business. The descriptor "Port of Tauranga – Port for the Future" encapsulated the company's values perfectly. Performance continued to improve. On the normal measures of efficiency, crane rate, containers handled per hour, ship loading rate and ship turnaround time, Tauranga soon became the most efficient port in Australia or New Zealand by a significant margin. Profit continued to grow and this was reflected in the share price. Port of Tauranga was consistently one of the highest "shareholder value creators" among companies listed on the NZX.

Globally, there was a strong movement to larger vessels which were more fuel and labour efficient. Vessels with 2800-container capacity were the largest visiting New Zealand. In the near future 6000 to 10,000-container vessels were likely. While it would take time for shipping lines to bring larger vessels to New Zealand, the sooner they came the sooner the benefits would be available to New Zealand shippers. It was critical that New Zealand was ready for larger vessels when they arrived. Port of Tauranga was much better placed than any other New Zealand port, but there was still much to be done. Larger vessels were wider and of deeper draught, so dredging to widen and deepen port channels was necessary. This required resource consent which was likely to take years. The wharf needed to be extended, more container cranes, straddle carriers, larger paved surface areas, and improved rail and truck interchange facilities would all be necessary. Port of Tauranga was determined to be ready when the big ships came, and it was.

Competition with Auckland for container business was intense, so margins were under pressure. There was a bigger issue. New Zealand could really only afford to have one North Island port which was large-ship capable. There was a significant risk that both Auckland and Tauranga would compete for that position. The capital cost to make either port large-ship capable was huge. While the cost was much lower at Tauranga, Ports of Auckland was owned by Auckland City which was demonstrably much less commercially demanding than Port of Tauranga shareholders. If both Auckland and Tauranga became large-ship capable there would be capital duplication and margin-destroying price competition from which the shipping lines would be the winners. Our aim was to put New Zealand shippers in the position to benefit from the lower operating costs of larger vessels. We decided to try to pre-empt that by exploring a merger with Auckland. On the face of it, we believed that there was likely to be a very strong economic case from the merger of the two ports. There would also be some disadvantages, while the difficulty in gaining Commerce Commission approval would be significant, even though most economic commentators believed that there was a strong need for rationalisation of New Zealand's ports. Our view was "let's understand the size of the prize of a merger with Auckland then consider the problems". A great deal of work went into the study. Our intuition proved to be correct. There were sizeable benefits from a merger, estimated at $20 million annually or a net present value of $320 million. There would be significant difficulties in agreeing valuations as Auckland City's high land values were not matched by the earning ability of their port assets. Negotiations faltered as the difficult issues were confronted and the Auckland team seemed quite unable to address them. As negotiations appeared to reach an impasse, we became increasingly concerned about what a merger would do to the efficiency and service ethic of Port of Tauranga and its focus on sound economic decisions. In the end, it was mutually agreed to suspend negotiations. The matter silently slid beneath the waves.

Then in 2013 the management team reached an agreement with the shareholders of PrimePort, Timaru to purchase a 51% holding in that company for $21.6 million and to lease for a term of thirty-five years the container facility, which had an annual throughput of 20,000 containers. It was an exceptionally good deal, both for the former shareholders who would receive a greater profit for their 49% shareholding than they had been receiving when owning 100%, and for Port of Tauranga, as profit increased sharply, making the purchase price appear modest. By 2015 container throughput had been lifted to 79,000 containers. Land was purchased at Rolleston for container storage and exchange and a large warehouse erected. Port of Tauranga was well on the way to becoming a significant player in the South Island freight industry.

Then a major play was set in motion. The company had developed a very good relationship with Maersk who were increasing their use of Tauranga. They planned to introduce big ships of up to 10,000 capacity to New Zealand. Studies showed that a saving to New Zealand of $340 million per annum could be expected from the larger ships. Tauranga would be ready and be the only port in New Zealand which could handle them. Fonterra had, in partnership with meat company Silver Fern Farms, established Kotahi to operate the logistics and shipping of their dairy and meat trade. In 2014 Kotahi entered into a long-term deal with Maersk under which Maersk would bring the large ships to New Zealand, berthing at Tauranga. By now Tauranga had been dredged to have a low-water draught of

14.5 metres, the deepest in Australia and New Zealand. Loading more containers on each port call required a larger number of containers to be accumulated to fill each vessel. They had to come from all over the North Island, which increased internal freight costs, thus reducing the shipping cost benefits gained from the larger vessels. A new approach to landside logistics to improve landside freight efficiency was needed. Port of Tauranga negotiated an agreement with Kotahi to merge Tapper Transport with Kotahi's transport business Dairy Transport Ltd to form CODA, which was to be the logistics operator for both Kotahi and Port of Tauranga. Kotahi was brought in as a 19.9% shareholder of Timaru Container Terminal. This brought Port of Tauranga, and Kotahi the country's largest shipper, together in a long-term strategic alliance with Maersk. Maersk would service New Zealand with larger ships using Tauranga Port. It was a major breakthrough.

I retired from Port of Tauranga in 2014. Container throughput had reached 759,000 with significant increase in the next few years baked in. Tax-paid profit was $78 million and by market capitalisation, Port of Tauranga was the tenth most valuable company on the New Zealand Stock Exchange. The shares I had purchased in 2002 for $1.55 were now worth more than $14 each. It was a record to be proud of.

FIFTY-SIX
CODA: THE LAST STANZA

HONOURS CONTINUED TO FLOW. IN 2010 ROTARY International honoured me with a Paul Harris Fellowship. In 2014 Waikato University bestowed upon me an Honorary Doctorate of Management. In 2017 I was admitted as a Laureate of the New Zealand Business Hall of Fame. Waikato followed in 2022 when I was admitted as a Laureate of the Waikato Business Hall of Fame.

Very early in my career, I observed that most people in leadership positions went on for too long. They were usually remembered for their last years, which were often not their best. There was no set period which was ideal. Staying too long was more about staying on after the best years have passed, rather the length of time served. I resolved then that I would never stay past my use-by date in any position. "Go out at the top" became my mantra, one which I followed throughout my career. As retirement grew closer, I resolved to halve my workload when I reached the age of sixty-five, to halve it again at seventy years of age and to retire completely by age seventy-five. I pretty much achieved all of those milestones. Retirement from Port of Tauranga in 2014 at the age of seventy-five completed my working career. Then, just as I was about to retire, Port of Tauranga and Kotahi established CODA, and they wanted an independent chairman. I believed that I would be acceptable to both parties so I put my hand up and was asked to take the chairmanship. My brief was to get CODA established. I did not intend it to be a long-term assignment. CODA is a musical term, meaning the last piece or stanza of a musical composition. This would definitely be my last act so CODA was an appropriate name for my last business.

CODA was effectively a start-up company, although it brought together two existing companies and the activities from a third. Each of the heritage businesses had their own values, culture and way of doing things, so welding them together into a single focussed entity with its own systems, values and culture was never going to be easy. To meet the needs of our shareholders, it was structured as a partnership rather than a joint stock company.

The Manager of Dairy Transport Ltd, Scott Brownlee, was appointed CEO. He pulled together a management team including a chief financial officer named David Choong. There was so much to do, but good progress was made in bringing the three entities together and establishing CODA in its own right. We needed to think differently from other transport firms. We were "intermodal", using both road and rail. We partnered with suppliers like KiwiRail and other transport firms, and customers such as Countdown, to more efficiently move freight and thus lower costs. Kotahi provided most of the business, but it was all export product which came from all over the North Island. We had to establish multimodal capability and use rail whenever economic. We needed to be flexible, innovative and agile to obtain rail costs which were economic. We would hire complete trains both on a regular longer term basis, or on a one-off contract basis. Where KiwiRail was unable to provide the right type of wagons for our goods we were prepared to purchase our own wagons and contract KiwiRail to move them. Our large export volume meant that trucks and trains were full on the journey to the port, but unless we could find freight to backload they would be empty on the return journey. We had to find the regular business which was moving away from the port, ascertain what those customers wanted and develop the ability to deliver it at a competitive price. Storage and distribution centres serviced by both road and rail were established in Rolleston, Christchurch and Otahuhu, Auckland. Large, high-quality warehouses were erected at each site.

We were operating in a very dangerous business so health and safety was most important and was the No. 1. item on every agenda and report. We set high standards and put huge efforts into keeping our workforce safe and reducing the frequency and severity of accidents. We had a pretty good record and a generally declining accident rate but tragically one of our drivers was killed when operating a swing lift used to lift containers onto and off the truck. A very prescriptive standard operating procedure (SOP) had been established to keep this activity safe. Although the driver had not completely followed the SOP, the company was found guilty under the Health and Safety at Work Act and was heavily fined. The whole investigation and prosecution process took over two years to play out and was most distressing for our management staff and the family of the deceased. We redoubled our efforts to keep our workers safe.

Laureate of the New Zealand Business Hall of Fame

Fonterra provided about 60% of the business, but it was at very fine margins of between 6% and 8% compared to the more than 20%

common in the industry. Farmers should take comfort that the common view of firms which service Fonterra is "while it is nice to have Fonterra's business you will never get rich from it". Such a low margin on 60% of the business made it very difficult to earn decent levels of profit. However, although undershooting our budgets, based on the original business case which had provided the basis for establishing CODA, by running a low-cost operation we managed to make net profit after tax of between $5 million and $8 million in most years. This provided a reasonable return on equity of 8% to 10%.

Annemarie, Lisa-Jane, Kevin, Gregory, Julie-Ann, Mark

By 2018 profit had flattened out and the directors became concerned that the financial information they were receiving did not show an accurate picture of CODA finances. They decided that CFO David Choong was not up to the job and needed to be replaced. We were fortunate to recruit Andrew Cleland, an experienced CFO from Fonterra. His impact on the business was immediate and revealing.

Since Coda had commenced business, it had a very high number of debtors in arrears. This had largely been inherited from the heritage businesses. Some progress in obtaining payment had been made, but the outstanding number remained large with little progress being made in further reducing it. Andrew quickly discovered that we had no documentation supporting most of the overdue amounts, which were being strongly disputed by the individual debtors concerned. We needed to write off about $2 million. It was little consolation that it should have been written off several years earlier. Then in 2018 Scott Brownlee resigned as CEO, ostensibly to go into business on his own account. He obviously knew something that the directors did not, for immediately the results took a turn for the worse. Costs were blowing out and we began to run monthly deficits which made a loss for the year likely, unless something could be done quickly to rectify the problem. Some of the problem was due to the new distribution centres which were not generating sufficient revenue to meet their operating costs. But there was also significant ongoing expenditure in developing TENEX, a new transport management system which was not delivering and which ultimately had to be totally written off.

We conducted a search for a replacement CEO and had the great fortune to attract Gerard Morrison, Maersk CEO for Australia, New Zealand and the Pacific Islands. He was an ideal CEO with extensive freight experience. He was very highly regarded within the New Zealand shipping and transport industries. We would normally have had no chance of attracting him from Maersk, but they wished to transfer him overseas while he was not prepared to leave New Zealand. As we concluded negotiations with him, CODA's results continued to deteriorate to the extent that just as he was about to sign the employment contract, we had to get him back in to disclose a more sombre picture of the state of CODA than we had previously presented. I was afraid that he might pull out but fortunately he did not, merely commenting that "the challenge had become just a little harder". Gerard commenced on 1 April, and by then the year-to-date loss had reached $800,000. He immediately began to make an impact, although monthly losses continued to October, when we returned to monthly profits with a modest profit for the year looking likely.

In October I turned eighty years of age. It was time for me to retire, which I did at the November board meeting. I was proud that we had successfully brought three different organisations together to form CODA which had been soundly established and was doing the job it had been set up to do. It had earned a good reputation with its customers for delivering quality service at very competitive rates. I would have preferred it to be delivering better financial results, but it had recovered from a tough period and looked likely to be in profit for the full year. I left it with a high-quality CEO. Overall, I was pleased with what CODA had achieved during my five years as chairman.

The author and former Prime Minister Jim Bolger

FIFTY-SEVEN
BLESSINGS

Never in my wildest dreams as a boy growing up at Paratu, Walton, or even in my early days as a young sharemilker, did I ever for one moment imagine the amazing career I would have. That I would become the leader of my industry, the dairy industry, and have a stellar business leadership career. That I would meet Her Majesty the Queen, Prince Philip, Prince Charles and Princess Anne; that I would know thirteen New Zealand prime ministers, most of them by their Christian names; that I would meet twenty-five foreign presidents and prime ministers, including the presidents of the three largest countries in the world: China, USA and Russia; that I would visit more than fifty countries.

To have those experiences, my life was blessed, blessed in many ways:

I was blessed to be born into a loving family, to God-fearing parents, whose Catholic faith was strong and central to their very being. They had very strong values and an exceptional work ethic. "Your own labour is the only thing you get for nothing so don't be afraid of work," my father said. Although Mum and Dad came from humble backgrounds, they were self-reliant individuals who understood that you were entitled only to what you earned. They were parsimonious, believing that you should not spend more than you earned. Their education was by today's standards modest, although adequate by the standard of those times, but they knew that knowledge was the key to progress and read widely. They were egalitarian, modest and unpretentious, regarding themselves as equal to all and superior to none. They had a strong sense of duty. Dad was not required to go to war in 1942, but he went regardless, because he believed it was his duty to serve his country. One of the great gifts our parents imparted to Michael, Denise, Paul and me was fluency in reading and a great love of it. That became the major source of knowledge for all of us. A strong social conscience and concern for others, especially those less fortunate, was ever present. While their care for our wellbeing was exemplary and their love unconditional, their greatest gift to my siblings and me was instilling their values in us. I have tried to live by those same values which made me what I became. My core values were learned at an early age from my parents. Foremost was honesty – always tell the truth; stand up for yourself and don't be pushed around; if a job is worth doing it is worth doing well; persevere – don't give up; be a giver not a taker; stand up for what you believe in; don't go along with what you believe to be wrong; stick up for those less fortunate. These values underpinned my whole approach to life and business.

I learned from experience: that integrity is the most precious virtue, it is priceless but costs nothing, it does, however, require courage; leadership is about doing the right thing, not the easiest or most popular; do not to be afraid to express a different view even if you are the only one to do so – the things I most regret usually occurred when I stayed silent and went along with something I disagreed with; that problems are more easily fixed early rather than late; always apply the TV test to ethical issues – how would I explain this on TV?; that people are the real asset of any business, always train, encourage and motivate them; that if you find out the facts, the answer to a problem is usually pretty clear; always put yourself in the other person's position and try to understand what really matters to them; why be mediocre when with little extra effort you can be good; always strive for excellence; the biggest cost in any business will probably be poor quality; a bad situation will almost certainly be worse than you believe it to be; unless you stretch yourself you will never know how good you can be; if you don't enjoy your job you should do something else.

I have had an amazing life. Growing up in the humble workers' town of Waitara, which was dominated by the freezing works. My father going to war when I was three and not returning until I was seven. My mother displaying great character to bring up three young children on a soldier's pay, helped by her father, my grandfather Tom Edge from whom my second name of Thomas came, who lived with us until he passed away when I was fifteen. He had a big influence on me. Then, at the age of nine moving to live on a farm in the picturesque farming district of Walton, where almost everyone was farming, people were generous, independent and very self-sufficient.

My siblings and I were fortunate to grow up in the country and I enjoyed the open air and freedom to roam widely. We lived outdoors almost every waking moment, made our own fun and learned to make a useful contribution to the never-ending work required by a farm. Despite the drudgery of milking twice a day, I never wanted to do anything but farm when I grew up. My education had been modest, but I received a different education and knowledge in my teens, doing casual work on farms around the district. I learned different ways of doing farming tasks and different farming practices. While working in a dairy factory and on a large construction site I gained practical knowledge in a range of skills. More importantly, I learned about life, labour and people. I learned that for many people work is a boring drudge, that many workers are demotivated and do not understand what is expected of them. That knowledge was to be a huge asset to me in my later leadership career because I understood that to achieve good performance, motivation was critical and leadership of, and communication with, one's team was the key to motivation. I was fortunate to start sharemilking on my own account when I was twenty, thus at an early age also gaining business experience. Then enjoying the good fortune of bringing up a family in the country in a secure and stable environment.

I virtually fell into leadership positions in Federated Farmers. The experience fitted well my enquiring mind and interest in the wider world. I began to enjoy being at the heart of major industry decision making and being able to influence events. Sport slipped in my priorities to be replaced by an enthusiastic participation in farming politics. I was a good public speaker and found that I could carry an audience, even a very large one. I seemed to have a knack of winning elections and being promoted to higher office. Dad gave me advice when I started playing senior rugby: "Through your career, Dryden, you will come up against many players who are more naturally talented than you are and there will be little you can do about it, but if you are fitter than them you will more than hold your own with them. Being fitter will always be totally within your own control." I applied that maxim to preparation and found if I put in the effort to know and understand the issues, I was able to hold my own with others whom I considered to be more talented; that solutions usually became more clear and I usually made good decisions. I am grateful to my early mentors, Colin Gordge for his encouragement, Max Hewitt for his inspiration, and the wise Sir William Dunlop from whom I learned about strategy and tactics. The experience of being provincial president of Waikato Federated Farmers at the age of thirty-three, during what was a difficult economic time for farmers and placed farming leadership under intense pressure, developed my leadership skills and shaped my future career.

Early in my career I seemed destined for politics, but when the opportunities came, and there were several, I realised that a political career did not fit well with the young family Christine and I were raising. But I had also realised that it would be commercial factors which would most influence the wellbeing of dairy farmers. That made it logical that I should turn my talents to the dairy manufacturing and marketing industry.

Presentation from Dairy Board staff

My commercial skills were developed as a director of New Zealand Cooperative Dairy Company and then applied when I became chairman of that company. By the time I became chairman of the New Zealand Dairy Board at age the age of forty-nine, I was an experienced businessman and leader, match fit and with boundless energy. I needed it all, for it was a tough and demanding job with 15,000 farming families and several thousand employees, all dependent on the Dairy Board for their livelihood. It was also very important to New Zealand, being our country's largest business, earning a massive 20% of our export income. So, the Dairy Board's influence on the New Zealand economy was huge.

Trade policy was a new area for me, but I soon loved it. It was exciting to participate in the Uruguay Round multilateral trade negotiations, the most comprehensive agricultural trade negotiation in the history of the world, and I am proud of what was achieved. That agreement more than doubled the returns New Zealand dairy farmers receive for their milk, so has been hugely beneficial to them and to New Zealand. I was privileged to represent New Zealand as member of the APEC Eminent Persons Group, tasked to advise the prime ministers and presidents of the twenty-one APEC countries, on a vision for, and pathway to, economic cooperation and trade liberalisation. To be involved with twenty high-achieving individuals, among them some of the best minds in the APEC region containing a total population of more than three billion people, was exhilarating.

Having completed thirty-two years working for farmers, ten years in Federated Farmers and twenty-five in the dairy industry, I embarked on a new career, as a director or chairman of a number of substantial companies in New Zealand and Australia over the next twenty years. This was hugely satisfying without the ever-present pressure which went with leadership roles in the dairy industry.

So, I have been blessed with a wonderful leadership career in the dairy industry and in New Zealand and international business.

I have been blessed also by the love of three remarkable women.

My mother Violet who nurtured and shaped me and was always there for me.

Christine was a city girl who became a farmer's wife and took to it as though she had been raised on a farm. Ours was a typical farming partnership in which she played a full role in our farming business. She milked cows, raised calves, undertook a myriad of other farming tasks, tended to our accounts, took dictation and typed up my submissions in our early days. But even more importantly, within ten years she bore six wonderful children. She was an exceptional mother, and it is largely due to her that our children grew into the outstanding individuals they became. Without her input, we would not have successfully built our farming business and without her my career would not have been possible. I owe much to her.

And more recently Marg. My soulmate, best friend and the love of my life. She makes me so happy. My dear mother, before she died, thanked Marg for "giving me my boy back and making him happy". She challenges me and stimulates my thinking. She has made me a much better person. My eldest son Mark, speaking at a family event, thanked her "for not only being the lovely person she is, but for making my father a better person". He was right. She has two children and three grandchildren of her own, but with me she inherited six children and twelve grandchildren. She treats them all exactly as if they are her own, and in fact she regards them as her children and grandchildren. She remembers their birthdays and buys the presents. I adore her.

I have been blessed with a wonderful family:

Mark, Julie-Ann, Gregory, Kevin, Lisa-Jane and Annemarie were respectful and well-behaved children. They have all matured into fine individuals with a strong work ethic and great character. They have all done well in their chosen career. The credit for that is largely due to Christine, not me. Christine and I are hugely proud of each of them, as is Marg. I regret that I did not tell them that in their earlier years. They have all chosen great partners and have rock-solid marriages. Johanne, Graham, Jennifer, Susan, Dean and Mike are all that we would ever have wished for our children's partners. We are proud to have them as our sons and daughters-in-law.

Then there are their children, our grandchildren. Adam, Melanie, Sean, Jessica, James, Hannah, Ruby, Joel, Olivia, Sophie, Nicholas and Harry are all fine young people, of good character, industrious with well-balanced and pleasant personalities, all successfully making their way in the world. They give us so much pleasure. We are so proud of them.

Gregory, Julie-Ann, Lisa-Jane, Mark, Kevin and Annemarie

I have been blessed with robust good health.

This enabled me to cope with an exceptionally heavy workload and considerable pressure for many years.

Do I have any regrets? Not many. I regret wasting my secondary schooling because if there is one thing I cannot abide, it is not delivering my best. Fortunately, it did not prove to be a major handicap. The experience I had gained instead, working in unskilled industrial jobs, gave me knowledge and understanding of what work is often like for the lower paid. That more than offset what I did not have in formal educational qualifications. It gave me empathy with workers that few in leadership positions ever experience. I would not have traded that for anything.

I do enormously regret that I was unable to keep the dairy industry united in the latter half of the 1990s, when dairy companies were single-mindedly pursuing their own interests in the mistaken belief that their own interests were all that mattered and industry cooperation was no longer important. That got Fonterra off to a bad start, created structural weaknesses and lost far too many of the industry's experienced personnel. That cost dairy farmers several billion dollars over the next decade and a half, before Fonterra lifted its performance to acceptable levels. That is the largest regret of my professional career and to this very day I feel that I let farmers down. My mistake was in respecting the fact that it was the cooperative dairy companies which were technically the board's shareholders so it was to them that I was accountable. Had I taken the fight directly to the farmers, as Warren Larsen wanted me to do, I have no doubt that the outcome would have been different.

But my biggest regret is that I did not spend more time with my children when they were young and that I was not a better father. My career came at a cost, a cost to my family. That they all turned out to be such great individuals is due to the love and skill of their mother. If I had my time over again, that is one thing I would definitely do differently, perhaps the only one.

So, I have had an amazing career. It has been at times hugely challenging, extending me to the very limit of my ability. But it has also always been interesting, mostly enjoyable and often exciting. As much as possible I tried to make it fun, believing that if you did not enjoy what you were doing you should get another job. Above all, it was hugely satisfying to be able to make a difference and benefit farmers. It has been a wonderful experience. Few people get to start at the very bottom of their industry and rise to the top. Even fewer get to lead an international business. Even fewer again get to lead the largest business in the country which is also a world leader in its sector. I was fortunate to have the opportunity to do those things. I will always be grateful to the dairy farmers of New Zealand for giving me that opportunity.

It has been an amazing experience for a farm boy from Walton.

Family celebrates my 80th birthday

ABOUT THE AUTHOR

Sir Dryden Spring, Doctor of Science, Distinguished Fellow of the Institute of Directors

Sir Dryden Spring is married to Margaret, Lady Spring. He has three daughters and three sons, twelve grandchildren and three great-grandchildren.

He was born in Waitara, grew up on a farm at Walton, was educated at Walton Primary School and Matamata College. He farmed at Walton and Elstow.

He began his public career as president of the New Zealand Sharemilkers Association in 1966, became president of Waikato

Federated Farmers in 1972, a position he held until 1976. He is a Life Member of Waikato Federated Farmers.

In 1973 he was chosen as New Zealand's Outstanding Young Man of the Year.

Sir Dryden was a director of New Zealand Cooperative Dairy Company Ltd, being chairman from 1982 to 1989. Under Sir Dryden's leadership the company was revitalised and transformed into one of New Zealand's best-performing dairy companies.

He was appointed a director of the New Zealand Dairy Board, of which he was chairman from 1989 to 1998. Under Sir Dryden's leadership the Dairy Board's turnover increased from $2.8 billion to $7.8 billion, while branded and premium product sales increased by more than 500%, from $400 million in 1989 to $2.1 billion.

Sir Dryden was a tireless campaigner for reform of agricultural trade and had a significant input into the Dairy Title of the WTO Uruguay Round which resulted in an increase in market access and a major reduction in tariffs for New Zealand dairy products. In 1993 he was appointed by the Prime Minister to the APEC Eminent Persons Group which drafted the APEC vision of "Free and Open Trade in The Asia Pacific", which was adopted by APEC leaders. From 2000 to 2006, Sir Dryden served as a member of the APEC Business Advisory Council which advised the leaders of the twenty-three APEC member countries. Sir Dryden was also a member of the prestigious International Policy Council for Agriculture, Food and Trade.

Sir Dryden was awarded the New Zealand 1990 Commemoration Medal and in 1994 was honoured by Her Majesty the Queen, with the award of Knight Bachelor for services to New Zealand and the New Zealand dairy industry.

Following his retirement as chairman of the New Zealand Dairy Board in 1998, Sir Dryden had extensive business interests. He was chairman of ANZ Bank New Zealand, Ericsson Communications NZ, Fletcher Forests Ltd, WEL Networks Ltd, Coda LLP and a director of several other New Zealand and Australian companies.

Sir Dryden has been a member of the Prime Minister's Enterprise Council, chairman of Asia New Zealand Foundation, ASEAN New Zealand Business Council of which he is a Life Member, Honorary Chairman of Philippines New Zealand Business Council and Patron of the Thailand New Zealand Business Council. He was a founding trustee of the Business and Parliament Trust, the Waikato Medical Research Foundation and a Distinguished Fellow of Massey University Academy of Agriculture.

Sir Dryden is a Distinguished Fellow of the Institute of Directors in New Zealand. He was awarded an Honorary Doctor of Science by Massey University and an Honorary Doctor of Waikato University Business School.

He has been inducted as a Laureate, of both the New Zealand Business Hall of Fame and the Waikato Business Hall of Fame. He was also awarded the Matamata Piako Business Person of the Year in 2016.

Sir Dryden has retired and now lives in Tauranga.

www.ingramcontent.com/pod-product-compliance
Lightning Source LLC
Chambersburg PA
CBHW062030290426
44109CB00026B/2579